ENGLISH "STANDARD" PRONUNCIATIONS: A Study of Attitudes

ENGLISH
LANGUAGE
CENTER

BY

MATS MOBÄRG

ACTA UNIVERSITATIS GOTHOBURGENSIS
GÖTEBORG SWEDEN

English
Language
Center

ISBN 91-7346-214-4
ISSN 0072-503X

Distributors:
ACTA UNIVERSITATIS GOTHOBURGENSIS
Box 5096
S-402 22 Göteborg, Sweden

✿ Goterna, Kungälv 1989

Abstract.

English "Standard" Pronunciations: a Study of Attitudes,
Mats Mobärg, University of Göteborg, Department of English, 1988 (1989)

This is a study of native English listeners' attitudes toward a sample of "standard" or "near-standard" English accents. 370 informants have listened to recordings of speakers describing a cartoon and answered a set of attitude questions about the speakers/accents. The questions concerned perceived age, occupation, psychological qualities, job suitability, social significance, etc. The speakers and listeners also supplied similar information about themselves, which made it possible to relate answer profiles to speakers' and listeners' background data.

The central concept of this study is DEGREE OF MODERNITY, i.e. the degree to which a speaker can be regarded as a traditional or a non-traditional, "modern", speaker. The DEGREE OF MODERNITY in a speaker was determined by means of a word pronunciation test including words that are in a process of phonetic change. On the basis of the result of this test, speakers were placed in either a MODERN or a TRADITIONAL group. In addition to this categorization, speakers were also subdivided according to age, sex and regional background, forming combinatory subgroups, such as OLD/MODERN, SOUTH/TRADITIONAL, etc.

The characteristic features of this study, then, are (1) that it deals with the standard area itself, rather than a wide standard-dialect spectrum; (2) that it presents an objective method of subdividing speakers according to DEGREE OF MODERNITY.

The introductory section contains a survey of relevant language attitude studies from around 1930 onwards and an introduction to the methods of this study. Then follow three basically parallel sections devoted to the age, sex and regionality aspects, respectively. In each of these sections, the informants are subdivided according to basically the same principle as the speakers. The main body of the text is a discussion, based on tests of significance, about how the various informant subgroups behave toward the various speaker subgroups and why. Tables accompany the discussion throughout.

The main tendency in the AGE section is an upgrading of the combinatory subgroup OLD/TRADITIONAL in comparisons related to status. Adult informants unexpectedly show greater acceptance of MODERN accents than do young people, however. There are also indications that subgroups in which AGE and DEGREE OF MODERNITY do not harmonize, e.g. OLD/MODERN, are downgraded by the informants.

In the SEX section we can notice a strong link between the subgroup MALE/TRADITIONAL and status traits. There are however interesting deviations in connection with traits to do with family and work relations.

SOUTH/TRADITIONAL is the speaker subgroup to receive the highest ratings for several, particularly status, traits in the REGIONALITY section, but there are also striking exceptions, e.g. in the case of PLEASANTNESS.

Key words: English language, sociolinguistics, language attitudes, RP, accent, dialect, age differences, sex differences, regional differences, status, solidarity, Wallace E. Lambert, Howard Giles.

Denna bok tillägnas
Mina barn
Karin och Gustaf
Och minnet av min pojke
Magnus
Som levde
Bland dessa sidor

Acknowledgments.

Embarking on a project of this kind is somehow like getting on a train whose destination is unknown and whose timetable has not yet come from the printer's. Even though the journey does not always develop the way you had expected, you cannot get off until you reach the station, or you'll be facing even greater problems.

On such a journey, you need good company, experienced travellers who have been on these trains before, but also people in the same situation as yourself with whom you can share your worries.

In this respect, I have been very lucky. On disembarking, I would therefore like to salute you all in gratitude for your company, friendliness and help.

Alvar Ellegård has been my supervisor throughout this project, cheering me up when my spirits were low, cooling me off when they were getting too high. I am particularly grateful for his generous offer to stay on as my supervisor after his retirement, thereby saving myself as well as other people from a lot of extra work.

I am grateful for financial support received from the University Foundation for Graduate Scholars and from the Arts Faculty Computer Service.

In the planning stages of this project, I was much helped by the advice of **Peter Trudgill**, who has also kindly taken the time to correspond with me on various matters in the course of the project.

David Isitt shared with me his experiences from his own fieldwork in England, which saved me from a lot of unnecessary setbacks.

The studio work in Gothenburg was expertly done by **Hugo Hansson** and **Nestor Cordero**.

Ulf Dantanus kindly helped me by finding and recording speakers for me in England. I would also like to thank him and his wife **Martha** for their hospitality when I was doing my fieldwork.

Bryan Errington, Alan J. Whysall and **David Wright** were helpful in arranging contacts in various parts of England.

Mr and Mrs P. Waller and my old friends **Leslie and Mavis Hamp** very generously let me stay in their homes during parts of my fieldwork session in England.

I am grateful to the **Longman Group UK Ltd** for permitting me to reproduce the cartoon on p. 62.

I have benefited much from discussing my project, formally as well as informally, with friends and colleagues at the English Department in Gothenburg, notably **Claes-Göran Engström, Harald Fawkner** (who also generously volunteered to read a proof), **Göran Kjellmer, Sölve Ohlander, Arne Olofsson, Mavis von Proschwitz, Aimo Seppänen, Mark Troy** and **David Wright** (who has read and commented on parts of the text and who will also proofread the finalized version). I am also grateful to my fellow students in the doctoral seminar for their interest.

Björn Areskoug of the University Computing Centre has been in charge of the computer processing of my material. He has also kindly and patiently answered innumerable layman's questions about statistics and related matters.

Anders Bäckman helped me to programme my statistical calculator.

Erland Hjelmquist and **Philip Hwang** of the Department of Psychology kindly undertook to read and comment on parts of the text.

Ulla Dahlbom, Lars-Erik Peterson and **Margareta Westberg** of the Department of Statistics have helped me with various statistical aspects.

Claes Göran Alvstam and **Sten Lorentzon** of the Department of Economic Geography advised me on matters relating to the section on regionality.

Lars-Gunnar Andersson of the Department of Linguistics has read and commented on the whole text, for which I am truly grateful.

My mother, **Majken Mobärg**, has supported me financially as well as otherwise.

My wife, **Ulla**, as well as helping me with this project in a multitude of ways, has had to carry a lot more than her fair share of our common burden during the last few years.

My final thanks are due to the **25 speakers** and **370 listener-informants** of my sample who without any compensation made this project possible.

Any drawbacks in the present report are my own responsibility.

Nödinge, May 1988

Mats Mobärg

Acknowledgments cont'd.

This dissertation exists in two versions: a preliminary photocopy version primarily intended for the public disputation in June 1988; and the present, definitive, version. Apart from minor alterations, the main difference between the two versions is that an overall summary has been added (pp. 331ff). On publishing the present version, I would like to extend my thanks to the following people:

Gunnel Melchers of Stockholm University acted as faculty opponent at the disputation. I valued our discussion highly because of the effort she had put into reading my text, her great knowledge of the subject matter, and, not least, the pleasant way in which she conducted the examination.

Lasse Ilonen and **Tore Hellberg** printed and bound the preliminary version in a most satisfactory way, despite a tight schedule.

My colleagues **Rhonwen Törnqvist** and **David Wright** read a final proof of the present version, revising my English. I am very grateful to them for taking on this task.

I remain solely responsible for any shortcomings in the book.

Nödinge, March 1989

Mats Mobärg

Table of contents.

1. Introduction.

> 'How could they make him an officer when he speaks broad Derbyshire?'
> 'He doesn't...except by fits and starts. He can speak perfectly well, for him. I suppose he has an idea if he's come down to the ranks again, he'd better speak as the ranks speak.'
>
> D.H. Lawrence, *Lady Chatterley's Lover* (1928)

This is a book about listeners' attitudes toward "standard" British English pronunciations.

370 native English informants, young people and adults of both sexes, from the South, the Midlands or the North, have been confronted with altogether 25 native English voices speaking in a standard or near-standard accent. On hearing the voices, the informants have answered a set of attitude questions about them, concerning conjectured age, occupation, psychological traits, job suitability, etc. In addition, the informants have also supplied information about themselves along partly the same lines.

The fundamental principle of the present analysis is one of variable subdivision: that is to say, the same material has been subdivided on a number of different parameters so as to create sets of mutually exclusive informant subgroups (e.g. males and females, young people and adults) who have assessed sets of mutually exclusive accent subgroups. The essence of the analysis is the comparison between ratings made by various informant subgroups with respect to various speaker subgroups.

My discussion pivots on the concept of DEGREE OF MODERNITY, i.e. the extent to which a speaker can be regarded as a traditional speaker or a non-traditional, "modern", speaker. Each speaker's DEGREE OF MODERNITY has been determined by means of a word pronunciation test, including words that are in a process of phonetic change, e.g. *lamentable*. Together with the speaker's status with regard to the other parameters of this study (AGE, SEX, REGIONALITY), DEGREE OF MODERNITY makes up a categorization that can be used to divide the full speaker group into various accent subgroups (e.g. YOUNG/MODERN, FEMALE/TRADITIONAL).

Superficially, my methods belong to the tradition formed in the early 1930s by T.H. Pear, Herta Herzog and others. These early studies were triggered by the coming of radio, which enabled people to hear speech that was not accompanied by visual or other stimuli, something which had been almost non-existent before. Indeed, several of the pioneers within this field used radio transmissions as part of their experiments.

Most studies carried out within this tradition have had a psychological inclination, i.e. scholars have tried to explore the significance of the human voice as part of the personality of the speaker.

From the early days onward, the techniques involved in investigations into attitudes to voices have been refined considerably, but many of the original approaches remain basically the same.

This study differs from the majority of language attitude studies in that its focus is on language, not on the relationship between social groups. As I shall point out elsewhere, this difference is perhaps not so rigid as it may seem, since there is no way of separating language from its speakers.

The linguistic area I set out to investigate is the standard area. Virtually all scholars who have studied attitudes to accents of British English have treated that area as synonymous with "RP", leaving any doubts as to the status of that concept without consideration. My method is the opposite one. I recorded 25 speakers, no questions asked (apart from their nationality). The speakers were asked to speak in a neutral voice, without putting on an accent. No speakers who had been recorded were discarded from the analysis. In this sense, we might claim that a certain amount of randomization was operative in the selection process, although there is a clear middle-class bias among the speakers, something which is hard to avoid in any experimental design, particularly so when the experimenter is a foreigner, as in the present case.

It seems reasonable to argue that what is "standard" when it comes to linguistic varieties is something that should be ascertained not from above but from below. That is to say, the standard is that which is believed to be standard by a given group of linguistic judges. From this it follows that there will most probably be disagreement between different sets of judges. If this is true, how do we go about defining the standard, if indeed it is possible, or even necessary to do so? One possible solution would be to simply use a majority system, so that an accent or an accent feature which is looked upon as standard by a majority of informants is considered standard. Another way would be to select a group of informants who for some reason or other could be said to represent greater linguistic maturity or some other relevant quality, and decide that their opinion as to the standard should be indicative of the general standard. The problem with the former solution is that it necessitates a statistically correct sample of informants in order for the majority decision to reflect the real situation. The problem with the latter suggestion is that it may result in a vicious circle. The traditional Jonesian definition of "RP" (cf p. 136) is an example of this in that it uses a narrow educational category as a pattern, not in this case as listeners but as speakers. One of the purposes of the present study is to see whether, owing to the various social changes in British society over the last century, it would be reasonable to suggest a standardization instrument other than the strict standard set by the Jonesians (cf Windsor Lewis 1985).

Furthermore, in this study I do not ask informants explicitly to assess the degree of "standardness", since that would mean begging the question. Instead various well-known techniques are used to elicit this information.

Since there is no way of stating once and for all by what criteria a standard accent should be defined, I believe it is wise not to settle for any one interpretative method in this type of investigation. Instead I think one should attempt to maintain an open attitude in one's discussion, trying to present as clearly as possible how the various informant subgroups respond to the accent samples. This means that we shall not expect the results to boil down to *one* distinct answer.

In brief, then, this project deals with people's attitudes to a sample of English standard or near-standard pronunciations. The questions underlying it are several: is there a recognized standard or shall we get different answers depending on who we ask; and if so, is there a pattern in this differentiation? Is it possible to discern a regular shift or other type of change according to some kind of pattern? Has the Jonesian education-based criterion, if indeed it ever existed other than as a scholarly artefact, given way to some other kind of criterion, such as the capital city being England's standard accent base? Has the accent ideal changed owing to changes in society and can such a change be reflected in differences in opinion between various informant categories?

The main purpose of this book, however, is to present the results of my field work. It is my hope that even the reader who finds the discussion deficient in some way will benefit from the facts on which it is founded.

Before continuing, the reader should study preliminarily section 1.9, below, entitled "A few notes on how to read this text" (p. 93).

1.1. The field of study.

Like most other branches of language-related study, the study of language attitudes has expanded markedly during its relatively brief existence. Since the starting-point around 1930, we have seen a rather insignificant scholarly brook grow into a major river, later to form a grand delta of substreams.

In the following survey, I choose to follow what from my point of view is the main stream, from the source of Pear and Herzog via the Lambert river of the 1960s to the major distributary of Giles in the present-day delta. For natural reasons such a presentation will be chronological.

This choice inevitably means that a certain part of what has been done within the field, particularly during the last couple of decades, will be left untouched in this presentation. It is my intention, however, to offer a sufficiently substantial background before which my own contribution to the field can be exhibited. The reader who wishes to find conveniently a more extensive survey of the field is recommended to study Giles & Powesland (1975). A brief presentation of language attitude findings with regard to the English language can also be found in Edwards (1982).

1.1.1. Early studies.
Scholarly preoccupation with the link between voice/speech and personality traits was largely brought about or at least strongly accelerated by the emergence of large-scale broadcasting, gramophone and telephone technology during the first few decades of the 20th century. Before then, voice and speech were necessarily accompanied by the speaker himself, in person, and so the idea of his voice and speech carrying in themselves features of psychological or other relevance was probably not even considered other than in very special circumstances. Sanford (1942:811) points out that "[b]efore 1900, [---] psychologists had little to say about linguistic phenomena."

That is not to say, of course, that people before the turn of the century did not find matters relating to voice and speech important. This is obvious and need not be elaborated. Let us however look at a fine pre-radio account of voice features actually winning over physical features in the attitude-formation of a person vis-à-vis another. This is how Frank Harris (1916) reacted on first meeting Oscar Wilde in 1884:

> His talk soon made me forget his repellent physical peculiarities;
> indeed I soon lost sight of them so completely that I have

wondered since how I could have been so disagreeably affected by them at first sight. There was an extraordinary physical vivacity and geniality in the man, an extraordinary charm in his gaiety, and lightning-quick intelligence. His enthusiasms, too, were infectious. Every mental question interested him, especially if it had anything to do with art or literature. His whole face lit up as he spoke and one saw nothing but his soulful eyes, heard nothing but his musical tenor voice; he was indeed what the French call a *charmeur*.

One wonders what impression Wilde would have made on radio! Indeed several early and later scholars have noted the feelings of disappointment that listeners often get when being confronted with the face of somebody whose voice they have admired on the radio.

I shall now go on to give a brief account of some of the most important early studies.

Setting the scene: Sapir 1927.
In 1927, Edward Sapir, the great American linguist, published an article, "Speech as a personality trait", in which he formulated the problems connected with the analysis of that type of human behaviour which is known as speech. The article is not explicitly founded on any experimentation; it could be seen as a kind of programme tract for much of the work that has since been carried out, not least within the field of sociolinguistics.

Sapir begins by suggesting a binary distinction between two branches of speech analysis: (1) the individual vs. society, and (2) the different levels of speech.

The first of these branches attempts to study the speech of the individual as a variant form of the speech pattern of the society he lives in. The speech society sets a standard which cannot be transgressed by the individual speakers, but nevertheless, each one of them has access to an infinite potential for variation within that standard. Sapir in other words is talking about the emics and etics of language in society.

The second branch is one whose most important feature is its analytical (although not uncontroversial) approach to the words *speech* and *voice*. Sapir shows how both these words in English tend to acquire popular interpretations which equate them or cause them to be used interchangably. This is something which becomes obvious to anybody working with informants and their attitudes: the task of making a division in the mind of the informants between, say, the linguistic and the non-linguistic aspects of speech is often overwhelmingly difficult. Maybe it is an impossible task.

5

Sapir does not think so. His idea is that it is our obligation as researchers to sharpen our analytical tools at all costs.

Allport & Cantril (1934; cf below) make use of this analytical approach to speech. However, their interpretation of Sapir (1927) is as far as I can make out not quite to the point. Allport & Cantril claim that Sapir (1927) draws a distinction between voice and speech, where voice represents the external *form* (pitch, rhythm, etc.) and speech the *content* (incl. dialect, vocabulary). In fact, Sapir (1927) makes no such explicit distinction.

What he does do, however, is devise a hierarchical structure to the phenomenon *speech*, where the basic level is *the voice*, i.e. those aspects of speech that are part of the speaker, whether he wants it or not, much the same way that a physiological quality is part of its possessor, for better or worse.

The second level is that of *voice dynamics*, e.g. intonation, rhythm, etc., which in turn can be analyzed into an individual and a social level.

The third level is *pronunciation*, the fourth *vocabulary*, and the fifth *style*. These levels too, according to Sapir, have an individual and a social aspect.

What makes Sapir's article particularly fascinating is the fact that it was written at a time when formal studies of speech were very thin on the ground, and a great deal of what scholars today consider part and parcel of their competence was still in its infancy. Sapir concludes (p. 905):

> It is possible that the kind of analysis which has here been suggested, if carried far enough, may enable us to arrive at certain very pertinent conclusions regarding personality. Intuitively we attach an enormous importance to the voice and to the speech behavior that is carried by the voice. We have not much to say about it as a rule, not much more than an "I like that man's voice," or "I do not like the way he talks." Individual speech analysis is difficult to make, partly because of the peculiarly fleeting character of speech, partly because it is especially difficult to eliminate the social determinants of speech. In view of these difficulties there is not as much significant speech analysis being made by students of behavior as we might wish, but the difficulties do not relieve us of the responsibility for making such researches.

Pear 1931.

T.H. Pear's (1931) study forms the genesis of experimentation into listeners' attitudes toward spoken language. In addition to the report on the experiment proper, the book contains a general discussion on voice, accent, radio drama and related matters, explicitly influenced by Sapir's (1927) article (cf above).

> It is a pity that this truly delightful book should be so hard to obtain in Sweden. It took me several attempts before I finally, at the eleventh hour, got the opportunity to read the text first hand. Second-hand information about Pear (1931) can be found in Allport & Cantril (1934), Taylor (1934), Stagner (1936), Kramer (1964), Giles & Powesland (1975), Brown & Bradshaw (1985).

Pear is not only the pioneer in the field; his "Radio-Personality" study is also the largest of all in terms of number of listener-informants: about 4,000 responses from all over Britain were secured. Obviously, such a scope of experimentation would be practically impossible without the assistance of a broadcasting organization. Indeed, the BBC took an active part in the experiment, which included reading-passages by 9 speakers selected on the basis of "definite and recorded success in their own calling". The speakers were judged for sex, age, occupation, leadership, place of birth and regional background. The listeners were also encouraged to supply free comments. The experiment was advertised in the *Radio Times*.

Unfortunately, the analysis and presentation of this gigantic material leave a lot to be desired. The main part of the result presentation consists of unstructured quotations from the listeners' free comments. The quantitative analysis is uneven, mixing percentages and absolute numbers rather haphazardly.

If we disregard these shortcomings, we find that in terms of accuracy, the results are often strikingly good. Sex, as expected, was judged quite accurately, apart from the voice of a child. Age, too, was accurately perceived on the whole, even though there was a marked central tendency of judgment, a common feature in all guessing experiments including my own (cf p. 98). Occupation was sometimes perceived with remarkable accuracy, but as the author notes (p. 167), "[t]he consistency of errors in the replies concerning occupation was as interesting as the consistency of correct judgments." Even in the cases where there were only chance correlations with the objective facts, informants tended to agree between themselves in terms of conjecture. Thus, *stereotyping*, a notion that has since permeated this type of study, entered the scene. Unlike most early scholars, Pear suggests an origin for some, not all, of these observed effects, viz. the conventional portrayals found in films and the theatre.

Herzog 1933.
In 1933, under the supervision of the famous Karl Bühler, the psychologist Herta Herzog of Vienna published a long article called "Stimme und Persönlichkeit". Most of the article was the fruit of a large-scale experiment carried out with the assistance of *Radio Wien*. Nine speakers of various backgrounds read a passage of text in German which was broadcast directly in the area. The experiment had been advertised in the Radio Wien magazine, where an answer form was also published. Some 2,700 people took part in the experiment. The influence of Pear (1931) on Herzog's method is obvious (and acknowledged by Herzog).

The listeners, on hearing the voices on the radio, were required to rate them with regard to a number of variables: *sex, age, occupation, liability to command, height, weight* and *pleasantness*. The questions were phrased in such a way as to facilitate quantitative analysis. On the answer form, the listeners also stated their own occupation, age, sex, and domicile.

We find in the results that as expected the sex conjecture produces answers that are basically correct. The age conjecture is less successful. In the same way as in several studies of this kind, including the present one, it suffers from a strong central tendency. As for the questions on bodily characteristics, the answers are surprisingly correct, but the analysis lacks an acceptable explanation of this state of affairs. The occupational guess is also mainly correct, but the seemingly obvious explanation that this is caused by a conventional judgment where not least the existence or absence of "dialect" plays an important part is not offered. In other words, "Stimme" is allowed to include both physiological features and linguistic features, which is of course perfectly true from the point of view of the listener, but which leaves a lot to be desired from the analytical aspect. Liability to command is judged in a way which largely, but not entirely, corresponds to the occupational guess, i.e. age and "dialect" play important parts. Finally, the pleasantness rating showed some deviations from the more career-related ratings.

When checking the relationship between ratings given and the people giving them, Herzog found certain interesting tendencies, for example that female listeners were better at guessing the age of the speakers, and that females and males respectively were more successful when guessing the occupational status of other females and males. Neither of these findings is corroborated in the present study. On the other hand, Herzog did find tendencies resembling "self-hatred" (Simpson & Yinger 1972) in the ratings given by lower-class informants of lower-class voices, and this type of result can be found in the present study, too.

The author concludes:

> [---] aus den Zuschriften zum Massenexperiment ergibt sich, daß in der Stimme die physiologische Daten des Sprechers [---], sein Milieu [...] und seine Innerlichkeit [...] in einer für den Hörer weitgehend richtig erfaßbaren Art zum Ausdruck kommen. [P. 345]

In view of the fact that no statistical analysis was carried out, and that no attempt was made to go into the complexity of the term "Stimme", as it is used here, we must argue that Herzog's conclusion is far too categorical (cf Brown & Bradshaw 1985:151 footnote). However, her experiment is a genuine piece of pioneering work in the field of listeners' attitudes to voices which, although suffering from certain technical, statistical and methodological shortcomings, has helped to set the scene for a great many subsequent studies, including the present one.

In addition to the "Massenexperiment", i.e. the large-scale quantitative part of the study, Herzog also undertook a "phenomenological" analysis of a number of voices, that is to say, a very detailed examination of the various things a listener feels and experiences when confronted with face-less voices. Although the present study is by no means characterized by such an approach, I think it would be beneficial to this entire field of study if more work were to be done along such lines.

Taylor 1934.
This is a brief article based on an experiment concerning listeners' reactions to spoken language. The author's intention is to show that even though we find a considerable degree of agreement between the judgments made by different listeners, this agreement is not based on factually accurate judgment. Technically, this is done by comparing listeners' ratings with self-evaluations supplied by the speakers. The results clearly show that Taylor's supposition is valid. The idea of *stereotyping* again appears, although Taylor himself does not use the word.

Allport & Cantril 1934.
The American experimental psychologists Allport & Cantril (1934) carried out an experiment in which informants were confronted with radio voices (and sometimes natural "face-less" voices, i.e. from behind a screen) reading a passage. The voices were to be graded with regard to a number of "Physical and Expressive Features" and "Interests and Traits". They were also to be matched against a set of summary sketches. The authors, drawing on what they claim to be Sapir's (1927; cf above) *voice* and *speech* distinction, where voice represents *form* (i.e. pitch, rhythm, vocal mannerisms, etc.) and speech *content* (i.e. subject-matter, vocabulary, dialect, etc.), make a point of not going into speech phenomena at all, which somewhat reduces

the relevance of their study for the present one. All gradings supplied by the informants were checked against their respective real values, which means that certain psychological traits in the speakers had had to be ascertained by means of standard tests.

Allport & Cantril found significant correlation between rated and real values in a number of cases, primarily in connection with *age* (where they also found a strong central tendency of judgment, cf the present study), *extroversion-introversion*, *ascendance-submission* and *dominant values*. Particularly strong correlation was found in informants' matching voices and *summary sketches*, which the authors take as an "argument against "segmental" and "atomistic" research upon arbitrarily isolated variables in personality".

In common with Taylor (1934), Allport & Cantril found that different groups of listeners tended to give similar ratings of a given voice (listeners were not selected according to a pre-defined system) and that listeners' impressions are uniform even though they may be factually wrong. This of course is a strong indication of stereotyping as a primary force in this type of judgment, which is also acknowledged by the authors. Moreover, it was found that a stereotype, once in existence in judging a certain speaker, tended to influence the judgment of other features regarding that speaker ("halo effect"); in other words, a stereotype is self-generating.

Bonaventura 1935.
Like the Herzog (1933) study, this Viennese study was performed under the auspices of Karl Bühler. Maria Bonaventura's experiment is in fact very similar to Herzog's in terms of overall method, but there is the difference that Bonaventura employs a technique of having listeners match recorded voices with photographs of the speakers. Moreover, Bonaventura's study is not a "Massen-experiment": the number of listeners is limited to 44. Using a method resembling Herzog's, Bonaventura carries out both quantitative and phenomenological analyses, i.e. she checks the way ratings were made, at the same time as she goes into the reactions of the informants when making the ratings. The group of 12 speakers can be divided into "Arbeiter" and "Akademiker", young and old speakers, and into the three Kretschmerian types (leptosomatic, athletic, pyknic), and consequently into any group made up of combinations of these categories. The general idea is to see to what extent accurate matchings are made with regard to the individual speakers and to the various subgroups.

The results show that the overall matching is successful; that the age matching is (as might have been expected) highly accurate; that Kretschmerian types give rise to considerably weaker but still clearly noticable tendencies; that the "Arbeiter" are somewhat more successfully matched than the "Akademiker". Furthermore, there seems to be a tendency for female informants to be better than males at matching photos and voices. A similar (less surprising) advantage is seen for old over young informants.

The phenomenological discussion is far too complex to be dealt with here. In it, the author tries to reach an understanding of why informants react the way they do, in what sequence they form their opinions, etc. Obviously, this discussion cannot be condensed into brief general statements; that would mean destroying the very idea governing it.

Stagner 1936.

Stagner's intention is to show how specific vocal cues, rather than an overall impression, produce certain responses about personality when confronted with listeners. His article is partly a reaction against the "holistic" perspective put forward by Allport & Cantril (1934; cf above). Stagner's method is to have male and female listeners rate voices for, basically, two kinds of traits: voice traits (e.g. flow of speech) and psychological traits (e.g. nervousness), and to check whether there is correlation between ratings of voice traits and of psychological traits, and also whether there are differences between male and female ratings. The results are somewhat uncertain, partly no doubt because of the small number of observations involved. Stagner however interprets the differences between different correlations as demonstrating "*the use of specific vocal cues in the process of making judgments about personality* [italics in original]". Apart from this, he too finds agreement of response which is not matched by accuracy of judgment—stereotyping.

Eisenberg & Zalowitz 1938.

In this experiment recordings of 8 speakers, half of whom were extremely dominant, the other half extremely non-dominant (according to a standard test), were played to 43 listeners. The task of the listeners was to judge the speakers for degree of dominance. The results show that no reliable degree of correctness of judgment could be found, but that again there was a considerable degree of agreement between listeners. In analyzing those voices that received a better-than-chance treatment, the authors found obvious stereotypes of dominance and non-dominance. They state (p. 629) that their findings "should disturb the faith of those who believe that if we have enough judges who agree we can learn the truth." From the point of view of the present study we would of course have to counter: truth about what? There are truths and there are truths (cf discussion on stereotyping below, p. 54).

Fay & Middleton 1939-1944.

The Fay and Middleton experiments were performed in the late 1930s and the first half of the 1940s in the Radio Research Laboratory of DePauw University, Indiana, USA. In all, over a dozen very similar experiments were carried out, the (brief) documentation of each one of them being published separately in a number of journals. Because of the similarity of the experiments, I will treat them jointly.

The experiments all concern "the ability to judge [something] from the voice as transmitted over a public address system". Among the things to be judged were the following: *Spranger personality types* (theoretic, economic, aesthetic, social, political, religious); *occupation; intelligence; Kretschmerian body types* (pyknic, leptosomatic, athletic); *rested or tired condition; sociability; truth-telling or lying; introversion; leadership; confidence; persuasiveness; emotional balance; effect of Benzedrine sulphate* (a type of amphetamine, i.e. a stimulant of the central nervous system, earlier erroneously believed to enhance mental achievement).

What made these experiments special compared with previous experiments was above all the greater sophistication of the sound transmission equipment. The authors claim that "high fidelity voice transmission was achieved" in their experiments (1940b:154).

The experimental set-up was largely the same throughout. Each experiment included passages of text read via a loudspeaker system by 5 to 27 speakers to groups of informants ranging in size from 28 to 155 people (in the odd case, recorded voice material was used). The informants were required to respond to the speech stimulus either by grading the voices along a 7-point scale (e.g. for *intelligence*), making a choice between options (e.g. *Benzedrine sulphate* or not), or by writing answers in full (e.g. for *Kretschmerian body types*). The assessment of the informants' responses was made in terms of reliability, i.e. responses were checked against real or estimated real values.

This is a brief account of the results of the experiments:

Spranger personality types: "There [was] a rather significant medium positive correlation between the listeners' ratings of Spranger value types and the actual types themselves." Certain voices gave rise to stereotyping.

Occupation: Some voices were easier than others to match accurately with a job label. In general, tendencies are too weak for any conclusions to be drawn. Certain voices (accurately or inaccurately) gave rise to stereotyping.

Intelligence: There was a weak overall tendency for informants to judge voices correctly for intelligence. The tendency was accentuated in connection with certain voices. A certain amount of voice stereotyping could be noticed.

Kretschmerian body types: A certain degree of correctness in judging the body types of speakers, notably in the case of pyknic and leptosomatic speakers, could be noticed. Certain pyknic and leptosomatic voices were found to be stereotypes.

Rested or tired condition: Judgments were unreliable. Certain voices were stereotyped as "rested" or "tired" irrespective of accuracy.

Sociability: No reliable ratings were found.

Truth-telling or lying: A slight tendency to judge truth-telling and lying accurately was noticed. Lying seems to be more easily judged than truth-telling.

Introversion: Judgments were not reliable, but a certain amount of agreement in excess of accuracy, i.e. stereotyping, could be found.

Leadership: Judgments were not reliable.

Confidence: The results indicate "that listeners have only slight ability to judge self-confidence from the transmitted voice." For about half the speakers, there was a "tendency toward consistency in judgment."

Emotional balance: Judgments were mostly unreliable. Certain tendencies towards stereotyping could be found.

Effect of Benzedrine: Judgments were not reliable. A certain amount of agreement in excess of accuracy, i.e. stereotyping, could be noticed.

The experiment concerning the perceived *Persuasiveness* of voices was conducted along somewhat different lines. Rather than simply asking listeners to judge voices with regard to a trait, etc., this experiment was founded on the idea that persuasiveness is best judged by checking to what extent listeners believe in the message of the various voices. To achieve this, a number of non-factual statements (e.g. "The Government should own all railroads") were selected and equated for perceived "credibility". In the first part of the experiment, the informants were confronted with the statements in writing and asked to mark them as "true" or "false" (which everybody did despite their non-factual status). Some months later, the same informants had to listen to recordings of the very same statements and mark them in a similar way. It turned out that when control of statement credibility was exercised, listeners differed in their belief of the various voices; in other words, people's voices are seen to be more or less persuasive regardless of speech content. The technique of this experiment, i.e. having informants act implicitly rather than simply answer questions, is closely related to that of Giles *et al.* (1975; cf below).

1.1.2. Wallace E. Lambert and the matched guise technique.

During the 1960s and 1970s, several very influential articles on language attitudes were published by the Canadian social psychologist Wallace E. Lambert and his colleagues (for convenience, I will use "Lambert" as an umbrella denomination of the work he has taken part in). What made these studies special as compared with earlier studies, apart from such improved sophistication as is a natural result of occupying a later stage in a research tradition, was the use Lambert made of the so-called "matched-guise technique" of confronting listeners with recordings of spoken language. In a matched-guise experiment, perfectly bilingual or bidialectal speakers record the same passage in the two varieties they command. These recordings are then arranged in experimental sets, often together with "filler voices", i.e. voices that are not part of the matched-guise experiment as such, but which are used to conceal from the listeners the fact that they are actually hearing the same voices twice. By using this technique, scholars claim that they can isolate relevant from irrelevant information.

Lambert's studies are primarily directed towards exploring the formation of attitudes in linguistically well-defined groups, using language as a convenient means of eliciting stereotyped views of one group vis-à-vis another:

> [...] evaluational reactions to a spoken language should be similar to those prompted by interaction with individuals who are perceived as members of the group that uses it, but because the use of the language is one aspect of behavior common to a variety of individuals, hearing the language is likely to arouse mainly generalized or stereotyped characteristics of the group. [Lambert *et al.* 1960:44]

Lambert, Hodgson, Gardner & Fillenbaum 1960.
In Lambert's pioneer study (Lambert *et al.* 1960), four bilinguals (in French and English) read a passage which was played to French Canadian and English Canadian informants. The informants were required to grade the voices for the following 14 traits: *Height, Good Looks, Leadership, Sense of Humour, Intelligence, Religiousness, Self-confidence, Dependability, Entertainingness, Kindness, Ambition, Sociability, Character, Likability*. They were also asked to answer various more or less open questions about their attitudes towards English and French

14

Canadians.

The most striking thing about the results is that both English and French informants grade the English guises significantly higher in a clear majority of the cases. At the overall level, there are only three cases where the opposite holds true (there are of course a number of cases where there are no significant differences): the English informants grade French guises significantly higher for Sense of Humour, and the French informants grade French guises significantly higher for Religiousness and Kindness. In addition, French informants tend to grade French guises less favourably than do English informants.

There was however little or no correlation between these gradings and the attitudes of the informants towards English and French Canadians as stated explicitly in their answers to the open questions. The authors conclude:

> The essential independence of evaluational reactions to spoken languages and attitudes is interpreted as a reflection of the influence of community-wide stereotypes of English and French speaking Canadians. [P. 51]

Anisfeld, Bogo & Lambert 1962.
In the next Lambert study (Anisfeld *et al.* 1962) the matched-guise experiment concerned the difference between non-accented and Jewish accented Canadian English. Four bidialectal speakers were selected to read a passage in each of these accents. The passages were then played to Jewish and non-Jewish informants who were asked to grade the voices according to the same principle as in Lambert *et al.* (1960). They were also asked to state what they thought was the religious affiliation of each speaker.

"Correct" ratings, i.e. ratings where the Jewish guises were believed to be Jewish by the informants, and vice versa, were treated separately from "incorrect" ones.

Among the "correct" ratings, Jewish informants rated non-accented voices significantly higher for Height, Good looks, and Leadership, and Jewish voices significantly higher for Sense of humour, Entertainingness, and Kindness. Non-Jewish informants rated non-accented voices significantly higher for Height, Good looks, Leadership, and Self-confidence. No Jewish accented voices were given higher ratings by non-Jewish informants.

In the case of incorrect ratings, i.e. where Jewish informants identified *both* guises in a pair as being Jewish, and non-Jewish informants identified them as being non-Jewish (these are of course not the only possible combinations, but for various reasons, they were the only ones to be analyzed), Jewish informants upgraded the non-accented guises for Height, Good looks, Leadership, and Self-Confidence, whereas the Jewish guises were upgraded for Kindness (the latter upgrading is not recognized as such by the authors in spite of a stated t value of 1.97—an error perhaps or a low number of observations?). Non-Jewish informants upgraded non-accented guises for Height, Good looks, Leadership, Self-confidence, and Dependability, whereas they did not upgrade Jewish guises at all.

In other words, regardless of whether informants identified guises correctly or incorrectly with regard to Jewishness or non-Jewishness, they tended to comparatively downrate accented guises, the exception being, as we have seen, a certain upgrading on the part of the Jewish informants of correctly perceived Jewish voices for Sense of humour, Entertainingness and Kindness, and of incorrectly perceived Jewish voices for Kindness.

From the discrepancy between ratings and explicitly stated attitudes towards Jews, the authors could conclude (p. 230) "that the technique used is especially sensitive to stereotypes rather than to attitudes."

Preston 1963.
In a follow-up study to Lambert *et al.* (1960), Preston (1963; reported in Lambert 1967) set out to investigate whether the sex variable, in speakers as well as listeners, had any effect on matched guise ratings. He also introduced a comparison between Canadian and Continental French. Apart from this, the general technique of the experiment was similar to that of the previous studies.

The results of this study somewhat confused the picture created by its predecessors: the virtually unanimous downgrading of French Canadians that was found in Lambert *et al.* (1960) was severely modified here. What happened was that the *female* French guises were more favourably rated for several traits to do with "competence" and "personal integrity", particularly by English Canadian males, but also by English Canadian females. This sexually based differentiation in the perception of French Canadian speakers is subjected to analysis by Lambert (1967), who suggests various sociocultural and sociopolitical explanations for it.

Webster & Kramer (1968) try to reconcile the apparently disparate findings of Lambert *et al.* (1960) and Preston (1963) by suggesting that ratings may be affected by the "degree of prejudice" in the informants. Their suggestion is further substantiated in an experiment in which 30 informants of 3 levels of prejudice listened to 5 voices, two of which were produced by one and the same speaker, "once with a French-Canadian accent and once without it", evaluating the voices along 10 bipolar six-step scales. The authors find that there are clear differences in informants' evaluations of the accented guise depending on which level of prejudice the informant belongs to. The most striking result is the relative upgrading of the accented guise by the "Medium prejudice" group of informants, which is explained by the authors as a case of "overcompensation" in order to balance the biases of their society which they recognize and somehow feel responsible for. The rather disturbing circumstance that the "Low prejudice" group joins the "High prejudice" group in responding less favourably to the accented guise is explained in the spirit of the biblical "Unto the pure all things are pure" (Tit. 1:15). However, as Giles & Powesland (1975:58f) point out, the limited number of observations on which this study is based necessitates great interpretational caution.

Anisfeld & Lambert 1964.

Together with Elizabeth Anisfeld, Lambert went on to carry out a new matched-guise experiment in which they concentrated on the attitudes of French Canadian children (Anisfeld & Lambert 1964). Four ten-year-old bilingual (French and English) girls read a passage from a fairy-tale in their two languages. In addition to the basic French-English distinction, there was also a certain distinction made between various French varieties. The passages were recorded and the recordings arranged in a set designed so as not to give away the fact that the same four speakers had spoken twice (in one case, three times). The recording was then played to 150 ten-year-old school children attending French schools. Half of these children were monolinguals in French, the other half bilinguals in French and English. The informants were required to rate the voices they heard for 15 traits of the same type as in the previously mentioned studies and, in addition, to answer a number of open attitude questions about the two languages concerned and the people who speak them.

The result of the experiment was that the French guises were upgraded for all traits except Height (as it happens, English Canadians according to statistics are genuinely taller), but that it was mainly in the judgment made by monolingual informants that this pro-French upgrading was significant. In addition to this basic result, there was also a certain tendency among bilinguals to be more favourably inclined towards Parisian French guises than towards Canadian French guises.

The answers to the open attitude questions show that bilinguals are more positively inclined towards English and English Canadians on the whole than monolinguals.

The authors note that the "self-hatred" that was present in the ratings made by adult French Canadians in a previous study (Anisfeld *et al.* 1962) cannot be found in the present results. They suggest that this is because ten-year-olds are in a stage of development which typically involves total rejection of all members of an outside group. From puberty onwards, according to this idea, young people gradually adopt the prejudiced attitudes of the society they are living in.

Lambert, Frankel & Tucker 1966.

In Lambert, Frankel & Tucker (1966), an attempt was made to explore the various ages in which this adoption is believed to take place. This time, the speakers were male and female bilinguals from 10 years of age and upwards. The informants were 373 French Canadian girls subdivided according to age, mono-linguality/bilinguality and private fee-paying vs. public (in the non-British sense) school (i.e. a kind of social grouping).

Since there are so many variables involved, the outcome of this study is less tidy than was the case in the previous studies. Furthermore, the interpretation of the results is rendered unnecessarily difficult by the circumstance that the authors have chosen to publish significant differences only, leaving non-significant differences out altogether. In view of the fact that even non-significant differences contribute to a trend, this method of presentation is, I feel, unfortunate.

The most conspicuous fact about these comparisons is that private school girls seem to be more English-minded than public school girls, i.e. there seems to be a social aspect to language preferences in Canada. Among the public school girls we notice a certain upgrading of adult male French guises, and of adult female English guises. In the 10-16 age bracket (for speakers and informants alike), there is a tendency among public school monolinguals to upgrade French guises, whereas virtually no such tendency can be seen in the ratings made by public school bilinguals.

Tucker & Lambert 1969.

A slightly different approach is used in Tucker & Lambert (1969). First of all, the research forming the basis of this study was carried out in the United States. Secondly, the study deals with differences between black and white speakers. Thirdly, this is not a matched-guise experiment (hence, it is more closely related to the present study).

15 traits were devised which were positively related to "success" and "friendliness": *Upbringing, Intelligent, Friendly, Educated, Disposition, Speech, Trustworthy, Ambitious, Faith in God, Talented, Character, Determination, Honest, Personality, Considerate*. On these traits, bipolar eight-step scales were based, much the same way as in the previously mentioned studies.

The voices of this study represented six dialect groups: (1) Network English; (2)

Educated White Southern; (3) Educated Negro Southern; (4) Black students from Mississippi attending Howard University, Washington D.C. (5) "Mississippi peer group", i.e. the dialect spoken at the Black college where the testing was carried out; (6) "New York alumni", i.e. people corresponding to (5) who had since lived for several years in New York City. There were four speakers of each dialect who recorded the 45-second reading passage used in the study.

In all, 258 informants listened to the voices. Of these, 150 were black students from a Southern college; 40 white students from New England; 68 white students from the South.

The most conspicuous result of this experiment is the unanimous top ranking of the Network English speakers among all three informant categories. Coming in second in the Northern white as well as Southern black judgment was Educated Negro Southern, whereas the Southern white informants placed their own peer group, Southern Educated White, in this position.

At the bottom of the ranking lists interesting differences occur. Educated White Southern was placed at the bottom position for every single trait by the black informants, whereas the white informants placed "Mississippi peer group" there.

The white informants were also asked to guess the race of each speaker. It turned out that the two white speaker groups were perceived as white by most informants; that about 50 per cent of "New York Alumni" and Educated Negro Southern, and about 70-90 per cent of "Howard University" and "Mississippi peer group" were perceived as black. In other words, there is a certain indication that "white judges [informants] can, in certain instances at least, distinguish white from Negro speakers." (p.468).

> Fraser (1973) is a replication of Tucker & Lambert (1969), using parts of the same stimulus material. To a great extent, Fraser's results tally with those of the original study, but there are some interesting deviations. Fraser found that when listeners misjudged the race of black speakers, i.e. guessed that they were white, they tended to downgrade them on several rating scales; however, when the race of white speakers was misjudged, there was no such downgrading. Fraser takes this to indicate that the "stereotypic pairing function" (between speech and character traits) is race dependent, so that expectations may differ with regard to the two groups. This seems to be another instance of the problem of "cognitive dissonance" that I shall return to on several occasions in the following pages (cf also Sebastian & Ryan 1985:123).

The first five of the Lambert studies discussed so far are treated jointly by W.E.

Lambert himself in Lambert (1967). A brief introductory discussion can also be found in Wardhaugh (1986:108ff).

Bourhis, Giles & Lambert 1975.

This study, which forms a bridge between the Lambert and Giles traditions, addresses the question of speech accommodation, i.e. the tendency for a speaker of a certain accent, etc., to converge toward or diverge from the accent of his interlocutor according to various social pressures (for a fuller account, see e.g. Beebe & Giles 1984:7ff). The study is divided into two matched-guise experiments, one with a French Canadian setting, the other with a Welsh setting.

The Canadian experiment had the form of a series of sports interviews with a French Canadian athlete. Each interview was conducted by a French Canadian *and* a European French interviewer, one after the other. There were six different experimental conditions depending on the order between the interviewers, and on the type and direction of accommodation taking place in the interviewee. The following is a schematic rendition of the six different accommodational conditions (FC=French Canadian, EF=European French, FCinf=informal French Canadian):

Interviewers:	1.FC 2.EF	1.EF 2.FC	1.FC 2.EF	1.EF 2.FC
Interviewee:	FC to FC	FC to FC	FC to EF	EF to FC
Interviewers:	1.FC 2.EF	1.EF 2.FC		
Interviewee:	FC to FCinf	FCinf to FC		

The recordings made of each of these situations were played to groups of French Canadian informants who were required to answer a number of socially relevant questions about the interviewee. They were also asked to comment on the accommodation as such.

The only significant differences that occurred concerned "intelligence" and "education". "Here the athlete was perceived to be more intelligent and educated when she shifted to European French [...] than when she did not [...] and least intelligent and educated when she shifted to Informal French Canadian." 65 per cent of the informants reported that they had perceived the direction of the accommodation the way it had happened.

The Welsh experiment was conducted largely along the same lines apart from the language involved. The following accommodational conditions were applied (MW=mild Welsh accent, BW=broad Welsh accent):

Interviewers:	1.MW 2.RP	1.RP 2.MW	1.MW 2.RP	1.RP 2.MW
Interviewee:	MW to MW	MW to MW	MW to RP	RP to MW
Interviewers:	1.MW 2.RP	1.RP 2.MW		
Interviewee:	MW to BW	BW to MW		

The results show that Welsh listeners perceive the speaker who converges towards RP as significantly more intelligent and as belonging to a significantly higher social class. Interestingly, however, shifting from a mild to a broad Welsh accent when answering the RP interviewer is perceived as an indication of significantly higher trustworthiness and kindheartedness.

Other Lambert studies.

In Frender *et al.* (1970) the authors set out to explore the "role of speech characteristics for scholastic success". The subjects of the study were two groups of 8-year-old French Canadian boys from low status areas of Montreal, one containing poor achievers, the other good achievers. The two groups were equated for non-verbal intelligence and then compared with regard to six speech variables, *Pronunciation, Accent, Speed of speech, Intonation, Individual characteristics*. The results indicate that the poor achievers show genuinely lower scores for three of these variables (speed, intonation, individual characteristics), and that this difference remains even when the groups are equated for verbal intelligence. The authors conclude (Frender *et al.* 1970:305):

> that a lower-class youngster's style of speech may mark or caricature him and thus adversely affect his opportunities to better himself in various situations, including the school environment.

In a follow-up study, Seligman *et al.* (1972) go on to find out what effects various speech styles and other traits in pupils have on teachers. They do this by selecting a number of voice recordings, photographs and compositions/drawings from a group of 8-year-old Montreal school boys. The material was then combined in various ways so as to create a number of "hypothetical children", e.g. good voice + good photo + good comp./draw., or good voice + bad photo + bad comp./draw., and so on, so that all possible combinations were acquired. These hypothetical children were then presented to student teachers as "authentic" children. The results showed that teachers seem to place great importance on voice cues when judging their pupils in particular with regard to intelligence; and that voice *and* physical appearance are of importance to teachers when evaluating the capability of their pupils.

Readers who wish to get convenient access to Lambert's writings are recommended to read Lambert (1972), which is a collection of essays by W.E. Lambert.

1.1.3. Other North American studies contemporary with Lambert.

Three studies carried out by Norman N. Markel and his colleagues (Markel *et al.* 1964, Markel *et al.* 1965, Markel *et al.* 1967) add to our knowledge of language attitudes.

The basis of the Markel *et al.* 1964 study is the assumption (p. 459) "that schizophrenics have distinct qualities in their voices that are distinguishable from the voice qualities [cf bottom of this paragraph] of nonschizophrenics", and the finding (Markel *et al.* 1965) that the *evaluative* factor of the semantic differential (Osgood *et al.* 1957), i.e. judgments about a speaker made along scales like *kind-cruel, nice-awful*, is influenced by the content of the spoken passage and the way it harmonized with the "voice set" of the speaker, i.e. the vocal features determined by the speaker's social, sexual, locational, etc., state. No such influence was found for the *potency* (*strong-weak*) and *activity* (*relaxed-tense*) factors. Furthermore, Markel *et al.* (1965) could show that the speaker's "voice qualities", i.e. more or less conscious (paralinguistic) features such as pitch range or tempo, had an effect on the specific impressions a hearer gets of a speaker.

Drawing on Osgood *et al.* (1957), the authors maintain the view that the evaluative factor is to all intents and purposes an "index of attitude", and speculate (drawing on Markel *et al.* 1965) that the potency and activity factors are thus rather to be regarded as markers of "specific impressions". This seems to make sense.

Their idea is that if there is a genuine difference in voice quality between schizophrenics and non-schizophrenics, this could be shown in listeners' attitudes to representatives of these two groups *equated for voice set* reading *one and the same passage*. This is the framework of the experiment reported in Markel *et al.* (1964). The recordings thus procured were played to a group of 40 judges who were required to grade the voices along three adjective-pair scales (evaluative, potency, activity; cf Osgood *et al.* 1957). In addition, the informants were asked to state whether they thought the respective speakers were schizophrenic or not.

The results show that there is a significant difference between schizophrenics and non-schizophrenics in terms of ratings of "potency". In general, there was also interaction between true and perceived diagnosis in terms of ratings for "potency" and "activity", that is to say, speakers who were perceived to be schizophrenic were given the expected ratings for potency and activity only in those cases when they were genuinely schizophrenic. The basic assumption, that the evaluative factor is not affected if content and voice set are held constant could also be confirmed.

Markel *et al.* (1967) is a study along much the same lines as the Lambert studies referred to above. However it goes one step further in purporting to examine (p. 33) "the hypothesis that regional dialect is a significant factor in judging personality from voice." The Lambert studies published prior to 1967 as we remember dealt primarily with French vs. English, or, in the case of Anisfeld *et al.* (1962), with Jewish accented English.

The speakers of this study are six female students born in Buffalo and six born in New York City. They recorded a short reading passage which was then played to the informants, 31 female students born and raised in Buffalo. On listening to the recording, the informants were required to rate the voices for nine adjective pairs referring to three adjective-pair scales: *evaluative, potency, activity* (Osgood *et al.* 1957; cf above).

The results indicate that there are significant differences in attitudes (according to Osgood's semantic differential) to speakers of different regional dialects. In this case, the speakers from Buffalo not unexpectedly got higher ratings than the New Yorkers for the evaluative factor, i.e. they were considered kinder, nicer and more pleasant; whereas they got lower ratings for potency (weaker, quieter, more delicate) and for activity (slower, duller, more passive). The authors conclude (p. 35) that "regional dialect elicits a stereotype which determines the evaluation of the speaker on each of the three major dimensions of semantic space."

1.1.4. Howard Giles.

The next few pages will cover some of the work carried out by, or under the auspices of, the British social psychologist Howard Giles. The work that I will refer to was produced during the 1970s and 1980s. As we have already noted, Giles also took part in one of the Lambert studies discussed above.

Giles 1970-1972: the "classic" experiments.

Giles (1970) is a matched-guise experiment of an extreme kind: one and the same speaker produces no less than 13 accent guises (RP, Affected RP, North American, French, South Welsh, Irish, Yorkshire, Somerset, Indian, Birmingham, Cockney, Italian, German) that are recorded and later played to a total of 177 listeners (school pupils) subdivided according to *age* (12-year-olds and 17-year-olds), *social background* (working class and middle class), and *regional background* (South West England and South Wales). The listeners were asked to name the accents and to grade them on three different 7-step scales, an *aesthetic*, a *communicative*, and a *status* scale. In addition, the informants were asked to grade 16 accent *labels* (the same (minus affected RP) as in the listening part of the experiment plus Scottish, West Indian, Liverpool, and "an accent identical to your own") on the same scales.

First of all, the results show that the 17-year-olds were significantly better at naming accents than the 12-year-olds. More importantly, there appeared highly interesting ranking-lists based on the informants' ratings. In order to elucidate these lists as economically as possible I have calculated the mean rating (7-step scale; positive pole: 1) for all three evaluational dimensions (italicized accent names appear in one set of comparisons only):

Vocal stimuli
1. RP (2.7)
2. French (3.6)
3. North American (3.9)
4. Irish (4.1)
5. S. Wales/*Affected RP* (4.2)
7. Northern England (4.4)
8. Italian (4.5)
9. Somerset (4.6)
10. German (4.7)
11. Indian/Cockney (4.8)
13. Birmingham (5.1)

Accent labels
1. RP ("B.B.C. accent") (2.2)
2. *Your own type accent* (2.6)
3. French (3.3)
4. *Scottish* (3.7)
5. Irish (3.9)
6. North American (4.0)
7. Northern England/German/ Somerset/S. Wales (4.1)
11. Italian (4.4)
12. *West Indies* (4.6)
13. *Liverpool* (4.7)
14. Indian (4.8)
15. Birmingham/Cockney (4.9)

We see that the two ranking-lists, based on the rating of voices and the rating of accent labels, respectively, have very much in common. We recall that in several early studies on listeners' attitudes to speakers (cf above), agreement of evaluation tended to outshine correctness as estimated in standard attitude tests, and this state of affairs was seen by most scholars concerned as an indication of stereotyping. However, as Giles (1970:224f) points out, we must be careful to distinguish between assessing the speaker and assessing the speech. Most of the research carried out within the field of attitudes towards speech has had as its aim to see to what extent a speaker's personality is reflected in the way he speaks. In such research, control has often consisted of comparisons between ratings of voice stimuli and the speakers' test scores in a standard test. Giles's (1970) set-up is one where accents, not speakers, are evaluated in two different ways, by rating voices and by rating accent labels. "So when techniques are actually measuring the same basic parameters, and socially-appropriate responses are not conducive to only one of these tasks, agreement is extremely high." (Giles 1970:224).

The aesthetic and the communicative dimensions receive remarkably similar voice ratings, the most drastic difference in terms of ranking being that "North

American" is judged considerably higher for communicative content than for aesthetic content. The status dimension, on the other hand, shows some deviation as compared with the other two. Thus, having occupied a close-to-bottom position for aesthetic and communicative content, "Affected RP" is moved up to a second position for status. A similar gain, although on a slightly smaller scale, is surprisingly made by "German", i.e. German-accented English. For Northern English we get the inversion of what happened to Affected RP and German: it receives a less favourable ranking for status than for aesthetic and communicative content.

If we want to relate Giles (1970) to the present study, we should also add another couple of results. As for the age variable in the informants, Giles found that the older informants (17 years of age) rated RP and "Affected RP" higher than did the younger informants, and that the younger informants seemed to exhibit more "accent loyalty" in upgrading (relatively) their own respective accent. Disregarding the age subdivision, we notice that both the Welsh and the English (Somerset) informants when compared tended to upgrade, relatively speaking, their own accent. In other words, the notion of "self-hatred" (Simpson & Yinger 1972), which I shall find several opportunities to return to in the pages to come, does not seem to have been operative in Giles's (1970) experiment.

> Ball (1983) can to a great extent be looked upon as a replication in an Australian setting of Giles (1970). In this study, which consists of several related matched-guise experiments, Australian listeners were confronted with various Australian, British, North American and non-native English accents which they were required to rate on Lambert-type competence, integrity and social attractiveness scales. "RP" was generally strongly upgraded for competence and integrity, but downgraded for social attractiveness (cf Giles 1970 and several other studies). Interestingly, a marked tendency toward "self-hatred" could be noticed with regard to competence and integrity in the clear downgrading of Australian English by the Australian informants, even as compared with their rating of a non-native accent, French. North American and Scots tended to occupy in-between positions.

Giles went on to carry out a modified replication of his (1970) study. This study, which formed the basis of his doctoral dissertation (University of Bristol 1971; unpublished), is briefly described in Giles & Powesland (1975:32). The main methodological novelties were the use of older (21 years of age) and regionally more heterogeneous listeners, and the non-use of the matched-guise technique. The accent samples were authentically produced by 13 different speakers (cf the present study). In spite of this "enormous amount of variability [...] in paralinguistic features" (*ib.*), the results of this study are reported to show great resemblance to those of the original (1970) study. A certain amount of deviation was found in the pleasantness ranking. This deviation Giles & Powesland (1975) suggest can be ascribed to "lack of control of paralinguistic features". There was also an overall tendency for the older listeners of the 1971 study to rate accents more favourably than the younger listeners, which is seen as an effect of a more "cosmopolitan social environment" (*ib.*).

In order to pursue this effect further, Giles set up a new experiment (1971a), in which he hypothesized that highly ethnocentric listeners, i.e. people with a strong sense of belonging to a certain ethnic group, would (1) be less favourably inclined towards regional accents; and (2) be more favourably inclined towards "RP". To test this, he selected out of a group of Somerset and South Wales sixth-formers 20 informants, 10 from each region, half of whom had a high, the other half a low, ethnocentrism score on a test specially designed to measure such things (Warr *et al.* 1967). These informants were then asked to rate accents according to exactly the same principles as in Giles (1970; cf above), i.e. for aesthetic, communicative and status content. The six voice recordings of Giles (1971a) were all selected from his (1970) experiment and thus read by one and the same person. Basically, both hypotheses were supported by the results of the experiment.

1971 saw another Giles experiment (1971b). This time Giles adapted to the methodology of Lambert in having listeners rate accented speech on a series of personality traits grouped together into the three personality categories, "competence", "personal integrity" and "social attractiveness". The technique used was that of matched guises. Having found (Giles 1970) that "RP", South Welsh, and Somerset represented roughly the top, middle and bottom, respectively, of a scale of perceived status based on accent, Giles confronted 96 South Welsh and Somerset listeners (12- and 17-year-olds) with matched-guise recordings of these varieties. The informants were required to rate the voices they heard along seven-point scales for each of 18 traits (e.g. intelligence, kindness, sociability). In summary, it was found (1) that the 17-year-olds (as compared with the younger informants) uprated RP on several competence traits; (2) that the Somerset informants, relative to the South Welsh ones, downgraded all three accents on as many as 10 traits (the author offers no explanation); (3) that RP was generally upgraded for competence; (4) that the two regional accents were upgraded on four traits concerning personal integrity and social attractiveness. In the present study we shall find several parallels to these results.

Giles (1972a) is a blend of his (1971a) and (1971b) studies. In it he attempts to find out whether the results of (1971b) will be affected by grouping the listeners according to their ethnocentrism scores. Practically, this could be done quite easily because of the fact that to a great extent the same listeners had been used in both experiments, and so it was mainly a question of reshuffling the material. Giles's main hypothesis was that highly ethnocentric listeners would rate regionally accented speakers less favourably on all personality traits and "RP" speakers more favourably. However, this hypothesis was supported on two traits only, intelligence and determination. Giles suggests (1972a:169) "that the personality complex of competence is probably the dominant dimension in the evaluation of standard and nonstandard accented speakers."

The same year, Giles performed yet another matched-guise experiment (1972b), this time in order to see to what extent the mildness or broadness of a mode of pronunciation might affect prestige and pleasantness ratings. One and the same speaker produced one mild and one broad version of each of three accents: South Welsh, Irish, Birmingham. In addition to rating the voices, the informants (12- and 21-year-old Welsh and non-Welsh persons) were asked to grade the voices for degree of broadness. This latter task was successfully carried out by the informants and there also turned out to be a clear correlation between accent mildness and perceived prestige. An interesting detail in the results was that although the 21-year-olds were better than the 12-year-olds at telling the difference between mild and broad versions, the 12-year-olds were more discriminating in their social evaluations. Giles suggests that "as the adolescent matures there develops an increasing sensitivity to vocal differences in accent usage, but concomitantly a greater tolerance to variations in broadness at a more cognitive level."

Giles and associates 1974-1975: Imposed Norm or Inherent Value?
Equipped with a strong case for the perceived supremacy of "RP" among British people, Giles went on to seek reasons for the formation of language prestige. There is a markedly practical vein in this research in that it attempts to propose educational measures to be taken in order to improve the social situation in terms of language among the linguistically deprived.

The first study I shall discuss was originally published in 1975 but will be referred to here as Giles *et al.* (1979a). The authors start out by acknowledging "two schools of thought concerning nonstandard usage", *Difference* and *Deficit*. Advocates of Difference claim that a nonstandard variety is no worse than a standard variety, it is simply different. Absence of scholastic success in nonstandard-speaking pupils can, according to this idea, be ascribed to lack of mutual understanding between pupils and teachers. The Deficit advocates, on the other hand, claim that the reason for such pupils to be unsuccessful is that their language puts them in a disadvantageous position because it is poorly suited to deal with scholastic matters (for a refreshing contribution to this debate, see Davies 1984). What Giles *et al.* (1979a) do now is to devise two hypotheses related to Difference and Deficit respectively which can help to explain the formative aspects of the two schools of thought: the *Imposed Norm* hypothesis and the *Inherent Value* hypothesis.

According to the Imposed Norm hypothesis, linguistic prestige, including aesthetic considerations, can be traced back to the prestige of the speakers of the language in question. It is in other words a sociopolitically loaded hypothesis. The Inherent Value hypothesis, on the other hand, claims that a prestigious variety is inherently superior at an aesthetic level. This hypothesis of course finds a great deal of support in popular notions of the foundations of aesthetic value.

Having established these hypotheses, Giles *et al.* (1979a) go on to suggest that their factual status can be tested by having listeners judge speech in languages they do not know. That way, the authors claim, it is possible to isolate any purely aesthetic features, if they exist, in the sense that if people who do not know the tested language at all grade varieties of it in a way similar to native speakers, then the Inherent Value hypothesis would be confirmed. If on the other hand they cannot distinguish in a native-like way between varieties, then the Imposed Norm hypothesis would be confirmed.

As a preliminary trial test, Giles *et al.* (1979a) confronted 35 Welsh listeners with matched-guise recordings of three varieties of French (plus a number of "filler voices" speaking other supposedly unknown languages). The listeners, who had virtually no knowledge of French at all, were asked to name the languages they heard and to rate them for pleasantness and prestige, and for a number of traits that had proved suitable in a native experiment concerning French varieties. The results show that unlike native listeners in an earlier experiment, the listeners were unable to make meaningful distinctions between the French varieties they heard. Quite a few were even unsure about French being French. The authors take these results as indicating that the Inherent Value hypothesis may be untenable in connection with the varieties tested.

I have certain doubts about the fundamental suppositions underlying these results. This thesis is however not the proper place for a thorough discussion on language aesthetics.

Giles *et al.* (1974), which in spite of its date is a later study than the one I have just been discussing, is a replication of that study using instead of French two socially relevant varieties of Greek that had been recorded according to the matched-guise technique. The recordings (including "filler voices") were played to a group of 46 British listeners, none of whom had any knowledge of Greek. The test procedure was the same as in the Giles *et al.* (1979a) experiment. The results show that none of the listeners managed to recognize the two voices under scrutiny as Greek. Moreover, there were no significant differences between the ratings for the two varieties (incidentally, the less than significant differences that did appear went in exactly the opposite direction from what would have been expected in a similar experiment using native Greek listeners). The authors interpret their results as clear support of the Imposed Norm hypothesis (cf also Trudgill 1983, ch. 12).

Giles *et al.* 1975: refining the matched-guise instrument.

In the course of their existence, matched-guise experiments have been subjected to criticism of various kinds (cf Giles & Bourhis 1973, Giles & Powesland 1975:101ff). Some of this criticism has dealt with the very principle of using matched guises (cf P.M. Smith 1985:89), but normally critics have focused on the artificiality of using tape recordings, thus leaving out important social information (cf Argyle *et al.* 1970); and on the circumstance that the technique, the way it has been practised, necessitates repetition of one and the same message which would seem to make listeners overly conscious of the *linguistic form* of the message. It has also been said that matched-guise experiments can deal with attitudes only, not with any action taken by people after receiving linguistic input (cf Fay & Middleton 1942b).

In order to test the validity of this criticism, Giles *et al.* (1975) performed an experiment designed to allow direct confrontation between a live speaker and his listeners. The general set-up was a classroom situation where one and the same bidialectal university psychologist (i.e. a high-status profession) addressed two different, but comparable, groups of 17-year-olds (N=28x2; having two different groups is of course a violation of the matched-guise principle, but the technique necessitates one hidden aspect). The content of his talk was simply a request to find out (allegedly on behalf of his University) how much high school students knew about psychology. To one of the groups the psychologist spoke "RP" and to the other he spoke with a Birmingham accent, attempting to maintain one and the same set of paralinguistic features. The speaker then handed out a sheet of paper and asked the students to write down what they thought psychology was all about; and then he left the room. The procedure took only a couple of minutes in each group.

The students were then addressed by another psychologist who said that her department was thinking of hiring a person to visit high schools in order to inform students about the subject of psychology; and did they think the man they had been listening to would be right for the job? The students were asked to write down their impressions of the first speaker and also to rate him on a number of scales.

The authors "found that the RP speaker was rated more intelligent than the same speaker using the nonstandard guise. Also, [the subjects] tended to write more to, and write significantly more about the former target person than the latter." About half the group of listeners commented on the high standard of the RP speaker's speech, whereas only two, out of courtesy it would seem, had anything to say about the speech of the Birmingham speaker.

Giles & Powesland (1975:104f) report on a follow-up experiment by Richard Bourhis in which real theatre audiences in the interval were asked to fill out questionnaires to do with the theatre. The message was transmitted via loudspeakers, certain nights in "RP", other nights in accented speech. Bourhis is reported to have found that a greater number of questionnaires were completed and more was written on the forms when the loudspeaker voice had an RP accent.

Giles and associates 1977-1980: the sexual aspect.

Most studies within the tradition presented here have dealt solely with the speech produced by male speakers (an exception is Cheyne 1970). In the wake of feminism, scholars naturally began to realize that such a limitation was highly detrimental to seriously intended social research, and so from around 1970 and onwards, several studies including or accentuating the sexual aspect have been carried out (for good surveys, see McConnell-Ginet *et al.* 1980, P.M. Smith 1985, Coates 1986). Many, but certainly not all, of these have a clear feminist inclination.

In 1978, Howard Giles and his associates (Elyan *et al.* 1978) produced a study which triggered a great deal of discussion both within the Giles group and outside it. The purpose of that study was to elicit listeners' reactions to "RP" and Lancashire accented female speech according to the matched-guise paradigm. What made the study special, apart from the fact that it had female speakers, was that among the traits tested were such positive and negative traits as those that had earlier (Williams *et al.* 1977) been found to be stereotypically associated with males and females respectively, e.g. aggressive/adventurous (male) vs. weak/gentle (female) (for a comprehensive list of such traits, see P.M. Smith 1985, pp 108-109).

The authors found that the "RP" accented guises were upgraded on competence and communicative traits but downgraded on traits to do with social attractiveness, as compared with the Lancashire guises. More interestingly, however, the "RP" guises were also seen to be more feminine in terms of the trait "femininity" but at the same time more masculine in terms of a number of stereotypical masculine traits. This rather unexpected finding gave rise to the notion of "perceived androgyny" as a feature of female "RP" speakers.

Giles & Marsh (1979) is a follow-up study to Elyan *et al.* (1978). In it, the authors attempt to find out whether another regional accent, South Welsh, produces the same type of contrast with "RP" as did the Lancashire accent of the original experiment. Also, they use both male and female voices in order to see to what extent, if any, androgyny is a universal feature of "RP" speakers. Apart from this, the experimental set-up is very much the same as in the Elyan *et al.* (1978) study (matched guises, reading).

The results of this experiment deviate in several ways from those of earlier studies. The general finding was that "RP speakers, irrespective of their sex, were rated as more competent, liberated and masculine [...] than South Welsh speakers [...]." However, there was no relative upgrading of the RP-speaking females for "femininity" (which, in Elyan *et al.* (1978) was what brought about the androgyny suggestion in the first place). Moreover, no connection was found either in Elyan *et al.* (1978) or Giles & Marsh (1979) between non-prestigious accents and masculinity; and in addition, there was no upgrading of regional speakers for social attractiveness. The authors regard the results as showing that "RP" in a woman creates certain features of masculinity—androgyny, even though the particularly strong polarization between simultaneously enhanced femininity and masculinity that was found in the original experiment was absent. As for the question of androgyny as a universal feature of "RP" speakers, male and female, the study offered no answer.

Having found that listeners were inclined to make this type of distinction between various forms of female speech, Giles and his colleagues (Giles *et al.* 1980a) went on to carry out a more specialized experiment, the basis of which was the idea that certain cues are particularly important for attitude formation when first meeting a person. A pilot study showed that in a woman, the presence or absence of "feminist ideals" was such an important initial cue. By means of a standard test, the authors therefore selected two groups of female speakers, one with attested feminist ideals, the other without such ideals. These speakers then recorded passages of free speech which were played to a small group of listeners who were asked to grade the voices on a number of scales. The results showed significant differences in favour of the feminist speakers with regard to "profeminism", "lucidity of argument", "intelligence" and "sincerity", whereas the non-feminists were graded higher on "frivolity", "superficiality" and "standard accent". Since this experiment involved free speech and hence a certain lack of control, the authors undertook a similar experiment, using reading passages. This time the "feminist speakers were perceived to be less fluent [...] and standard accented [...], lower in pitch [...], less precisely enunciated [...], more masculine [...] and less feminine-sounding [...] than the nonfeminist speakers." In addition, they were also rated lower for "intelligence". The authors interpret the differences as indicating that "feminists have a more assertive, nonstandard, "masculine-sounding" speech style than nonfeminists." Now, obviously, feminism as such does not necessitate a certain style of speech. It is, the authors suggest, rather a question of assimilating toward what is considered a dominant type of behaviour. It is also possible that "the voice of feminism" is not that at all, but rather the voice of sharing certain values and not sharing others.

In Giles *et al.* (1980b), which also summarizes the line of research, the authors set out to question the interpretations offered in the previous studies of the Giles group. What brought about this reconsideration was the circumstance that "perceived androgyny" with its rather disturbing internal assymetries might be seen as an effect of class, rather than sex, pressures, in which case "androgyny" would no longer be needed as an explanatory model. In order to achieve control over the various factors involved, Giles *et al.* (1980b) had groups of students mark adjectives from a standard list (a) for masculinity and femininity; (b) for Middle Class and Working Class relevance. In this way it was possible to create combinatory subgroups of adjectives, e.g. masculine *and* WC, feminine *and* MC, etc., and also subgroups which showed no association with class and sex respectively.

With the new sets of adjectives as tools, the authors reinterpreted the results of both Elyan *et al.* (1978) and Giles & Marsh (1979). It turned out that their new suppositions were largely valid: it was primarily in connection with adjectives that were *both masculine and MC* that the androgyny phenomenon had appeared, and so there were strong indications that class, rather than sex, was operative.

In order to substantiate this new interpretation further, Giles *et al.* (1980b) performed another matched-guise experiment in which a group of listeners were confronted with recordings in "RP" and Yorkshire accents, rating the voices with regard to the four combinatory subgroups of adjectives that had been created (M/WC, F/WC, M/MC, F/MC). The results showed that males and females were upgraded on their respective sex-appropriate adjectives, and that "RP" speakers were upgraded on MC adjectives, whereas Yorkshire guises were upgraded on WC adjectives. The authors claim that "[...] class-based attributions appear to have predominated over sex-based attributions in this study, since there were fewer significant effects for speaker sex than for accent guise."

Giles *et al.* (1980b) also carried out an experiment to supplement the 1980a study concerning perceived feminism (cf above). We recall that the results of that study had given rise to two strands of interpretation, one of *assimilation* and one of *sharing values.* One way of finding out which strand is the most feasible one is to check *male* speakers with varying degrees of feminist values. Since males would seem to have no reason to assimilate as it were toward themselves, but as good a reason as anybody to share values, a perceived differentiation of speech styles in feminist and non-feminist males would indicate that the sharing of values is the operative factor in what seemed to be "the voice of feminism".

This experiment included speech samples recorded by two groups of males, one with high standard test scores for feminism, the other with low scores. The samples were played to small groups of listeners who rated them according to the same principles as in the studies mentioned above.

The results show basically the same tendencies as in the Giles *et al.* (1980a) study. The authors conclude:

> [---] it would seem that "the voice of feminism" [---] is not **unique** to women who are attempting to redefine their status in society. In other words, it can be tentatively suggested that [---] the so-called "feminist" voice is more likely to be causally linked to a more broadly-based liberal ideology than to feminism *per se.* [p. 272f]

The authors, in summarizing their discussion, interestingly utilize a Gestalt psychological approach to the importance of sex differences in perceived language variation. According to this idea, "[---] sex is sometimes the figure and other times the ground in the display of that name." Also, what we refer to as sex differences may or may not be governed by sex at all, but by correlating entities. Moreover, there is always the possibility of variation according to the social context.

Giles & Farrar 1979: speech and other variables.
Giles & Farrar (1979) is an expanded follow-up study to the Giles *et al.* (1975) study reported above. Like the earlier study, it differs from the typical kind of matched-guise experiments in that it does not utilize recorded speech but rather direct confrontation between speaker and informant. Also, informants' attitudes toward the speakers are elicited not by means of rating scales, but by checking the length and style of their written answers to questions put to them by the speakers.

In addition to these techniques, Giles & Farrar (1979) add a non-linguistic variable to the attitude measuring project: dress style.

In this experiment the speaker, who was bidialectal in "RP" and Cockney, pretended to be conducting an attitude survey in a middle-class area in Berkshire. She would knock on people's doors, describe the project, hand over a questionnaire, and tell them she would pick up their responses in half an hour. For each call she would use one of the following combinatory guises: (1) "RP"/smart dress, (2) "RP"/casual dress, (3) Cockney/smart dress, (4) Cockney/casual dress.

The results, in terms of the length and style of the informants answers, show that informants wrote almost 50 per cent more in response to the "RP" speaker, but that dress style had no such distinguishing effect. When answering questionnaires handed over by "RP" speakers, however, people tended to adjust their style according to the speaker's dress: the casually dressed "RP" speaker elicited an informal style, whereas the smartly dressed "RP" speaker received formally styled responses. As for the two Cockney guises, responses were equivalently placed at an in-between stylistic position.

These results are of particular interest with regard to the present study, in implicitly supporting the notion of *harmony/disharmony* (Festinger's terms: "cognitive consonance" and "dissonance" are probably related to this notion) between two variables as an operative factor in certain kinds of attitude analysis, which I shall return to in the section entitled "Age and degree of modernity" (cf also Aboud *et al.* 1974).

Giles, Wilson & Conway 1981: manipulating the linguistic variable.

In the studies by the Giles group that I have reported on so far, language has been treated holistically. There have been no attempts to manipulate the speech variable other than by having a speaker produce different guises. In Giles *et al.* (1981) a first step in the direction of an analysis of speech variables is taken in that lexical diversity is introduced as an object of study, in addition to accent.

The stimulus material was four recordings by one and the same speaker representing the following factors: accent ("RP" vs. South Welsh), lexical diversity (high vs. low). The recordings were played to four groups of listeners, respectively, who were asked to "put themselves in the place of a personnel officer working for a large industrial firm." Going by the voice recordings, this imaginary person was to select applicants for four different jobs within that firm, "industrial plant cleaner", "production assembler", "industrial mechanic", "foreman". This was done by rating the speaker on a number of job-related scales, e.g. suitability and competence. In addition, the listeners rated the speakers on scales concerning social and psychological qualities.

Beginning with the general traits we notice that the "RP" guises were significantly upgraded for "aggressiveness" and "status", whereas the Welsh accented guises were upgraded for "sincerity", "generosity" and "goodnaturedness". Moreover, low diversity speakers were upgraded for being more "agreeable" and "good-natured".

The job selection proper had as a result that the South Welsh speakers were perceived as more suitable than the "RP" speakers for "assembler" and that their ability to get on with equals and inferiors with regard to "cleaner" and "assembler" was perceived as higher. Low diversity speakers were seen to have a better ability to get on with superiors with regard to "cleaner", "assembler" and "mechanic", which the authors speculatively ascribe to a higher degree of (perceived) malleability and obedience among this category. The "RP" guises did not attain very high ratings in connection with these job labels. By means of a supplementary experiment, the authors manage to show that this was because of the socially inferior level of the labels.

Giles & Sassoon 1983: accent, social class and style.
From a methodological viewpoint, Giles & Sassoon (1983) is a blend of the two previously discussed studies. In addition to the typical ingredient of a matched-guise experiment, accent variation, this study treats simultaneously the explicitly stated social class of the speaker as well as the degree of formality of his speech. The experiment is an attempt to expand and replicate on British soil an American experiment by Ryan & Sebastian (1980, cf below), who found that Mexican-American speakers were more strongly downgraded for status by middle-class informants if it was known to the informants that the speakers were lower class than were middle-class speakers about whom the same information had been supplied. That is to say, in the case of harmony between social class and speech, the attitude-forming effect was seen to be accentuated.

Hypothesizing a result deviating from that of Ryan & Sebastian (1980), Giles & Sassoon (1983) set up a British matched-guise experiment in which a bidialectal speaker recorded a formal and an informal version of the same message in each of his two accents, "RP" and Cockney, which were played to groups of listeners respectively. In addition to these variables, the social class of the speaker was indicated to the listeners. The informants were required to rate the voice they heard along five different types of scales: (1) *control scales* indicating the extent to which the listeners noticed the class, accent and formality of the speaker; (2) *social evaluation scales* of the type we have grown used to; (3) *belief similarity scales* indicating the listeners' degree of agreement with the speaker on social issues; (4) *social distance scales* placing the speaker in a more or less close relationship to the listener (cf the CHILD/BROTHER/SISTER scale of the present study); (5) *social role scales* indicating the listeners' willingness to work together with the speaker (cf the FELLOW WORKER/STUDENT scale of the present study).

The results on the control scales show that informants were generally able to distinguish between the guises in the expected way. More interestingly, the ratings on the social evaluation scales seem to refute the findings of Ryan & Sebastian (1980): there was no interaction effect between perceived class and accent. Middle class and "RP" speakers were rated higher for status (only) than lower class and Cockney speakers, but the combination of Cockney and lower class did not accentuate this relative downgrading, nor did a middle class background save the Cockney from the downgrading brought down on him by his accent. As for belief similarity, informants tended to agree somewhat more with middle class and "RP" speakers, but there was some variation depending on the issue. The social distance and social role scales generally gave rise to no significant differences. An interesting exception was a tendency for informants to prefer an "RP" speaker to a Cockney as subordinate. There was also an interesting exponent of the harmony/disharmony idea in that "RP speakers were evaluated the most favourable of all when speaking the formal passage and lowest of all when speaking the informal one; differences between the nonstandard speakers were insignificant and intermediate to the standard speakers [...]." This low evaluation of informally speaking "RP" speakers seems to be a parallel to a persistent finding in the present study (AGE section) with regard to my combinatory subgroups OLD/MODERN and YOUNG/TRADITIONAL which are often downrated as compared to the more harmonious OLD/TRADITIONAL and YOUNG/MODERN.

Giles and associates 1983: manipulating the test situation.

Giles *et al.* 1983 is a regular matched-guise experiment with certain modifications. First of all, the listeners were children (from Bristol) seven to nine years of age. Secondly, the test context was manipulated by allowing some of the listeners to discuss their evaluations before writing them down. The stimulus was made up of two recordings of identical content by one and the same speaker, one in "RP", the other in South Welsh. The children were required (1) to rate the voices along scales relating to competence and social attractiveness, respectively; and (2) to make a drawing of the respective speakers. Going by earlier research, it was hypothesized that the "RP" guise would be upgraded for competence, and the Welsh guise for social attractiveness; that those children who were given the opportunity to discuss their evaluations would give more pointed responses than the others; that the "RP" speaker would be drawn taller than the Welsh speaker.

Among the results we find a tendency for the youngest children to (relatively speaking) downgrade the "RP" speaker on the traits "funny" (=peculiar) and "successful". This tendency is interestingly inverted in the judgment made by the slightly older children, and so it seems that children are socialized gradually into accepting "RP" as the norm, at least in connection with certain (competence?) traits. The "group discussion" seems to have promoted a couple of differences too. Firstly, the speakers in general were considered less "nasty" by the children who had been given the opportunity to discuss. Secondly, older children who had discussed "found the speakers [...] to be more likeable and less lazy than in the other two conditions." The drawing project showed no significant differences.

Slightly older children (12-14 years of age; from Bucks) participated as informants in a similar experiment (Creber & Giles 1983). This time the manipulation of the test situation was arranged by having half the experiment take place at school, the other half at a local youth club. The accent guises used were, again, "RP" and South Welsh, the informants being required to rate the voices they heard on status and solidarity scales and, in addition, on scales relating to accent preference and social distance. It was hypothesized that the "RP" guise would be upgraded for status traits and the Welsh guise for solidarity traits; furthermore, it was hypothesized that the school setting would accentuate the upgrading of "RP", and vice versa.

The "RP" guise was indeed upgraded for status, but there was no corresponding upgrading of the Welsh guise for solidarity. Interestingly (but perhaps not altogether unexpectedly, considering the regional location of the experiment) the children selected "RP" as the accent they would like to speak themselves. The test manipulation had as an overall result that the children who were tested at school generally rated the voices higher than did the youth club children. More interestingly, certain interaction effects between accent and test situation were found, viz. a tendency for the school group to accentuate their upgrading of "RP" as hypothesized. The solidarity dimension did not give rise to any significant differentiation, which the authors, probably rightly, ascribe to the circumstance that the test was carried out in Buckinghamshire, whereas the regional accented guise was South Welsh. This finding is related to the "second choice principle" suggested in the present study, i.e. the standard often being the second choice in preference judgments, after one's own accent.

Giles and associates 1981-1984: the "Retroactive Speech Halo Effect".

The main principle of a matched-guise experiment is, we remember, to confront listeners with what they believe are the voices of different speakers, but what in actual fact is one and the same multilingual speaker producing different language, dialect or accent guises. A related method is to have a speaker consciously manipulate his language output, e.g. in terms of speech rate, in order to elicit differentiating responses. A similar technique further refined also enables scholars to manipulate recorded speech by means of various methods (e.g. by computer, cf Graff *et al.* 1986), so that the *very same passage* can be presented to listeners in different guises. By doing this, researchers claim to be able to isolate certain features of speech that are of particular interest for their study, without having to worry about "irrelevant" variation.

We have seen (Giles & Bourhis 1973) that several aspects of the matched-guise technique have been subjected to criticism, for example the tendency to repeat one and the same reading passage over and over again to listeners, which would seem to distort reactions in various ways. The very principle of the matched-guise technique has also been criticized for not sufficiently considering the possibility of the multilingual speakers modifying their output in more ways than one when going from one language form to another (P.M. Smith 1985:89), i.e. a holistically coloured critique. Vocal manipulation has been criticized for insufficient control of those vocal aspects that are not being studied (Brown *et al.* 1985) and synthetic manipulation of lacking "ecological validity", i.e. real life relevance (*ib.*).

In the early 1980s, the Giles group started out on a new series of experiments which did not utilize the matched-guise technique, but which in all other respects were founded on listeners' attitudes to speech, much the same way as the earlier studies. The first three experiments I shall discuss sought to investigate what has been called the "retroactive speech halo effect" (Ball *et al.* 1982): the tendency for listeners to modify their opinion of a speaker retroactively after receiving some additional, socially loaded information about her.

In Thakerar & Giles (1981), a recording of a speaker with "a mild degree of British regional accent broadness" describing a test he had been subjected to was played to three isolated groups of listeners. The first group, *after* hearing the recording, was told that the speaker had been very successful both in the test he had been describing and in his university studies in general. The second group was told that the speaker had done badly; and the third group was given no additional information. The listeners then filled in a questionnaire containing scales measuring perceived status, speech style, competence and benevolence with regard to the speaker. They were then asked to listen to the speaker and fill in an identical questionnaire once again.

The results show that there is a significant upgrading of the speaker for status, speech style and competence in the judgment of the group who had been supplied with the positive information, and a corresponding downgrading by the negatively informed group. Furthermore, listeners tended to accentuate their ratings after listening a second time. The authors claim that "[t]hese data clearly indicate that induced affective states have a retroactive effect on judgements."

Ball *et al.* (1982) is a replication in two phases of the Thakerar & Giles (1981) study, in an Australian setting. This time the speaker was a woman speaking in a "General Australian" accent about her impressions before and after an employment interview. *After* hearing the recording, half the informants were told that the speaker had been offered the job but turned it down for something better; the other half that she had not got the job and that she had been trying to find employment for six months prior to this interview. They then filled in the same type of questionnaire as in the previous study. The positively and negatively informed groups were then divided into three subgroups respectively. The first subgroup heard the speaker and answered the questions once again (cf Thakerar & Giles 1981); the second subgroup was asked to *think* about the speaker and then answer the questions once again; the third subgroup was given a "distracting task" after which they too answered the questions a second time. Intergroup control was exercised by means of calibrating responses toward a filler voice that was not part of the experiment proper.

The result:

> It was found that when the speaker was known to have been successful, she was perceived to have had a more refined accent [...] and a faster rate of talking [...] than [the] person having failed the interview. In addition, the high status group rated the speaker as kinder [...], more confident [...], more dependable [...], more active [...] more intelligent [...], more ambitious [...] and more upper class [...] than the same speaker as rated by the low status group.

In the second phase of the study, the same recording was played to two other groups of listeners. The first ("formal") group, after hearing the recording was told that it had been taken from a radio programme; the second ("informal") group, that it was part of a surreptitiously recorded chit-chat. These two groups were then further divided into four subgroups respectively, receiving the following information: (1) control, no further information; (2) the speaker is a native Australian; (3) the speaker's family had moved to Australia before the speaker was born; (4) the speaker had first arrived in Australia when she was nine years old. The listeners were required to rate the voice along the same kind of scales as in phase one of the study.

The only reliable finding was that "the native Australian and control speakers were perceived as more broad and Australian in accent than the apparently more foreign-sounding "new" and "old" immigrants."

The authors conclude:

> [The retroactive speech halo effect] appears to be most responsive to status attributes of speakers, less to their ethnic background characteristics, and not at all to the social contextual features in which the voice is produced. [---] These data clearly suggest that we do not passively listen to someone's voice, we actively construct and reconstruct our impressions of it according to our predispositions. What we think someone's voice sounds like can be more influential in determining our attitudes and behaviour [...] towards them than what can be measured objectively as his or hers.

Giles & Fitzpatrick (1984) is a further development of the same basic technique devised in order to investigate the "retroactive speech halo effect". As this study does not manipulate accent/dialect at all, I shall be very brief in my report.

The purpose of the Giles & Fitzpatrick (1984) study is to see to what extent listeners' responses to one and the same dialogue, produced by one and the same married couple, were influenced retroactively by information about the couple's internal socio-emotional relationship (whether they embraced traditional values on marriage, etc.). The results indicate that listeners tend to differentiate their attitudes toward the couple on many scales in accordance with the additional information supplied after listening to the recording. The innovation in this study is that it deals with group interaction rather than individuals in isolation. The authors rightly suggest a strong need for empirical expansion in this area.

Brown *et al.* 1985: speech rate, accent and speech context.
The relationship between speech rate and perceived personality has been subject to several investigations (e.g. Smith *et al.* 1975, Apple *et al.* 1979). The most persistent finding of these investigations is the clear positive relationship between increased speech rate and increased perceived competence. As for the benevolence dimension, results have been less clearcut, but there are certain signs of a so-called "inverted U" relationship between speech rate and benevolence, i.e. slower speech promoting higher benevolence ratings to a point, after which a further decrease in speech rate also decreases benevolence ratings.

In a recent study by the Giles group (Brown *et al.* 1985) which also includes a good general survey of the field, these findings were again put to the test. In this study the group returns to the matched-guise technique, albeit in a form slightly different from the classic experiments (cf however discussion on Giles *et al.* (1975) above). The experiment was conducted along the following lines:

A bidialectal speaker recorded six versions of one and the same passage. These versions differed in terms of accent ("RP" and South East Welsh) and speech rate (slow, medium and fast). Each of the six combinatory subcategories thus created (e.g. RP/slow, Welsh/medium) was played to two isolated groups of listeners who were required to rate the voice they heard on competence and benevolence scales. Of these 12 groups of listeners, six listened to the recording without any further information. The other six groups were told that the passage they were about to hear had been recorded at a lecture in which a psychologist was discussing communication between dentists and children.

The results corroborate earlier findings concerning the positive relationship between high competence ratings on the one hand and "RP" accent and fast speech rate on the other. However, no inverted U effect for speech rate and benevolence ratings was found, but rather a straight inversion of the competence ratings: fast speech rate - low benevolence ratings, and vice versa. Contrary to several earlier indications, the Welsh guise did not promote higher benevolence ratings (cf Creber & Giles 1983 and above), which again would seem to indicate that benevolence (or solidarity) requires a closeness aspect and not just a regional one in order to yield the expected results. Most importantly from the point of view of this study, it was shown that the additional information on context (i.e. the lecture) that was supplied to half the informants neutralized the impact of speech rate on certain competence traits: listeners who were informed about the context of the speech could more easily accept a slower speech rate without interpreting it as a sign of reduced competence.

1.1.5. Other workers in the field.

As I have already pointed out, "language attitudes" as a scholarly field has expanded dramatically since the 1960s. It is therefore neither possible nor desirable even to attempt full coverage in the present context. This in turn means that several worthy workers in the field have not been and will not be treated here. What I have been trying to do so far is offer a background to my own study, which means that I have laid particularly great emphasis on such central studies as have a bearing on the English language and especially the British situation, which is my present concern.

With even smaller pretentions as regards coverage than hitherto, I will now go on to present another couple of contributions to our knowledge of language attitudes.

William Labov.

The extremely influential sociolinguistic work of William Labov is largely of a different kind from most of the work I have referred to so far (for an introduction, see e.g. Wardhaugh 1986). Labov's approach to language variation is analytical, rather than holistic. In his classic New York study (1966) he set out to investigate the social relevance of certain aspects of the phonemic variation in New York speech. This work involved recording speech in various ways and relating it to the social situation of its speakers. It is not a study of listeners' attitudes, but it does contain a section entitled "Social evaluation", which has some relevance to the present study.

The basic idea of Labov's (1966) social evaluation is to elicit the subjective attitudes towards New York City speech from people who have acted as informants, (speakers), in other parts of the study, in order to investigate the relationship between language attitudes and language behaviour.

The stimulus material consisted of tape-recordings of five female speakers, selected on the basis of their accents, reading a passage specially designed to elicit responses about the phonemic variation at issue: (1) pronounced vs. mute post-vocalic /r/; (2) the vowel of *beer, bear, bat, pass*, etc.; (3) the vowel of *sure, for, hot*, etc.; (4) the quality of voiced and voiceless <th>. The recordings were cut and mixed so as to reduce the risk of informants' attitudes to one feature influencing their ratings of another.

The finalized version of the recordings was played to a total of 122 native New Yorkers, a majority of whom had participated as speaker informants in earlier stages of the study.

Their task was to rate each spoken sentence on a scale indicating the "occupational suitability" of the speaker with regard to six job labels, ranging from "Television personality" to "Factory worker", plus a waste basket, "None of [i.e. lower than] these".

The interpretation of the ratings was based on the contrast between ratings of a "neutral" calibrational passage and ratings of passages each containing a high degree of a certain phonemic test item, all of which was uttered by one and the same speaker. This way, it could be ascertained which informants were more sensitive than others to, for example, a close, diphthongized variety of the vowel in *back*, or a mute /r/ in *heart*, and this information could in turn be used to draw various social conclusions about the variation.

The results show "a great many close correlations" between a speaker's own linguistic behaviour and his subjective evaluations. A couple of examples:

representatives of the "lower classes" who tend to show no style-related variation in their use of the "(oh)" vowel also do not rate differentiatingly such variation in other speakers. Similarly, the clear correlation between relatively lower age, higher status and pronounced post-vocalic /r/'s that could be found in the earlier parts of the study were accompanied by subjective evaluations going in the same direction. There was also an ethnic aspect to the analysis. Jews and Italians were shown to relate differently to the "(eh)" and "(oh)" vowels respectively, depending on the formality of the speech situation. This difference was reflected in their attitudes towards the two sounds, repectively, when spoken by others. In Labov's (p. 448) own words: "The degree of correction which occurs in speech is thus paralleled by the consistency of negative response to stigmatized forms."

20 years later, Labov and his colleagues published a matched-guise study (Graff *et al.* 1986) designed to investigate the importance of the variation of two diphthongs in the assessment of the ethnic background of the speakers.

The basis of this study was made up of the two diphthongs /aw/ (*house*) and /ow/ (*home*) in certain types of Philadelphian English. These vowels are in a process of change, and it has been possible to show that there is an ethnic differentiation in this development: white speakers seem to have gone farther in terms of phonological innovation than black speakers, who seem to have remained closer to the "standard" form. Phonetically, the most advanced form of /aw/ has a first element [e], that is to say a close, fronted articulation, as compared with the "standard" [a] and the less advanced Philadelphian [æ]. The /ow/ diphthong is going in the direction of the RP vowel in *home*, i.e. it has an unrounded, fronted starting-point, as compared with the "General American Standard" vowel.

The questions that the study set out to address were (1) whether "members of the two groups [blacks and whites] were aware of [the differences]" and (2) "whether these two variables in themselves might be sufficiently prominent to serve as markers of a speaker's ethnicity within the community."

In order to make for total isolation of the phonemes under scrutiny the authors decided to manipulate a recording of natural speech by means of advanced speech synthesis. Two short sentences, one containing two /aw/ phonemes, the other two /ow/ phonemes, were selected from a recording made by a 25-year-old black speaker. The critical parts of the sentences were subjected to formant manipulation in order to make the two diphthongs more advanced, i.e. white-sounding, without making any other alterations. This way, two guises for each sentence with a high degree of control of paralinguistic features, etc., were produced.

In addition to these semi-synthetic guises, there were also a number of bidialectal black and white speakers who recorded regular matched-guise material to be used in the same experiment as a comparison between methods.

In all, 70 black, white and Puerto Rican informants listened to the recordings, rating the speakers on a scale going from "sounds very black" to "sounds very white", and deciding whether the person was black or white.

The overall results show that the "natural" guises were readily and significantly identified according to expectations. The same effect, although generally weaker, was found for the synthetic /aw/ guises, whereas the /ow/ guises did not give rise to any significant effects: "The responses of both blacks and whites demonstrate that a difference in the position of the nucleus of /aw/, between front (tense) and central (lax), is a prominent cue to the ethnic identity and affiliation of a speaker among the members of this community." The authors suggest that the reason for /aw/ being a stronger ethnic marker than /ow/ is that it (/aw/) is "phonetically peripheral" among white speakers, whereas it is non-peripheral among blacks; /ow/, on the other hand, is non-peripheral among both groups, which enables blacks to adapt to a white style of speech without going to phonetic extremes. This in turn would seem to reduce the reliability of /ow/ as an ethnic marker.

Strongman & Woosley 1967; Cheyne 1970.
These two brief but often quoted studies both concern the attitudinal relationship between various British regional accents. Between them they triggered a lot of the early work done by Howard Giles (cf above).

In the Strongman & Woosley (1967) study, two bidialectal speakers each recorded a London and a Yorkshire guise. It is not clear whether "London" represents an English standard accent or whether it is supposed to have certain non-standard connotations (Giles & Powesland (1975:66f) in their discussion assume the former interpretation). These recordings were played to listeners from the North and from London and the Home Counties who were required to rate the voices on a number of mainly psychological scales. In brief, the results show that Northern and Southern informants agreed that the London speakers were more self-confident and that the Yorkshire speakers were more honest and reliable. The Northern informants upgraded the Yorkshire voices for industriousness, generosity, goodnaturedness and kindheartedness, whereas they rated the London voices higher for meanness, irritability and hardness. The Southern informants rated the Yorkshire voices higher for seriousness.

Cheyne (1970) is a study conducted along very much the same lines as the previously discussed study. The chief difference is that this time the comparison concerns Scottish and English accents (it is less than clear from the text what is meant by "English accent"; I again follow Giles & Powesland (1975:66f) in assuming that it stands for an English standard accent).

Cheyne had four drama students read a passage, once with an English accent, once with a Scottish accent. To these eight guises were added two authentic English and two authentic Scottish voices reading the same passage. The 12 voices thus procured were played to 170 informants in Glasgow and London who were asked to rate the voices on 21 Lambert-type scales.

In his result presentation, Cheyne distinguishes between ratings of male and female speakers. English and Scottish informants agreed between them that English male voices should be rated higher than Scottish male voices for wealth, prestige, intelligence, height, occupational status, ambition, leadership, cleanliness, good looks and self-confidence. They also agreed on rating Scottish males higher for friendliness. In addition to this agreement, the Scottish informants upgraded Scottish males for sense of humour, generosity, good-heartedness, likeability and nervousness.

As for the female speakers, Scots and Englishmen agreed that English female voices should be rated higher for wealth, prestige, intelligence and height. The Scottish informants also upgraded the English females for occupational status, ambition, leadership, cleanliness and good looks, and the Scottish females for entertainingness and sense of humour.

The author noted that "differences tended to be greater and occur for more scales with the two different-speaker pairs than with the four same-speaker (=matched-guise) pairs of voices", which would seem to indicate that the authentic voices carried with them stronger markers of regional significance than the matched-guise voices.

Shuy & Williams 1973.

This American study has many features in common with the present one. Its purpose was to elicit informants' responses with regard to five accent stimuli: Detroit speech, White Southern speech, British speech (presumably "RP"), Negro speech, and Standard speech. The voices were rated on 12 semantic differential (adjective) scales by a total of 620 Detroit informants, who were further subcategorized according to race (black/white), socioeconomic status (upper middle, lower middle, upper working, lower working), age (10-12, 16-18, 21+) and sex.

The first question addressed was whether the traits tested were judged independently

45

or whether there was an implicit system in the informants' judgments. Factor analysis "led to the identification of four factors characterizing interrelated use of scales": (1) *value* (e.g. good-bad), (2) *complexity* (e.g. easy-difficult), (3) *potency* (e.g. strong-weak), (4) *activity* (fast-slow).

The next step was to see how the five accents under scrutiny averaged across these four factors. As for the value factor, Standard, British and Detroit were rated significantly higher than Negro and Southern. In the complexity comparison, British headed the league, Standard, Southern an Negro assuming an in-between position, Detroit speech finishing last (a reasonable peer-group effect). British, Detroit and Standard were rated highest for potency, Negro and, particularly, Southern falling notably behind. A similar tendency, apart from an even higher position for British was found in the activity comparison. It is interesting to notice the extremely high ratings received by British in this American investigation. Similar results can be found in Stewart *et al.* (1985).

The ethnicity of the informants gave rise to certain interesting tendencies, primarily with regard to Negro speech. Black informants rated this variety significantly higher than did whites. This is particularly interesting as it would seem to contradict findings of "self-hatred" which are frequent in connection with minority groups (Simpson & Yinger 1972:227). However, if we look at the adjectives used by Shuy & Williams (1973), we see that they are leaning more towards the personal and less towards the social side, which might explain this apparent anomaly. In addition to this, there was a tendency for black informants to downgrade Southern (white), which would seem to corroborate the findings of Tucker & Lambert (1969).

In the comparison based on the social class of the informants, there was an interesting correlation between high social class and favourable attitudes towards British (potency and value) (cf Stewart *et al.* 1985); and similarly between low social class and favourable attitudes towards Detroit/Negro (potency).

The age comparison showed that adult informants tended to upgrade Standard and British for value and potency relative to youths and children, who in turn thought that these accents were more complex than did adults.

The sex variable, finally, showed no significant interactions.

Ellen Bouchard Ryan.

The work of the American social psychologist Ellen Bouchard Ryan and her colleagues is worthy in itself of much more attention than can be provided in the present context. Among other things, the Ryan group has devoted itself to the age aspect of language perception and to the study of Spanish-accented American

English and its attitudinal and social consequences (see Ryan 1973 for a general manifesto. A summary of recent research into ethnicity, social class and age markers in speech can also be found in Sebastian and Ryan 1985). Together with Howard Giles, Ellen B. Ryan has edited the important monograph *Attitudes towards Language Variation* (1982).

Ryan & Capadano (1978) is a study which seeks to elicit listeners' attitudes to adult speakers of various ages by means of bipolar rating scales (e.g. Insecure—Self-assured) and open-ended questions on voice characteristics and perceived age. The authors found that there was "[...] strong agreement among subjects about the relative ages of the speakers" and conclude that their "[...] results indicate that listeners have the ability to discriminate between members of different age groups through vocal stimuli and are aware of some voice traits which allow the listener to perceive speaker age." Like many students of age conjecture, including the present writer, Ryan & Capadano noticed a strong tendency among listeners to guess conservatively, i.e. "underestimat[e] the highest and over-estimat[e] the lowest ages." Discussing this phenomenon, they suggest that the apparent attribution of characteristics to elderly people should really be interpreted as relating to middle-aged people. Both old male and old female speakers, particularly females, were subjected to a certain amount of downgrading on the rating scales as compared with younger, or less old, speakers.

In the section on Howard Giles above, I referred to studies in which rate of speech was used as a variable. We recall for instance that several scholars have found a positive correlation between speech rate and perceived competence. In Stewart & Ryan (1982), speech rate was manipulated in a similar fashion in order to elucidate any differentiation in informants' perception of younger and older speakers.

The stimulus material was based on six recordings, three of young (20-22), and three of old (60-65) speakers. Each speaker read the spontaneous-sounding text in three different versions, one slow, one medium, and one fast. This yielded 18 unique cells which were combined into six sections with three different speakers/rates in each.

Each of these six sections was played to a unique group of ten listeners, which means that the total number of informants was 60. On hearing the voices, the informants were required to rate them on scales measuring competence, benevolence, age stereotyping, belief similarity, social distance and social class. Moreover, the informants were supplied with three hypothetical situations in which the speaker either succeeded or failed, and they were asked to rate the extent to which they thought success and failure were caused by ability, effort, task difficulty, and luck, respectively. Finally, there were questions concerning perceived age and voice characteristics.

Among the results was a clear correlation between speech rate and competence traits, most notably in the ratings of young speakers. As for the benevolence traits, we see similar but weaker tendencies. An interesting detail is the clear downgrading of the combinatory subgroup young/slow in almost all comparisons, which, according to the authors (p. 105) "appears to reflect the consequences of a disconfirmation of the stereotype that young people speak relatively quickly." In the AGE section of the present study, I shall suggest on several occasions that disharmony between a speaker's age and her language output might be conducive to a drop in informants' ratings. It would seem that such a suggestion finds a certain amount of support in Stewart's & Ryan's results concerning disharmony between age and speech rate. The overall finding of this study, however, is that there exists a strong tendency for young informants to downgrade old as compared with younger speakers.

I have already mentioned the Ryan & Sebastian (1980) study in connection with the British-based replication of it carried out by Giles & Sassoon (1983). It is a study designed to investigate the perceived relationship between a speaker's standard or non-standard accent and his social class.

Two standard-speaking Americans and two Americans with a Spanish accent were recorded reading a short passage of rather formal text. The recordings were played to 120 "middle-class, Anglo-American" informants who in the regular fashion had to rate the speakers on traits of status, solidarity, stereotyping, speech, and social distance.

The special feature of this experiment was that the 80 listeners in the experimental condition, prior to hearing the voices, were informed implicitly about the social background of the speakers. In this way, a 4-cell matrix was obtained in which each of two social classes, middle and lower, had two types of accent, standard and "accented", attached to it. The 40 listeners in the control condition heard the voices without this additional information.

The authors found that, as expected, standard voices were upgraded as compared with accented voices; and similarly, middle-class voices were upgraded relative to lower-class voices. Interestingly, however, there was a strong interactive effect between non-standard accent and lower class: non-standard, lower-class speakers were downgraded particularly strongly. Ryan & Sebastian conclude that "[---] being *either* a person with a middle-class background *or* a speaker of standard English results in relatively favourable evaluations while [...] being *both* a member of a different ethnic group *and* an individual with a lower-class background results in decidedly negative evaluations." As we have already seen, Giles's and Sassoon's (1983) replication did not yield a similar outcome for the British situation. From the point of view of the present study, however, Ryan's & Sebastian's suggestion is interesting, because it seems to be cognitively related to my own suggestions about "social markedness" (cf p. 316), even though the parallel should not be exaggerated, in view of the fact that my concern is not the conflict between standard and non-standard, but rather conflicts within the standard area itself.

Melchers 1985.
This study is part of a larger project set up in order to elucidate the Scandinavian element in the dialect of Shetland. It is of interest to the present discussion because of the highly special status of Shetland as a semi-isolated linguistic area which would seem to promote less, or at any rate differently, biassed language attitudes than in the mainland dialectal areas. The main body of the study is descriptive of various, chiefly social, aspects of the Shetland dialect, but there is also a brief section on the attitudes of Shetland informants towards other British accents. Interestingly, genuine Shetlanders are reported to have no sense of prevailing opinions about the status of various English accents (cf Giles 1970, etc.). Thus, for example, Birmingham, generally the least appreciated among English accents (*ib.*), was not commented on in any negative way by the informants. Unfavourable comments were however made about certain *Scottish* urban accents, such as Aberdeen and Glasgow. It should be noted that these attitudes were not founded on hearing recorded material, and so they are of course primarily of social psychological interest.

When asked to rate the "BBC accent" on a number of semantic differential scales, the informants (350 high school students) gave non-committal answers on the scales friendly-hostile, clever-stupid, hard-soft, and weak-strong; negative answers on ugly-beautiful, cold-warm, slow-quick; positive answers on smooth-awkward and careful-careless. The same task with regard to the "Shetland dialect" produced non-committal responses on beautiful-ugly, hard-soft, careful-careless; and positive answers on the scales friendly-hostile, warm-cold, clever-stupid, quick-slow, smooth-awkward and strong-weak. Positive attitudes towards the Shetland dialect were accentuated in the ratings made by *native* Shetlanders. It might be argued that these findings reflect the circumstance that Shetland, in being a small, close and partly isolated society, is characterized by solidarity to a greater extent than areas situated in the midst of large-scale socioeconomic life. In the section on REGIONALITY, I shall return to the possibility of linguistic oppression being stronger close to a linguistic power centre. It would seem that the rather neutral, or non-committal, responses supplied by the geographically and culturally peripheral Shetland informants regarding standard English accents constitute some support for such a suggestion.

An interesting detail from the point of view of the present test battery was that most students, when asked in what situations it would be inappropriate to speak dialect, answered "job interviews" and when "talking to important people, like the headmaster." The Shetland dialect, on the other hand, was preferred in close, family-type situations, etc.

Christer Påhlsson.

The two studies I am going to refer to here, Påhlsson (1982) and (forthc.) have one important feature in common with the present study: the use of a language-based criterion for subdividing groups of people, in Påhlsson's case listeners, in mine, speakers. The pivot of the present study is what I refer to as DEGREE OF MODERNITY (cf p. 83), i.e. on the basis of the linguistic behaviour of my speakers in a test, I assign them either to the category MODERN or TRADITIONAL. Påhlsson, on the other hand, doing his field-work in the burring area of Northumberland, subdivides his group of listener-informants on the basis of the degree to which they use the burr in their own speech.

The two later studies are spin-offs from his major (1972) study on the Northumbrian burr. In the original study, Påhlsson related the burr to the social (in a wide sense) situation of its users. A couple of years later, he returned to the same area in Northumberland in order to use his old speakers as listener-informants in an attitude investigation concerning eight English accents: Scottish, South-East, Midlands, RP, London, North-East, American, Tyneside. This investigation forms the basis of the two studies discussed here.

Påhlsson's (1982) study seeks to elicit informants' subjective preferences and non-preferences, as well as their evaluation of their own language, whereas the (forthc.) study investigates the perceived suitability of the voices with respect to a number of job labels.

Påhlsson divided his informants into five basic groups according to their use of the burr (= a posterior articulation of /r/): (1) burr used equally often in all positions; (2) burr used more often in initial, intervocalic and post-consonantal positions than in pre-consonantal and final, post-vocalic positions; (3) same as (2), but with a particularly low use of the burr in a final, post-vocalic position; (4) same as (2)/(3) but with a slight increase in the use of the burr in a final, post-vocalic position; (5) burr used more often pre-consonantally and finally than elsewhere. In addition, Påhlsson distinguished between "high" and "low" burrers according to how often the burr was used in general.

Påhlsson's analysis is based on the idea that it is possible to notice a socially relevant structure corresponding to these five burr variables. This structure includes place of birth, age, social class, education, etc. In other words, if you use the burr in a certain way, you are likely to belong to a certain structural category. The criticism that could be levelled at this method of analysis is that, in view of the fact that the total number of informants was 90 and that they were not evenly distributed across the five categories, certain subgroups of listeners seem to be much too small for the analysis to prove rewarding. It seems to me that a bipartite analysis would have been preferable under the circumstances.

Overall averages (i.e. disregarding subcategorization) show that 45 per cent of the informants (N=80) rate "RP" as the most attractive among the accents tested, that 26 per cent go for Scottish, and that the remaining six accents get between 1 and 6 per cent of the votes, the bottom position for preference being held by Tyneside, i.e. the local urban accent.

As for non-preference, i.e. which accent the informants liked the least, the basic configuration is one of inversion of the preceding ranking, but tendencies are less marked. The least-preferred accent is Tyneside (by 22 per cent of the informants; N=77), closely followed by American (21 per cent), North-East (20 per cent) and Midland (17 per cent). Then there is a long leap to the remaining four accents which get between 4 and 7 per cent of the votes. "RP" and Scottish hold the bottom positions for non-preference with 4 and 5 per cent, respectively.

Thus, there seems to be no doubt that a principle of self-hatred is operative in these ratings, in addition to the more expected upgrading of "RP". As I have already indicated, the subcategorization cannot be used statistically because of small numbers, which is a pity, since the categorization as such is very elegant.

The self-evaluations show that a majority of the informants consider themselves to be dialect speakers (91 per cent; N=90); are positively inclined to their dialect (60 per cent); have not tried to modify their dialect (79 per cent); adapt to their interlocutors (66 per cent); take no notice of comments about their dialect (64 per cent).

In Påhlsson's (forthc.) study, the informants were asked to state (yes or no) whether each of the eight accents was suitable with regard to each of 11 occupations: surgeon, sales manager, firemaster, farmer, shop assistant, lorry driver, wood bailiff, hotel waiter, bus conductor, farm worker, stevedore. The job labels were selected so as to represent the non-manual, manual and agricultural aspects of the various socio-economic classes in the 1966 *Classification of Occupations*.

The version of the study that I have kindly been given access to is preliminary, and so I shall have to treat the results rather summarily. Påhlsson in his presentation uses diagrams representing each tested accent which he refers to as "social profiles". From these diagrams one can deduce the perceived suitability of the accents with respect to the 11 job labels. "Scottish" receives a rather flat set of averages broken up by a considerable uprating for agricultural job labels. "South-East" is primarily perceived as being positively related to a relatively high social class, but also has certain overall non-manual qualities. "Midlands" is negatively related to a high social class. "RP" is extremely well correlated with high socio-economic positions. "London" is basically flat across the job spectrum. "North-East" grows more suitable the farther toward the non-professional end of the scale we go. "American" is basically flat. "Tyneside" is very similar to "North-East".

Påhlsson also discusses subgroups (cf above) and their differentiation, but again I hold that such a neat method of subdivision as his would really require a larger material (or fewer subcategories) in order to prove its point.

1.2. Sociolinguistics vs. social psychology.

The student of language attitudes who has his home base somewhere within the area of linguistics (e.g. the present writer) soon discovers that in trying to find reports on language attitude research, he will have to leave his home territory virtually straight away. There is no doubt that of all that has been written on this subject since it took on a formal methodological guise in the early 1930s, the lion's share has been produced by psychologists. The above survey is a clear indication of this state of affairs.

The reason for a psychologist to devote time and effort to the study of language may be different from that of a linguist. As far as language attitudes are concerned, psychologists regard them as a methodological device used in order to gain enhanced understanding of the attitude formation between social groups. In particular the matched guise technique, i.e. eliciting informants' attitudes to various language forms produced surreptitiously by one and the same speaker, has over the last few decades been regarded as a good way of getting information about "[---] the stereotyped impressions or biased views which members of one social group hold of representative members of a contrasting group", primarily because it "[---] appears to reveal judges' more private reactions to the contrasting group than direct attitude questionnaires do [---]" (Lambert 1967:93f). In other words, language is used as a decoy in order not to frighten off the game the social psychologist really wants to catch, human interaction. The matched-guise technique is then a way of making sure that informants' varying responses are not based on voice or personality idiosynchrasies. This methodology is founded on the idea of language being part of a system of social norms, a background against which individuals can act and vary within certain limits (cf Sapir 1927, Hudson 1980:ch. 4).

The pure sociolinguist, if indeed such an animal exists, will approach language attitudes in order to find out things about language, e.g. principles governing language change and variation. In doing so, he will be equipped with the tools of theoretical linguistics, e.g. the structuralist theory of language which allows analysis at various levels. But in order to suggest tenable explanations as to the question "why?" in the first place, he will also have to fall back on whatever information he might procure concerning human interaction, power relations, etc., which means that he will be dealing with very much the same entities as his colleague on the psychological (or sociological) side (cf Ryan, Giles & Sebastian 1982).

A lot of effort has gone into attempts toward reconciling social psychology and sociolinguistics (see e.g. Giles 1979). It is not altogether clear to me why there should be felt to be a need for reconciliation in the first place, as that would seem to imply a will toward the contrary among the trend-setters of either field. Is there such a will? The matter can, I think, be resolved by means of a historical analysis which shows that social psychology and sociolinguistics have developed side by side over the years only because they are sprung from two different scholarly traditions, not because there are, necessarily, differences in the matter they work with. Insofar as language is a type of human behaviour which can only exist in social interaction, it is a social psychological as well as a sociolinguistic concern, the difference between the two subjects in that context being primarily one of tradition. It is my belief that this difference in tradition is, if anything, beneficial to the work as such, as it will promote a wider variety of aspects than would otherwise appear.

There is no doubt that both subjects have their methodological specialities for studies of language attitudes, linguistics perhaps mainly in its extensive analytical apparatus with regard to language; psychology in the "[...] sophisticated statistical techniques [that] are a hallmark of social psychological methods [---]" (Giles 1979:16). To the extent that workers from either side trespass in the methodological domains of the other side (as, for instance, in the present study), there will inevitably be a certain amount of awkwardness, but it is to be hoped that there will also be some degree of freshness of approach that might promote more expert developments on both sides.

1.3. On stereotyping.

I would like to draw attention to one important issue with many implications both in the present study and in much of the work that has been carried out within the field of language attitudes: that of *stereotyping*.

One of the typical findings of research into language attitudes from the pioneer days and onwards has been that the degree of unanimity between listener-informants is often much greater than is the accuracy of their ratings (cf survey pp. 7ff), accuracy being determined by the degree of correlation between ratings and results on standard psychological tests. From the start and with few exceptions this state of affairs has been interpreted as indicative of stereotyping, i.e. simplified and often prejudiced opinions founded on social and cultural expectations and beliefs.

> One exception is Kramer (1964) which is a "reconsideration" of earlier data (from the 1930s, 40s, 50s; strangely enough, no mention is made of Lambert's work). Kramer claims that "[...] interjudge agreement is not without validity, and that the role of seeking correlations with external criteria [= psychological tests] has not been fully understood [...]". His point is that standard psychological tests must not be regarded as the final verdict of what is a true personality trait, but rather as a component in an aggregate of methods to judge personality, voice assessment being another. It should be noticed that Kramer does not discuss "factually verifiable traits" such as social class, profession, etc., which are also seen to be treated stereotypically in listeners' responses.

> More recently, Brown & Bradshaw (1985) reached similar conclusions. They claim that the circumstance that objectively measurable characteristics give rise to accurate voice judgments should be interpreted as an indication of *general* accuracy in such judgments. If "paper and pencil measures" show deviant results, they should be put to doubt, particularly in view of the fact that "the concept of personality is itself rooted in the perception one person has of another" (p. 153).

The point I would like to make is that stereotyping means "different things to different people". It is natural that social psychologists are highly concerned with the distinction between stereotypes and "real" judgments based on voice, as they use voice as an instrument to gain knowledge about persons, i.e. the persons assessing the voices and the persons possessing them. If there is something dubious (which stereotyping is implicitly regarded as) about the link between voice assessment and personality, then the scholarly project is in danger. A linguist, on the other hand, who seeks to gain knowledge about language, will be content with whatever responses a language sample elicits, as long as he knows how to describe and define the sample.

1.4. The recordings. The voices. What they say.

Altogether, the voice material of this investigation consists of 25 different voice recordings. The recordings were made in Gothenburg and in Brighton, England. The Gothenburg recordings were made either in the recording studio of the English department or at external sessions. The Brighton recordings were all made externally. This means that the recording quality varies considerably within the material. The studio recordings are by far the best, followed by the external Gothenburg recordings and last the Brighton recordings. The quality variation was caused by variation in recording facilities and recording equipment (ranging from Revox studio recorder, via Tandberg reel recorder, to Philips cassette recorder). There was also variation in recording environment, as several of the external recordings were made in a "natural" environment. I have not made any attempt to control for recording quality. It is possible that a relatively bad recording quality might affect voice assessment negatively, and vice versa. Sebastian & Ryan (1985:124ff) report on studies in which the experimental use of "white noise" in recordings had a significantly negative effect on speaker evaluation.

The objective requirement for the speakers was that they were to be native speakers of English from England (in the strict sense). The odd case where the person was born outside England but where the family had moved to England very early on was also accepted.

Since this is not a matched-guise experiment (Lambert 1967), it was not necessary to find speakers with an especially developed skill in producing many different accent guises. This of course facilitated procedures considerably, British English perfectly bidialectal speakers being thin on the ground in Sweden (as well as elsewhere).

Not using the matched-guise technique was however primarily the result of a conscious methodological choice. First of all, this study is devoted to the "standard" pole of each speaker's accent variation spectrum, which is as it were only *one*, and so matched guises would probably be somewhat off target, as they would seem to require variation between pre-defined varieties. Second, matched guises are naturally more interesting to social psychologists doing language attitude research, since to them, language is an instrument used in order to gain information about people and as such it should be "held constant" as much as possible. To a linguist, on the other hand, the variation between speech samples is the object of study.

Third, even if these two points could be shown to be invalid, the matched-guise technique can be put to doubt as it is based on an atomistic idea of personality, i.e. that somebody's personality is built up of isolated and interchangable chunks of features, accent being one. According to this idea, we are supposed to be able to remove one such chunk and replace it with another one, without disturbing either what is left or the whole. It would lead too far to go into this problem in detail here (and I would not pretend to have the competence to do so), but I would like to express a certain amount of scepticism toward that idea. There is, I feel, a great risk of constructing a non-person by using this technique, a non-person who would no doubt cause informants to react in a certain pointed way when listening to him, perhaps partly owing to confusion, but who would nevertheless be a non-person. I think that a case in point might be the theory put forward by the scientist and philosopher Michael Polanyi, who says (1967:85) that

> all our higher principles [e.g. personality; my comment] must rely
> for their working on a lower level of reality and this necessarily
> sets limits to their scope, yet does not make them reducible to the
> terms [e.g. those governing accent variation; my comment] of the
> lower level.

In Gothenburg, speakers were obtained through various channels, e.g. evening schools, the English School, the University, and individual personal contacts. In Brighton, the speakers were contacted individually in various ways that were convenient. Gothenburg and Brighton speakers can be distinguished by the G or B in their personal speaker ID code.

The Gothenburg recordings were made between March 11 and April 22, 1982, and the Brighton ones around April 20, 1982.

Before making the recordings, the speakers were asked to fill out a form containing questions about themselves. The information obtained thus will later be used in the informant-speaker comparisons. In fact, the form is in principle the same as the one used by the informants. The items in the form were the following:

1. Speaker ID code number.
2. Date of recording.
3. Speaker sex.
4. Year of birth.
5. Place of residence, age 0-20.
6. Place of residence, last ten years.
7. Place of residence, time of the recording.
8. Occupation.
9. Father's (or mother's) occupation.
10. Husband's/wife's occupation.
11. Primary education (number of years/type).
12. Secondary education (number of years/type).
13. Post-school education (number of years/type).

Questions (5) and (6) on place of residence might of course be hard to answer in a uniform way by speakers who have moved a lot. For convenience, therefore, speakers were asked to state the place where they had lived longest during the period in question.

In the working-out that followed, several of the answers had to be transformed into numerical values in order for them to be statistically processible. Thus, the answers to questions (5)-(7) on residence were transformed into four different categories: country, area within country, county within area, and community size. For example, somebody answering "Barrow-in-Furness, Cumbria" would get the regional code E 6 03 2, meaning England, North, Cumbria, 50,000-100,000 inhabitants. Community sizes were mostly obtained from *Pears Cyclopedia* or *The Reader's Digest Complete Atlas of the British Isles*. (As it later turned out, this codification is characterized by a certain amount of investigational overkill, since the only regional level that is used actively in the present study is the one concerning area within country, e.g. North.)

Similarly, answers to questions (8)-(10) regarding occupation, which of course are of limited interest in themselves, but which may make up reasonably good indicators of social status, were transformed into numerical values for all occupations involving gainful employment, according to to the system set up in *Classification of Occupations 1980* :

I.	Professional etc. (e.g. lawyer, doctor);
II.	Intermediate (e.g. teacher, businessman, actor);
III.	Skilled non-manual (e.g. secretary, clerk, sales representative);
IV.	Skilled manual (e.g. decorator, bricklayer);
V.	Partly skilled (e.g. factory worker);
VI.	Non-skilled.

Category IV is a slight deviation from the subdivision used in *Classification of*

Occupations 1980, where "Skilled" forms one category (III) with the two subcategories "Non-manual" and "Manual". (Macaulay (1976:174) claims that the manual—non-manual distinction is "considered one of the most important in a modern industrial society.")

In addition to these numerical values, the following characters were used:

> X. Not gainfully employed (mostly housewife);
> Z. Zero entries (i.e. no answer supplied);
> S. Student.

In the questions on educational background, numerical labels were tagged to the various types of education:

Primary
1. State
2. Private

Secondary
1. Secondary modern, secondary technical, elementary
2. Grammar, direct grant
3. Comprehensive
4. Public
5. Other

Post-School
1. Academic
2. Non-academic

These numerals are simply labels in numerical form, used in order to facilitate coding, i.e. they are not intended for computation.

To the 13 question items was added a 14th: a percentage figure representing "Degree of modernity" with regard to the pronunciation of a number of words with controversial pronunciation. A higher percentage is suggested to indicate a more traditional type of pronunciation in general than a lower. It is this figure that forms the systematic backbone of this study (cf pp 83ff).

In table 1, the 25 speakers of our sample and the information supplied by each one of them are presented. Some irrelevant information has been omitted, and certain answers have been codified in accordance with the presentation above in order to secure confidentiality.

Speaker ID	Sex	Year of birth	Res age 0 to 20	Res last 10 yrs	Res now	Occupation
7G	F	1922	London	Sweden	Sweden	2
9B	M	1925	Sussex	Kent	Sussex	1
7B	F	1928	Sussex	Sussex	Sussex	3
8G	M	1929	Sussex	Sweden	Sweden	2
16G	M	1930	Essex	Sweden	Sweden	2
17G	F	1935	Cheshire	Sweden	Sweden	2
15G	F	1936	Cumbria	Lancs	Lancs	1
11G	M	1939	Sussex	Sweden	Sweden	2
12G	F	1942	Liverpool	Sweden	Sweden	2
15B	M	1942	London	Notts	Notts	2
1G	F	1946	Warks	Warks	Sweden	3
3G	F	1946	Yorks	London	Sweden	2
5G	F	1946	London	London	Sweden	2
12B	F	1946	Warks	Sussex	Sussex	2
13G	M	1948	Birmingham	Sweden	Sweden	2
4G	F	1949	Essex	Essex	Sweden	3
2G	F	1950	Beds	Beds	Sweden	2
6G	M	1950	London	London	Sweden	2
14B	M	1950	Derbyshire	Sussex	Sussex	2
9G	F	1952	London	London	Sweden	2
10G	M	1954	Liverpool	Liverpool	Sweden	2
14G	F	1954	Liverpool	Liverpool	Sweden	2
6B	F	1954	Sussex	Sussex	Sussex	3
13B	F	1961	Manchester	Manchester	Sussex	S
8B	F	1965	Sussex	Sussex	Sussex	3

Sp ID	Father's occ	Spouse's occ	Primary ed	Secondary ed	Post school ed	Trad pron
7G	2	1	State	Grammar	Acad.	93
9B	2	X	State	Grammar	Non-acad.	60
7B	2	1	State	High school	Non-acad.	47
8G	1	2	Private	Public	Acad.	80
16G	2	1	Private	Dir. grant	Acad.	90
17G	2	1	Other	Grammar	Acad.	63
15G	4	2	State	Grammar	Acad.	70
11G	1	2	Private	Public	Acad.	77
12G	4	1	Private	Grammar	Non-acad.	67
15B	2	2	State	Public	Acad.	60
1G	2	2	Private	Grammar	Non-acad.	70
3G	1	1	State	Grammar	Acad.	60
5G	2	Z	State	Grammar	Acad.	70
12B	2	1	State	Grammar	Non-acad.	60
13G	4	S	State	Grammar	Acad.	70
4G	4	1	State	?	Non-acad.	53
2G	5	1	State	Compr.	Non-acad.	47
6G	1	2	Private	Public	Acad.	47
14B	2	Z	State	Grammar	Non-acad.	57
9G	2	3	Other	Private	Acad.	70
10G	5	3	State	Grammar	Non-acad.	53
14G	3	Z	State	Grammar	Non-acad.	40
6B	2	4	State	Other	Non-acad.	43
13B	2	Z	State	Compr.	Non-acad.	50
8B	4	2	State	Grammar	- -	50

Table 1. Presentation of the 25 speakers ordered by age. See p. 57f for an explanation of codes.

The speaker ID code numbers were given at the time of the recording. Since recordings were made at two different places, Gothenburg and Brighton, and I was able to supervise the Gothenburg recordings only, there are two numerical sequences within the speaker group. To distinguish between the Gothenburg sequence and the Brighton sequence, the letter G or B was added to the sequential number of the speakers. The reason for the seemingly erratic distribution of ID code numbers in the Brighton sequence of speakers (several numbers are "missing" in the sequence) is that there were certain problems of communication between myself in Gothenburg and my colleague in Brighton who helped me with the Brighton recordings. For better or worse, however, I decided to retain the ID codes originally given, particularly since they are actually quoted by the speakers themselves on the tapes, rather than risk such mishaps as might result from translating them into new, more orderly ones.

It will be noticed that several of the speakers are resident in Sweden at the time of the recording, and that quite a few of them have lived in Sweden at least for the better part of the last ten years. It may be a matter of debate whether such speakers ought to be used in a project of this kind. It is my decided opinion that all but one of the speakers are linguistically very stable, and that this state of affairs is further enhanced by the fact that many of them are actually teaching English in Sweden. The one case which is less than satisfactory in this particular respect is speaker 17G, who, in addition to having lived in Sweden for a considerable number of years, also has a very mixed international background in general. This was to become evident in connection with the informant assessment of speaker 17G. In retrospect, I am inclined to admit that some further editing of the speaker material might have been beneficial to the project. On the other hand, there is undoubtedly a great advantage in the principle of non-interference, which would have been lost in the case of such editing.

The occupational codification also involves some problematic points. In the English language there exist a number of job labels that are very frequent, but unfortunately very loose in terms of exact semantic content. Examples of this are *engineer* and *salesman*, labels which without qualification can lead one astray altogether. In cases where job labels of this kind have been used without further explanation, I have had to resort to common-sensical interpretations, or even flipping a mental coin.

The information obtained about the educational background of the speakers is sometimes blurred, which goes to show that asking people about how many years they went to this or that kind of school is not as clearcut a question as one would tend to expect. From the point of view of the present study, however, this inexactitude is of no consequence, since the educational variable within the speaker group has not been used other than marginally.

Content of recording

In the overwhelming majority of attitudinal studies based on tape-recorded language, reading-passages rather than free speech have been used. The reason for this is probably twofold: (1) it will enable the investigator to maintain uniformity to a greater extent than would otherwise be the case; (2) it is a method of greater practical convenience. This to me is somewhat like the proverbial drunkard, who looks under a streetlight for the coin he has lost, even though he knows that he has probably dropped it elsewhere. I believe it is highly essential to use a language rendition type which as closely as possible resembles spontaneous language if spontaneous language is what we are interested in. There are to my mind enough inauthenticity problems involved in the recording methodology as it is, without our actually adding another one to the very linguistic core of that which we are going to investigate. Or in the words of Romaine (1980:229) on a related problem: "If we [separate paralinguistic features from their segmental context], then the experimental situation is very much removed from reality, since people never hear speech of this type, let alone evaluate it." The circumstance that free speech in certain attitude experiments has yielded similar results as reading passages (cf Giles & Bourhis 1973:337) should not, I think, be taken as proof that this will always happen. However, uniformity and convenience are no doubt important factors which should be catered for in any investigation design. It is in other words important to see to it that uniformity of a kind is maintained even if we want to use free speech (cf Aronovitch 1976). And it is of course important to limit the time during which you have to bother people who almost invariably have other things to do, both in connection with the recording sessions and the listening sessions.

Now, how do we make different speakers produce similar speech other than by asking them to read aloud? This is a question which is often raised in a foreign language department in connection with oral testing. Retelling stories and describing pictures are two methods that have been employed at the English department of Gothenburg University. Both methods have their advantages, retelling stories mainly in that the student is supplied with some linguistic input that might help her along in the rather tense test situation; description mainly because it is very convenient to administer. Since linguistic input is an irrelevant factor in connection with native speakers, and since I did not want to provide a linguistic model, I decided that describing a picture would be a suitable way for the speakers of this project to produce reasonably uniform language. The picture selected for the purpose was one which had been used in a very great number of oral tests and which had proved appropriate in that it tended to stimulate most speakers to keep on talking for a couple of minutes:

(From J.B. Heaton, Composition through Pictures (1966). Reproduced with the permission of the Longman Group UK Ltd.)

As for the problem of lexical diversity promoting an undesired differentiation in informants' responses, the available evidence does not appear to point in any one direction (Giles *et al.* 1981). The reader is invited to judge the degree of lexical diversity in the present speech passages, transcripts of which can be found in an appendix.

The speakers were also asked to read eight sentences designed to give an indication about the degree of linguistic modernity in the speakers. The principles governing this particular activity, which is central to this project, are described more thoroughly on pp. 83ff.

The only component of the recording that will be played before informants is the description of the picture. The description was to go on for 90 seconds, which, in the great majority of cases, was what really happened (cf discussion on irregularities below).

Before making the recording, the speakers were given the following instructions in writing:

> [---] Try to speak in as natural a voice as possible. Do not put on an accent. If you are "multi-dialectal" and feel that you must make a choice between different stylistic registers, use the voice that you would consider proper when discussing a serious matter with a stranger, i.e. a fairly neutral, basically non-dialectal, voice. But again: do not put on an accent. [---] Describe the situation in the picture in some detail. [---]

It is clear that this passage of instruction contains several points which might be said to reduce the speech authenticity it is there to create. On the other hand, there is no doubt that the notion of a more or less official linguistic register is clear to most people, and furthermore, that they would be very likely to use a "higher" style in, say, conversation with a person in a position of authority than otherwise (cf Wakelin 1972:154, Bolinger 1975:330). And indeed, informants' reactions to standard-type accents are what we are after in this study. It was not felt at the time of the recording sessions that these instructions caused any problem on the part of the speakers.

Organization of recordings into programmes

For practical reasons it was necessary to devise a way of organizing the 25 voice specimens into programmes of a length suitable for the sessions in which informants were to listen to the voices. Since brevity is of vital interest when it comes to asking outsiders for assistance, these programmes had to be concentrated. At the same time, it was essential that each informant got an opportunity to listen to as many voices as possible, in order for the comparative aspect to be properly provided for. Similar fieldwork, although with written material, carried out by researchers from the English department in Gothenburg suggested that 30 minutes was probably the maximum period during which to interrupt a regular activity at a school, a university department, or a business establishment, which were to be the principal types of setting for the listening sessions.

Since each speaker had recorded a 90-second passage, and since there would naturally be a need for time to organize seating arrangements, explain what was going on in general, allow informants to think and fill out questionnaires, etc., it was decided that five voices would be the maximum number in each programme, i.e. each session. It was assumed that a five-voice programme would fit into a 30-minute framework for the informant session as a whole. As it turned out, this was a reasonably valid assumption: 30 to 40 minutes was the normal time span of each session.

25 voice specimens arranged in programmes of five in each would bring about a set of five different voice programmes, in the most basic kind of design. However, since such a design would be totally devoid of potential for internal check, in that there would be no way of comparing the scores from two different sessions using different programmes, I decided to have an overlap of one voice between the programmes, so that voice number five in programme number one would recur as voice number one in programme number two, and so on:

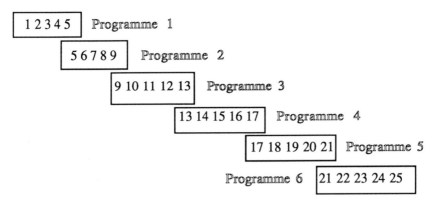

This also means that the five overlapping voices get extra thorough treatment, which was believed to be an asset in the interpretation process (as it turned out, this overlap has not been further elaborated in the present report). This leaves us with six five-voice programmes which contain three or four entirely new voice specimens and one or two which are shared between programmes according to the illustration above.

It could be argued here that a more reliable design would have been to use the same, say, five voices throughout. No doubt this would have made for greater comparability in general and of course a larger number of informants exposed to each voice. On the other hand, such an arrangement would have involved selecting voice specimens according to some sort of principle, rather than recording a fair number of voices and using all of them, the way I have done. It is my belief that planned selection would have been detrimental to the purpose of this investigation in that it would have created a greater risk of begging the question (cf also discussion on statistics below p. 87).

The next step was to decide how to combine voice specimens so as to form six reasonably equivalent five-voice programmes. I have already mentioned that in addition to describing a picture, the speakers were required to record eight sentences containing words whose pronunciation is subject to some controversy (in fact *controversy* is one of them). It was hypothesized that the percentage of words pronounced traditionally might be an indicator of the "degree of modernity" in the language of the speakers. It turned out that among the 25 speakers, there was a span from 40 to 93 per cent traditionally pronounced words. Following the percentage figure five categories were made up:

(1) 40-47 per cent;
(2) 50-57 per cent;
(3) 60-63 per cent;
(4) 67-70 per cent;
(5) 70-93 per cent;

thus creating five categories with five speakers in each, each category with reasonably equivalent degree-of-modernity percentages (for a fuller account of Degree of modernity, see p. 83). From each of these five categories one speaker was selected to form the first five-voice programme, and then another to form the second one, and so on. In addition to this restriction, it was seen to that there would be reasonable equality in recording standards between the six programmes, so that each programme got its fair share of good and not so good recordings.

It was felt to be appropriate not to play a full recording to the informants at one fell swoop, but allow for thinking and rethinking. Therefore each 90-second voice specimen was split into two halves. Technically, this was done by having a brief pause on the tape in the middle of the recording so that the investigator could turn off the machine at that point. In other words, each five-voice programme was presented in the following order:

Voice 1: speech - pause - speech;
pause;
Voice 2: speech - pause - speech;

and so on.

Irregularities in recordings
The time stipulated for the recordings was as I have already mentioned 90 seconds. This stipulation was adhered to in most of the recording sessions. There are however a couple of recordings that are marginally shorter, and also one that is somewhat longer than 90 seconds. One recording, speaker 8B, is only 40 seconds in all. In this particular case, I decided to use that 40-second passage twice, before and after the break in the edited programme.

In all but one of the recordings, the speakers did exactly what was required of them, simply to describe the picture in some detail. In one case, though, viz. the recording made by speaker 15B, there is some unfortunate deviation from this pattern. Transcripts of this passage and all other passages can be found in appendix 1, where there is also an indication of the duration of each speaker's unedited recording.

1.5. The questionnaire.

In each informant listening session, there were two different forms that the informants were asked to read and fill out, (1) a single sheet containing on the front a very brief introduction to the project and a number of items to do with the informant himself, and on the back written instructions about the things required of the informants together with the drawing that the speakers were going to describe (cf p. 62); (2) a set of five sheets making up the questionnaire proper, each sheet containing questions about one individual voice in the five-voice programme that the informant was going to listen to. At the end of each informant session, the informants were asked to fasten the single sheet to the five-sheet set by means of a stapler provided by myself, thus creating an identifiable, individual set of answers. Copies of all forms can be found in appendices 3-7.

The single sheet.
The purpose of the single sheet was to collect information about the informant believed to be useful in the assessment. Basically the informants were asked to answer the same set of questions as that which the speakers were confronted with before making the recording, viz. sex, year of birth, residence, educational background, occupation. The main idea governing the design of this form was to try and obtain a good amount of valid information without causing a great many interpretational problems on the part of the informants. For this reason it was considered wise to construct a modified version of the form to be used by youth informants, so as to avoid uncertainty about the applicability of certain items, such as "occupation", etc. In retrospect, I think I can state quite confidently that this modification caused more problems than it helped to alleviate in that the two versions had to be somehow equalized in the analysis. This again stresses the importance of keeping procedures simple.

As was the case with the speakers, informants were asked to state their place of residence in three different ways, which could be referred to as *childhood residence, recent residence* and *present residence*, respectively. For youth informants (i.e. sixth-formers), childhood residence meant residence up to the age of ten, for adults up to the age of 20. Recent residence for youth informants referred to residence since the age of ten, for adults the last ten years. Present residence is of course the same for both informant categories. In addition to these differences, there was also a modification of the wording of the questions in order to make the youth version sound somewhat less formal, thus "where did you live?" rather than "place of residence".

As it could be expected that informants who had moved a lot might find it hard to answer the question on residence in a uniform way, such informants were asked to state the place where they had lived longest within the period in question.

Occupation, too, was subjected to a threefold question, but only for adult informants, who were asked to state (1) their own occupation, (2) their husband's/wife's occupation, and (3) their father's (or mother's) occupation. This was done in order to ensure that we would get an answer regarding occupational status, regardless of such factors as might otherwise have prevented this, e.g. informants without gainful employment. In the case of the youth informants, in view of the fact that they were all secondary school pupils, it was not necessary to ask about husband's/wife's occupation, or indeed about their own occupation, since that was given from the start. Here, father's/mother's occupation had to suffice.

The educational background of the informants is a factor which undoubtedly is of some significance, but which proves difficult to investigate without going into great detail. The reason is that the educational system has changed and is changing, so that comparisons are often less than easy to make. Adult informants were asked to state the type of primary, secondary and post-school education they had had, and how many years of each. Youths, who, as we have seen, are secondary school pupils themselves, were simply asked whether their primary and secondary education had been "local state", "private" or "other".

Informants' answers about residence, occupation and education were then tranformed into characters and numerals in order to be computable and in order to secure confidentiality. This was done in the same way as in connection with the speakers (see p. 57-58).

In addition to these questions on personal background, there was also a set of questions intended to elucidate the informant's opinion of herself as a judge of varieties of spoken English. There were three such questions and they were phrased: (1) How much do you notice a person's accent? (2) How much are you influenced by a person's accent? (3) Do you find it easy or difficult to make a rough judgment about where a person comes from by the way he speaks? The first two were to be answered along a four-step scale going from "not at all" to "very much", the third along a six-step scale going from "very difficult" to "very easy". Apart from the factual aspect, these questions also served the purpose of making the informants acquainted with the kind of scale that they would encounter throughout the questionnaire proper, which will be discussed more thoroughly below.

When discussing the form filled out by the speakers, I used the expression "investigational overkill" to describe the phenomenon of asking more questions than you can practically take care of in the working-out process. Investigational overkill is a feature of the single-sheet form filled out by the informants as well. Some of the questions asked were only used for reference in the course of the project, without actually being brought up in the report. Others are used marginally. The three informant variables that make up the structure of this study are AGE, SEX and REGIONALITY. They were selected because they were felt to lend themselves most favourably to the analysis, in view of the fact that there had to be limitation of the scope of the report. The alternative would have been to discuss more variables more superficially. The choice was mine, and I decided to concentrate on these three variables.

It could be argued that investigational overkill is a case of bad planning. Within reasonable limits I do not think that is the case. Investigations happen over time and there is no way that the investigator can know before what he knows after. A much greater misfortune would be to be so narrow in the preparatory phases that you end up with a substantial amount of material that for various reasons you cannot use.

A way of going about this kind of problem which I do not approve of, but which is sometimes used in research reports, is to weed the report of anything that falls outside the limits set by the finalized product. This method has the advantage of appearing neat and well-planned, but of course the disadvantage of hiding from the reader the process behind that product, which may be a necessary prerequisite for understanding it properly.

On the front of the single-sheet form, space was also provided where I could fill in details about recordings used, test place and date, etc.

On the back of the single-sheet form were the following instructions:

You are about to hear five different English voices. The speakers all describe the picture you can see below. Each speaker will speak for about *80 seconds*. After about *40 seconds*, there will be a one-minute pause (or slightly longer, if necessary). During this pause, you should try to answer the questions on the answer sheet (nos. 1-9, front and back). *There is one anwer sheet for each speaker*. After the pause you will hear *another 40 seconds by the same speaker*, so that you can make up your mind about doubtful questions.

Then you go on to the next answer sheet and the next voice, and the procedure is repeated; and so on.

Before you start listening, take a quick look at the picture and one of the answer sheets, so that you get acquainted with the material.

THIS IS THE PICTURE THAT THE SPEAKERS DESCRIBE:
[Picture, see p. 62]

The questionnaire proper.
The questionnaire in which the informants are asked to answer questions about the five voices they are going to hear consists of five identical sheets, each sheet containing nine different questions and a blank where the informants could fill in the ID code of the respective speaker as it was quoted by the speaker on the tape. Here follows a presentation of the nine questions with some discussion.

1. How old do you think the speaker is? Answer: about .... years of age.

Since the age aspect can be closely associated with language change, which is one of the phenomena this study seeks to explore, it was considered useful to check whether informants' age conjectures were in any way affected by factors other than those which we normally associate with age. For instance, speakers who are believed to be considerably younger than they actually are might display linguistic features which could be looked upon as indications of modernity, and vice versa.

In a pilot study preceding this one, some of the question items were tried out. In that pilot study, the age question was presented as a tick-off question where the informants were asked to place the voices they heard in one out of a number of age brackets, each with a five-year span. However, this method proved to add complication without promoting interpretational clarity, so I decided to use a fully open-ended question design here.

> Asking for an unrestricted AGE guess, or for that matter any numerical guess or estimate, will give rise to what is known as "digit preference" or, in the case of AGE, "age heaping", that is to say, informants will tend to overuse certain digits at the expense of others. Thus, in Western cultures, age guesses ending in 0 or 5 will by far outnumber guesses ending in other digits. This happens in the present study as well, but since we are not after meticulous accuracy, guessing not being compatible with such accuracy, we need not be concerned about age heaping. For a thorough discussion on these matters, see Shryock *et al.* (1980:204ff).

2. What part of England do you think the speaker comes from? (Choose between (a), (b) and (c))
(a) I am fairly certain he/she comes from ,....................................
(b) I should think he/she probably comes from ....
(c) I have no idea ☐ (tick off box)

In the pilot study just mentioned, a map of England was given instead, with the five major dialect areas indicated (Northern, Midland, Western, Eastern, Southern) and the informants were asked to place the voice they heard in one of those areas. It turned out, however, that that kind of method, although very suitable from the point of view of comparison and neat in that it adhered to a traditionally accepted pattern of dialect distribution, did not fit well into the informant—voice confrontation, since it tended to impose on informants a pattern with which many of them were unfamiliar, thus causing them to answer in categories they would never have chosen of their own accord. It was therefore decided to employ an open-ended design instead, accepting the risk of getting answers of a variety of types which would have to be sorted out in the assessment.

Guessing is a business which may make people feel uncomfortable if they are faced with a situation where they have to guess, willy-nilly. It therefore seemed prudent to soften the question somewhat by introducing a weighting system, whereby informants could choose to answer in one out of three answer alternatives, depending on how certain they felt about the question. It was believed that such a system would be particularly beneficial in connection with the question on regional background, since that question deals with a distinctive ability which is recognized by most people as a real ability, i.e. many people would find it natural to assume that accent can reveal regionality, although they may feel that their competence in making the distinction themselves is lacking. If informants have a choice between different degrees of certainty in their answers, it would seem reasonable to expect answers which are more in accordance with their actual distinctive potential than would otherwise be the case. In the result analysis, the three degrees will be referred to as AREA HIGH POWER, AREA LOW POWER, and AREA ZERO POWER, respectively.

As will be seen later on, it is my belief that non-committal answer alternatives should be avoided in this kind of study. I was therefore reluctant to introduce the "I have no idea" alternative in this question. However, since we are dealing with a real ability, and since the (b) alternative, "I should think....probably,...." would seem to be loose enough to attract informants with a fair amount of uncertainty, I decided to leave open the possibility to state explicitly that the voice in question has no regional significance for a certain informant. This would also seem appropriate in view of the fact that the "RP" accent is often defined as an accent which does not give away the domicile of its speakers. It was felt that this three-level design might make it possible to judge more efficiently the significance of regionality in spoken standard British English.

3. What do you think the speaker does for a living? Suggest an occupation that seems reasonable to you.

This question is one which should be expected to create some distress in the informants, as there is of course no one-to-one relationship between occupations and accents. What we are after is a rather general indication as to possible associations between accent and socio-economic status. The pilot study showed that an explicit use of class categories (Working Class, Upper Middle Class, etc.) is not altogether fortunate, probably because informants are often put off by the assumptions hidden in such categories, which they may not agree with. Also, class categories are necessarily abstract entities, which, in order to be manageable, should be subjected to rather thorough definitions (Macaulay (1976) in a sociolinguistic study in Glasgow chose occupation as a social class indicator because of the practical convenience of this technique when working with school children, and because it was felt to be the best *single* class indicator). I decided, therefore, to use an open-ended type of question, facing up to whatever objections informants might have about answering it.

In the working-out process, the answers to questions (2) and (3) were transformed into characters and numerals in the same way as was done in connection with the speakers (cf p. 57).

4. What qualities do you think the speaker possesses? (For example, if you think he probably has very high qualities of leadership, you put a tick in the rightmost box; if you think he has high, but not *very* high qualities, you put a tick in the second box from the right, and so on.) [Then followed ten labels for psychological or related qualities, each with a scale made up of six boxes, going from "very little" to "very much". The labels were: LEADERSHIP, DEPENDABILITY, HONESTY, SENSE OF HUMOUR, FRIENDLINESS, INTELLIGENCE, SELF-CONFIDENCE, AMBITION, DETERMINATION, EDUCATION.]

The ten quality labels make up a selection borrowed from the writings of Lambert and his colleagues (Lambert *et al.* 1960, Tucker & Lambert 1969). The principle underlying this selection was mainly to get a reasonably wide spectrum of qualities that would be applicable to British speakers and informants, and to avoid such qualities as could, I think, rightly be criticized for being too far-fetched, such as

"Faith in God" (Tucker & Lambert 1969; a relic of the Spranger typology, perhaps? For a view in support of using such quality labels, see Giles & Bourhis 1973:340). It was further thought necessary for practical reasons to limit the scope of the questionnaire as much as possible. Synonymous or near-synonymous labels were therefore discarded in several, although not all, cases: there was also the counteracting wish to consider, to provide for the facilitation of internal check, i.e. the possibility of being able to compare informants' answers with regard to near-synonymous labels to see whether the difference was unduly great, which would reduce the predictive power of the material.

One of the ten labels, EDUCATION, is obviously not a psychological quality. Indeed, in the pilot study, education was allotted a section of its own, in which informants were asked to guess the educational background of the speakers in a rather detailed way. Since education is a cultural phenomenon which means different things to different people, and since details about educational systems are often less than clear to many people, this turned out not to be very successful. Instead I decided to use the less exact, but more convenient, method of simply asking informants whether they thought that the speakers had more or less "education".

Education seems intuitively to fit well into the general semantic field made up of psychological qualities, and so it was thought to be convenient to place it there. This is also the way Tucker & Lambert (1969) treat the concept.

In a study (Preston 1963) carried out at McGill University and referred to by Lambert (1967), "[t]he 18 personality traits [...] were grouped for the purpose of interpretation into three logically distinct categories of personality: (a) *competence* which included intelligence, ambition, self-confidence, leadership and courage; (b) *personal integrity* which included dependability, sincerity, character, conscientiousness and kindness; (c) *social attractiveness* which included sociability, likeability, entertainingness, sense of humor and affectionateness." (Lambert 1967: 95) This grouping has since been used in several studies of attitude. It seems to me that (b) and (c) should rather be regarded as parallel subcategories to a more general category which would in turn be on an equal footing with (a). I have decided in this study to divide psychological qualities into two categories, *individually significant qualities* and *socially significant qualities*. Individually significant qualities are: INTELLIGENCE, SELF-CONFIDENCE, AMBITION, DETERMINATION, and, for convenience, EDUCATION. Socially significant qualities are LEADERSHIP, DEPENDABILITY, HONESTY, SENSE OF HUMOUR and FRIENDLINESS. Obviously, there is bound to be a great deal of semantic overspill between these two categories, but the basis of the subdivision seems rational, in that the socially significant qualities can only be applied in a multi-person context (there is as it were no point in being friendly or dependable on one's own), whereas the individually significant qualities can exist more independently of people other than the subject herself. This binary subdivision would seem to fit well into the framework of this study, since attitudes towards accents, which make up the core of this study, could be expected to differ according to whether the stimulus voice is looked upon in a social or non-social situation.

Informant response to the ten qualities in this section, and indeed to all closed-category questions in the questionnaire, is given along six-step scales, where the leftmost step represents the negative extreme ("very little") and the rightmost one the positive extreme ("very much"). In the questionnaire, no degree tags were attached to the second through fifth box of the scale, and so the informants were encouraged implicitly to look upon the scale as a scale, rather than a set of labelled boxes. "Response-order effects" of the kind discussed by Schuman & Presser (1981:36ff), i.e. the risk of the position of a given alternative within the answer scale creating undesirable effects can, I believe, be disregarded here because of the great simplicity of the scales—which in turn is an effect of not labelling the boxes. As has already been mentioned, scales of this kind were also used in the single-sheet form on which the informants presented themselves, but then they were supplied with explicit labels, so as to give informants, some of whom may have been new to scales of this kind, an opportunity to acquaint themselves with the scale design.

The scale we are using is a bipolar, symmetric, six-step scale whose extremes are true opposites. It is sometimes argued (Langlet & Wärneryd 1983:45ff) that such scales are deficient in that they do not contain a mid alternative, and thereby force informants to assume opinions they do not genuinely hold. This might make them adverse to the questionnaire as a whole, which would reduce the predictive power of the investigation.

In a thorough investigation into the formal aspects of attitude surveys, Schuman & Presser (1981) discuss the pros and cons of having and not having a mid alternative in a closed answer scale. Really, the problem is twofold. It is first of all a matter of offering explicitly a "Don't know" option or not. Secondly, it is a matter of having or not having a mid alternative for informants who genuinely take the mid position. Schuman & Presser show that a Don't know alternative attracts considerably more respondents than would be prepared to give a spontaneous Don't know answer if such an option was not offered, but that this tendency normally does not affect the balance between positive and negative answers. They also show that a genuine mid alternative tends to attract respondents who would otherwise express a more polarized opinion, rather than respondents who would give (spontaneous or filtered) Don't know answers.

The experiments on which Schuman & Presser base their findings are mostly taken from the field of politics in a wide sense, for example, the relationship between Russia and America or between Israel or the Arab nations, communists in America, divorce, and so on. What could generally be said about such subject matters is that they would normally seem to constitute isolated phenomena which might or might not be part of the respondent's experience. People are not necessarily exposed to such subject matters (cf Bogart 1967). It is also the case that political matters of this kind are normally conveyed as *information* via more or less official information channels, which means that there will be great variation in the way people receive the message, if indeed they receive it at all. Furthermore, the reason why information campaigns are carried out in the first place is hopefully to promote clarity and understanding of something which is a matter of fact. It is in other words possible to check to what extent a message has attained its informative goal, and this is probably the objective of many investigations into attitudes.

The present study differs from Schuman's & Presser's examples in that it deals with a subject matter, voices and accents, which is there all the time, not as self-sufficient showpieces, but as coveyers. This in turn has at least two important consequences: (1) it is to be doubted that anybody within a given linguistic environment could truthfully claim ignorance about voices and accents; (2) most people, in particular people with no explicit interest in linguistic matters, will probably be unaccustomed to making formal, explicit judgments about voices and accents, other than such common popular beliefs as "this is a nice voice", etc. It could also be argued that the idea of associating voice and/or linguistic phenomena with matters that are factually important, such as psychological qualities, or, which we shall come to later on, suitability in connection with various jobs, is repulsive to many people for ideological reasons. This is not to say, I believe, that they do not have an opinion; it is merely to say that it is not considered good taste to express it.

On the basis of these points, I decided to refrain both from having a Don't know option and a genuine mid alternative in my attitude scales. It is my belief that people do have an opinion, because my subject matter is not made up of external information; it is something which is part not only of people's experience, but of their basic cognitive repertoire. In order to avoid informants taking the easy way out by means of choosing the mid alternative, which is probably what a great number of people would do, quite naturally, had they a choice, not because they do not have an opinion, but because they are unaccustomed to discussing it, or indeed unwilling to state it, I settled for a six-step design. And it turns out that even Schuman & Presser, having been busy advocating a Don't know option and a genuine mid alternative, have to admit that

> [...] whether filtered [with Don't know, etc.] or standard [without it] questions should be used in a questionnaire would seem to depend on whether an investigator is interested mainly in "informed opinion" on an issue or mainly in underlying dispositions[; thus] there may be no general solution to the problem of which form of question is better. (1981:160)

In terms of average calculations, the present design of course means that 3.5 is the "non-committal" mid position that we should expect in a group of informants who, as a group, do not have a marked opinion in either direction.

5. How acceptable do you think the speaker's accent would be in different positions? Put a tick in the correct box.

How acceptable would you consider this accent to be in:

> (a) a teacher of English
> (b) an actor/actress
> (c) a grocer's assistant
> (d) a BBC newsreader
> (e) a disc jockey
> (f) a barrister
> (g) a rock singer
> (h) a government official
> (i) a workingman/-woman
> (j) a fellow worker/student of yours
> (k) your child (or brother/sister)

[For each of these job (or related) labels, a six-step scale of boxes was provided, with the poles "not acceptable" and "highly acceptable" given in the first instance.]

Many readers will find the formulation of this question less than entirely fortunate. At one point in the preparatory phases, the word *suitable* was substituted for "acceptable", which undoubtedly made the questions sound better from a stylistic point of view. On the other hand, *suitable* would, to my mind, place the matter of debate more within the speaker, rather than the listener, and what we are after here is the attitudes of listeners.

Also, this is a question which many informants would be reluctant to answer, since doing so might be felt to indicate some association with what is believed to be prejudice.

From the point of view of this study, the question is crucial, in that it aspires to elucidate how informants look upon the relationship between accent and social position. Here we are not merely after the connection with socio-economic status, but also, perhaps primarily, the traditional-modern and official-personal dichotomies. There may well be ways of eliciting informants' attitudes to these matters without exposing one's flank to charges of either looseness or pointlessness, but probably not without going into a degree of detail which was beyond the practical scope of this project. For better or worse, therefore, this is the question the informants were required to answer, with no further information or instruction provided.

The eleven labels, as we have seen, can be placed within different socio-semantic categories. BBC NEWSREADER and ACTOR/ACTRESS are job labels which are traditionally very closely associated with the "RP" concept, in the case of BBC NEWSREADER, more or less by definition. BARRISTER is a label which stereotypically possesses strong Oxbridge undertones, thereby being associated with the "RP" type of accent. TEACHER OF ENGLISH and GOVERNMENT OFFICIAL might be seen as belonging to an in-between category. GOVERNMENT OFFICIAL turned out to be an unfortunate label, since it is semantically loose, having the capacity of meaning anything from a top-ranking civil servant to local government secretarial staff. GROCER'S ASSISTANT and WORKINGMAN/-WOMAN were selected as belonging to traditional non-"RP" areas. GROCER'S ASSISTANT was intended to represent a type of job with a more or less clear oral aspect, something which you will find in many service jobs. WORKINGMAN/-WOMAN was thought of as being a convenient generic name for a man or woman of the working class. This, too, turned out to be less than fortunate, but for other reasons. It appears that the word *workingman* has lost its specific meaning for a great number of people. The selection of the word was based on definitions such as:

> A man of the working classes; a man employed to work for a
> wage, esp. in a manual or industrial occupation: a term inclusive
> of 'artisan', 'mechanic', and 'labourer'.
> (from *A New English Dictionary on Historical Principles*);

or:

> A man who works for wages, especially at manual labor.
> (*The American Heritage Dictionary of the English Language*).

But, somewhat surprisingly, it turned out that this meaning was not obvious to a number of, primarily young, informants, who professed themselves confused. Maybe the female form, WORKINGWOMAN, added to the confusion, since for historical reasons it has never been as set a concept as WORKINGMAN. The fact remains, however, that a majority of the speakers were female, and so I considered it necessary to include the female form of this job label. DISC JOCKEY and ROCK SINGER were chosen to represent jobs which could be associated with modern, youth-based culture, thereby possibly exhibiting a contrast with the "RP" area of a kind different from the traditional socio-economic contrast. FELLOW WORKER/STUDENT and CHILD/BROTHER/SISTER, finally, were chosen to represent the peer-group and/or individual area, which could also be expected to be different from the traditional socio-economic contrast (cf Giles's & Sassoon's (1983) "social role"/"social distance").

6. How pleasant do you think this accent is? [followed by six-step scale going from "very unpleasant" to "very pleasant"].

Pleasantness is a variable that has been frequently used in dialect/accent research, notably by Howard Giles and Peter Trudgill and their colleagues (for a summarizing account, see e.g. Trudgill 1983, ch. 12). It is of course virtually impossible to decide whether an informant answering this question actually does so with regard to the accent as such or to other voice-related features. On the other hand, this uncertainty is what we are up against all the time in realistic situations, so there may be a point in not being too specific in the formulation of this question. One great advantage with the PLEASANTNESS variable is that it will not create any interpretational uncertainty among informants, unless they are very sophisticated judges of meaning.

Giles (1971b) and other scholars have shown that "RP" speakers tend to get higher ratings than dialect speakers on a number of Lambert-type (Lambert 1967) personality traits, including pleasantness . It is therefore reasonable to expect relatively high average ratings in this material, since all speakers in it speak standard-type accents. If the PLEASANTNESS variable manages to distinguish between different kind of neutral, standard-like accents, and not only between such accents and regional ones, then we are up against a problem complex whose subtlety is far greater than what has hitherto been established.

7. Do you think this accent is heard very often (a) in your part of England?; (b) in England as a whole? [six-step scales going from "very seldom" to "very often"].

One of the most prevalent ideas about the British "RP" accent is that it is an accent that cannot be regionally defined; this in fact is sometimes used as a definition of "RP". It is also true, of course, that there is a regional base for the RP-type accent as such, even if its speakers come from a wide variety of areas, and this base is London and the South-East of England. One way of checking whether informants attach a regional label to standard-type accents or not is to ask them these questions. Using his by now classic Norwich material, Trudgill has estimated that "RP" "is an accent used natively by only 3 per cent to 5 per cent of the population of England" (Trudgill & Hannah 1982:9). This estimation is used to devalue "RP" as a pattern for foreign students of English. Of course, the question whether "RP" is a common accent or not is one which cannot be answered solely by checking how many its speakers are. Its usualness has also to do with how usual it is perceived to be, and this is where this question comes in.

8. Do you think the speaker's accent would be a disadvantage or an advantage for him/her in a job interview with an employer? [six-step scale going from "disadvantage" to "advantage"].

It is a well-known phenomenon in attitude research that it is sometimes better to ask questions which do not directly seem to involve the respondents themselves, but which even so elucidate their opinion. This technique, humorously referred to as "the 'Other People' Approach" (Barton 1958), is used in this question. It would seem reasonable to expect informants to give a straight answer to a question of this kind, even though they may find the idea of accent influencing an employer in an interview ludicrous.

As was the case in question (5) above, this question is open to counter-reactions for not specifying what type of situation is intended. To my mind, such counter-reactions are not quite valid here, as it would be hard to think of an accent which would be advantageous in one job interview, but disadvantageous in another (cf Labov 1966:410; for partly opposed views, cf Hopper & Williams 1973:301, Giles *et al.* 1981). What is undoubtedly the case is that it may be hard to envisage a speaker of a certain accent in a certain job interview, but that is a different matter.

9. Do you think the speaker's accent is like (a) your own accent? (b) the accents of most of your friends? [six-step scale going from "very different" to "very like"].

Since the regional base of the British standard accent is South-Eastern, we might expect answers to these questions to differ according to the regional background of the different informants. However, since "RP" is often said to be unlimited by regional boundaries, this effect should be expected to vary according to the socio-economic situation of the informant, but only, of course, if the assumption is valid. It may well be that certain informant categories have a view of this matter which does not fit into the traditional pattern. For instance, the egalitarianism which is said to be permeating society might have caused young people's opinions to change. This and related questions will hopefully be elucidated in the assessment of informant answers.

1.6. The informants. The test sessions.

As we have seen in the discussion of the questionnaire, informants were required to state a number of facts concerning their background which were believed to make up interesting points of comparison, e.g. age, regional background, socio-economic background. Regional background is of course highly interesting in connection with a study of accent. However, in order for regionality to display a reasonable degree of differentiation, it was necessary to have a certain regional spread in the organization of test sessions. The North-South dimension was considered sufficiently multifarious to serve the purpose, and so, three areas along that dimension were devised, viz. North, Midland, South. "Midland" should be looked upon as nothing more than a convenient label for the mid part of the North-South axis. It does not necessarily signify all the meanings normally put into the name *Midland*.

For practical reasons, such as already existing networks of personal contacts, Brighton (E. Sussex), Sleaford (Lincolnshire) and Newcastle-on-Tyne (Tyne & Wear) were selected as "home bases" in the respective test areas. The idea was to travel from these bases to places that might be rewarding from the point of view of finding informants. This in turn means that normally the test sessions were held within relatively easy reach of the home base. Only in one case, in Midland, was it necessary to spend a night away from the base.

The informant sessions were carried out between May 11 and May 27, 1982. Prior to this period, inquiries were sent to a large number of school authorities, universities, companies and individuals within reach of the three home bases. In these inquiries the project was outlined and there was a request that I be allowed to visit a school, company, etc., during my stay in England. Positive and promising replies to these requests were followed up by telephone calls immediately on my arrival in England, and soon a time-table to the following effect could be established:

South
May 11   University College London, Scandinavian Department
                 Alfa-Laval UK, Brentford, London

May 12   Boundstone School, Lancing, W. Sussex
          Worthing Sixth Form College, W. Sussex
          Royal Insurance, London
          Private sessions, London
May 13   Brighton Polytechnic, E. Sussex
          Collyers Sixth Form College, Horsham, W. Sussex
May 14   Christ's Hospital, Horsham, W. Sussex
          Private sessions, Horsham, W. Sussex
May 17   Steyning Grammar School, W. Sussex

Midland
May 18   Carre's Grammar School, Sleaford, Lincolnshire
          Kesteven & Sleaford High School for Girls, Sleaford,
              Lincolnshire
          County Secondary School, Sleaford, Lincolnshire
May 20   Speedwell Tool Co., Preston, Lancashire
          Peter Craig, Preston, Lancashire
          Central Lancashire New Town Development
          Corporation, Preston, Lancashire
May 21   Wright-Robinson Comprehensive School, Manchester
May 22   Private sessions, Sleaford, Lincolnshire

North
May 25   Cramlington High School, Tyne and Wear
May 26   Springfield Comprehensive School, Jarrow, Tyne and Wear
          Private session, Hebburn, Tyne and Wear
May 27   Private session, Corbridge, Northumberland

In all, this meant that 370 individual informants were subjected to the test, 109 of whom were adults, and 261 young people (secondary school, normally Sixth Form, students). It will be noticed that there is a certain bias in the informant selection in the direction towards theoretical education. It is also clear that the age spread is not so wide as would have been desired from the comparative aspect. As is usual in a majority of language investigations requiring the participation of informants (cf Davis 1986), availability often wins over desirability. This drawback is something which I genuinely regret and which will of course mar the outcome of this study. However, within the framework of this project, there was no scope for further refinement. Davis (1986) points out that to date, no dialectology investigation has lived up to a true statistician's idea of random sampling, and that it is highly essential that every investigator who uses a "convenience sample" takes care to instruct his readers about "deficiencies involved" (cf also Wardhaugh 1986:145ff). He concludes: "[---] classic random sampling is [...] not really feasible for us [=dialectologists, sociolinguists]; instead our efforts should be spent in eliminating *destructive* bias [...]." (p. 47).

In the letters of inquiry that were sent to the various authorities, companies and individuals, I had said that a session would take about 30 minutes. This was intuitively felt to be the maximum period of time during which to interrupt a regular activity going on there. I have described elsewhere (p. 63) how voice recordings were put together so as to form five-voice programmes and discussed other details about the time allotted to the various parts of the test procedure. It turned out that it was possible to keep within this 30-minute limit, give a couple of minutes at the odd session.

Most of the time, I used a standard cassette player (Sankyo ST-60) which I brought with me. At a few of the test places, such facilities were (sometimes excellently!) provided by the hosts. In addition to the cassette player, I had to carry with me questionnaires and extra pencils and erasers, in case informants should want such equipment.

A typical test session would begin with a very brief introduction by a person in charge (e.g. a teacher), followed by an almost as brief introduction to the project by myself. I would try to draw the informants' attention to the quite common phenomenon that you often get a visual impression of a person you hear on the radio or on the telephone, even though you may have no real idea as to his/her physical appearance, background, etc., and that this was what I wanted to explore. I also stressed that I was more interested in what the informants actually answered than in the correctness of their answers. This was done in order to avoid the changing of answers or the copying of neighbours' answers. Then I handed out the single-sheet form (cf p. 66) on which informants were asked to provide some information about themselves. At the same time the questionnaire was handed out so that the informants could have a quick look at it, and then the tape would roll with as little interruption as possible (cf p. 65). After listening and filling out questionnaires, the informants would normally be curious as to whether they had answered "correctly", and so I would tell them what a "right" answer to the factual questions would be like, taking care that no changes were made at this point.

The number of informants to listen to a programme at any one session varied considerably. In the private sessions, there were normally but a handful of people, whereas in the school sessions, there could be up to about 30 students present, depending on the facilities and other practical constraints. The average number of informants per session was 16.

As explained above, the voice material was divided into six programmes, each with five voices. It was attempted that all five-voice programmes were to be subjected to reasonably equal numbers of informants, in order to achieve as good comparability as possible. Obviously, this could only be done very roughly, as there was no way of influencing informant numbers at a given session. The number of informants to listen to each individual voice can be found in table 2. An asterisk by the speaker ID code means that that particular speaker is present in two different programmes, as an overlapping voice (cf p. 63f).

Speaker	Number Informants	Number adults	Number youths
4G*	155	35	120
17G*	140	63	77
15G*	136	39	97
6G*	125	11	114
7G*	106	36	70
5G	94	4	90
9G	94	4	90
9B	94	4	90
8G	79	32	47
14G	79	32	47
13B	79	32	47
1G	61	31	30
11G	61	31	30
6B	61	31	30
10G	57	7	50
7B	57	7	50
15B	57	7	50
2G	49	29	20
3G	49	29	20
13G	49	29	20
14B	49	29	20
12G	31	7	24
16G	31	7	24
8B	31	7	24
12B	31	7	24

Table 2. Number of adult and young informants to listen to each speaker. * see above.

It will be noticed from the table that some voices get very limited informant treatment, particularly by the adult informants. This is of course a factor which has to be taken into account when assessing the figures we get in the investigation. However, since the assessment will solely deal with group averages, both regarding speakers and informants, no major drawback should result from this, exept from the odd case where even groups happen to be unduly small.

General points on interpretative method.
After the test sessions in England, the questionnaires were to be codified in order to be processible by means of a computer. In practice, this meant that all the answers in the questionnaires had to be turned into numerical values and printed on each questionnaire so that the punching procedure was facilitated. For various reasons, lack of time being one, the questionnaires had not been supplied with numbered boxes for this purpose in advance, so this had to be done manually after the test sessions. Although this brought the good thing with it that all the questionnaires had to be individually scrutinized very thoroughly, so that flaws could be, and were, revealed, there is every reason to advise anybody planning an investigation of this

kind to see to it that the preconditions for coding and punching are planned and checked thoroughly before the material is actually used. To achieve this after the investigation is extremely arduous and time-consuming.

The material was punched and processed at *Göteborgs Datacentral*. The computer program used for the purpose was the well-established statistical program SAS. Apart from producing general lists of all answer items in the material, SAS can create tables of comparison between any groups of items: speakers, informants, answers, etc., that are identifiable within the framework of this study. The typical table produced is one which yields a group mean (M), standard deviation (SD), and group size (N), with regard to a certain subgroup. For example, we can order the computer to produce a table which compares the average ratings of a male and a female group of informants with regard to male and female voices, and so on. Thus we can check whether attitudes to accents defined in a certain way vary systematically according to the listener. This is the stuff of this study.

Depending on how we count, there are about ten to fifteen informant variables that can be checked against about as many speaker variables. This means that the number of theoretically possible combinations is very high. Further treatment of all of these, or even a majority of them, would go far beyond the scope of this project, and it would in many cases be less than interesting, either because of the variables themselves being uninteresting in certain combinations, or because of the smallness of certain possible subgroups.

I therefore decided that the main scope of this study was to be devoted to three variables, AGE, SEX, and REGIONALITY, and their relationship to its central concept: DEGREE OF MODERNITY, as defined below.

1.7. Degree of modernity.

It was found necessary to employ some kind of method to attempt to pinpoint certain features of linguistic significance which might serve as indicators of the degree of modernity in the speech of the respective speakers. In order to avoid subjectivity to some extent, word pronunciation was chosen as a suitable exponent of degree of modernity.

It is fairly easy to find a number of reasonably frequent words which over the last few decades (or the last century) have changed or are now in the process of changing their pronunciation (cf Safire 1986). A list of such words can be found in Burchfield, *The Spoken Word. A BBC Guide* (1981). In this booklet, Burchfield has compiled a list of such words as often give rise to public irritation when pronounced in an unorthodox way by BBC broadcasting staff. Furthermore, among these words he has indicated the ones most often subjected to criticism when thus pronounced. From this list, 30 allegedly controversial words were selected in order to be read aloud by all the speakers of the present project, thereby indicating whether each speaker preferred the "traditional" or the "non-traditional" pronunciation of the words. *A speaker with a higher percentage of traditionally pronounced words would be regarded as linguistically more traditional in general than someone with a lower percentage. This principle is the chosen anchor point of this study.*

In order to avoid a pentasyllabic technical term, the word "modern" will henceforth be used to represent what should really be referred to as "non-traditional". This is an important qualification, since the origins of the non-traditional forms vary so that some of them are not really "modern" in any temporal sense but rather regionally based deviations from an accepted norm.

The words selected were the following:

Word	Trad pron	Mod pron
Arctic	1st <c> pronounced [k]	1st <c> mute
aristocrats	1st syll stress	2nd syll stress
capitalists	1st syll stress	2nd syll stress
comparable	1st syll stress	2nd syll stress
composite	[-it]	[-ait]
contribute	2nd syll stress	1st syll stress
controversy	1st syll stress	2nd syll stress
decades	1st syll stress	2nd syll stress
deficit	1st syll stress	2nd syll stress
deities	[di:-]	[dei-]
disastrous	[-str-]	[-stər-] ([ə] = 1st V in *about*)
dispute	2nd syll stress	1st syll stress
distribute	2nd syll stress	1st syll stress
economic	[i:k-]	[ek-]
exquisite	1st syll stress	2nd syll stress
February	[febr-]	[febj-]
genuine	[-in]	[-ain]
government	<n> pronounced	<n> mute
inherent	[-hiər-]	[-her-]
jewellery	[-u:əlri]	[-u:ləri]
kilometres	1st syll stress	2nd syll stress
lamentable	1st syll stress	2nd syll stress
occurrence	2nd syll V short	2nd syll V long
primarily	1st syll stress	2nd syll stress
research	2nd syll stress	1st syll stress
Soviet	1st syll [səuv-]	1st syll [sov-]
spontaneity	[-ni:-]	[-nei-]
status	1st V [ei]	1st V [æ]
temporarily	1st syll stress	3rd syll stress
trait	final <t> mute	final <t> pronounced

The following table shows how, as a group, the traditional and modern pronunciations of these words were treated in three editions of Daniel Jones's pronouncing dictionary (1924, 1956, 1977) and in Kenyon's & Knott's American counterpart (1953), respectively:

TRADITIONAL	1st choice	2nd-Nth choice	Pron not given	Word not entered
Jones 1924	27*	2 *	0	1 * *
Jones 1956	30	0	0	0
K-K 1953 (US)	21	6	3	0
Jones 1977	29	1	0	0
MODERN				
Jones 1924	0	7	22	1 * *
Jones 1956	0	16	14	0
K-K 1953 (US)	5	10	15	0
Jones 1977	1	21	8	0

*) Jones here has even older forms of the two words *decade* and *jewellery*
**) The word not entered is *Soviet*

Table 3. Treatment of "traditional" and "modern" words in various pronouncing dictionaries.

This table would seem to confirm Burchfield's impression of the pronunciation development of these words. Also, it indicates that American influence is a probable source of change for some of the words (e.g. *primarily*).

As it could be expected that a list of nothing but these 30 words might perhaps arouse suspicion, at least among speakers with a certain degree of linguistic sophistication, so that pronunciations otherwise used would this time be meticulously avoided, it was decided that the words were to be "hidden" in sentences with reasonable, though perhaps somewhat strained, contexts. For this purpose, the following eight sentences were constructed:

1. *This government doesn't want to contribute to any sort of controversy or dispute.*

2. *Primarily, we shall have to find out if there are any comparable deities in the religions of the Arctic peoples of the Soviet Union.*

3. *Next February, five decades will have passed since that lamentable occurrence.*

4. *Dr Parker is carrying out some research on the economic status of 19th century European aristocrats and capitalists.*

5. *This jewellery is really exquisite!*

6. *It would be a good thing if at least parts of Britain would use kilometres instead of miles on road signs.*

7. *Inherent spontaneity is a composite but genuine trait.*

8. *The disastrous deficit makes it impossible to distribute wealth equally.*

It could be argued that a linguistically sophisticated person would immediately realize that these sentences, with their high concentration of moot points, have been made up to test the "correctness" of her pronunciation, and would thus make her overly cautious; it could be argued that the test words should have been distributed less densely and less conspicuously into more sentences. Limitation, however, is a crucial factor when it comes to asking outsiders for assistance, and so I decided to stick to the eight sentences, particularly in view of the fact that in addition to the sentences, the speakers were also required to read a passage (which has not been utilized in this study) and describe a picture (cf p. 61f), an undertaking which in all took the better part of an hour.

The speakers were then divided into two groups according to the percentage of traditionally pronounced words from the list of 30 words above. There turned out to be a spread from 40 to 93 per cent in the speaker sample, and so it was decided to split the full group into two subgroups, one with a percentage of traditionally pronounced words ranging from 40 to 66 per cent, the other from 67 to 93 per cent, that is to say, the percentage span of the full group was split into two equally wide halves. Hereby we get one subgroup with ten members, TRADITIONAL, and one with 15 members, MODERN (the subgroup names do not pretend to be anything more than convenient labels). The reason for dividing the full group at that particular point was that it created two reasonably homogeneous groups of reasonably equal size, without having to make a split within one and the same percentage group.

In table 1, the personal information about all the speakers is presented, one part of which is the percentage figure on which the DEGREE OF MODERNITY subdivision is based. One thing that should be noticed when looking at these figures is that there is a high degree of correlation between AGE and DEGREE OF MODERNITY: eight out of ten (80 per cent) members of TRADITIONAL also belong to the subgroup OLD; and ten out of 15 (67 per cent) members of MODERN belong to YOUNG (see p. 96 for an explanation of OLD and YOUNG). This ought to lend at least some weight to the method of estimating modernity employed here, as it seems to show that older people generally (and naturally) use older forms of pronunciation than do younger. But we also get interesting objects of study in the groups of speakers who occupy the areas which do not exhibit this correlation, that is to say, the speakers who are OLD *and* MODERN, YOUNG *and*

TRADITIONAL.

1.8. Some remarks on the statistics of this study.

This is a study of averages (mean values). Groups of informants' observations are related to groups of accent samples according to various methods of subdivision. This is a fact which must be kept in mind when reading this study. Averages do not exist in reality; they are statistical symbols of group features. As such, they can be more or less representative of these features. A measure of the degree to which they are representative is the standard deviation, which is also a kind of average, viz. of the deviation of the individual observations from the average value (a simplification; for a more detailed account, see e.g. Butler 1985:36f). Thus, a relatively low standard deviation value indicates that a large proportion of the individual observations are placed relatively close to the average value.

The mean values of the present study are based on the *perceptions* and *attitudes* of a number of people who meet certain requirements set up by myself towards a number of accents spoken by people who also meet such requirements.

There is no difficulty at all involved in the calculation and presentation of attitude-based mean values as such. The problem arises when we apply them to the real world we want to describe, that is to say, in the interpretative phases of our work. A well-known example from the world of hard facts can serve as an apposite illustration of this problem: In the 1950s the Ford Motor Company carried out a market analysis of unprecedented dimensions in order to find out what type of car the typical American car owner really wanted. On the basis of the results of this survey, Ford created a car model, the Edsel, which was an attempt at a car that would suit "everybody". The model was launched in the late 1950s, and it turned out to be the all-time sales flop of the American motor industry. The Edsel was probably acceptable to a lot of prospective buyers, but it did not tickle the individual buyer enough to make him buy it, which makes a great difference if you are in the motor business (cf also discussion on commercial TV, p. 318f). This goes to show that attitudes and preferences are part of a very complex structure which allows no one interpretation. In order to draw sensible conclusions from a large material of attitude-based mean values, we must always try to keep in mind the situation in which the attitudes were stated as compared with the real world as we know it, or else we may end up producing another Edsel.

Statistical significance and related problems.

When we get a difference between two mean values, we want to find out to what extent it is likely that this difference is "genuine" or whether it is created by chance factors: we want to know if the difference is "statistically significant". In the present study, two types of comparison will be made. First, I will compare the mean of one informant group with the mean of another with regard to one and the same item in the material. For example, a male and a female group of informants have answered a certain attitude question concerning a certain group of accents and I want to find out whether the difference between the male and the female answer is significant. Second, I will compare the answer made by one informant group concerning a certain group of accents with their answer to the same question concerning another group of accents. In the first case I am interested in the difference between two informant groups; in the second in the variation within an informant group. As long as the means compared concern mutually exclusive groups and we do not compare incompatible answers, we can test the significance in a convenient way, by means of a so-called t-test.

The t-test is a test which utilizes the mean, the standard deviation, and the number of samples for each of the two groups being compared in order to produce a value (t) which indicates the level of significance. The formula, awe-inspiring as it may seem, can be programmed into a pocket-size statistical calculator (e.g. Canon F-300P) for convenient access:

$$t = \frac{M_1 - M_2}{\sqrt{S^2} \; \sqrt{\dfrac{1}{n_1} + \dfrac{1}{n_2}}}$$

M = mean
S = standard deviation
n = number of observations

$$S^2 = \frac{(n_1 - 1)S_1^2 + (n_2 - 1)S_2^2}{n_1 + n_2 - 2}$$

The formula as it is given here presupposes reasonable balance between the tested samples in terms of number and standard deviation. Also, the value for n should not be lower than about 30 in any group.

The level of the t value determines whether the difference between the two means is significant (cf however discussion on what is an observation below):

$t \geq 1.96$ — difference significant at the 5 per cent level (*)
$t \geq 2.58$ — difference significant at the 1 per cent level (**)
$t \geq 3.29$ — difference significant at the 0.1 per cent level (***)

A difference significant at the 1 per cent level means that there is one chance in a hundred that the difference is created by chance factors, and so on. In the present study, a difference significant at the 5 per cent level will be regarded as a true difference (cf Butler 1985:71). Some scholars (e.g. Cheyne 1970) would argue that in as large a material as the present one, only 1 per cent levels of significance should be considered "in view of the high probability of obtaining spurious 0.05 significance values." I believe however that as long as we do not regard certain significance levels as God's Own Truth, but rather as statistical measures indicating the predictive power of the really interesting values, the differences between means, we are on the safe side. This is particularly true if all underlying values are explicitly stated, as in the present study.

What is an observation?
If you carry out a study designed to elicit attitudes toward, say, immigrants, and you categorize your (native) informants according to the colour of their hair and eyes, in order to see whether this subcategorization has any bearing on their attitudes, you must always remember that if for example you compare a mean given by the blond group with one given by the blue-eyed group, these two means will not be independent of one another, since the blond and blue-eyed groups are not mutually exclusive. Hence, the difference between the two cannot be tested for significance (or rather, a significance test will not be reliable). This means that you should either compare the attitudinal mean of the blond group with that of the dark group or the brown-eyed mean with that of the blue-eyed group; or you have to resort to combinatory subgroups (intersecting groups), i.e. blue/dark, blue/blond, brown/dark, brown/blond, whose attitude means can all be compared with one another and tested for significance as they are all mutually exclusive. This example can be seen as a parallel to my various subcategorizations based on AGE and DEGREE OF MODERNITY (OLD/MODERN, OLD/TRADITIONAL, etc.).

In the present study, there is however another complication caused by the organization of the fieldwork, which should be made clear to the reader, as it involves a certain amount of violation of the principle of non-circularity.

The voices that were played to the listener-informants were organized in programmes of five in each. Altogether the voices of 25 speakers were confronted with listeners (cf p. 63f for a more detailed account). Since (1) each informant listened to and rated 5 separate voices, and (2) both informants and voices in the various parts of the analysis were subdivided on several different parameters (e.g. AGE, SEX,

REGIONALITY; in the case of the voices into a four-cell matrix of combinatory subgroups, e.g. NORTH/MODERN), it follows that one and the same listener-informant will be responsible for more than one observation with regard to a certain accent subgroup. In other words, it is bound to happen that an informant, let us call her Sue, in one set of comparisons appears as a representative of the informant category, female; in another of the category Northern, and so on. Similarly, when Sue's ratings are analysed in the SEX comparison, she may have listened to, say, two voices which both represent the same accent subgroup (e.g. MALE/MODERN); whereas in the REGIONALITY comparison, the voices she listened to may be categorized in a different way, so that another two or so voices belonged to one and the same subgroup (e.g. SOUTH/TRADITIONAL).

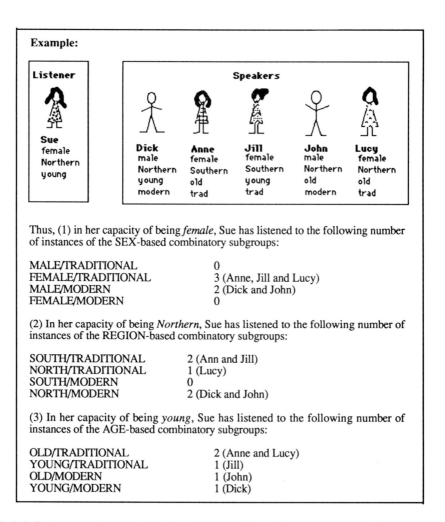

Example:

| Listener | Speakers | | | | |

Sue
female
Northern
young

Dick	Anne	Jill	John	Lucy
male	female	female	male	female
Northern	Southern	Southern	Northern	Northern
young	old	young	old	old
modern	trad	trad	modern	trad

Thus, (1) in her capacity of being *female*, Sue has listened to the following number of instances of the SEX-based combinatory subgroups:

MALE/TRADITIONAL	0
FEMALE/TRADITIONAL	3 (Anne, Jill and Lucy)
MALE/MODERN	2 (Dick and John)
FEMALE/MODERN	0

(2) In her capacity of being *Northern*, Sue has listened to the following number of instances of the REGION-based combinatory subgroups:

SOUTH/TRADITIONAL	2 (Ann and Jill)
NORTH/TRADITIONAL	1 (Lucy)
SOUTH/MODERN	0
NORTH/MODERN	2 (Dick and John)

(3) In her capacity of being *young*, Sue has listened to the following number of instances of the AGE-based combinatory subgroups:

OLD/TRADITIONAL	2 (Anne and Lucy)
YOUNG/TRADITIONAL	1 (Jill)
OLD/MODERN	1 (John)
YOUNG/MODERN	1 (Dick)

In brief, then: an observation (an instance of N) in the present material represents *one rating made by a listener answering a certain description of a voice answering a certain description*. In some cases, an informant rates one voice only belonging to a certain subgroup; in other cases, she rates more than one, depending on the subdivision.

Strictly statistically, this will reduce the predictive power of the material, since, in every comparison, certain informants' opinions with regard to a given subgroup are,

91

so to speak, accentuated by their rating more than one speaker belonging to that group, or, to put it more in accordance with a statistician's view, certain observations are not entirely independent of certain other observations. On the other hand, the informants are not aware of this when making the ratings: the categorization is part of the analysis.

The magnitude of this phenomenon can be described in terms of a percentage, viz. the listeners to a certain combinatory accent subgroup who out of the five voices in the programme they have been subjected to, have heard more than one voice belonging to that subgroup (cf example above). There are twelve such combinatory subgroups in the material and the percentages of "informants-listening-to-more-than-one-instance-of-a-subgroup" are indicated beside each subgroup name in the list below:

OLD/TRADITIONAL	228 out of 371 (61 per cent)
YOUNG/TRADITIONAL	0 out of 143 (0 per cent)
OLD/MODERN	57 out of 371 (15 per cent)
YOUNG/MODERN	314 out of 371 (85 per cent)
MALE/TRADITIONAL	0 out of 220 (0 per cent)
FEMALE/TRADITIONAL	151 out of 371 (41 per cent)
MALE/MODERN	151 out of 231 (65 per cent)
FEMALE/MODERN	220 out of 371 (59 per cent)
SOUTH/TRADITIONAL	94 out of 371 (25 per cent)
NORTH/TRADITIONAL	0 out of 277 (0 per cent)
SOUTH/MODERN	243 out of 292 (83 per cent)
NORTH/MODERN	128 out of 277 (46 per cent)

This means that an average of 40 per cent of the informants who have listened to a certain subgroup have heard two instances of it (in some cases, three) within the framework of each five-voice programme.

It should be noticed that this is not tantamount to comparing groups which are not mutually exclusive, something which would be a serious infringement on fundamental statistical (and common-sensical) principles. It is simply a question of somewhat diluting the predictive strength of the material as a sacrifice to the subcategorization which is part and parcel of the present method.

In order to escape this problem within a system of variable subcategorization, one would either have to use a "one-voice-one-listener" approach, which would seem hazardous from the point of view of comparability; or else, all informants would have to listen to all voices, which, for practical reasons, would necessitate a considerable reduction of speaker numbers, which in turn would render variable subcategorization very difficult, if not impossible.

What this boils down to, then, is that the statistical significance values of the present study are slightly overestimated, to the effect that what looks like significance at, say, the 1 per cent level should be interpreted somewhat more critically than the figure implies. From the point of view of tendencies, however, this can be disregarded altogether.

1.9. A few notes on how to read this text.

The present text can be seen either as a large body of tables accompanied by a text commentary; or vice versa. In either case, it is essential that the reader is familiarized with certain principles guiding text and tables.

One important distinction is that which exists between speaker/voice/accent sample etc. on the one hand, and informant/listener/listener-informant on the other. This dichotomy is the methodological starting-point of the present study: speakers have recorded speech passages; informants have listened to them, rating them on various scales. It is particularly important to remember throughout that the word *informant* is used to denote *listener-informant*. In some studies, especially studies which include speech analysis, the word informant may be used for speaker. However, since this study is about listeners' attitudes, I thought it appropriate to reserve the term *informant* for the listeners.

The scales used in the tables are six-point scales (cf pp. 73ff for a detailed account as to why). With the exception of the scale concerning Occupational Conjecture, all scales are arranged so that a high rating (e.g. 5.67) indicates a high proportion of whatever is being rated, whereas a low rating (e.g. 2.34) indicates a low proportion. This would seem to me to be a commonsensical system of representation. The reason why I make this point is that many studies which utilize statistical rating, not least within the field of psychology, have 1 as their highest pole.

The Occupational Conjecture, I admit, "violates" this principle, but for a good reason: the scale used here is based on the *1980 Classification of Occupations*. Thus, it is an official social index which should not be altered.

Often, when discussing six-point scales, I use the expression "the non-committal 3.5". This should be seen as a technical term used to denote the middle of such a scale.

In principle, two types of comparison will be made for each attitude item: (1) the average ratings of one subgroup of listeners with regard to a speaker subgroup will be compared with those of another listener subgroup (vertical comparison); (2) the various average ratings made by a subgroup of listeners will be compared between them (horizontal comparison).

In the first case, statistically significant differences will be indicated typographically in the tables according to the following system: (1) two mean values in the same column which show a difference at the 5 per cent level (*; t≥1.96) will be underlined; (2) two mean values in the same column which show a difference at the 1 per cent level (**; t≥2.58) will be italicized; (3) two mean values in the same column which show a difference at the 0.1 per cent level (***; t≥3.29) will be underlined and italicized.

In the second case, i.e. when the various subgroup ratings made by the same group of listeners are compared with each other (horizontally), there will be no indication of significant differences in the tables. This is because there are normally four horizontal items of comparison in each table and there is no convenient way of indicating which item is significantly different from which. Instead, this will be taken up in the surrounding text and/or in special tables of comparison (SEX and REGIONALITY sections only).

Here follows as an example a table (from p. 284) with the comparative dimensions indicated:

| Intelligence | SPEAKER VOICE CATEGORY Combinatory subgroups | | | | |
	NORTH/MOD	NORTH/TRAD	SOUTH/MOD	SOUTH/TRAD	ALL SPEAKERS
South'n inf's M	4.29	4.31	4.09	4.46	4.27
South'n inf's SD	1.07	1.12	1.30	1.15	1.19
South'n inf's N	114	106	251	184	715
North'n inf's M	4.40	4.58	4.30	4.74	4.48
North'n inf's SD	1.19	1.00	1.25	1.17	1.19
North'n inf's N	248	153	313	238	952

What this table states, then, is that two informant subgroups, Southerners and Northerners, have rated four combinatory accent subgroups, NORTH/MODERN, NORTH/TRADITIONAL, SOUTH/MODERN, SOUTH/TRADITIONAL, on a six-point scale for INTELLIGENCE. A vertical comparison shows that in terms of overall ("ALL SPEAKERS") ratings Northerners rate the voices significantly higher than do Southerners (***); and that there are (*) significant differences in the ratings of NORTH/TRADITIONAL and SOUTH/TRADITIONAL (the two "TRADITIONAL-combinations") to the effect that Northerners give the higher average ratings. Significant differences in the horizontal comparison cannot be deduced straight from the table, but will be discussed in the text. I will sometimes use the expression "rating profile" to denote the relationship between the various subgroup ratings made by an informant subgroup.

The symbols *, **, *** are used in the text to denote significance at the 5, 1, and 0.1 per cent levels, respectively.

Indentation of a portion of text from both margins indicates (1) a *quotation* if the text is printed in *full type size* (see e.g. p. 21); (2) a *supplementary note*, etc., if the text is printed in *reduced type size* (see e.g. p. 19).

There are no numbered notes in the text; whatever has to be said is said in its context. The reference system is of the Harvard type.

Capital letters are used to denote and distinguish terminological items (e.g. MODERN, NORTH, YOUNG).

The three report sections of this study (2. AGE, 3. SEX, 4. REGIONALITY) can be read separately. The AGE chapter, however, is more detailed in its approach. Thus, it serves as an introduction to the type of discussion that will follow in the SEX and REGIONALITY sections.

2. Age and degree of modernity

The present subdivision of the material is based upon two, probably related, features in the speakers of the sample, their AGE and the DEGREE OF MODERNITY in their speech as defined on pp. 83ff.

2.1. Age

Each of the 25 speakers of the sample was asked to state his/her year of birth. The years thus obtained ranged from 1922 (age at the time of the experiment: 60) to 1965 (17). The average age of all speakers was 38.04. The group of 25 speakers was then split into two parts according to the AGE of the speakers, so that all speakers born between 1922 and 1946 made up the subgroup OLD, and all speakers born between 1947 and 1965 the subgroup YOUNG (the subgroup names have been chosen as convenient labels only). The reason for dividing the group between the years of birth 1946 and 1947 was that this created two subgroups relatively similar in size (OLD: N=14; YOUNG: N=11) without arbitrarily placing speakers with the same year of birth in different subgroups.

In table 1 (p. 59), the speakers are presented in AGE order, so that the reader can check which speakers belong to which subgroup (cf also appendix "Speaker subgroups"). It will be clear from the table that there is a certain amount of inequality in the male/female distribution of the speaker sample and that this inequality is reflected fairly equally in both subgroups. There is also some difference in age spread between YOUNG and OLD: YOUNG ranges from 1948 to 1965 (17 years; M=28.63; SD 5.28), whereas OLD ranges from 1922 to 1946 (24 years; M=45.43; SD 8.52).

To make for an interesting set of comparisons, the listener-informants were also divided into an "adult" (N=109) and a "youth"(=6th formers; N=261) group. *The word "youth(s)" will henceforth be used as a technical term for any member, male or female, of the young informant group or for the group as a whole.*

> Comparing the language attitudes of two age groups of informants within the framework of one test is one way of investigating empirically how and why language might change. We should however make sure that we realize that there is more to the age comparison methodology than that. Changes may take place "within" a person as a result of aging; or they may be brought about by changes in the impact of society on a given age group as compared with the same age group, say, 50 years earlier, etc. Thus, finding or not finding tendencies in a test of the present kind may or may not be indicative of genuine language change (see Lieberson 1980: a very good article on socio-

linguistic methodology).

Subgroup comparison.

We are now going to see how the AGE and DEGREE OF MODERNITY variables behave when confronted with the 36 questions of our investigation. In doing so, we will discuss both variables together, question by question. Some questions will generate only very limited discussion, owing to their content. Wherever it is suitable, one or more mini-hypotheses will be presented for the point at issue.

The discussion in this chapter will be rather detailed and step-by-step oriented. There are two reasons behind such a procedure: (1) it reflects some of the processes of work and thought that form the basis of the interpretation. As I have stated before, I do not believe in weeding a report of everything but some sort of crystallized final result; (2) it serves as an introduction to my current methodology. Later chapters will be more structural.

Age conjecture.

The informants were asked to guess the age of each speaker in the sample. Hypotheses: (a) it ought to be possible for listeners to guess the approximate age of a speaker; (b) speakers with a DEGREE OF MODERNITY in their speech which does not harmonize with their AGE ought to get an age rating that deviates from what might otherwise be expected; (c) if there is awareness, conscious or unconscious, among listeners, of linguistic modernity, it seems reasonable to expect an exaggerated reaction to such varieties as are considered marked from the point of view of the age group one belongs to; in other words, a young listener might overstate the age of somebody who has a low DEGREE OF MODERNITY, more so than an older listener, whereas an old, rather than young, listener might understate the age of a speaker with a high DEGREE OF MODERNITY; (d) there may be a tendency toward greater conjectural accuracy in older informants, simply owing to a greater experience of life.

| Age guess | SPEAKER VOICE CATEGORY Non-combinatory subgroups | | | | |
	OLD	YOUNG	TRADITIONAL	MODERN	ALL SPEAKERS
Adult inf's M	32.95	*28.17*	*34.67*	27.80	*30.69*
Adult inf's SD	9.19	5.66	7.99	6.83	8.08
Adult inf's N	223	201	178	246	424
Youth inf's M	31.65	*25.49*	*30.07*	28.09	*28.90*
Youth inf's SD	8.70	5.53	7.61	8.26	8.06
Youth inf's N	710	573	524	759	1283
Sp's real age M	45.43	28.64	43.00	34.73	38.04

The first thing to be noticed about the age conjectures is the rather great understatement of the age of the speakers belonging to the OLD category: the average age suggested by adult informants is 32.95, and by youth informants 31.65. These figures should be compared with the authentic average age, which is 45.43. Thus, we have here an understating of speaker age by 12-13 years. These figures should be compared with the ones based on YOUNG speakers: 28.17 (adults' conjecture) and 25.49 (youths' conjecture) versus 28.64 (authentic average age). This very conspicuous difference is however chiefly created by a well-known phenomenon within the field of the psychology of guessing: a tendency to make so-called conservative guesses, i.e., overstate the values of items whose real values are low and understate the values of items whose real values are high, to an extent which correlates proportionally to the degree of deviation of the real value from some sort of mean. This tendency has been widely noticed by scholars, mainly in sociologically or psychologically inclined subjects. An early discussion on the phenomenon can be found in Hollingworth (1910). He talks about

> a general law—*the central tendency of judgment.* In all estimates of stimuli belonging to a general range or group we tend to form our judgments around the median value of the series—toward this mean each judgment is shifted by virtue of a mental set corresponding to the particular range in question. [p. 462]

He concludes:

> The tendency seems explicable only in terms of itself. [---] in an experiment on sensible discrimination we become adapted to the median value of the series, tend to expect it, to assimilate all other values toward it, and to greater or less degree to substitute it for them. [---] The error to which it leads is distinctly an error of judgment, and is quite independent of sensory or physiological conditions which may of themselves be sources of other types of errors. [p. 468f]

More recently, and in a field more related to the present study, conservative guesses have been dealt with by Ryan and her colleagues (Stewart & Ryan 1982; Ryan & Capadano 1978). They noticed that age is often clearly underestimated in relatively old speakers: "Thus, the characteristics attributed to the older voices are more probably related to stereotypes of middle-aged individuals than to those of the elderly." (Ryan & Capadano 1978:101)

It is obvious that the conservative guess phenomenon must be taken into account when assessing informants' conjectures. I shall return to this problem below.

The second thing we notice is that there is a significant difference of 1.79 years between the adult and youth overall averages (***; t=3.96), to the effect that adults guess higher, youths lower. Since we are dealing with an open-ended question here, I think it is fair to claim that there is a certain amount of egocentricity in these figures; it seems reasonable that in a choice without restrictions, you tend towards your own age. From this it follows that it is primarily figures deviating from this pattern that are interesting.

If we look at the four speaker categories, we see that the category OLD gets ratings that lie very close to the expected pattern in terms of youth—adult difference. If there is any difference at all, it is mainly that the distance between youths and adults has diminished when compared with the overall average. YOUNG shows an increasing difference; MODERN gets about the same rating from adults and youths, which means either that the adults have gone "down" or the youths "up" in relation to the overall average. Finally TRADITIONAL, where the difference is greater than in any other category. If we use the overall averages as a starting-point, there are three voice subgroups for which we can see a tendency:(1) there seems to be a downward trend in the youth rating of YOUNG; (2) a clear downward trend in the adult rating of MODERN; (3) a clear upward trend in the adult rating of TRADITIONAL.

The real average age of TRADITIONAL is 43.00, and of MODERN, 34.73; thus, the real average age difference between these two categories is considerably smaller than was the case in the OLD-YOUNG comparison (45.43 v. 28.64). Now, if there are no other age-marking factors in the speakers than those caused by physiological or other non-linguistic factors, it would seem reasonable to expect that a certain average rating of, say, YOUNG and a *similar* average rating of, say, MODERN are both based on reasonably equal real values; in other words, if we get an adult conjecture for MODERN of 27.80, and an adult conjecture for YOUNG of 28.17, the circumstance that these two figures are close to being equal ought to indicate that the underlying *real* values are also fairly equal. But this is not the case: the real age value of MODERN is 34.73 and of YOUNG, 28.64. So there must be something in MODERN, which is not as present in YOUNG, which makes adult informants guess "lower", a differentiating age marker of linguistic relevance. The problem at this point is that this phenomenon is not present in the youth assessment. In fact, the youths have guessed very much in accordance with what should be expected if the labels TRADITIONAL and MODERN were arbitrary.

As I have already indicated, the tendency to make conservative guesses is a factor which must be taken into consideration when assessing the age guess figures. Thus it is necessary to compare the age figures obtained in the MODERN-TRADITIONAL comparison with the ones we should *expect* in a group with that real age mean. An indication of the expected age guess can be obtained by means of linear regression analysis. Practically, this is done by plotting all the individual data onto a system of co-ordinates, where the x axis represents real age, and the y axis, age guess. Any individual age guess has a real age counterpart, and so, a point in the system of co-ordinates represents the set of data made up of these two values. Linear regression analysis is based on the idea that a scatterplot can be represented by a straight line. Obviously the degree to which a scatterplot lends itself to linear representation is dependent on what it looks like. If points are spread in a way which conveys little or no direction, then linear regression analysis will be of no help. On the other hand, if points take on a pattern with an internal direction, then a straight line can be a good representation and simplification of the scatterplot. Statistically, the straight line is achieved by determining the minimum square sum of vertical deviations from the individual points to the line, and the line itself can be described by means of the formula $y=A+Bx$, where A represents the place of intersection of the line on the y axis, and B, the change in y for every change of 1 on the x axis of a point along the line. The coefficients A and B can be conveniently determined by means of an advanced statistical calculator, in the present case a Canon F-300P, which also gives the correlation coefficient, r, i.e. the numerical indicator of the predictive power of the line in relation to the scatterplot. The correlation coefficient is a numerical expression between -1 and +1. Values close to 0 indicate bad correlation; values close to +/-1 indicate good correlation.

In the present material, we get the following values based (for practical reasons) on every second set of data within the age guess:

N=909
A=14.72
B=0.38
r=0.52

The value 0.52 for r indicates that a straight line is neither a good nor a bad representation of the scatterplot. As usual, interpretational caution is necessary.

The speaker subgroup, TRADITIONAL, has a real age mean of 43.00, and MODERN, a real age mean of 34.73. If, by means of the linear regression coefficients, we check what would be the *expected* average guess by *all* informants, corresponding to these real age means, we get the following results:

TRADITIONAL: 31.06
MODERN: 27.92

These age guess values are what we should on an average expect for these two speaker subgroups. It is deviation from these expected values that is interesting, rather than deviation from the real values, which, as we have seen, are subject to conservative guessing.

Similarly, the real age mean for OLD is 45.43, and for YOUNG, 28.64, and these values correspond to the following expected average ratings:

OLD: 31.98
YOUNG: 25.60

What we can notice when looking at adults' and youths' mean ratings of the four subgroups, OLD, YOUNG, TRADITIONAL, MODERN, is that the youths place their ratings very close to what should be expected from the point of view of our present discussion; that is to say, there seems to be no other distinctive factor operative in the youth assessment than the age factor. The adults, on the other hand, deviate from the expected pattern with regard to two subgroups: YOUNG and TRADITIONAL. The strongest tendency is that which we find for TRADITIONAL. The adults place this subgroup 3.61 years higher than the expected mean, which is a great deal considering that, owing to conservative guessing, the spread of ratings is much smaller than the spread of real age. YOUNG, too, is placed higher than expected by the adult informants, although not quite as much higher as in the rating of TRADITIONAL: 2.57 years. Again, we must be careful in assessing these differences, since the expected value is based on a linear analysis with a correlation coefficient of no more than 0.52. If, however, for the sake of argument, we say that the adults have genuinely overstated the age of TRADITIONAL and YOUNG, we might perhaps suggest the following: The apparent overstatement of the age of TRADITIONAL is what we should expect if TRADITIONAL conveys what its name implies. The circumstance that this is observed by adults, but not by youths, could, as was hypothesized above, be ascribed to the adults having greater experience in general. It seems reasonable to assume that a person who has witnessed a development will find it easier to recognize the phases of that development than somebody who has only seen, as it were, one phase. But what about YOUNG? Does not the overstating of the age of this subgroup ruin the argument? I think not. YOUNG and OLD are the result of a subdivision based on age only. It may well be the case that the overstating of the age of YOUNG can be ascribed to its containing a large proportion of TRADITIONAL. We now go on to check the possibility of intersecting subgroups adding to our understanding the problem.

Age conjecture: combinatory subgroups

In order to see to what extent DEGREE OF MODERNITY functions as a differentiator *within* each AGE category, we can go deeper into the material and check the average conjectures concerning the particular groups of voices that belong to OLD *and* TRADITIONAL, OLD *and* MODERN, YOUNG *and* TRADITIONAL, YOUNG *and* MODERN. Henceforth such intersecting subgroups will be written with a slant (e.g. YOUNG/MODERN), and referred to as "combinatory subgroups" as opposed to the "non-combinatory subgroups" that we have been discussing so far. It would seem reasonable to expect deviations from expected values to be   concentrated to those subgroups in which AGE and DEGREE OF MODERNITY do not match, e.g. OLD/MODERN.

Age guess	SPEAKER VOICE CATEGORY Combinatory subgroups				
	OLD/MOD	OLD/TRAD	YOUNG/MOD	YOUNG/TRAD	ALL SPEAKERS
Adult inf's M	*27.78*	*35.73*	*27.82*	30.00	*30.69*
Adult inf's SD	9.61	7.66	5.08	7.84	8.08
Adult inf's N	78	145	168	33	424
Youth inf's M	*32.66*	*30.90*	*25.05*	27.19	*28.90*
Youth inf's SD	9.62	7.88	5.38	5.79	8.06
Youth inf's N	303	407	456	117	1283
Sp's real age M	45.00	45.75	27.89	32.00	38.04

If we do this, we notice that adult informants give almost identical age conjectures for both OLD/MODERN (27.78) and YOUNG/MODERN (27.82). This is interesting in view of the fact that the *real* average age of OLD/MODERN is 45.00, and of YOUNG/MODERN, 27.89. However, as we have seen (p. 97f), we must also take conservative guessing into account: we know that speakers with a relatively high age will be thought of as being considerably younger than they actually are, etc., so that we tend to get a concentration of average conjectures that lies much closer to the "middle" than in the real situation. The "expected" average adult conjecture for OLD/MODERN is 31.82, and for YOUNG/MODERN, 27.89. This means that such MODERN speakers as exhibit agreement between AGE and DEGREE OF MODERNITY, i.e. YOUNG/MODERN, receive an average adult age conjecture (27.82) that is almost identical with the average real age of this subgroup. On the other hand, the group of MODERN speakers who do not exhibit such agreement, i.e. OLD/MODERN, are given an average adult age conjecture (27.78) which is markedly lower than the expected age conjecture (31.82), in fact they get the same adult average conjecture as YOUNG/MODERN.

If we carry out the same operation on OLD/TRADITIONAL (AGE— DEGREE OF MODERNITY agreement) and YOUNG/TRADITIONAL (AGE— DEGREE OF MODERNITY disagreement) we notice that adult informants give an average age conjecture of 30.00 for the speaker subgroup YOUNG/TRADITIONAL. This conjecture should be compared with the real average age of this subgroup, 32.00, and, above all, with the expected average conjecture, 26.88. OLD/TRADITIONAL gets an average adult conjecture of 35.73, to be compared with the real average of 45.75, and the expected average of 32.11. With an obvious risk of overinterpreting small deviations within a statistically unstable material (cf discussion on linear regression and correlation above p. 100f), we might suggest that adult informants tend to overrate the age of TRADITIONAL speakers in relation to the age conjecture we should expect after allowing for conservative guessing. This tendency seems to be about as strong in OLD/TRADITIONAL as in YOUNG/TRADITIONAL. In other words, a traditional linguistic output might seem to serve as an age marker stronger than the physiological voice features of the speaker.

We have already pointed out that the conjectures made by the youth informants on an average lie very close to the expected values, which would seem to indicate that young people pay less attention to linguistic differences of the kind discussed here. There is, however, one disturbing deviation in the youth assessment: the youths actually give a lower average conjecture (30.90) for OLD/TRADITIONAL than for OLD/MODERN (32.66). Furthermore, the difference between the two is significant (**; t=2.68). It is very hard to explain this within the present framework, but I would like to offer two *highly tentative* suggestions: (1) the youths are disturbed by the lack of harmony between AGE and DEGREE OF MODERNITY in OLD/MODERN, and being young themselves they feel that the language treatment of OLD/MODERN leaves a lot to be desired from a modernity point of view (imagine Vera Lynn singing a tune by The Rolling Stones); (2) the youths may be attracted by the neutral correctness of OLD/TRADITIONAL and thus want to place it closer to themselves.

2.2. Regional conjecture.

In the second group of questions, informants were asked to speculate as to the regional background of the speakers. Here it was found necessary to qualify the concept, regionality, somewhat, so that the subjective power of informants' conjectures could be taken into account. This was done by employing a three-level technique, whereby informants were given three differently weighted options for answering the question, "What part of England do you think the speaker comes from?":

(1) I am fairly certain he/she comes from.....
(2) I should think he/she probably comes from.....
(3) I have no idea   ☐   (tick off box)

These answer levels are referred to as AREA HIGH POWER, AREA LOW POWER, and AREA ZERO POWER, respectively. The three-level system was based on the assumption that the ability to make regionally based accent distinctions, being a real ability rather than a "gut feeling", varies a lot from person to person, and that it would be unfortunate not to manifest this variation in the answers.

The questions on AREA HIGH POWER and AREA LOW POWER are both open-ended, and during the experiment sessions, no further instructions were supplied as to the length and degree of detail of the intended answers. This means that answers ranging from rather loose regional descriptions, such as "South", down to place-names, had to be accepted and in the working-out transformed into parallel entities. For our present purpose, no greater degree of detail than that which is conveyed by the area names, LONDON, SOUTH, SOUTHWEST, EAST, MIDLANDS, NORTH was necessary. In order to make these names arithmetically manageable, they were given numerical values according to the principle "near London—low number"; "far from London—high number":

LONDON - 1   SOUTHWEST - 3   MIDLANDS - 5
SOUTH - 2   EAST - 4   NORTH - 6

Although the question was phrased "What part of *England* do you think the speaker comes from?" (no italics in questionnaire), it did happen on the odd occasion that informants suggested areas outside England. The present discussion, however, deals solely with regions within England, leaving out deviant answers altogether.

Hypotheses: (1) adults are both subjectively and objectively better than youths at making correct guesses of regional background; this ought to manifest itself in a greater tendency among adults to choose to answer the AREA HIGH POWER alternative, rather than AREA LOW POWER or AREA ZERO POWER; it also ought to mean that the answers given by the adult informants should come closer to the real regional values, which can be estimated fairly accurately. (2) Since accent correctness is associated with London and the Home Counties (Daniel Jones; Windsor Lewis 1985:250), it would seem reasonable to expect conjectures about TRADITIONAL voices to get relatively low regional ratings; MODERN voices, on the other hand, may simply by displaying qualities that are different from TRADITIONAL be more closely associated with what is generally known as "regional accents" (an unfortunate term, since there is a regional element in all accents), thereby getting higher regional coefficients; this distinction should in turn be expected mainly in adult conjectures, since youth informants, for reasons suggested above, could be expected to possess less power of distinction and/or less interest in making the distinction, which in turn should create a greater tendency among youths to choose the ZERO POWER answer alternative, "I have no idea".

We begin by checking the extent to which adult and youth informants have chosen to answer in AREA HIGH POWER, AREA LOW POWER, and AREA ZERO POWER, respectively, thereby indicating how subjectively confident they were:

	Area High Power	Area Low Power	Area Zero Power
Adults	35.35%	49.34%	15.31%
Youths	20.67%	51.45%	27.88%

Adults' and youths' answers per area answer category. Per cent of answers total.

This table shows that adult informants to a considerably higher degree than youths choose AREA HIGH POWER; and that the reverse is true about AREA ZERO POWER. In other words, confidence in one's own ability to make accent distinctions is a more conspicuous trait in adults than in youths, which was hypothesized above. It also shows that AREA LOW POWER is by far the most attractive answer category for both adult and youth informants, in getting about 50 per cent of total answers from both informant groups. This circumstance also indicates that it is in AREA LOW POWER that the most reliable scores can be found, for merely quantitative reasons: the smaller the group, the harder it is to find tendencies and draw conclusions.

It is also interesting to see whether there is a regional tendency in the choice between the three answer categories, i.e. whether the regional background of the informants in any way affects the certitude of their answers. This can be done simply by estimating the regional mean of the informants themselves according to the same principle as in connection with the informant conjectures, i.e. a 1-to-6 scale with London as its starting-point and North as its termination. If we do this, we get the following figures for adult and youth informants:

A D U L T S

	N	M	SD
Area high power answers	182	2.99	1.86
Area low power answers	259	3.13	1.85
Area zero power answers	78	4.04	1.75

Y O U T H S

	N	M	SD
Area high power answers	260	3.85	1.90
Area low power answers	647	4.04	1.79
Area zero power answers	355	4.29	1.65

Average **regional coefficient (M)** of adult and youth **informants** who chose to answer questions on regional background of speakers in answer category **HIGH POWER, LOW POWER**, and **ZERO POWER**, respectively, thereby indicating how confident they were.

These figures seem to show that the willingness to choose high-certitude answer alternatives diminishes the farther away from the London area the informant lives. This tendency is particularly strong in the adult informants. This circumstance ought reasonably to be an indication that there is felt to be a certain Southern bias in the accents of this study.

Area HP	SPEAKER VOICE CATEGORY Non-combinatory subgroups				
	OLD	YOUNG	TRADITIONAL	MODERN	ALL SPEAKERS
Adult inf's M	2.49	2.75	2.38	_2.77_	_2.60_
Adult inf's SD	1.42	1.73	1.29	1.73	1.57
Adult inf's N	103	84	79	108	187
Youth inf's M	_1.98_	2.09	2.05	_2.01_	_2.03_
Youth inf's SD	1.26	1.37	1.23	1.38	1.31
Youth inf's N	142	122	114	150	264
Sp's real age M	45.43	28.64	43.00	34.73	38.04
Sp's real area M	3.14	3.18	3.00	3.27	3.16
Sp's real area SD	1.81	1.70	1.90	1.65	1.76

Area HP

SPEAKER VOICE CATEGORY
Combinatory subgroups

	OLD/MOD	OLD/TRAD	YOUNG/MOD	YOUNG/TRAD	ALL SPEAKERS
Adult inf's M	2.56	2.45	2.86	1.75	2.60
Adult inf's SD	1.61	1.34	1.79	0.46	1.57
Adult inf's N	32	71	76	8	187
Youth inf's M	1.82	2.08	2.13	1.96	2.03
Youth inf's SD	1.05	1.38	1.54	0.51	1.31
Youth inf's N	56	86	94	28	264
Sp's real age M	45.00	45.75	27.89	32.00	38.04
Sp's real area M	3.33	3.00	3.22	3.00	3.16
Sp's real area SD	1.70	1.87	1.62	2.00	1.76

Area LP

SPEAKER VOICE CATEGORY
Non-combinatory subgroups

	OLD	YOUNG	TRADITIONAL	MODERN	ALL SPEAKERS
Adult inf's M	2.83	3.09	2.74	3.08	2.95
Adult inf's SD	1.55	1.64	1.51	1.64	1.60
Adult inf's N	143	118	101	160	261
Youth inf's M	2.54	2.60	2.54	2.58	2.57
Youth inf's SD	1.59	1.62	1.57	1.62	1.60
Youth inf's N	353	304	267	390	657
Sp's real age M	45.43	28.64	43.00	34.73	38.04
Sp's real area M	3.14	3.18	3.00	3.27	3.16
Sp's real area SD	1.81	1.70	1.90	1.65	1.76

Area LP

SPEAKER VOICE CATEGORY
Combinatory subgroups

	OLD/MOD	OLD/TRAD	YOUNG/MOD	YOUNG/TRAD	ALL SPEAKERS
Adult inf's M	2.95	2.75	3.16	2.69	2.95
Adult inf's SD	1.61	1.52	1.66	1.54	1.60
Adult inf's N	58	85	102	16	261
Youth inf's M	2.48	2.58	2.65	2.40	2.57
Youth inf's SD	1.52	1.64	1.69	1.29	1.60
Youth inf's N	148	205	242	62	657
Sp's real age M	45.00	45.75	27.89	32.00	38.04
Sp's real area M	3.33	3.00	3.22	3.00	3.16
Sp's real area SD	1.70	1.87	1.62	2.00	1.76

Let us first look at overall differences and similarities between AREA HIGH POWER and AREA LOW POWER answers. First of all it turns out that the general level of ratings is higher (i.e. indicating more "away-from-London" weight) in the AREA LOW POWER conjecture. The reason for this is perhaps simply that informants are more willing to make a wild guess in the LOW POWER category without risking to commit themselves, and that this willingness might tend to attract them to accents with which they are less familiar, but which they may have a more or less vague idea of. It is also the case that in both answer categories, youths give considerably lower, i.e. closer to London, regional means at the overall level than do adults. This state of affairs is furthermore (and expectedly) reflected in all but one of the subgroup average ratings. The one case where it is not (YOUNG/TRADITIONAL in the AREA HIGH POWER conjecture) we can quite confidently discard from the discussion because of a very low N value in the adult conjecture. So it seems to be clear that youths generally (as always, on average) place their regional ratings closer to London. So we must ask ourselves why this should be. One possible way of finding a solution to the problem is to check the regionality of the informants to see if they tend to give egocentric conjectures. Indeed, we find that the adults have a regional coefficient of 3.24 (SD 1.90) and the youths 3.98 (SD 1.85), which means that it is in fact the youths who, on an average, are based farthest from London. This in turn shows that at any rate we are not seeing a direct exponent of egocentricity here. There is however a slightly different but related possibility, viz. that their greater distance to London might cause youth informants to alienate themselves from the fairly neutral accents of our sample to a greater extent than the adults. Metaphorically, this could be described as a rebound: the longer the distance from the starting-point to the place of impact, the longer the rebound.

It is clear that there is a South-Eastern bias in the outlook of the informants on our voices. This is probably caused by a certain over-representation of the name "London" as an answer by the informants. It seems reasonable to expect London to possess stronger power of attraction than any other single place-name, simply by virtue of the Metropolis being the socio-political and cultural epicentre of England.

Success rate of regional conjecture.

So far, I have been discussing the subjectively felt degree of conjectural confidence among informants and general tendencies in informants' regional ratings. I have however not discussed the relationship between informants' ratings and the "correct answer", i.e. the *real* regional background of the speakers. This will be my next concern.

Unlike most of the questions asked in this study, the one on regionality allows comparisons with reality, since all speakers before making the recordings were required to supply information about themselves, one part of which concerned their regional background (the question used here is the one in which speakers were asked to state their place of residence at age 0-20). Since all speakers by definition had to be English in the strict sense, it was possible to use the same numerical representation for speakers as for informants (a scale going from 1 (London) to 6 (North)), which enables us to estimate the real average value of the variable REGIONALITY within the various speaker subgroups. The values obtained thus can be found in the tables above (p. 106-107).

When we compare the average conjectures given with the real regional coefficients for the respective subgroups, we immediately notice that *all* conjectures, by adults and youths alike, are lower than the corresponding real value. Thus, informants seem to place more London weight on the voices than the voices actually possess. We have already noted that youths give lower average ratings than adults throughout, and so it follows that the youths are seemingly worse at guessing the regionality of speakers, something that was hypothesized above.

The subgroup ratings closest to their real counterparts are adults' ratings of YOUNG and MODERN, and the combinatory subgroup YOUNG/MODERN in the LOW POWER assessment, so it is perhaps possible to argue that to the adult informants, that characteristic, whatever it is, which generally forces ratings in the direction of London, is felt to be weakened in those particular subgroups. In other words, the neutrality of the other subgroups, although not matched by real near -London REGIONALITY, causes the adult informants to place them closer to London; YOUNG, MODERN, and YOUNG/ MODERN, on the other hand, get the regional ratings they genuinely deserve: REGIONALITY is more apparent in them.

The differentiation discussed in the previous paragraph concerned adult conjectures only. The youth informants give a much flatter set of ratings of the subgroups. I do not believe it is possible to draw any conclusions from whatever differences we might be able to discern within the youth assessment. This indicates that my hypothesis was correct: we do get a differentiation in which DEGREE OF MODERNITY seems to play a part, but only from the adults. Now, whether youths are genuinely worse when it comes to making accent distinctions, or whether they simply do not care, cannot be ascertained within the present framework; it remains an open question.

Adults vs. youths.
I shall now look into similarities and differences between adults' and youths' subgroup ratings. By difference, I mainly mean statistically significant difference at the five per cent level ($t \geq 1.96$); similarity refers to cases where there is no such difference. I shall use both AREA HIGH POWER and AREA LOW POWER conjectures as starting-points in this discussion (tendencies are very much the same in both).

For three subgroups, two of which are non-combinatory and one combinatory, we get very clearly significant differences (** or more; t≥2.58) between adults' and youths' ratings, both in AREA HIGH POWER and AREA LOW POWER. It is the subgroups YOUNG and MODERN, and, as a consequence, YOUNG/MODERN, which receive this treatment. What seems to be the case, judging by the deviation of subgroup ratings from the mean, is that adults tend to place these three subgroups significantly farther from London than do youths. We remember that it was also these three subgroups that got the highest conjectural success rate (in the adult conjecture), a fact which is obviously related to these subgroups exhibiting significant differences between adults and youths. I believe it can be argued here too that YOUNG, MODERN, and YOUNG/MODERN contain elements which reduce their potential London weight when judged by adults. It is possible that adults are more sensitive to certain features in these subgroups with regard to degree of neutrality/standardness, thereby placing them farther from the correctness epicentre, London. It is also possible that we are in fact seeing a rebound of the kind discussed above (p. 108): our adults, on an average, are based closer to London than our youths. Perhaps this circumstance makes them less inclined to alienate themselves from YOUNG, MODERN, and YOUNG/MODERN, who in fact have a very similar regional base as the adult informants. It is probably not possible to sort out the particulars in any greater detail at this point.

We have seen that youths generally place subgroups at a lower (i.e. closer to London) level than do adults. This could be explained as a rebound effect brought about by youths living farther from London, thus wanting to alienate themselves from the neutral types of accent that our speakers exhibit. It is also possible to argue that youths give a more stereotypical response in associating neutral voices to a higher degree with London. In this context, it is interesting to see which subgroups present markedly small differences, or great similarity, when comparing adults' and youths' average conjectures. It turns out that it is TRADITIONAL and TRADITIONAL-combinations that do not give rise to a great deal of difference between adults and youths (as for YOUNG/ TRADITIONAL, we have to be careful when making judgments because of the smallness of the group). Adults place their lowest (closest to London) ratings on these subgroups, and there may be a similar (but much weaker) tendency in the youth assessment, which is however blurred by what seems to be a downward (London) tendency in the youths' rating of OLD/MODERN. It is hard to offer a satisfactory explanation of this tendency, so I think we had better leave the matter open.

Area zero power.

Area ZP	SPEAKER VOICE CATEGORY Non-combinatory subgroups				
	OLD	YOUNG	TRADITIONAL	MODERN	ALL SPEAKERS
Adult inf's M	- -	- -	- -	- -	- -
Adult inf's SD	- -	- -	- -	- -	- -
Adult inf's N	44*)	37*)	37*)	44*)	81
Youth inf's M	- -	- -	- -	- -	- -
Youth inf's SD	- -	- -	- -	- -	- -
Youth inf's N	214*)	142*)	142*)	214*)	356
Sp's real age M	45.43	28.64	43.00	34.73	38.04

*) Numerical similarity is coincidental.

Area ZP	SPEAKER VOICE CATEGORY Combinatory subgroups				
	OLD/MOD	OLD/TRAD	YOUNG/MOD	YOUNG/TRAD	ALL SPEAKERS
Adult inf's M	- -	- -	- -	- -	- -
Adult inf's SD	- -	- -	- -	- -	- -
Adult inf's N	17	27	27	10	81
Youth inf's M	- -	- -	- -	- -	- -
Youth inf's SD	- -	- -	- -	- -	- -
Youth inf's N	99	115	115	27	356
Sp's real age M	45.00	45.75	27.89	32.00	38.04

The answer alternative "I have no idea" differs from the other two alternatives (AREA HIGH POWER and AREA LOW POWER) in that it requires a binary answer and not an open one. This of course leads to a situation where we cannot place answers along a scale. All we can do is check how many informants, adults and youths, chose to answer the question on regional background by means of this alternative, or rather, how many answers were given by the two groups of informants stating that they had "no idea" as to the regional background of the speaker in question.

As we have already seen, 15.31 per cent of adults' answers and 27.88 per cent of youths' answers fall within this answer alternative, which vindicates what seemed to be a self-evident hypothesis: that higher age in informants makes for greater certitude, probably simply owing to wider experience.

The way AREA ZERO POWER answers are distributed does not seem to be explicable either from the point of view of speakers' real regionality or real age. The figures seem to be haphazardly varied across the table of comparison. However, the explanation we are looking for is probably to be found in the number of *members* in the various subgroups. It turns out that AREA ZERO POWER answers are relatively frequent in subgroups with a relatively high number of speakers, and that they are relatively infrequent in subgroups with a relatively low number of speakers. This means that informant uncertainty leading to AREA ZERO POWER answers is distributed equally over the speakers, which in turn means that AREA ZERO POWER answers, rather than being associated with any specific speaker subgroup, functions as a wastepaper basket for informants who are generally weak when it comes to making area judgments.

2.3. Occupational conjecture.

In this question, informants were asked: "What do you think the speaker does for a living? Suggest an occupation that seems reasonable to you." This question was open-ended so that informants had to think of an answer themselves. Apart from this, there is of course a strong general resemblance between this item and the one concerning acceptability with regard to a set of job labels (cf pp. 142ff). In the following discussion, only such informant answers as could be translated into numerical socio-economic values are taken up, leaving out suggestions such as *student, housewife.*

Hypotheses: If no other clues than purely physiological ones exist, it would seem reasonable to expect answers to be fairly arbitrary, apart from such restrictions as might be caused by sex or age considerations. If, on the other hand, there are linguistic or other dynamic features in the voice samples that can give away the social status of the speakers (cf Laver 1968:50), we might expect this to be reflected in the selection of job labels suggested for the various voices. Since all the speakers in our material by definition speak in a fairly neutral type of accent, we should expect average conjectures to lie closer to the "professional" end of the scale (indicating high-status professions), than to the opposite end. The scale, which is based on the 1980 *Classification of Occupations,* goes from 1 (professional) to 6 (unskilled). Hence a low value on the scale indicates high status. When it comes to possible differences between adult and youth conjectures, it would seem likely to expect youth informants to be less fussy about the significance of language variation than adults. On the other hand, life experience might be a decisive factor here, so that perhaps adults find it easier to make fine distinctions of the kind required here.

Occupation	SPEAKER VOICE CATEGORY Non-combinatory subgroups				
	OLD	YOUNG	TRADITIONAL	MODERN	ALL SPEAKERS
Adult inf's M	2.22	2.59	2.13	2.59	2.39
Adult inf's SD	0.68	0.76	0.66	0.74	0.74
Adult inf's N	216	184	173	227	400
Youth inf's M	2.36	2.71	2.41	2.59	2.51
Youth inf's SD	0.79	0.93	0.71	0.98	0.87
Youth inf's N	551	412	421	542	963
Sp's real age M	45.43	28.64	43.00	34.73	38.04

Occupation	SPEAKER VOICE CATEGORY Combinatory subgroups				
	OLD/MOD	OLD/TRAD	YOUNG/MOD	YOUNG/TRAD	ALL SPEAKERS
Adult inf's M	2.50	2.08	2.63	2.37	2.39
Adult inf's SD	0.61	0.68	0.79	0.49	0.74
Adult inf's N	70	146	157	27	400
Youth inf's M	2.37	2.35	2.74	2.61	2.51
Youth inf's SD	0.93	0.68	0.98	0.76	0.87
Youth inf's N	225	326	317	95	963
Sp's real age M	45.00	45.75	27.89	32.00	38.04

Discussion. We notice first of all that the overall averages, *and* all subgroup averages, for both adult and youth informants, lie clearly towards the lower end of the scale, thereby indicating that both informant categories regard the voices as, on the whole, more "professional" than not. In addition to this, there is a significant difference (*; t=2.42) between the adult overall average of 2.39 and the youth overall average of 2.51, that is to say, the adults indicate a stronger connection between the voices and the "professional" end of the scale than do the youths. If we go into the individual subgroup averages, we notice that the only subgroups for which there are significant differences between adult and youth average ratings are OLD (*; t=2.29), TRADITIONAL (***; t=4.46), and the combinatory subgroup OLD/TRADITIONAL (***; t=3.99). For all these, adults give lower, i.e. more "professional" averages. It is very difficult to say whether these differences are caused by a stronger genuine sense of sociolinguistic levels among the adults, or whether it is simply a question of adults being able to suggest a wider variety of job labels for their answers. It would seem natural, for instance, if youths were to choose the job label "teacher" more often than the adults and, say, the label "barrister" less often, and that might affect averages in this way. A third possibility is of course that youths, as I suggested in the hypothesis above, are less fussy about these matters in general, which would direct their ratings more toward the middle of the scale.

If we look at the way adults and youths have distributed their ratings over the different subgroups, we notice first of all that they all distinguish clearly between OLD and YOUNG, and between TRADITIONAL and MODERN, so that OLD and TRADITIONAL get significantly lower, i.e. more "professional", ratings than YOUNG and MODERN. Interestingly, though, we do not find any difference worth mentioning between the youth ratings of the combinatory subgroups OLD/MODERN and OLD/TRADITIONAL. It seems that it is the AGE aspect that plays the most important part here. The same goes for YOUNG/MODERN and YOUNG/TRADITIONAL: they get very equal ratings from the youth informants. The adults, on the other hand, while making no significant difference between YOUNG/MODERN and YOUNG/TRADITIONAL (t=1.65), present a very clear difference (***; t=4.39) between OLD/MODERN and OLD/TRADITIONAL (2.50 v. 2.08). In other words, it is the type of accent which is exhibited by those speakers in our sample who combine a relatively old age and, according to our method of defining DEGREE OF MODERNITY, a relatively traditional linguistic output, which adults associate most strongly with a "professional" type of job.

The circumstance that the adults' differentiation between YOUNG/MODERN and YOUNG/TRADITIONAL is not significant at the five per cent level (t=1.65) is to a very great extent an effect of YOUNG/TRADITIONAL being small in number, statistical significance being closely related to group sizes. However, whether significant or not, there is a clear distinction between the adults' ratings of YOUNG/MODERN and YOUNG/TRADITIONAL too (2.63 v. 2.37). That is to say, YOUNG/TRADITIONAL is looked upon as being more "professional" than YOUNG/MODERN. Youth informants, as we have seen, seem rather to base their distinction on AGE.

This difference between adult and youth informants could be partly explained in terms of environmental pressure: the adult category that youths come in close contact with, apart from their own parents, mainly consists of school teachers, which might lead to a strong link between the notion *old* and the notion *authority* in the outlook of young people on society. Adults, on the other hand, should not be expected to attach as great importance to the age distinction as such; for them, social classification is a much more multifarious business, which could explain their greater distinctive ability with regard to accent. A less sophisticated but by no means less probable explanation has to do with maturity and life experience: adults have been exposed to greater diversity both in social and linguistic terms than youths, and this is maybe what is reflected in the present figures. Torbe (1984:101f) touches on the same phenomenon:

[---] it is not so clear how young people identify those who hold 'authority' once they have left school. In schools hierarchy corresponds to age, pivoting around the formal distinction between adult and school student; and authority is vested in those who are clearly not children. In the eyes of young people in school, hierarchy is typified by the relationship between teacher and pupil; and it is, of course, generally easy for them to tell one from the other. Those who are 'our age' are 'us', those who are adults, and over 21, are 'them'. But in industry, young people have to adjust to working with people who are of various ages, and whose status as superiors or equals they are sometimes not clear about. Uncertainty about these relationships brings with it uncertainty about the social context in which communication takes place.

2.4. Psychological qualities.

In the next section of the investigation, informants were asked to rate the voices along a six-step scale with regard to certain psychological (or related) qualities. The six-step model was chosen to avoid a non-committal mid alternative (cf pp 73ff). The qualities tested were the following:

Leadership	
Dependability	
Honesty	Social
Sense of humour	
Friendliness	
Intelligence	
Self-confidence	
Ambition	Individual
Determination	
Education	

As indicated, the list can be divided into subcategories according to the "socio-semantic" content of the qualities: the first five, LEADERSHIP, DEPENDABILITY, HONESTY, SENSE OF HUMOUR, and FRIENDLINESS, could all be referred to mainly as *socially significant* psychological traits; the remaining five, INTELLIGENCE, SELF-CONFIDENCE, AMBITION, DETERMINATION, EDUCATION, as basically *individual* traits (cf p. 71f). Some of the qualities, e.g. DEPENDABILITY and HONESTY, are semantically similar. This fact could be used as a means of internal check, so that discrepancies between two such qualities in the judgment of the informants might be said to point towards a lack of reliability.

EDUCATION is really the odd man out in the list, since it cannot be regarded as a psychological quality. It was entered in the list for practical convenience, and because it was felt to belong to the same general field, not least from the viewpoint of the informants, as the nine preceding qualities. Furthermore, EDUCATION is particularly interesting as it is the only item in the list that allows comparison with a real value within the framework of this study.

It is necessary to point out here that YOUNG and OLD in the present set of comparisons are labels designated in order to differentiate between two subgroups bordering on one another. They must therefore not be interpreted as meaning *markedly* young or *markedly* old. A consequence of this is that we do not get results downgrading OLD for lack of various aspects of effectiveness, etc. O'Connell & Rotter (1979) have shown that when asked to grade 25-, 50-, and 75-year-old men and women (stereotypes, not real people) on various traits, informants tend to perceive a very obvious positive relationship between increasing age and low values for particularly "effectiveness", and also, to a lesser degree, "autonomy" and "personal acceptability". Such tendencies should not be expected here, simply because we have not looked for them.

LEADERSHIP.
Hypothesis: it would seem reasonable to expect higher LEADERSHIP ratings of OLD than of YOUNG voices, as this quality can be expected to correlate with seniority. It would also seem likely that TRADITIONAL receives higher ratings than MODERN, because of the assumed relationship between influential social position and traditional, "correct", language treatment. Youths, for reasons discussed above (e.g. p. 114) would be expected to pay more attention to the AGE distinction as such; whereas they might attach less social significance than adults to sociolinguistic differentiation.

Leadership	SPEAKER VOICE CATEGORY Non-combinatory subgroups				
	OLD	YOUNG	TRADITIONAL	MODERN	ALL SPEAKERS
Adult inf's M	3.66	*3.65*	*3.93*	3.47	*3.66*
Adult inf's SD	1.47	1.20	1.37	1.32	1.36
Adult inf's N	294	237	214	317	531
Youth inf's M	3.62	*3.32*	*3.65*	3.38	*3.49*
Youth inf's SD	1.48	1.28	1.38	1.41	1.40
Youth inf's N	707	572	519	760	1279
Sp's real age M	45.43	28.64	43.00	34.73	38.04

Let us begin by looking at overall average ratings, disregarding for the time being subgroup ratings. Adult informants give an overall average rating of 3.66 (SD 1.36), and youth informants an average of 3.49 (SD 1.40).

The difference is statistically significant (*; t=2.37), which seems to indicate that on the whole adults are more inclined to associate the neutral, standard-type accents of the sample with LEADERSHIP than are youths.

Both overall average ratings lie very close to the expected non-committal average, 3.5, which we would get if, say, 50 per cent of the informants ticked the number three box and the other 50 per cent the number four box. Thus, as a group, these voices do not seem to stand out as being particularly marked with regard to LEADERSHIP, which in turn means that a subgroup which does stand out is interesting. The circumstance that the LEADERSHIP ratings of our voices are the lowest ratings in the Psychological Qualities section, with the exception of SENSE OF HUMOUR, could, I suspect, be ascribed to the fact that a majority of the speakers in the sample (16 out of 25) are women, whereas the LEADERSHIP stereotype is most certainly male (cf Baroni & D'Urso (1984) for a somewhat modified view of this matter based on an Italian investigation).

Turning to non-combinatory subgroups, we notice that adult informants make no distinction at all between OLD and YOUNG (3.66 [SD 1.47] vs. 3.65 [SD 1.20]), and furthermore, that their subgroup average ratings are very close to 3.5. It seems therefore that to the adults, the OLD-YOUNG subdivision is fairly arbitrary in connection with LEADERSHIP.

The two subgroups, TRADITIONAL and MODERN, on the other hand, receive adult average ratings that are markedly disparate, 3.93 (SD 1.32) and 3.47 (SD 1.37), respectively (***; t=3.88). It is TRADITIONAL that stands out here: it seems that speakers whose language output, according to our way of defining DEGREE OF MODERNITY, is relatively traditional are looked upon as possessing a notably higher degree of LEADERSHIP than the subgroup with less traditional output.

The youth informants' treatment of the OLD-YOUNG configuration is virtually the same as their treatment of TRADITIONAL-MODERN: OLD and TRADITIONAL get higher ratings, YOUNG and MODERN lower, and the levels of average ratings are almost identical in both configurations. Both differences are statistically significant (***; t≥3.39). Thus, the chief difference between adults and youths in this particular set of comparisons is that the adults do not regard the AGE distinction as conducive to differentiation of LEADERSHIP judgment, whereas this is very much the case in the youth assessment.

As for our hypotheses, we see that they all hold good, with the qualification that the one which suggested that youths might pay less attention to linguistic variation is true in degree only, not in any absolute way; both adults and youths distinguish clearly, as we have seen, between TRADITIONAL and MODERN, but the adults, by elevating TRADITIONAL especially much, more so than the youths (*; t=2.50).

I believe it is fairly safe to say that the apparent difference between adults and youths with regard to LEADERSHIP judgment is one which reflects the differences in social power between the two groups. To young people, LEADERSHIP is something exerted by "them" (cf the quotation from Torbe (1984) above, p. 115), that is to say, the over-21's, because that is the situation young people are in.

Leadership	SPEAKER VOICE CATEGORY Combinatory subgroups				
	OLD/MOD	OLD/TRAD	YOUNG/MOD	YOUNG/TRAD	ALL SPEAKERS
Adult inf's M	3.01	4.07	3.72	3.21	3.66
Adult inf's SD	1.40	1.37	1.20	1.12	1.36
Adult inf's N	114	180	203	34	531
Youth inf's M	3.41	3.78	3.36	3.18	3.49
Youth inf's SD	1.58	1.39	1.28	1.23	1.40
Youth inf's N	304	403	456	116	1279
Sp's real age M	45.00	45.75	27.89	32.00	38.04

Let us go on to look at combinatory subgroups instead (OLD/TRADITIONAL, OLD/MODERN, YOUNG/TRADITIONAL, YOUNG/ MODERN). Here we can see that OLD/TRADITIONAL gets the clearly highest average ratings from both informant groups, but that the rating of the adults (4.07) is significantly higher than that (3.78) of the youths (*; t=2.34). The only combinatory subgroup to which the youths give a higher average rating than the adults is OLD/MODERN. So, as we have already noted in connection with non-combinatory subgroups, youths seem to place more importance on AGE, whereas adults certainly seem to go by DEGREE OF MODERNITY.

However, if we check how adults and youths have distributed their ratings internally, rather than how they compare with each other, we notice that it is in fact only OLD/TRADITIONAL that stands out significantly from the other combinatory subgroups in the youth assessment; the other three cannot be statistically distinguished. In the adult judgment, OLD/TRADITIONAL holds a supreme position, as we have seen, significantly higher than in the youth assessment; then follows YOUNG/MODERN, which in fact occupies about the same absolute level as did OLD/TRADITIONAL in the youth assessment; and finally OLD/MODERN and YOUNG/TRADITIONAL, which cannot be distinguished statistically.

Why should there be considered to be more LEADERSHIP in YOUNG/MODERN than in OLD/MODERN and YOUNG/TRADITIONAL? First of all, in terms of number of speakers, YOUNG/TRADITIONAL is a small subgroup (N=2), and the number of observations made of it is consequently relatively small, particularly in the adult assessment, so there may be an undesirable sampling effect here. Another possibility, which suggests itself later on in this study (cf p. 174) in connection with ratings for preference, where YOUNG/TRADITIONAL in fact gets top preference, is that it may be something about the very label, LEADERSHIP, that causes confusing responses. A more sophisticated explanation has to do with what we might call "age-language harmony": perhaps attitudes can sometimes be affected negatively, or less positively, if it is (more or less) obvious that a speaker dissociates linguistically from his regular peer category. In an attitude experiment involving the use of photos and voice recordings, Aboud *et al.* (1974) found that certain effects on attitude ratings were created by discrepancies between the apparent social class of a speaker (as conveyed by a photo) and his speech. However, in that experiment discrepancies tended to produce more, rather than less, favourable impressions in listeners, particularly in the combination working class photo/middle class voice. This is confusing but at any rate it shows that the overall idea of harmony or discrepancy may be a productive differentiator in attitude judgment. Aboud *et al.* (1974:240) state that even though "[e]valuative reactions to discrepancy have been an important theoretical focus in a variety of contexts, [...] there is little consensus as to their effects." It is probably wise to leave the door open to such a possibility in the present study.

DEPENDABILITY.
Hypotheses: Both LEADERSHIP and DEPENDABILITY belong to the social category of qualities, the difference being that whereas LEADERSHIP is a quality whose chief characteristics lie within the superior-inferior paradigm, DEPENDABILITY is associated with a greater degree of equality between the parties. It could therefore be expected that DEPENDABILITY might present a different kind of overall picture from LEADERSHIP, so that for instance peer group (age group) solidarity might boost estimates. It seems reasonable, therefore, to expect that YOUNG and, particularly, MODERN will receive DEPENDABILITY values that are relatively higher than the LEADERSHIP values these two subgroups received earlier, but not necessarily higher than those of OLD and TRADITIONAL. Since DEPENDABILITY is less associated with power relations, we might even

expect a flat distribution of ratings.

Dependability	SPEAKER VOICE CATEGORY				
	Non-combinatory subgroups				
	OLD	YOUNG	TRADITIONAL	MODERN	ALL SPEAKERS
Adult inf's M	4.31	4.22	4.37	4.20	4.27
Adult inf's SD	1.07	1.01	1.03	1.05	1.04
Adult inf's N	294	239	214	319	533
Youth inf's M	4.28	4.01	4.33	4.04	4.16
Youth inf's SD	1.20	1.10	1.13	1.17	1.16
Youth inf's N	705	573	758	520	1278
Sp's real age M	45.43	28.64	43.00	34.73	38.04

The overall average ratings (adults 4.27 [SD 1.04]; youths 4.16 [SD 1.16]) show that the general opinion about the voices in terms of DEPENDABILITY is strongly favourable. The difference between adults and youths is not quite significant at the five per cent level (t=1.89).

The adults present a set of subgroup ratings that is relatively flat, YOUNG and MODERN getting slightly lower (not significantly so, t≤0.99) ratings than the other two subgroups. The youth informants, on the other hand, rate YOUNG and MODERN considerably lower than OLD and TRADITIONAL (***; t≥4.15). In fact, the internal differentiation in terms of numerical value is almost exactly the same as in the LEADERSHIP assessment, whereas the general level of assessment is markedly higher.

Our hypothesis can thus be said to be corroborated with regard to the adult informants, whose distribution of ratings is flat. The youth informants, in uprating OLD and TRADITIONAL, do not fit into this pattern at all. I would like to suggest two tentative explanations of this: (1) DEPENDABILITY to a young person is more associated with a parent-child (or similar) relation, and therefore the OLD and TRADITIONAL voices, symbolizing, possibly, society's "parental" sector, receive relatively higher ratings. The stress is on "relatively", of course: what has happened in *absolute* terms is that the youths have downgraded YOUNG and MODERN to a level significantly (** and *, respectively) lower than that of the adults. What comes to mind are the

> feelings of inferiority and even of self-hatred, often deeply unconscious or disguised by assertions to the contrary, in many members of minority groups who have come to see themselves from the point of view of the majority. [Simpson & Yinger 1972:227]

The problem here is that if indeed youths are a "minority" group, then the adults, the representatives of the "majority" in this study, have in fact been more favourable towards them than they have themselves. So perhaps "majority" and "minority" should be interpreted not as concepts of number, but as concepts of what might be called "cultural power". This is the standpoint taken by many feminist sociolinguists with regard to the status of women and women's language (cf Smith P.M. 1985:55).

Something which further complicates the matter somewhat is the circumstance that the informants whom we refer to as "adults" in fact are of an average age of 33.4, which makes them more equal in age to YOUNG than to OLD. Theoretically, this could lead one to believe that there is an element of peer group identification in the flatness of the adult ratings. But in that case, where does that leave the youths? Perhaps in a situation where they feel they have no peer group, and therefore go for the conventional option, which is my second suggestion; (2) the youth informants may simply have made a more conventional assessment. This could be explained as a result of not having any voices to associate with; or limited experience and hence limited subtlety in making linguistic distinctions; or both.

Dependability	SPEAKER VOICE CATEGORY Combinatory subgroups				
	OLD/MOD	OLD/TRAD	YOUNG/MOD	YOUNG/TRAD	ALL SPEAKERS
Adult inf's M	4.11	4.43	4.24	4.06	4.27
Adult inf's SD	1.08	1.05	1.03	0.89	1.04
Adult inf's N	114	180	205	34	533
Youth inf's M	4.09	4.42	4.01	4.02	4.16
Youth inf's SD	1.22	1.17	1.13	0.96	1.16
Youth inf's N	302	403	456	117	1278
Sp's real age M	45.00	45.75	27.89	32.00	38.04

Is it possible that an analysis of the combinatory subgroups (OLD/TRADITIONAL etc.) might add to our explanation here? If we start off with the youth ratings, which are more straightforward than their adult couterparts, we at once see that one combinatory subgroup stands out markedly from the rest, viz. OLD/TRADITIONAL. The remaining three subgroups get very similar ratings from the youth informants. This seems to show that to the young informants of this investigation, a relatively old person with a relatively traditional linguistic output is stereotypically more dependable than other speakers. I do not think it is too far-fetched to suggest that what we have here is a mixture of parent-child and teacher-pupil relationships. Having said that, we must remember that all four combinatory subgroups get good youth ratings in the sense that the average ratings are higher than 4 throughout. But OLD/TRADITIONAL does stand out. There is no doubt about that (***).

The adult informants, too, place OLD/TRADITIONAL highest. But then there is the disturbing circumstance that the adults seem to be more favourably inclined towards YOUNG/MODERN than towards YOUNG/TRADITIONAL. In other words, we have a situation that resembles the one that we have just been discussing in connection with LEADERSHIP above: TRADITIONAL seems to function differently in combination with YOUNG as compared with OLD. However, it is not possible to make sufficiently strong statistical distinctions here. If the tendency should prevail, that YOUNG/MODERN wins over YOUNG/TRADITIONAL, even though OLD/TRADITIONAL is clearly the overall "victor", then we might be obliged to postulate a hypothesis of age-language harmony. At this point we must remember that the speaker subgroup YOUNG/TRADITIONAL is very small (N=2), so there is a good chance that the oddities we see in informants' reactions to it are caused by sampling deficiencies.

The really interesting difference, though, is the one we find if we compare adults' and youths' ratings with regard to combinatory subgroups. It turns out that there is very little difference indeed apart from one subgroup, viz. YOUNG/MODERN, for which the youths give a significantly (**; t=2.49) lower rating than do the adults. Conventionalism and "self-hatred" on the part of the youths are the only explanations I can offer at this point.

HONESTY.

Hypotheses: HONESTY, too, is a socially significant trait, in many ways similar to DEPENDABILITY, but one which, at least superficially, seems to be more associated with internal peer-group relations, honesty being an especially desirable quality in friends. It would therefore seem reasonable to expect a higher degree of peer-group solidarity, displayed as relatively high ratings of YOUNG and MODERN by youth informants, etc. A flat distribution of values would also seem likely, as HONESTY would seem to belong to the personal sphere, in which prestigious linguistic features ought to play a smaller part than elsewhere. As HONESTY and DEPENDABILITY belong to the same overall category of traits, there ought also of course to be some correlation between these two qualities in terms of ratings given.

Honesty	SPEAKER VOICE CATEGORY Non-combinatory subgroups				
	OLD	YOUNG	TRADITIONAL	MODERN	ALL SPEAKERS
Adult inf's M	4.45	4.40	4.45	4.41	4.43
Adult inf's SD	1.07	0.91	1.04	0.97	1.00
Adult inf's N	294	240	215	319	534
Youth inf's M	4.65	4.33	4.65	4.41	4.51
Youth inf's SD	1.07	1.05	1.03	1.09	1.07
Youth inf's N	708	571	523	756	1279
Sp's real age M	45.43	28.64	43.00	34.73	38.04

Discussion. First of all we notice that the average ratings of *all* speakers are higher than was the case in the DEPENDABILITY comparison (adults 4.43 [SD 1.00]; youths 4.51 [SD 1.07]; difference not significant: t=1.48). This may simply be an effect of HONESTY being a more everyday concept, about which people are more willing to make distinct judgments. It could also be explained as a result of the individual-level connotations of the word: you rate the speakers as acquaintances rather than as people on whom you depend or who depend on you.

The adult informants give a very flat set of ratings of all four voice subgroups. That is to say, they do not distinguish between the voice subgroups with regard to HONESTY, but give all voices, on an average, favourable ratings.

The youth informants too give favourable ratings, more so, in fact, than the adults. Here though, we can notice a tendency towards differentiation: OLD gets 4.65 (SD 1.07) vs. 4.33 (SD 1.05) for YOUNG (**; t=2.69); TRADITIONAL gets 4.65 (SD 1.03) vs. 4.41 (SD 1.09) for MODERN (*; t=2.39); or in other words, youth informants seem to attach more HONESTY to OLD and TRADITIONAL than to YOUNG and MODERN. I think that what we have here is a more conventional judgment on the part of the youth informants. It is obvious that they experience some difference between the voice categories which they probably attach to a stereotype pattern. Apart from the general difference in level, the ratings on DEPENDABILITY and HONESTY present a notably similar pattern.

Honesty	SPEAKER VOICE CATEGORY Combinatory subgroups				
	OLD/MOD	OLD/TRAD	YOUNG/MOD	YOUNG/TRAD	ALL SPEAKERS
Adult inf's M	4.43	*4.46*	4.40	4.38	4.43
Adult inf's SD	1.04	1.08	0.93	0.82	1.00
Adult inf's N	113	181	206	34	534
Youth inf's M	4.51	*4.75*	4.33	4.32	4.51
Youth inf's SD	1.14	1.00	1.04	1.06	1.07
Youth inf's N	302	406	454	117	1279
Sp's real age M	45.00	45.75	27.89	32.00	38.04

An analysis of attitudes towards combinatory subgroups (OLD/TRADITIONAL, OLD/MODERN, etc.) does not yield any new information in the case of the adult informants: they give virtually identical ratings of the four combinatory subgroups (in the area of 4.4). The youth informants on the other hand give notably higher ratings of OLD-combinations than of YOUNG-combinations, particularly so in the case of OLD/TRADITIONAL, which is in fact the only combinatory subgroup for which there is a significant difference (**; t=3.16) between adult and youth assessments. It seems that we are getting a more conventional response from the youths, which should perhaps be expected in view of the subordinate and rather passive situation of school pupils.

Thus, our hypothesis on peer-group solidarity was refuted, whereas the one on flat ratings was supported, but only by the adult informants.

SENSE OF HUMOUR.
Hypotheses: Although SENSE OF HUMOUR belongs to the socially significant qualities, it bears little resemblance to the qualities we have just discussed. It is something that you associate very strongly with the close, personal sphere, and that you might perhaps be rather surprised to find in situations where, say, dependability and honesty are stressed. Traditionally it is associated not with the stiff upper lip but with a wish to twist reality and play around with fact, and so, the speech-styles in which it is conveyed are often different from those used to convey grimmer matters. The joke, according to Scholes (1974:48) "is essentially antiformal in its operation." It would seem reasonable to expect this to colour the present comparison. For instance, AGE would seem to be of little consequence when judging SENSE OF HUMOUR, unless there is an element of group solidarity involved. Also, TRADITIONAL might perhaps not be a typical choice of voice in this context, for reasons just mentioned.

S. of humour	SPEAKER VOICE CATEGORY Non-combinatory subgroups				
	OLD	YOUNG	TRADITIONAL	MODERN	ALL SPEAKERS
Adult inf's M	3.46	_3.59_	3.48	_3.54_	_3.52_
Adult inf's SD	1.32	1.17	1.29	1.23	1.25
Adult inf's N	287	234	209	312	521
Youth inf's M	3.33	_3.38_	3.41	_3.30_	_3.35_
Youth inf's SD	1.34	1.25	1.25	1.33	1.30
Youth inf's N	709	572	522	759	1281
Sp's real age M	45.43	28.64	43.00	34.73	38.04

S. of humour	SPEAKER VOICE CATEGORY Combinatory subgroups				
	OLD/MOD	OLD/TRAD	YOUNG/MOD	YOUNG/TRAD	ALL SPEAKERS
Adult inf's M	3.44	3.48	3.60	3.52	_3.52_
Adult inf's SD	1.27	1.35	1.20	0.94	1.25
Adult inf's N	111	176	201	33	521
Youth inf's M	3.15	3.46	3.40	3.26	_3.35_
Youth inf's SD	1.42	1.26	1.25	1.23	1.30
Youth inf's N	304	405	455	117	1281
Sp's real age M	45.00	45.75	27.89	32.00	38.04

Discussion. The adult average for *all* speakers is 3.52 (SD 1.25), that is, the non-committal average just on target. The youth overall average is 3.35 (SD 1.30), also close to 3.5, but lower than the adult rating (**; t=2.54). When it comes to the four non-combinatory subgroups, OLD, YOUNG, TRADITIONAL, MODERN, the adult ratings all lie evenly distributed around 3.50.

If we compare adults and youths with regard to their respective subgroup averages, we notice that the only subgroups of which adults and youths give significantly different average ratings are YOUNG and MODERN. In both cases, youths give lower ratings than adults (* and ** respectively). As for the combinatory subgroups, we do not get any fully significant differences, but both OLD/MODERN and YOUNG/MODERN are close to getting significantly lower youth ratings (t=1.89 and t=1.91, respectively). The youth SD value in connection with their rating of OLD/MODERN is markedly high (1.42), indicating a great deal of group vacillation.

It is a bit surprising that the only differences between adults and youths manifest themselves as lower SENSE OF HUMOUR ratings of YOUNG, MODERN, and the two MODERN-combinations in the youth assessment.

We have seen that internally, adults give a very flat set of average ratings, all of which lie close to 3.5. There are no significant differences within adults' subgroup ratings. The youths differ from this pattern in downgrading OLD/MODERN and YOUNG/TRADITIONAL while giving close-to-middle ratings of OLD/ TRADITIONAL and YOUNG/MODERN.

I think it can be argued that the adult assessment is a genuinely non-committal assessment: all their averages lie very close to 3.5. And indeed, it does seem reasonable to get a non-committal response in a judgment of SENSE OF HUMOUR based on a neutral voice material.

As for the youths, we can note that they seem to have downgraded those combinatory subgroups whose speakers exhibit lack of age-language harmony, i.e. OLD/MODERN and YOUNG/TRADITIONAL. Although it is dangerous to draw heavily on such a loose notion, I would venture at least to suggest the possibility of negative responses being caused by the possible presumption hidden in age-language *dis*-harmony. Maybe this is something which is felt to be less than fully agreeable in a close, personal context.

What matters in the end, though, is how this judgment relates to the other judgments, and there is no doubt that we get a lower general level of ratings for SENSE OF HUMOUR than for any other quality in this set of comparisons. This state of affairs is especially stressed in the judgment made by the youth informants. In the overall respect, then, we can say that our hypothesis holds good, as the standard-type voices of this study do not easily lend themselves to SENSE OF HUMOUR stereotyping. As for the youth informants' downgrading of OLD/MODERN and YOUNG/TRADITIONAL, this was something I had not hypothesized, but which adds further weight to the idea of age-language harmony that I have been tentatively proposing (cf p. 119).

FRIENDLINESS.
Hypotheses: FRIENDLINESS certainly belongs to the socially significant qualities. By definition it is chiefly associated with the personal sphere in a way similar to SENSE OF HUMOUR. If we should expect any difference at all from SENSE OF HUMOUR, slighty higher ratings of MODERN and, perhaps, YOUNG would seem likely, as these subgroups are perhaps less associated with official status and other similar factors than TRADITIONAL and OLD. It should be remembered also that FRIENDLINESS is something which is at least stereotypically linked with a person's voice quality and other non-linguistic vocal factors. This circumstance will complicate the interpretation.

Friendliness	SPEAKER VOICE CATEGORY Non-combinatory subgroups				
	OLD	YOUNG	TRADITIONAL	MODERN	ALL SPEAKERS
Adult inf's M	3.97	3.90	3.93	3.94	3.94
Adult inf's SD	1.21	1.10	1.22	1.12	1.16
Adult inf's N	294	240	214	320	534
Youth inf's M	3.95	4.02	4.11	3.90	3.99
Youth inf's SD	1.28	1.13	1.19	1.23	1.21
Youth inf's N	710	572	523	759	1282
Sp's real age M	45.43	28.64	43.00	34.73	38.04

The average ratings of *all* voices lie very close to 4.0, both in the adult and youth assessment, which means that on the whole, these voices are regarded as friendly voices. The difference between adults' and youths' overall averages is negligible, as is most of the difference in SD values. When it comes to the four non-combinatory subgroups, the adults present virtually no spread at all. The youths, on the other hand, upgrade TRADITIONAL at the expense of MODERN (the difference is significant (**; t=3.04)).

Friendliness	SPEAKER VOICE CATEGORY Combinatory subgroups				
	OLD/MOD	OLD/TRAD	YOUNG/MOD	YOUNG/TRAD	ALL SPEAKERS
Adult inf's M	<u>4.02</u>	<u>3.93</u>	3.90	3.91	3.94
Adult inf's SD	1.10	1.28	1.13	0.88	1.16
Adult inf's N	113	181	207	33	534
Youth inf's M	<u>3.69</u>	<u>4.15</u>	4.04	3.95	3.99
Youth inf's SD	1.36	1.18	1.11	1.22	1.21
Youth inf's N	304	406	455	117	1282
Sp's real age M	45.00	45.75	27.89	32.00	38.04

Let us see whether an analysis of combinatory subgroups can contribute to our understanding the problem. We see at once that the adults give very even ratings to the four combinatory subgroups too. The only subgroup average to stand out at all from the rest is that concerning OLD/MODERN, which is slightly higher than the other adult ratings (difference not significant). Interestingly, it so happens that OLD/MODERN is the subgroup which receives the *lowest* youth rating, whereas OLD/TRADITIONAL gets the highest youth rating.

As we have already noted, there is virtually no difference at all in overall averages between adults and youths. In view of this, it is of course particularly interesting if there are individual subgroups which present clear differences. And there are. What we have is an interesting "topsy-turvy" configuration if we compare adults and youths with regard to (1) OLD/MODERN AND (2) OLD/TRADITIONAL. The adults give a significantly higher (*; t=2.31) average rating of OLD/MODERN, whereas the youths rate OLD/TRADITIONAL significantly higher (*; t=2.03). That is to say, what seems to happen is that the adults maintain their general level for both subgroups, whereas the youths "lower" their level for OLD/MODERN and "raise" it for OLD/TRADITIONAL. It is very hard to explain this phenomenon, unless we see it as a result of formal deficiencies in the method used in this study to form groups (cf pp. 83ff). Why should the same subgroup, OLD/MODERN, get the highest (if not significantly so) adult average and the lowest youth average? Something which might elucidate the problem somewhat is the youth SD value for OLD/MODERN, 1.36. It is clearly the highest SD figure in the table, which would seem to indicate a considerable amount of group vacillation among the youth informants when rating OLD/MODERN. A possible, but by no means self-evident, explanation is that FRIENDLINESS might mean different things to different people; that for example the youths might associate the term more with somebody being "friendly" to them, whereas the adults might think of it in terms of a friendship relation between equal parties. It is possible that OLD/TRADITIONAL conveys more of "friendliness from above" to youth informants, thus causing a higher rating; and that OLD/MODERN has more of a "friendliness on equal terms" in it to the adults, thereby raising their rating.

It seems that it is the adults who support our hypothesis by upgrading (relatively speaking) OLD/MODERN. The main impression of adults ratings of FRIENDLINESS, though, is that they do not present a great deal of variation. The youths again seem to follow an unhypothesized principle of age-language harmony by upgrading such combinatory subgroups as exhibit harmony.

INTELLIGENCE.
Hypotheses: Here we have a quality which is basically of individual, rather than social, significance. A traditional approach would be to ascribe higher INTELLIGENCE values to such accents as would normally be associated with intellectual work, education, etc. Within the framework of the present study, it will be hypothesized that TRADITIONAL typifies such accents, thus getting high INTELLIGENCE ratings. Even though AGE objectively cannot be seen to co-vary with INTELLIGENCE, social pressure probably causes some, particularly young, informants to upgrade relatively old voices for INTELLIGENCE. If a shift has taken place, or is taking place, in the direction of increased social equality, we might expect a more flat distribution of ratings by youths than by adults. On the other hand, we have already noticed on several occasions a tendency in the assessment of the youth informants that could be regarded as conventionalism or stereotyping,

which would of course work in the opposite direction.

Intelligence	SPEAKER VOICE CATEGORY Non-combinatory subgroups				
	OLD	YOUNG	TRADITIONAL	MODERN	ALL SPEAKERS
Adult inf's M	4.39	4.19	4.52	4.15	4.30
Adult inf's SD	1.12	1.04	1.06	1.09	1.09
Adult inf's N	293	233	214	312	526
Youth inf's M	4.53	4.24	4.56	4.29	4.40
Youth inf's SD	1.23	1.23	1.16	1.27	1.24
Youth inf's N	709	571	523	757	1280
Sp's real age M	45.43	28.64	43.00	34.73	38.04

Discussion. The overall average ratings (adults 4.30 [SD 1.09]; youths 4.40 [SD 1.24]) show that on the whole, the voices of the sample get favourable ratings for INTELLIGENCE, and that the difference between adults and youths is not so great. The youths give a slightly higher average, but the difference is not significant (t=1.61). If we compare youths and adults with regard to the four non-combinatory subgroups, we find no significant differences, but there is a less than significant (t=1.68) upward tendency in the youth rating of OLD, which would seem to support our hypothesis that AGE functions as a general prestige marker when judged by young informants. There also seems to be a gap between adults and youths when rating MODERN (not significant, though; t=1.71), to the effect that adults seem to downgrade this subgroup for INTELLIGENCE more strongly than the youths, which might be a slight indication of a more egalitarian view on the part of the youths, which in turn would support another of our hypotheses. These suggestions must be taken with a pinch of salt, though, since, as we have seen, differences are not significant at the five per cent level.

If instead we make a "horizontal" comparison, we notice that the difference between OLD and YOUNG and that between TRADITIONAL and MODERN in the youth assessment are very similar in magnitude (*** in both cases), whereas the adults distinguish more clearly between TRADITIONAL and MODERN (***) than between OLD and YOUNG (*). It seems therefore that DEGREE OF MODERNITY is a more potent distinguisher for adults in this particular case. The youths, as we have already noted, seem to be influenced just as strongly by AGE.

In this context, the reader may ask what we mean by INTELLIGENCE. The answer is that we have not made any attempt to define or otherwise elaborate on our quality labels; the informants were not supplied with any such information, and so, whatever vagueness blurs the labels has to be faced when discussing and assessing the various ratings.

Intelligence	SPEAKER VOICE CATEGORY Combinatory subgroups				
	OLD/MOD	OLD/TRAD	YOUNG/MOD	YOUNG/TRAD	ALL SPEAKERS
Adult inf's M	4.04	4.60	4.21	4.09	4.30
Adult inf's SD	1.10	1.09	1.08	0.80	1.09
Adult inf's N	112	181	200	33	526
Youth inf's M	4.39	4.63	4.22	4.33	4.40
Youth inf's SD	1.29	1.17	1.26	1.11	1.24
Youth inf's N	302	407	455	116	1280
Sp's real age M	45.00	45.75	27.89	32.00	38.04

Let us now go on to the combinatory subgroups instead. We then notice at once that what in the youth assessment seemed to be a fairly straightforward case of overlap between AGE and DEGREE OF MODERNITY is notably modified: it turns out that the clearly highest youth rating goes to OLD/TRADITIONAL (4.63), whereas the lowest goes to YOUNG/MODERN (4.22), OLD/MODERN and YOUNG/TRADITIONAL assuming an in-between position. Thus, it seems that the youth informants associate INTELLIGENCE most strongly with traditional linguistic output by relatively old speakers, and least strongly with the subgroup that would seem to be closest to the youths themselves, YOUNG/MODERN, which would add further weight to a hypothesis of self-hatred among youths.

Interestingly, there are some differences worthy of notice in the adult ratings as compared with the youth ones. What is not different is the ranking of OLD/TRADITIONAL: the adults give this subgroup an even higher rating than was the case in the youth assessment. Both OLD/MODERN and YOUNG/TRADITIONAL, though, are placed notably lower by the adults than by the youths; in fact, they are the lowest-ranking subgroups in the adult judgment, whereas YOUNG/MODERN, although numerically at the same level as in the youth assessment, ranks higher, although the difference here is not very great.

We noted earlier on that there were no significant differences between adults and youths, either in overall averages or in non-combinatory subgroup ratings. The situation is slightly different for combinatory subgroups, viz. in the case of OLD/MODERN. It turns out that the youths place this subgroup exactly on their overall average level, whereas the adults lower considerably the rating of this subgroup as compared with *their* overall average (the difference between adults' and youths' ratings of OLD/MODERN is significant: *; t=2.55). A similar thing happens with YOUNG/TRADITIONAL, although the difference between adults and youths is not quite as marked here (t=1.16).

If there is truth in the figures, we once again get an indication of the need for a hypothesis of age-language harmony, since the adult informants seem to downrate for INTELLIGENCE those subgroups (OLD/MODERN and YOUNG/TRADITIONAL) in which such harmony does not exist. There is an obvious risk of over-interpretation in this kind of discussion. It is of course only if the small irregularities take on a regular pattern between them that any conclusions worthy of the name can be drawn.

SELF-CONFIDENCE.

Hypotheses: This is another individually significant quality. Traditionally, the typical "RP" voice is believed to convey a great deal of it. If our system of organizing the voices is in agreement with the traditional view, then we should expect high SELF-CONFIDENCE ratings for TRADITIONAL. It is also possible that the AGE variable may be regarded, by young informants in particular, as a differentiator, for the same social reasons as we have suggested on a number of occasions. Sociopolitical egalitarianism may have brought about a change here too, so that perhaps young people attach less importance to accent differentiation in this respect.

	SPEAKER VOICE CATEGORY				
Self-confidence	Non-combinatory subgroups				
	OLD	YOUNG	TRADITIONAL	MODERN	ALL SPEAKERS
Adult inf's M	4.24	4.16	4.54	3.97	4.21
Adult inf's SD	1.44	1.25	1.26	1.37	1.35
Adult inf's N	294	237	215	316	531
Youth inf's M	4.14	4.04	4.21	4.02	4.10
Youth inf's SD	1.48	1.30	1.38	1.41	1.40
Youth inf's N	708	574	521	761	1282
Sp's real age M	45.43	28.64	43.00	34.73	38.04

Discussion. Again we get high overall ratings from both informant groups (adults 4.21 [SD 1.35]; youths 4.10 [SD 1.40]). Interestingly, it is the adults who this time make the highest rating (the difference is however not significant; t=1.54). Thus, it seems that SELF-CONFIDENCE is a more salient feature in neutral accents to adults than to youths, whereas the opposite is the case for INTELLIGENCE. A possible reason for this difference is that the adults, to a lesser degree than the youths, have accepted the idea of INTELLIGENCE being transmittable in a speaker's accent, an idea which obviously suffers from a great deal of conventional thinking; whereas they recognize the possibility of SELF-CONFIDENCE being associated with accent, which would seem to be a better-founded idea, in that SELF-CONFIDENCE normally takes on an *active* and *explicit* aspect on the part of the possessor of the quality, and this aspect is in fact often conveyed verbally.

The general profile of adult and youth ratings with regard to non-combinatory subgroups is one where the expected pattern appears: OLD and TRADITIONAL relatively high; YOUNG and MODERN relatively low. Both adults and youths make very little distinction between YOUNG and OLD, but between TRADITIONAL and MODERN the distinction is clearer, especially among the adults (adults: ***; youths: *). Both youths and adults rank TRADITIONAL as the category in which SELF-CONFIDENCE is most strongly stressed, the adults very much so. So we seem to get support both for the "traditional" hypothesis and the one which suggested a lesser degree of traditionalism on the part of the youths.

Self-confidence	SPEAKER VOICE CATEGORY Combinatory subgroups				
	OLD/MOD	OLD/TRAD	YOUNG/MOD	YOUNG/TRAD	ALL SPEAKERS
Adult inf's M	3.47	4.72	4.26	3.59	4.21
Adult inf's SD	1.48	1.17	1.22	1.26	1.35
Adult inf's N	113	181	203	34	531
Youth inf's M	3.96	4.28	4.06	3.93	4.10
Youth inf's SD	1.58	1.38	1.28	1.34	1.40
Youth inf's N	304	404	457	117	1282
Sp's real age M	45.00	45.75	27.89	32.00	38.04

However, if we look at the ratings of combinatory subgroups, we notice that such a statement requires some qualification. It so happens that the youth informants give fairly equal ratings of OLD/MODERN, YOUNG/TRADITIONAL and YOUNG/MODERN (3.96, 4.06, and 3.93, respectively), whereas OLD/TRADITIONAL gets a considerably higher rating (4.28). The adults, on the other hand, present a much wider spread of ratings, from 3.47 to 4.72. Their ratings fall onto three levels: (1) the highest level, 4.72, with OLD/TRADITIONAL as its sole occupant; (2) the mid level, 4.26, occupied by YOUNG/MODERN; the lowest level, 3.47/3.59, with OLD/MODERN and YOUNG/TRADITIONAL. This means that the youths' ability to distinguish between our accents seems to be more limited than the adults' ability, which would corroborate the hypothesis of youths taking a more egalitarian view on linguistic differences. On the other hand, the one combinatory subgroup to stand out in the youth assessment is OLD/TRADITIONAL, that is, the variety which should have the strongest upper-crust connotations of the four combinatory subgreoups.

The main difference between adults and youths in terms of combinatory subgroup ratings is to be found in the two OLD-combinations, where adults give significantly (***) higher ratings of OLD/TRADITIONAL and significantly (*) lower ratings of

OLD/MODERN than do the youths. Or, in plain English, SELF-CONFIDENCE seems to be a more conspicuous feature in OLD/TRADITIONAL than in OLD/MODERN, as far as the adult informants are concerned. Now, if this is a genuine opinion, why should YOUNG/MODERN end up significantly higher (**) than YOUNG/TRADITIONAL in the adult assessment? Again, it seems that the adults favour those subgroups which exhibit age-language harmony at the expense of those which do not. But there is also the aspect of peer/age group attraction to be considered. We have already seen that the adults are closer in terms of age to the YOUNG subgroup than are the youth informants. On the other hand, they are closest to YOUNG/TRADITIONAL, not YOUNG/MODERN. We do get an adult average rating of YOUNG/MODERN which lies very close to the overall adult average, which in a sense could be regarded as a non-committal position, from the point of view of the comparison in question.

To sum up, we notice (1) downgrading of subgroups with age-language *dis*harmony by the adults; (2) strong adult upgrading of OLD/TRADITIONAL; (3) close-to-average rating of YOUNG/MODERN in the adult assessment; (4) similar, but much weaker tendencies in the youth assessment.

AMBITION.

Hypothesis: AMBITION is another one of the individually significant traits of this section. It seems reasonable to expect an outcome similar to the previous ones, AMBITION being semantically related to SELF-CONFIDENCE.

Ambition	SPEAKER VOICE CATEGORY Non-combinatory subgroups				
	OLD	YOUNG	TRADITIONAL	MODERN	ALL SPEAKERS
Adult inf's M	4.02	3.91	4.22	3.81	3.97
Adult inf's SD	1.30	1.26	1.24	1.28	1.28
Adult inf's N	291	235	212	314	526
Youth inf's M	4.03	3.88	4.08	3.88	3.96
Youth inf's SD	1.38	1.24	1.27	1.35	1.32
Youth inf's N	703	570	518	755	1273
Sp's real age M	45.43	28.64	43.00	34.73	38.04

Discussion. The overall average ratings are lower than was the case for SELF-CONFIDENCE and INTELLIGENCE, just under 4.00 for adults and youths alike. In fact the overall average values given by the two informant groups are remarkably similar and this goes for most of the subgroup ratings as well. It is only the adult rating of TRADITIONAL that stands out somewhat from the rest. It is also a fact that both adults and youths distinguish more clearly between TRADITIONAL and MODERN than between YOUNG and OLD, the adult informants particularly so.

Ambition	SPEAKER VOICE CATEGORY Combinatory subgroups				
	OLD/MOD	OLD/TRAD	YOUNG/MOD	YOUNG/TRAD	ALL SPEAKERS
Adult inf's M	3.47	4.36	3.99	3.42	3.97
Adult inf's SD	1.24	1.21	1.27	1.09	1.28
Adult inf's N	112	179	202	33	526
Youth inf's M	3.87	4.15	3.89	3.83	3.96
Youth inf's SD	1.49	1.27	1.25	1.22	1.32
Youth inf's N	301	402	454	116	1273
Sp's real age M	45.00	45.75	27.89	32.00	38.04

Again, though, an analysis of combinatory subgroups gives rise to further elaboration. In fact we get the same general pattern here as in our previous discussion on SELF-CONFIDENCE, although the spread of ratings is narrower. Thus, youth informants give almost exactly the same average ratings of OLD/MODERN, YOUNG/MODERN and YOUNG/TRADITIONAL. OLD/ TRADITIONAL, however, gets a significantly (**) higher average youth rating. And in basically the same way as before, the adult informants present a three-level pattern in their ratings, a high level with OLD/TRADITIONAL, a mid level with YOUNG/MODERN, and a bottom level with OLD/MODERN and YOUNG/ TRADITIONAL. Both adults and youths thus distinguish between OLD/ TRADITIONAL on the one hand, and the other three combinatory subgroups on the other, but adults more markedly so. The youth informants are less extreme than the adults both in terms of high and low average ratings, but they do mark OLD/TRADITIONAL as being the subgroup with the highest average degree of AMBITION.

It seems therefore that a traditional type of output by a speaker in whom such output can be expected is conducive to high ratings for AMBITION both by adults and youths. In addition, adults downgrade such subgroups in which age-language harmony is lacking, leaving YOUNG/MODERN as an in-between, close-to-average, category. Such downgrading does not take place in the youth assessment.

DETERMINATION.

Hypotheses: DETERMINATION is semantically very similar to AMBITION. This is therefore one of the internal checkpoints of the material: if there should be a great deal of difference between the scores for AMBITION and those for DETERMINATION, we should suspect that something was wrong. If there is a difference between the two qualities, I think it is true to say that it is mainly a difference along the scale personal-official, DETERMINATION containing more of the former, AMBITION more of the latter. If this is the case, we should expect a more even distribution of ratings throughout, since informants would tend to react not in association with official status, but on a more personal basis.

Determination	SPEAKER VOICE CATEGORY Non-combinatory subgroups				
	OLD	YOUNG	TRADITIONAL	MODERN	ALL SPEAKERS
Adult inf's M	4.08	3.96	4.19	3.92	4.03
Adult inf's SD	1.25	1.18	1.24	1.19	1.22
Adult inf's N	290	236	212	314	526
Youth inf's M	4.06	3.85	4.11	3.87	3.97
Youth inf's SD	1.30	1.20	1.17	1.31	1.26
Youth inf's N	704	571	520	755	1275
Sp's real age M	45.43	28.64	43.00	34.73	38.04

Discussion. The internal check shows that there is consistency in the informant evaluations: the DETERMINATION ratings are very similar to those on AMBITION, the overall averages lying just around 4.00. The rating profile for the four non-combinatory subgroups is also similar to those of the preceding tables: OLD and TRADITIONAL get higher ratings, YOUNG and MODERN lower (no significant differences). In detail, there is a slight difference between this table and the previous ones in that the adult distinction between TRADITIONAL and MODERN is not quite as strongly marked this time. The youth informants distinguish about as much between YOUNG and OLD as between TRADITIONAL and MODERN. Now, why should suddenly DEGREE OF MODERNITY cease to have a stronger power of distinction than AGE? One possible explanation might have to do with voice quality, DETERMINATION being a psychological quality which is stereotypically associated with certain rather harsh vocal features which in turn may not be typical of this predominantly female speaker sample.

Determination	SPEAKER VOICE CATEGORY Combinatory subgroups				
	OLD/MOD	OLD/TRAD	YOUNG/MOD	YOUNG/TRAD	ALL SPEAKERS
Adult inf's M	3.65	4.35	4.06	3.30	4.03
Adult inf's SD	1.23	1.18	1.15	1.21	1.22
Adult inf's N	111	179	203	33	526
Youth inf's M	3.90	4.17	3.85	3.87	3.97
Youth inf's SD	1.44	1.18	1.22	1.11	1.26
Youth inf's N	301	403	454	117	1275
Sp's real age M	45.00	45.75	27.89	32.00	38.04

An analysis of combinatory subgroups shows that it is really OLD/TRADITIONAL that stands out from the rest. As was the case in the previous discussion on AMBITION, this is particularly true about the assessment made by the youth informants, in the sense that they have very little variation in average subgroup ratings as a whole, with the exception of OLD/TRADITIONAL. The adult informants this time place the four combinatory subgroups at four different levels, each level seemingly distinct: (1) OLD/TRADITIONAL; (2) YOUNG/MODERN; (3) OLD/MODERN; (4) YOUNG/TRADITIONAL; i.e. the same ranking as before, but this time with OLD/MODERN and YOUNG/TRADITIONAL at different levels. However, the difference in level between OLD/MODERN and YOUNG/ TRADITIONAL is not statistically significant (t=1.44). It seems therefore that the aforementioned tendency prevails: combinatory subgroups which exhibit age-language harmony the way it is defined here get higher adult ratings for DETERMINATION than combinatory subgroups without such harmony.

As has been the case in the last few comparisons, YOUNG/MODERN ends up very close to the adult overall average, which would seem to indicate that *within* this comparison, YOUNG/MODERN is looked upon as being neutral.

EDUCATION.
Hypotheses. EDUCATION differs systematically in two ways from the nine qualities discussed up to now: (1) it is not a "quality" in the psychological sense, but was entered in this section for reasons of convenience; (2) unlike the preceding nine qualities, EDUCATION is a factor which can be checked within the framework of this investigation, since all speakers were required to state their educational background at the time of the recording.

What is traditionally known as "RP" is an accent, or class of accents, which is by definition closely linked with the educational background of its speakers. Thus Daniel Jones talks about "everyday speech in the families of Southern English people who have been educated at the public schools" (Jones 1963:XV). Among certain categories of people, the expression "an educated accent" seems to be widely used. If there is correlation between "RP" and the subgroup TRADITIONAL of the present study, it would not seem unreasonable to expect relatively high ratings of TRADITIONAL with regard to EDUCATION. Because of degree of EDUCATION to some extent being a function of AGE, and because of the subgroups OLD and TRADITIONAL overlapping, we might also expect high ratings of OLD. Also, there is the ambivalence hinted at earlier on, that young informants will either give vent to a more egalitarian view which might show itself as an even distribution of subgroup ratings; or they will be more conventional in their judgment.

	SPEAKER VOICE CATEGORY				
Education	Non-combinatory subgroups				
	OLD	YOUNG	TRADITIONAL	MODERN	ALL SPEAKERS
Adult inf's M	4.57	4.16	4.70	<u>4.17</u>	<u>4.38</u>
Adult inf's SD	1.06	1.05	1.03	1.05	1.07
Adult inf's N	291	235	213	313	526
Youth inf's M	4.67	4.30	4.72	<u>4.36</u>	<u>4.51</u>
Youth inf's SD	1.19	1.24	1.10	1.28	1.22
Youth inf's N	710	571	523	758	1281
Sp's real age M	45.43	28.64	43.00	34.73	38.04

Discussion. On the whole, the voices of the sample are regarded as "educated" voices. The adult informants have an overall average of 4.38 (SD 1.07) and the youths one of 4.51 (SD 1.22). This means that there seems to be fairly good agreement between adults and youths in this particular respect, youth informants giving a slightly higher rating (the difference is significant: *; t=2.13). If we look at the four subgroups we see that the greatest difference between adults and youths can be found in their ratings of YOUNG and MODERN, where the adult informants present lower ratings (it is only in the case of MODERN, though, that the adult-youth difference is statistically significant: *; t=2.32). When it comes to distinguishing between between OLD and YOUNG on the one hand, and TRADITIONAL and MODERN on the other, the youth informants show no difference between the two. The adults are more distinguishing: although in both cases the distinction is absolutely clear (***), there is a notably wider gap between MODERN and TRADITIONAL (t=5.73) than between OLD and YOUNG (t=4.43) in the adult assessment. This means that the adults seem to possess a power of distinction, or willingness to distinguish, that makes it easier, or more relevant, for them to base judgment about degree of EDUCATION upon language features. Contrary to what was the case in the previous comparisons, it is now the adults who seem to be more conventional by strongly upgrading TRADITIONAL and downgrading MODERN. Tendencies are similar in the youth assessment, but less extreme.

At this point it should again be remembered that EDUCATION is different from the previous qualities in several ways, one of which is that it can be looked upon as a process that people participate in for a longer or shorter period of time. The informant category that I refer to as "youth informants" are all secondary school pupils (6th formers), which means that they have limited experience of education compared with many of the adults. It should also be noticed that there is a consistent tendency in SD values for adult and youth informants: adults' SD's are lower, indicating a lower degree of group vacillation, or a higher degree of common certitude.

It is probably the case that in discussing education in connection with accent, we suddenly enter into a situation which is sociopolitically loaded to a much greater extent than the discussion on psychological qualities, since psychological qualities and vocal features for many listeners would be easier to connect than a sociopolitical quality and a set of vocal features. As I have stated earlier on, the informants probably do not distinguish between the physiological and the linguistic aspect of speech when making their conjectures. That distinction is part of our business in interpreting the ratings.

What then is the relationship between the informants' ratings of the educational status of the speakers and their real educational status? A convenient way of indicating this is to state the average total number of years in education for each of the four speaker categories. We can also easily check how many percent of each speaker category have an academic background. These figures can then be compared with the informant ratings of the four categories.

	OLD (N=14)	YOUNG (N=11)	TRAD (N=9)	MOD (N=16)
Adult av rating	4.57 (SD 1.06)	4.16 (SD 1.05)	4.70 (SD 1.03)	4.17 (SD 1.05)
Youth av rating	4.67 (SD 1.19)	4.30 (SD 1.24)	4.72 (1.10)	4.36 (SD 1.28)
Yrs in education	17.4	14.8	17.7	15.4
% acad backgr.	64	27	89	25

Adult and youth informants' educational conjecture; speakers' average educational background in terms of (1) average no. of years in education, (2) percentage of academics in each subgroup.

This table shows first of all that there is a difference in real educational status (average) between the four speaker categories. OLD and TRADITIONAL on average have two to three more years of education than YOUNG and MODERN, something which of course to some extent might be explained by the fact that if you are young, you have not had as much time at your disposal for education as if you are old. However, checking the real AGE values of the speakers, we see that YOUNG and MODERN are not so young on the whole that their age would not allow a rather extended period of education, so we are probably right in saying that there is a genuine difference in EDUCATION in favour of OLD and TRADITIONAL. Interesting to notice are the percentages representing the academic status of the four speaker categories: they show that YOUNG and MODERN are very similar in terms of academic status, whereas there is a clear difference between OLD and TRADITIONAL, OLD having 64 percent academics, TRADITIONAL 89 percent. It should be remembered here that we are talking about a total number of speakers of no more than 25, which may reduce the impact of these percentages somewhat.

A comparison between informant conjectures and real values goes to show that both adult and youth informants present a conjectural profile which matches rather well the real situation, but that the adults are notably more exact in their conjectures. Their ratings present a striking similarity with the profile made up of the percentages for real academic background.

Education	SPEAKER VOICE CATEGORY Combinatory subgroups				
	OLD/MOD	OLD/TRAD	YOUNG/MOD	YOUNG/TRAD	ALL SPEAKERS
Adult inf's M	4.20	4.79	4.15	4.21	4.38
Adult inf's SD	0.97	1.04	1.09	0.78	1.07
Adult inf's N	111	180	202	33	526
Youth inf's M	4.51	4.79	4.26	4.48	4.51
Youth inf's SD	1.28	1.11	1.28	1.05	1.22
Youth inf's N	303	407	455	116	1281
Sp's real age M	45.00	45.75	27.89	32.00	38.04

Now, let us turn to the combinatory subgroups. We then notice straight away that the ratings take on a different profile. Before, we had two peak categories, TRADITIONAL and OLD, and two low categories, MODERN and YOUNG. In the present arrangement of ratings, it turns out that the only outstanding combinatory subgroup in the adult assessment is OLD/TRADITIONAL (4.79). The remaining three combinatory subgroups get virtually equivalent average ratings from the adult informants (in the area of 4.2).

As we have already noted, in this particular comparison the general level of ratings is somewhat higher for the youths than for the adults. The youth informants too place OLD/TRADITIONAL highest and at exactly the same average level as do the adults. Interestingly, though, the youth informants place OLD/MODERN and YOUNG/TRADITIONAL at an in-between, close-to-average level, whereas YOUNG/MODERN finishes last at about the same level as that at which all but one of the adult ratings were placed.

This means that we have here a situation very different from the ones we have seen in several of the previous comparisons, since this time it is the adult informants who do not seem to distinguish between three of the combinatory subgroups, whereas the youth informants do.

Before we go on to discuss this, we should take a look at the *real* educational status of the four combinatory subgroups. It turns out that three of them, OLD/TRADITIONAL, OLD/MODERN, and YOUNG/TRADITIONAL are very equal in terms of average number of years in education (17.5, 17.2, and 17.0 years, respectively), whereas YOUNG/MODERN falls slightly behind (15.3 years). The *academic* status of the four combinatory subgroups is such that OLD/TRADITIONAL (N=8) has 75 percent academics; OLD/MODERN (N=6) 50 percent; YOUNG/TRADITIONAL (N=2. i.e. a very small and thus statistically unstable group) 100 percent; and finally YOUNG/MODERN (N=9) 11.1 percent academics.

This would seem to show that in this particular case, the youth informants might be said to be more fortunate in their ratings, since they manage to indicate distinctions which are very close to the real distinctions in terms of the educational status of the speakers.

Now, why should this be? Why should all of a sudden the youth informants be better than the adults at rating the voices? First of all, it is essential to remember that it is only in the present comparison, on EDUCATION, that it is possible to judge success in relation to a real value. Secondly, it should be remembered that we are dealing with average ratings which are all high up on the six-step scale (4.15-4.79) and that the youth ratings, as they are less polarized than the adult ratings, can all be contained within the spread of the adult ratings. Thus, it is not the case that the adults are unwilling to make distinctions; in fact they have marked out OLD/TRADITIONAL more clearly than the youths; but they have not distinguished between the remaining three combinatory subgroups.

I would like to offer the following tentative explanation, which is based on the assumption (which need not be correct) that there is nothing wrong with the figures from the point of view of statistical representation: Both adults and youths agree that the educational top and bottom positions should be occupied by OLD/TRADITIONAL and YOUNG/MODERN, respectively. This is obvious and need not be gone into any further, apart from the qualifying remark that the span between the two is larger in the adult assessment. The principle of age-language harmony hinted at earlier is operative in the adult ratings, but not (so much) in the youth ratings. This causes adults to downgrade those combinatory subgroups in which age-language harmony is lacking, i.e. OLD/MODERN and YOUNG/TRADITIONAL. These two subgroups ending up at approximately the same level as YOUNG/MODERN is, according to this explanatory model, a coincidence.

If this explanation is acceptable, it would seem to indicate that what is new about this comparison is not so much the adults giving a more flat distribution of ratings, as the circumstance that the youth informants mark negatively the combinatory subgroup YOUNG/MODERN. Maybe the fact that we are now dealing not with a psychological quality but with an objectively verifiable class has changed the profile of the youth assessment this way. Informants may feel that here it is possible to "know", and thereby be more willing to commit themselves.

The impact of this discussion is reduced somewhat by the fact that the difference in youth average ratings between YOUNG/MODERN and YOUNG/TRADITIONAL (4.26 and 4.48, respectively) is not statistically significant at the five per cent level (t=1.71). This means that random factors may play a more decisive part than would be desired, so that we may not be seeing a difference at all in real terms (as always, statistical significance is a matter of degree, but I believe it is wise to stick to the five per cent significance boundary, primarily for reasons of convenience and consistency). If that is the case, we have here a situation where youth informants rate OLD-combinations higher, YOUNG-combinations lower. The only marked difference between adult and youth ratings would in that case be the ratings of OLD/MODERN, where youth informants have a significantly higher figure (*; t=2.32).

In fact, it turns out that the youth ratings for EDUCATION follow much the same pattern as their ratings for INTELLIGENCE. The adult ratings are also very similar to the ones concerning INTELLIGENCE, but there is the difference of YOUNG/MODERN finishing relatively lower in the EDUCATION comparison. It seems superficially reasonable to expect a certain association between INTELLIGENCE and EDUCATION in informant responses. If, even so, we do get differences that can be attributed to factors other than chance, we might explain these differences as a result of EDUCATION being easier to "know" something about. If this is what has caused the drop in the adult rating of YOUNG/MODERN, it would seem to indicate that adults find it a little bit harder to associate the accents represented by YOUNG/MODERN with the concept of EDUCATION than do the youths. This might very well be a question of the adults genuinely "knowing" that these accents are not as "educated" as some of the others, whereas, by comparison, they would not be as prepared to downgrade the same accents with regard to psychological qualities. The same could basically be said about the youth informants, only that, as we have seen, they do not rate YOUNG/MODERN quite as low, and that they rate OLD/MODERN and YOUNG/TRADITIONAL higher. In fact, the only clearly significant (*; t=2.32) difference between adult and youth ratings of combinatory subgroups is the one concerning OLD/MODERN. In order to explain this, it is probably wise to resort to a theory that we have discussed before: that it is natural for young people to associate higher age with various aspects of authority, EDUCATION being one.

It must however be remembered that we are dealing with differences that are mostly too small for any ultimate suggestion to prove rewarding.

2.5. Rating of acceptability.

This section of the questionnaire and the interpretation belonging to it probably make up the most crucial part of the present investigational procedure. In it, the informants were asked to state how acceptable they thought the various accents would be in certain professional or other situations. Answers were given along the same kind of six-step scales as in the preceding section. The exact wording of the question was as follows: "How acceptable do you think this speaker's accent would be in different positions? Put a tick in the correct box. How acceptable would you consider this accent to be in....."; and then followed a list of eleven "job labels" or "group labels", viz. *a Teacher of English; an Actor/Actress; a Grocer's Assistant; a BBC Newsreader; a Disc Jockey; a Barrister; a Rock Singer; a Government Official; a Workingman/-woman; a Fellow Worker/Student of Yours; Your Child (or Brother/Sister).* These labels were chosen in order to create a spread across the social, economic, and cultural field, but also to make the task of the informants less arduous and time-consuming than would be the case with a more codified system of categorization.

In retrospect, it is possible to claim that two of these job labels were not so fortunate, namely GOVERNMENT OFFICIAL and WORKINGMAN/-WOMAN. It turned out that they were both semantically too loose, that they embraced too much, or, in the latter case, that particularly young informants were uncertain as to the meaning of the word (cf Introduction, p. 76).

I shall now go on to discuss each one of these eleven test items and how adult and youth informants responded to them with regard to non-combinatory and combinatory speaker subgroups.

TEACHER OF ENGLISH.
Hypotheses: It would seem reasonable to expect high acceptability ratings of all the voices of the sample as they are all neutral voices with little "regional" colouring. The degree to which informants are particular with regard to the acceptability of the voices in TEACHER OF ENGLISH could be expected to vary according to the familiarity of the informants with the school environment, so that e.g. adults by being alienated from the school environment tend to regard it more conventionally and stereotypically than youths, thereby being more demanding when judging a "teacher's" language. Counteracting this hypothesis is the circumstance that many of the adult informants of this study are in fact teachers themselves, which would seem to promote a more liberal view of teachers' language. We have seen on several occasions that the youth informants tend to associate AGE with prestige (cf Torbe 1984, quotation p. 115 above), and so we might also expect youths to upgrade OLD in this context.

142

Teacher of Engl.	SPEAKER VOICE CATEGORY Non-combinatory subgroups				
	OLD	YOUNG	TRADITIONAL	MODERN	ALL SPEAKERS
Adult inf's M	4.60	4.35	4.87	4.23	4.49
Adult inf's SD	1.40	1.40	1.29	1.43	1.41
Adult inf's N	295	238	214	319	533
Youth inf's M	4.52	4.09	4.78	4.01	4.33
Youth inf's SD	1.43	1.46	1.25	1.51	1.46
Youth inf's N	712	573	525	760	1285
Sp's real age M	45.43	28.64	43.00	34.73	38.04

Discussion. The average figures for all speakers regardless of speaker category show that on the whole the speakers receive favourable ratings from adults and youths alike. In fact, these are the highest overall acceptability ratings in this section. The adult informants are somewhat more favourable (4.49 [SD 1.41]) than the youths (4.33 [SD 1.46]). The difference is significant at the five per cent level (*; t=2.15). If we look into the four speaker subgroups, we see that there is a clear pattern in favour of OLD and TRADITIONAL both in the adult and the youth assessment. The chief difference between adults and youths is that the youth informants give significantly (*) lower ratings of YOUNG and MODERN. When it comes to the distinguishing power of AGE and DEGREE OF MODERNITY, we can notice a strong tendency both among youths and adults to distinguish particularly clearly between TRADITIONAL and MODERN, and a slightly less strong tendency to distinguish between YOUNG and OLD.

Now, why should the youth informants be more particular than the adults in distinguishing between subgroups? First of all, since we are discussing TEACHER OF ENGLISH, we are on the home ground of the youth informants, who are all secondary school pupils. It may well be that they judge partly according to other criteria than strictly linguistic ones, such as voice quality, or degree of pleasantness (which we shall return to below). And we can be sure of one thing: their frame of reference is more distinct since they are actually in the school system themselves. Another possible explanation is that youth informants experience a wish to dissimilate YOUNG, who they may associate with themselves, and the concept of TEACHER. This would tally with certain suggestions made by Labov (1966:493) about New York children resisting middle class norms because of their teachers' advocating "a language, and an attitude towards language, which is quite remote from everyday life." And then we have of course conventionalism, pure and simple.

Teacher of Engl.	SPEAKER VOICE CATEGORY Combinatory subgroups				
	OLD/MOD	OLD/TRAD	YOUNG/MOD	YOUNG/TRAD	ALL SPEAKERS
Adult inf's M	4.07	4.93	*4.32*	4.55	4.49
Adult inf's SD	1.45	1.27	1.41	1.35	1.41
Adult inf's N	114	181	205	33	533
Youth inf's M	4.05	4.86	*3.98*	4.51	4.33
Youth inf's SD	1.53	1.24	1.50	1.24	1.46
Youth inf's N	304	408	456	117	1285
Sp's real age M	45.00	45.75	27.89	32.00	38.04

Let us now see how an analysis of combinatory subgroups may affect this interpretation. One thing is clear, both in the adult and in the youth assessment: OLD/TRADITIONAL is the combinatory subgroup which gets the clearly highest ratings for TEACHER OF ENGLISH. The ratings of this subgroup are significantly different from those of most other subgroups. Both adults and youths seem to prefer a relatively traditional linguistic output by relatively old speakers in connection with TEACHER OF ENGLISH. This is perhaps not to be wondered at. Interestingly, though, the second position, both in the adult and youth assessment, is taken by YOUNG/TRADITIONAL, a combinatory subgroup which, as we remember, was downgraded in many of the comparisons of the previous section on psychological qualities. The smallness of this subgroup (N=2) obviously reduces the predictive power of any statement made about it, and, for natural reasons, it also reduces the number of listener responses made about it. Therefore, it is only natural that the adult rating of YOUNG/TRADITIONAL, which is based on a very small number of responses (33), does not bring about a statistically significant difference when compared with the other adult ratings here (statistical significance of the difference between two mean values is calculated by means of a formula which includes the two mean values and their respective SD and N values; high SD values and/or low N values reduces the chance of getting statistical significance). However, there is some harmony between adult and youth ratings with regard to TEACHER OF ENGLISH, so perhaps we might still venture to accept the adult figure in spite of its statistical limitations. It appears that it is the TRADITIONAL element that makes for the enhanced acceptability in TEACHER OF ENGLISH, more so than the AGE element.

The two remaining subgroups, OLD/MODERN and YOUNG/MODERN, get a slightly different treatment by the two informant groups: the youths place both of them at about the same level (around 4), whereas the adults seem to be more favourably inclined towards YOUNG/MODERN in connection with TEACHER OF ENGLISH, turning it into an in-between category. However, the adult difference between OLD/MODERN and YOUNG/MODERN cannot be statistically established at the five per cent level (t=1.50). If we disregard this statistical shortcoming, it seems as if the one combinatory subgroup really to stand out negatively from the rest in the adult assessment is OLD/MODERN (4.07). In comparison, as we have seen, the youth informants are equally negatively inclined, relatively speaking, to both subgroups.

The only difference between adult and youth ratings of combinatory subgroups that is statistically significant is that concerning YOUNG/MODERN (**; t=2.75). What happens here is mainly that the youths downgrade this subgroup markedly, both in relation to the adults and to their own overall average. We have already suggested reasons for youth informants not wanting to give high TEACHER ratings of such voices as can be associated with themselves. Now, since we are discussing the difference between adults and youths, we should of course consider not only the latter group. There may also be a tendency among the not-so-old adult informants of this study, many of whom are in fact teachers, *not* to downgrade YOUNG/MODERN as it may be felt to represent something desirable, although not traditionally so. The fact that the attention of teachers focuses on students, and vice versa, might create a situation where teachers internalize students' behaviour as some kind of norm, whereas students, more expectedly, regard teachers' behaviour as their norm. Such speculation is corroborated by the fact that teachers often testify that the company of young people makes them feel young themselves. Another way of explaining the adult informants' relatively favourable rating of YOUNG/MODERN is to look at the cultural history of this informant category: the average age of the adult informants is 33.4, which means that on an average (as the tests were carried out in 1982), many of them may be close to the spirit of '68. If so, they will probably be farther from accepting a traditional evaluation of people than virtually any other group. Giles & Powesland (1975:33) report studies carried out in the mid and late 60s which indicate that "the educational opinions of student teachers tend to change in the direction of radicalism and liberalism during their courses."

ACTOR/ACTRESS.
Hypotheses: The acting profession is perhaps, together with certain jobs within broadcasting, the profession to be most strongly associated with correctness of pronunciation. In Britain, as in many other countries, prospective actors are actually taught to speak with an approved accent, a *Bühnenaussprache,* which traditionally was the only acceptable form of speech for use on the stage, unless a part required a more marked "rustic" variety of speech. Most linguists would equate the traditionally approved British *Bühnenaussprache* with "RP". In Wells's (1982) terminology, the British *Bühnenaussprache* would be called "Adoptive RP", as it is normally learnt in adult life. Wells also claims that Adoptive RP has certain

distinctive features that are not present in other types of "RP", most of which however seem to be elocutionary rather than dialectal. Apart from such "adoptive" features, there are also a number of novelties of pronunciation in the speech of younger as compared to older actors. Such features are often subjected to severe criticism by believers in tradition and hard-to-define concepts such as "clarity" (cf Burgess 1983). A good example of such a feature is the vowel in *back, cat*. This vowel often takes on a kind of shibboleth function so that its open and close varieties are seen as symbols of modernity and tradition, respectively (cf Amis 1983). Now if our way of categorizing speakers manages to create a similar division, we might expect informants to distinguish clearly between TRADITIONAL and MODERN. In addition, youth informants might perhaps be expected to be more permissive with regard to MODERN, as they have been brought up listening to actors who do not sound the way actors used to.

Actor	SPEAKER VOICE CATEGORY				
	Non-combinatory subgroups				
	OLD	YOUNG	TRADITIONAL	MODERN	ALL SPEAKERS
Adult inf's M	4.24	3.87	4.45	3.82	4.07
Adult inf's SD	1.58	1.54	1.51	1.57	1.57
Adult inf's N	294	240	215	319	534
Youth inf's M	4.19	3.82	4.36	3.79	4.02
Youth inf's SD	1.48	1.48	1.37	1.53	1.49
Youth inf's N	710	573	523	760	1283
Sp's real age M	45.43	28.64	43.00	34.73	38.04

Discussion. We notice straight away that the difference between the ratings by the two informant groups is very small indeed, both as regards the overall average and the ratings of the four subgroups. In fact, there are no statistically significant differences between adult and youth average ratings in this comparison. Secondly, the pattern that we have grown used to up to now still prevails: there is a clear difference in ratings between on the one hand OLD and TRADITIONAL and on the other YOUNG and MODERN. The overall averages (adults 4.07 [SD 1.57]; youths 4.02 [SD 1.45]) show that even if we are now dealing with figures slightly lower than in the TEACHER discussion above, we are still on the clearly positive side of the six-step scale, that is, these voices on an average are considered acceptable in an ACTOR. The only individual non-combinatory subgroup rating that does seem to stand out on its own at all is the adult rating of TRADITIONAL, 4.45 (SD 1.51). Both adult and youth informants place TRADITIONAL in a top-ranking position. OLD gets the second highest ratings, whereas YOUNG and MODERN fall behind. Taken together, these figures, considering the great unanimity of the verdict, clearly show that the voices/accents belonging to TRADITIONAL are associated with the acting profession by adults and youths alike, and that the differentiation hypothesized above does not take place. What we get is a fairly conventional profile. From the point of view of internal check, as we know about the strong connection between language correctness and acting, we also get some justification of the method employed to divide the speakers according to DEGREE OF MODERNITY, TRADITIONAL attaining higher ratings than OLD.

Actor	SPEAKER VOICE CATEGORY Combinatory subgroups				
	OLD/MOD	OLD/TRAD	YOUNG/MOD	YOUNG/TRAD	ALL SPEAKERS
Adult inf's M	3.78	4.53	3.85	4.00	4.07
Adult inf's SD	1.64	1.47	1.53	1.62	1.57
Adult inf's N	112	182	207	33	534
Youth inf's M	3.85	4.45	3.75	4.07	4.02
Youth inf's SD	1.57	1.36	1.50	1.38	1.49
Youth inf's N	304	406	456	117	1283
Sp's real age M	45.00	45.75	27.89	32.00	38.04

Do combinatory subgroups reveal anything new about youth and adult informants' opinion of the voices with regard to ACTOR/ACTRESS? The first thing that turns out is that there is very little difference indeed between youths and adults in this particular set of comparisons. Both adults and youths place OLD/TRADITIONAL highest. This is probably absolutely clear, although the smallness of the YOUNG/TRADITIONAL subgroup (N=2) and the ensuing low number of responses by mainly adult informants seem to upset statistics somewhat (in fact, the adult rating of OLD/TRADITIONAL, 4.53, is not significantly different from the adult rating of YOUNG/TRADITIONAL, 4.00; t=1.88). Furthermore, both adult and youth informants place the remaining three combinatory subgroups at about the same average level (3.75-4.07). The only significant difference among the ratings of these three subgroups is that between the youth rating of YOUNG/MODERN (3.75) and YOUNG/TRADITIONAL (4.07) (*; t=2.09). It seems that the youth informants attach somewhat more ACTOR weight to YOUNG/TRADITIONAL than to YOUNG/MODERN. The same tendency can be found in the adult ratings, although the differences there are not significant.

What we seem to have here, then, is a situation where combinatory subgroups containing TRADITIONAL get higher ACTOR ratings than subgroups containing MODERN, and where OLD/TRADITIONAL gets the clearly highest ratings of all. Both adult and youth informants tend to downgrade combinatory subgroups containing MODERN, irrespective of AGE. It seems therefore that if there are modernity features in modern actor's pronunciation of the kind suggested above, these features are not sifted out in the present system of judging DEGREE OF

MODERNITY. Alternatively, it may be the case that since we are in a sense asking about an "ideal", informants may be making their judgments with a stereotypical ACTOR in mind, rather than the real actors they watch on television every night, and this might affect ratings in a conservative direction. In any case, it seems to be clear that the traditional coupling between "correct language" and the acting profession is highly present in popular opinion, which is perhaps not terribly surprising.

GROCER'S ASSISTANT.

Hypotheses: The job label GROCER'S ASSISTANT was chosen in order to project a professional category which could be associated with spoken English, but which does not belong to the traditional "RP" area. If this was a correct choice, it ought to show itself in the ratings, provided informants agree to the assumption. We might expect the adult informants to be more conscious of the social implications, thence downrating TRADITIONAL, whereas youth informants might be expected to adopt a more egalitarian view. Conventionalism and stereotypicality are of course factors which will tend to overshadow the ratings to a greater or lesser extent.

Grocer's ass.	SPEAKER VOICE CATEGORY				
	Non-combinatory subgroups				
	OLD	YOUNG	TRADITIONAL	MODERN	ALL SPEAKERS
Adult inf's M	3.25	3.86	3.07	3.82	3.52
Adult inf's SD	1.72	1.54	1.70	1.58	1.67
Adult inf's N	293	239	213	319	532
Youth inf's M	2.91	3.56	2.98	3.35	3.20
Youth inf's SD	1.64	1.60	1.61	1.66	1.65
Youth inf's N	707	568	521	754	1275
Sp's real age M	45.43	28.64	43.00	34.73	38.04

Discussion. The overall averages indicate that in general, adults look upon these accents as neither acceptable nor unacceptable in a GROCER'S ASSISTANT, whereas youths give notably lower ratings. The difference between adults' and youths' overall ratings is significant (***; t=3.74), which is also true of three out of four non-combinatory subgroups. It is in fact only TRADITIONAL which does not give rise to a significant difference between adult and youth ratings, the direct reason being that the adults give their clearly lowest rating in connection with this subgroup, i.e. TRADITIONAL stands out as being particularly unacceptable in a GROCER'S ASSISTANT in the eyes of the adults.

As for the remaining three subgroups, adults maintain a significantly higher level of rating than youths. This adult-youth difference manifests itself mainly in the youths downgrading OLD, and the adults upgrading (as always, relatively speaking)

YOUNG and MODERN. As for the youths' downgrading of OLD, we might speculate that they have made a more context-based, less linguistic, judgment in dissociating the label GROCER'S ASSISTANT from relatively old age. The adults, on the other hand, have remained nearer to the non-committal 3.5. In the case of YOUNG, we notice a related pattern: the youths place their average rating very close to 3.5, whereas the adults place theirs significantly (*) higher. It seems that the youths chose to mark OLD as being *in*appropriate in a GROCER'S ASSISTANT, whereas the adults rather mark the appropriateness of YOUNG. In other words, both adults and youths appear to be socioculturally restricted in terms of AGE by youths downgrading OLD and adults upgrading YOUNG; regarding their own peer subgroup (which is not as clearcut a relationship as would be desired because of the low average age of the adult informants) both adults and youths seem to be more non-committal. This pattern is further supported by the circumstance that neither adults nor youths differentiate in terms of average ratings between their two respective non-peer subgroups, which would seem to indicate that their judgment of those subgroups is more conventional.

The greatest difference between adult and youth ratings of one non-combinatory subgroup is that of MODERN: adults 3.82 (SD 1.58); youths 3.35 (SD 1.66) (***; t=4.30); that is to say, a majority of the adults placed MODERN on the positive half of the scale, thereby indicating that on an average, they considered the accents of MODERN acceptable in a GROCER'S ASSISTANT, whereas a majority of the youth informants placed MODERN on the negative half. Now, why should the accents represented by MODERN be regarded as more acceptable in a GROCER'S ASSISTANT in the judgment of adults than in that of youths? Let me suggest a tentative explanation beginning with a new question: what would make a given accent *un*-acceptable in a GROCER'S ASSISTANT in the first place? If we assume that we are dealing with a unidimensional sociocultural scale (which is most probably an oversimplification), and also that GROCER'S ASSISTANT is felt to be a job label signalling a humble social position, the answer can be one out of two: (1) the accent is either too uppercrust for such a humble position; (2) or it is too lowly even for such a humble position. The question whether an accent is *acceptable* cannot be answered along quite the same lines: either the accent has got what it takes *and more,* or it has got what it takes, *but no more* (the theoretical possibility that an accent is just on target for a certain job label—and that only—can, I think, safely be discarded for lack of realism). There is no way to decide within the present framework which of these answer principles was used by the informants, but we can always speculate. We have seen on a number of occasions that contrary to expectations the adult informants seem more favourably inclined towards MODERN. This favourable inclination is perhaps a reflection of openmindedness on the part of the adults, i.e. they *accept* MODERN in various contexts, even though they may not always *expect* it there. The youths, on the other hand, have consistently been expressing less favourable opinions towards this subgroup, and will be doing so in the comparisons to come. It seems as if they feel generally uncomfortable about MODERN. Maybe there is a normality or lack of flashiness about this subgroup which from a stereotypical aspect it is hard to connect to job labels of the type we have here, regardless of the social connotations of the labels.

The general impression to be drawn from the table is however that OLD and, particularly, TRADITIONAL are looked upon as not acceptable in a GROCER'S ASSISTANT both by adults and youths.

Grocer's ass.	SPEAKER VOICE CATEGORY Combinatory subgroups				
	OLD/MOD	OLD/TRAD	YOUNG/MOD	YOUNG/TRAD	ALL SPEAKERS
Adult inf's M	*3.85*	2.87	3.81	4.15	*3.52*
Adult inf's SD	1.64	1.67	1.55	1.46	1.67
Adult inf's N	113	180	206	33	532
Youth inf's M	*2.91*	2.91	3.64	3.25	*3.20*
Youth inf's SD	1.67	1.62	1.60	1.55	1.65
Youth inf's N	303	404	451	117	1275
Sp's real age M	45.00	45.75	27.89	32.00	38.04

If we go on to look at combinatory subgroups instead, we see at once that adults seem to mark "relative inappropriateness", whereas youths seem to mark "relative appropriateness": the only outstanding adult rating is the one of OLD/TRADITIONAL (2.87), that is, a figure considerably lower than the other adult ratings (***; $t \geq 4.12$). In the youth assessment, differences are somewhat smaller, but the one figure to stand out clearly here is the rating of YOUNG/MODERN (3.64), which is significantly higher than the other three youth averages ($t \geq 2.36$).

Another way of looking at these ratings has to do with levels: adults seem to place their averages at three different levels; a high level with YOUNG/TRADITIONAL (4.15), a mid level with OLD/MODERN and YOUNG/MODERN (3.85 and 3.81, respectively), and a low level with OLD/TRADITIONAL (2.87). Youths, on the other hand, also have three levels, but with a different distribution of subgroups at each level. We have also seen that the youth ratings are generally lower. At the high level of the youth informants we have YOUNG/MODERN (3.64); at the mid level we have YOUNG/TRADITIONAL (3.25); and at the low level we have OLD/MODERN and OLD/TRADITIONAL (both 2.91). In other words, it seems as if the AGE variable is inversely proportional to acceptability in a GROCER'S

ASSISTANT in the youth assessment, whereas OLD/TRADITIONAL assumes that position in the adult assessment. In general, the adult assessment contains some confusing figures, such as the rating of YOUNG/TRADITIONAL. Why should YOUNG/TRADITIONAL receive the clearly highest (4.15) adult ratings? We have already seen that this particular combinatory subgroup is very small (N=2), and that the number of adult responses with regard to it is also (consequently) small (33). This may have caused undesirable random effects. And indeed, if we check the figures for statistical significance, it turns out that it is only the rating of OLD/TRADITIONAL that differs significantly from the other adult ratings; so statistically, the adult rating of YOUNG/TRADITIONAL (4.15) cannot be distinguished from the ones of OLD/MODERN (3.85) and YOUNG/MODERN (3.81). There is however another disturbing figure here, viz. the SD value for the adult rating of YOUNG/TRADITIONAL (1.46), which is notably lower than any of the other SD values in this comparison. This makes it seem as if there was less "group vacillation" in the assessment of this subgroup.

BBC NEWSREADER.

Hypotheses: Although things have changed over the last few decades, there still exists a situation which encourages the use of a standard type of accent among certain staff in broadcasting. Newsreaders on the national radio and television channels normally belong to this type of staff. In a comparative discussion on British and German radio language, Leitner (1980) suggests that BBC English is more homogeneous than its German counterpart, and that this can partly be explained by a stronger tendency to stress upper-class values in Britain. He also suggests that there is a tendency in British radio to be "message-oriented" (rather than "addressee-oriented"), i.e. to stress the credibility of the message, and that this tendency will promote the use of "RP". Bell (1983) enumerates a number of reasons why broadcasting adopts standard language, e.g. that it is authoritative and widely understood; and why broadcasting language is identified as standard: it is public and available, it earns prestige from its subject matter (news especially), radio prescribes explicitly correct speech; etc. Shosteck (1974) rates "voice and speech" as the most important characteristic in a TV news personality, more important than "professional attributes", "personal appeal" and "appearance". Similar tendencies can be found in a recent Swedish radio listener poll (Wigren et al. 1987). All this is not tantamount to saying that all newsreaders sound the same, or that newsreaders today sound the same as newsreaders forty or fifty years ago (cf Cheshire 1984). Or in the words of Robert Burchfield (1981:6f):

> It can no longer be assumed (as Alvar Lidell did) that all broadcasters should speak R.P. [...]. Most BBC newsreaders and announcers in London do so, but there are exceptions, and many

of the presenters, correspondents, weather forecasters and so on,
use entirely acceptable regional accents.

This can be compared with a quotation from A. Lloyd James's *Broadcast English*
(1935), which, although liberal and scientifically openminded when it comes to
explaining the nature of pronunciation change, nevertheless stresses the desirability
of uniformity in broadcast speech:

> The Advisory Committee on Spoken English has discussed each
> word on its merits, and it recommends that announcers should use
> the pronunciations set out below.

In general and in practice, the sentiment within the field of nationally broadcast
newsreading must still be said to be strongly in favour of a standard type of accent.
In this respect things have changed but little (Davies 1984:234).

If our suppositions regarding DEGREE OF MODERNITY are correct, and we have
indeed used words causing debate when pronounced in an unorthodox way on radio
and television to estimate DEGREE OF MODERNITY (see above p. 83f), we
should expect the voice category TRADITIONAL to get high acceptability ratings at
the expense of MODERN. Even though AGE is perhaps not a decisive characteristic
of a newsreader, we might still expect OLD to be more favourably received than
YOUNG, partly because of the overlapping between OLD and TRADITIONAL and
between YOUNG and MODERN, partly because OLD may convey authority better
than YOUNG. If there is a tendency among youth informants to be more egalitarian,
this should show itself in smaller variation in the distribution of ratings.

BBC newsreader	SPEAKER VOICE CATEGORY Non-combinatory subgroups				
	OLD	YOUNG	TRADITIONAL	MODERN	ALL SPEAKERS
Adult inf's M	4.05	3.50	4.41	3.39	3.80
Adult inf's SD	1.67	1.59	1.53	1.62	1.65
Adult inf's N	297	239	216	320	536
Youth inf's M	4.05	3.43	4.24	3.46	3.78
Youth inf's SD	1.64	1.55	1.52	1.63	1.63
Youth inf's N	711	572	524	759	1283
Sp's real age M	45.43	28.64	43.00	34.73	38.04

The overall averages (adults 3.80 [SD 1.65]; youths 3.78 [SD 1.63]) show that
these voices as a group on average lie fairly close to the non-committal 3.5. Both
adult and youth informants however give higher ratings of OLD and

TRADITIONAL than of YOUNG and MODERN, TRADITIONAL getting the highest rating of all non-combinatory subgroups. Here it should be noticed that the adults make a considerably greater difference between TRADITIONAL and MODERN than do the youths, whereas in the case of the AGE-based comparison, adults and youths give strikingly similar average ratings. Thus it seems that the adults are more sensitive to such correctness features as are displayed by TRADITIONAL, or, to put it slightly differently, that youths are less concerned about the difference between MODERN and TRADITIONAL. This would seem to support the "egalitarian" hypothesis above. We must however not make too much of it, since there is no non-combinatory subgroup for which there is a significant difference between adults' and youths' ratings.

Another general observation in connection with this table is that the average ratings are relatively low, lower than those for ACTOR and considerably lower than those for TEACHER OF ENGLISH. This is probably due to the fact that whereas TEACHER and ACTOR, in spite of their being in some way associated with language correctness, can, and often do, present variation, a BBC NEWSREADER is typically looked upon as *the* standard, a "correctness archetype", thus creating greater particularity in informants.

BBC newsreader	SPEAKER VOICE CATEGORY Combinatory subgroups				
	OLD/MOD	OLD/TRAD	YOUNG/MOD	YOUNG/TRAD	ALL SPEAKERS
Adult inf's M	3.23	4.56	3.49	3.58	3.80
Adult inf's SD	1.66	1.46	1.59	1.62	1.65
Adult inf's N	114	183	206	33	536
Youth inf's M	3.63	4.37	3.34	3.81	3.78
Youth inf's SD	1.70	1.53	1.57	1.40	1.63
Youth inf's N	304	407	455	117	1283
Sp's real age M	45.00	45.75	27.89	32.00	38.04

From checking combinatory subgroups, it becomes clear that it is really OLD/TRADITIONAL that is the outstanding category here, rather than OLD and/or TRADITIONAL. Adults have given this subgroup an average rating of 4.56, youths one of 4.37. The reason why OLD and TRADITIONAL both got high ratings in the non-combinatory comparison was of course that there was a great deal of overlapping between the categories. But now we can see that it is exactly the overlap between the two that caused the high ratings. In other words, OLD/MODERN and YOUNG/TRADITIONAL fall notably behind.

The adult informants have placed their average ratings at basically two levels, one consisting of OLD/TRADITIONAL, and another consisting of the remaining three subgroups, which get ratings in the area of 3.4, i.e. close to the non-committal 3.5. The youth informants, on the other hand, have three statistically separable levels, a high level with OLD/TRADITIONAL, a mid level with OLD/MODERN and YOUNG/TRADITIONAL, and a low level with YOUNG/MODERN. It could probably be argued here that the youths recognize the newsreader stereotype in OLD/TRADITIONAL in a way similar to the adults, but that unlike the adults they attach more BBC NEWSREADER weight to any group of voices containg OLD, possibly for reasons of "AGE-based authority" and "self-hatred". It also seems that the TRADITIONAL element promotes acceptability in the youth assessment, since YOUNG/TRADITIONAL gets the second highest youth rating, although the distance between this rating and the one of OLD/TRADITIONAL is great. In brief then: adults clearly differentiate between OLD/TRADITIONAL and other com-binatory subgroups; youths too upgrade OLD/TRADITIONAL but in addition place OLD/MODERN and YOUNG/TRADITIONAL higher than do the adults; YOUNG/MODERN finishes last. Maybe there are two kinds of impetus here: one which favours OLD, i.e. the "authority" impetus; and another which favours TRADITIONAL, which might be called the "stereotypicality" impetus. Where both of these are lacking, which is the case in YOUNG/MODERN, we get a low youth rating.

Apart from the outstanding rating of OLD/TRADITIONAL, there are no significant differences among the adult averages (t≤1.38). The clearly lowest rating, however, is that of OLD/MODERN (creating the only significant (*) difference between adults' and youths' ratings of combinatory subgroups). This might be an indication (1) that the authority aspect (naturally) does not play as important a part in the adult assessment; (2) that MODERN is less acceptable in OLD speakers in a formal BBC NEWSREADER situation, whereas it might be more acceptable in speakers whose age harmonizes with their speech.

DISC JOCKEY.
Hypotheses: Disc jockeys like other people show individual linguistic variation in everyday life. Once in the studio, though, it seems that many of them put on an accent to be used there and nowhere but, virtually. As Philip Howard (1984:12) humorously points out:

> As well as giving the listeners and viewers of the world bugs with which they can eavesdrop on pronunciations and dialects of English from all round the world, mass broadcasting develops its own registers, from GodSpeak, the trendy but solemn elongated vowels of religious broadcasting, to PopSpeak, the matey,

classless, chirpy mid-Atlantic of disc jockeys, that was never spoken by anybody outside a broadcasting studio.

Even though Howard makes a good job of trying, it is of course hard to describe an accent in writing, particularly since so many crucial features have to do with intonation, rhythm, and so on. Even so, many people would I am sure be prepared to agree with him as to the existence of a DISC JOCKEY voice or accent.

Since the business of a DISC JOCKEY has very much to do with promoting music to young people, music which belongs to a culture which is often strictly separated from the traditional culture of adults, we would expect both the AGE and the DEGREE OF MODERNITY variables to be operative in the present comparison, to the effect that YOUNG and MODERN get higher ratings than OLD and TRADITIONAL. We might also expect youth informants to give more pointed verdicts in general, since we would now seem to be, as it were, on their home ground.

To counteract this expectation, there is the circumstance that DISC JOCKEY normally belongs to the broadcasting sphere, which, as we have seen, is closely linked up with traditional correctness ideals.

Disc jockey	SPEAKER VOICE CATEGORY				
	Non-combinatory subgroups				
	OLD	YOUNG	TRADITIONAL	MODERN	ALL SPEAKERS
Adult inf's M	2.50	3.17	2.66	2.89	2.80
Adult inf's SD	1.47	1.52	1.48	1.55	1.53
Adult inf's N	296	239	215	320	535
Youth inf's M	2.56	2.92	2.77	2.68	2.72
Youth inf's SD	1.38	1.46	1.44	1.42	1.43
Youth inf's N	710	572	521	761	1282
Sp's real age M	45.43	28.64	43.00	34.73	38.04

Discussion. The overall averages (adults 2.80 [SD 1.52]; youths 2.72 [SD 1.43]) clearly show that we are now dealing with a professional category that does not fit our voices. Among the four non-combinatory voice subgroups, the highest average rating is the 3.17 (SD 1.52) that the adult informants give of YOUNG, and the lowest the 2.50 (SD 1.47) they give of OLD. The difference is significant (***; t=5.16). The youth informants too rate these two subgroups highest and lowest, repectively (***; t=4.52). The difference between MODERN and TRADITIONAL is notably smaller both among adults (t=1.71) and youths (t=1.11). Unexpectedly, TRADITIONAL gets slightly higher youth ratings than MODERN, but the difference (t=1.11) is so small that it can probably be ascribed to random factors.

What we have here is a situation where the main dividing-line goes between

YOUNG and OLD, so it seems that AGE rather than DEGREE OF MODERNITY is decisive in the rating of acceptability with regard to DISC JOCKEY. If however we return for a moment to our discussion on AGE conjecture (p. 97ff), we recall that there was very little difference between YOUNG and MODERN in the AGE conjectures, and indeed between OLD and TRADITIONAL too. This leads to the rather disturbing question: is there a good reason why YOUNG should be considered more suitable in a DISC JOCKEY than MODERN, when there is virtually no conjectural age difference between the two according to the AGE guess table above? In other words, what apart from AGE can be operative in YOUNG, causing it to be more acceptable in a DISC JOCKEY? One possibility is of course that there may be strongly deviant individuals in a group who could cause an unexpected average. Another possibility is that the technique that I have employed to estimate DEGREE OF MODERNITY is not sufficiently effective. It may be that DISC JOCKEY is such a special job label that other and subtler techniques would be necessary to pinpoint its characteristics. A third possibility is that the AGE conjecture (in view of conservative guessing etc.) is too erratic to be taken into consideration in this context. An analysis of individual speakers, rather than group averages, might offer an explanation of this problem, but would go beyond the scope of the present study.

Disc jockey	SPEAKER VOICE CATEGORY Combinatory subgroups				
	OLD/MOD	OLD/TRAD	YOUNG/MOD	YOUNG/TRAD	ALL SPEAKERS
Adult inf's M	2.48	2.51	3.12	3.48	2.80
Adult inf's SD	1.55	1.42	1.50	1.58	1.53
Adult inf's N	114	182	206	33	535
Youth inf's M	2.35	2.71	2.90	2.98	2.72
Youth inf's SD	1.32	1.41	1.44	1.52	1.43
Youth inf's N	304	406	457	115	1282
Sp's real age M	45.00	45.75	27.89	32.00	38.04

A step in that direction, however, is to see how the ratings of combinatory subgroups behave with regard to DISC JOCKEY. It turns out that the adult informants do not present any significant differences apart from what has been indicated already, i.e. between subgroups containing YOUNG on the one hand, and subgroups containing OLD on the other. There is a tendency, though, if less than significant (t=1.27), for adults to give a higher average rating of YOUNG/TRADITIONAL (3.48) than of YOUNG/MODERN (3.12). In fact, the adult rating of YOUNG/TRADITIONAL is clearly the highest average rating in this comparison. Unfortunately, as we remember, YOUNG/TRADITIONAL is a small subgroup (N=2) which tends necessarily to contribute to creating non-significant differences. If we disregard that problem for a while, we might speculate that a stereotypical DISC JOCKEY in the eyes (ears) of many people is somebody who puts on an accent in addition, of course, to the indigenous qualities and activities of this job. This could in other words be an exponent of the age-language harmony discussion we have pursued earlier on: the coupling between relatively young age and relatively traditional linguistic output might for certain listeners signal a kind of hard-to-define "MediaSpeak" (cf Howard quotation above) which might fit into the DISC JOCKEY stereotype.

Youth informants, on the other hand, while distinguishing between YOUNG-combinations and OLD-combinations, do not especially mark out YOUNG/TRADITIONAL. Instead, they choose OLD/MODERN for *their* special treatment. This combinatory subgroup receives the clearly lowest youth rating, and indeed, the lowest rating in the entire comparison (2.35). Thus, OLD/MODERN is significantly different (***; t≥3.46) from any of the other youth averages. Keeping in mind that we are clearly on the negative half of the scale throughout when discussing ratings for DISC JOCKEY, we might still argue that the low youth rating of OLD/MODERN is caused by a lack of "broadcasting features" in the voices of this subgroup, in addition to the more obvious age aspect. That is to say, if a relatively old speaker is to participate vocally in a public speaking or broadcasting activity in which you would rather have younger participants, he should at any rate possess the speech qualities appropriate for such an activity, even though his age may not be suitable for the activity. There had better be harmony between who you are and how you speak.

There is a detail here that might be worth some discussion: the youth informants throughout exhibit DISC JOCKEY ratings that are ranked inversely from the youth AGE conjectures of the four combinatory subgroups, i.e. subgroups with a relatively high youth AGE conjecture get relatively low DISC JOCKEY ratings, and vice versa. If this is more than a coincidence, it would seem to show that the youth informants maintain an age-based approach to the voices which harmonizes with the AGE conjectures they have given. And this approach in turn corroborates the suggestion that AGE rather than DEGREE OF MODERNITY is the crucial thing in a DISC JOCKEY, at least in the assessment of the youth informants.

The adults present a less orderly picture if we compare their DISC JOCKEY ratings of combinatory subgroups with their AGE conjectures regarding these subgroups. We do get higher DISC JOCKEY ratings of YOUNG-combinations than of OLD-combinations, but the individual subgroups are not clear in this case. The only strong conclusion that can be drawn here is probably that both adults and youths seem to attach less DISC JOCKEY weight to OLD than to YOUNG speakers. In the case of the youths, this is done in a way which reverses their AGE ranking. In the case of the adults, it is not possible to discern any such relationship, but nevertheless, they make basically the same distinction.

BARRISTER.

Hypotheses: The legal professions are traditionally strongly associated with the more conservative forms of pronunciation. This is particularly true of barristers and judges in the courtroom. The strong link between Oxbridge and the legal career can partly be responsible for this state of affairs. True, most people have never, or very rarely, been in contact with a barrister other than through films, which probably tends to accentuate the expected stereotype, so we must be aware that the label BARRISTER in the present context is one mainly to do with tradition-based expectation and stereotype.

All this taken into account, we should expect high acceptability ratings of TRADITIONAL and lower for MODERN. Since the legal professions are associated with authority, which is in turn probably associated with older age, we might also expect relatively high ratings of OLD. Even if most people as we have said will have but little personal experience from courts and the people working in them, it is reasonable to assume that whatever experience there is will be greater among the adults than among the youths. This might lead to adults presenting a wider scope of ratings than youths.

Barrister	SPEAKER VOICE CATEGORY Non-combinatory subgroups				
	OLD	YOUNG	TRADITIONAL	MODERN	ALL SPEAKERS
Adult inf's M	3.95	3.44	4.36	3.29	3.72
Adult inf's SD	1.78	1.64	1.65	1.67	1.74
Adult inf's N	296	237	215	318	533
Youth inf's M	3.94	3.32	4.03	3.41	3.66
Youth inf's SD	1.70	1.64	1.62	1.70	1.70
Youth inf's N	706	571	519	758	1277
Sp's real age M	45.43	28.64	43.00	34.73	38.04

Discussion. Our voices, as a group, end up slightly above the non-committal 3.5. The non-combinatory subgroup figure to stand out most clearly from the others is the adult rating of TRADITIONAL (4.36 [SD 1.65]). This figure is by far the highest rating of a non-combinatory subgroup in this comparison, significantly higher (*; t=2.50) than the youth rating of this subgroup. Likewise it is the adults who give the lowest figure, 3.29 (SD 1.67) for MODERN. The distinction made by the adults between YOUNG and OLD is clear (t=3.40), but not so clear as that between TRADITIONAL and MODERN (t=7.29). In other words, as far as the adult informants are concerned, there is a very strong tendency towards associating

BARRISTER with TRADITIONAL. If we recall our discussion on EDUCATION above (p. 136ff), we remember that there was strong correlation between TRADITIONAL and academic background. It also turns out that BARRISTER is the most clearcut case of a profession requiring academic training in this set of comparisons. It might therefore be argued that what we have here is to a great extent a judgment on academic accent.

The youth informants present a less widespread distribution of averages, which was also hypothesized above. Thus, the difference between MODERN and TRADITIONAL is somewhat smaller in the youth assessment, but still highly significant (***; t=6.52). Also, the youths distinguish as clearly between YOUNG and OLD (***; t=6.58) as they do between MODERN and TRADITIONAL. This would seem to indicate that the "age authority" aspect is stronger among the youths.

A related, interesting detail is the fact that whereas both adults and youths give their highest rating to TRADITIONAL, they are not in agreement as to their lowest rating. The adults give it to MODERN and the youths to YOUNG. Even if the differences are too small for any strong conclusions to be made, it could perhaps be argued that the adults make a more sophisticated linguistic assessment, whereas that of the youths is socioculturally based, in that it dissociates BARRISTER from a young AGE. Of course the informants did not know the age of the different voices when listening to them, and as we have already seen, the conjectural AGE of YOUNG and OLD was very similar to that of MODERN and TRADITIONAL, which causes an interpretative problem that I shall discuss in some detail in connection with ROCK SINGER below.

Barrister	SPEAKER VOICE CATEGORY Combinatory subgroups				
	OLD/MOD	OLD/TRAD	YOUNG/MOD	YOUNG/TRAD	ALL SPEAKERS
Adult inf's M	3.06	4.50	3.42	3.58	3.72
Adult inf's SD	1.73	1.59	1.62	1.77	1.74
Adult inf's N	114	182	204	33	533
Youth inf's M	3.64	4.17	3.26	3.53	3.66
Youth inf's SD	1.77	1.60	1.64	1.61	1.70
Youth inf's N	303	403	455	116	1277
Sp's real age M	45.00	45.75	27.89	32.00	38.04

Let us now see how combinatory subgroups react with regard to BARRISTER. In both the adult and the youth assessment, it is quite clear that OLD/TRADITIONAL is the combinatory subgroup that is regarded as most "acceptable", and most markedly so in the adult assessment. If we disregard statistical significance for the time being, it seems as though the adult informants place their ratings at three levels, a high level with OLD/TRADITIONAL, a mid level with YOUNG/MODERN and YOUNG/TRADITIONAL, and a low level with OLD/MODERN. Maybe what we have here is a reflection of social change: of a relatively old person who aspires to exhibit BARRISTER traits, it is required that he use TRADITIONAL language, simply because that is the way it is (probably rightly) believed to have been; younger people probably do not have to face up to that requirement. Acceptability may be less tense here. However, as it turns out, the only significant differences found among the adult ratings are those between OLD/TRADITIONAL and the remaining three subgroups. OLD/MODERN is close (t=1.85) to being significantly lower than YOUNG/MODERN, however.

The youth informants too seem to have three levels of rating here: a top level with OLD/TRADITIONAL, a mid level with OLD/MODERN and YOUNG/TRADITIONAL, and a low level with YOUNG/MODERN. The difference between YOUNG/MODERN and YOUNG/TRADITIONAL is not significant, however (t=1.59). One might suggest the explanation that the youth informants present the traditional stereotype, coupled with a certain amount of age authority. Indeed, age authority seems to play a part when comparing adults and youths, as the youths give a significantly higher (**; t=3.00) average rating of OLD/MODERN than do the adults, whereas they give a significantly lower average rating (*; t=2.31) of OLD/TRADITIONAL. In fact, the treatment of these two combinatory subgroups is what primarily constitutes the difference between youths and adults in the BARRISTER comparison.

ROCK SINGER.
Hypotheses: It is a well established fact that the pronunciation of pop singers when singing follows principles other than those regulating their speech. We do not know the details of these principles, but much light is shed on the matter by Peter Trudgill in his book *On Dialect* (1983) in which he devotes a chapter to this issue: "Acts of conflicting identity. The sociolinguistics of British pop-song pronunciation". Trudgill claims that this deviation in pronunciation can mainly be described as a wish to identify with a group which is desirable in some ways but which the singers themselves normally do not belong to, e.g. Americans or the urban working class. Incidentally, even Swedish rock singers, *singing in Swedish,* sometimes put on what seems to be Anglo-American features of pronunciation, which adds to the idea of a deviant pattern of cultural identification within the field of rock music. There is also a strong wish to dissociate oneself from certain undesirable groups and values, primarily to do with the middle class. The strong relationship between youth and rock music is a further factor to be considered.

Since our voices are all fairly neutral, we should expect low ratings in all cases, particularly so in connection with OLD and TRADITIONAL. It might of course be argued that although everybody knows that there are typical pop-song pronunciations, this says very little about the genuine accents of the singers. In most cases, people will have heard rock singers sing only, not talk. This situation is in many ways similar to the one discussed when dealing with BARRISTER above: a great deal of our discussion has to do with expectations and stereotype.

Rock singer	SPEAKER VOICE CATEGORY Non-combinatory subgroups				
	OLD	YOUNG	TRADITIONAL	MODERN	ALL SPEAKERS
Adult inf's M	2.15	2.90	2.11	2.74	2.49
Adult inf's SD	1.43	1.56	1.41	1.57	1.54
Adult inf's N	2.90	236	212	314	526
Youth inf's M	2.07	2.64	2.16	2.44	2.32
Youth inf's SD	1.38	1.50	1.37	1.51	1.46
Youth inf's N	710	570	522	758	1280
Sp's real age M	45.43	28.64	43.00	34.73	38.04

Discussion. These ratings are the lowest in this section. The overall averages do not come anywhere near the non-committal 3.5. The youth overall average (2.32) is significantly lower (*; t=2.21) than the corresponding adult figure (2.49). I take this to indicate a stronger dissociation on the part of the youths between these accents and ROCK SINGER.

No single non-combinatory average reaches above 2.90, which is the adult rating of YOUNG. Both adults and youths give their highest rating to YOUNG, but differ in giving their lowest ratings: adults choose TRADITIONAL, wheras youths go for OLD. The differences are so small, however, that nothing can made of them.

Apart from the fact that the general level is lower in this table, there is not unexpectedly great similarity between the ratings for DISC JOCKEY and those for ROCK SINGER. However, this similarity again raises the question why YOUNG should get a top rating in this comparison, considering the fact that YOUNG and MODERN got very similar AGE conjectures (cf pp. 97ff). We may be dealing with two age categories, *marked* and *unmarked* age. Unmarked age would basically be neutral, biologically based age, whereas marked age would be a socially loaded category indicating a certain inclination on the part of the speaker. It would in other words be possible for somebody to sound young so that it would be reasonable to guess that his age is relatively low, at the same time as he has few features in his speech that are especially associated with youth.

| Rock singer | SPEAKER VOICE CATEGORY Combinatory subgroups | | | | |
	OLD/MOD	OLD/TRAD	YOUNG/MOD	YOUNG/TRAD	ALL SPEAKERS
Adult inf's M	2.50	1.93	2.87	3.09	2.49
Adult inf's SD	1.57	1.30	1.56	1.59	1.54
Adult inf's N	111	179	203	33	526
Youth inf's M	2.05	2.09	2.70	2.42	2.32
Youth inf's SD	1.42	1.36	1.52	1.39	1.46
Youth inf's N	303	407	455	115	1280
Sp's real age M	45.00	45.75	27.89	32.00	38.04

An examination of combinatory subgroups shows that youth informants make their only significant distinction between OLD-combinations and YOUNG-combinations. Within OLD, there is virtually no distinction at all, and the seemingly substantial difference between YOUNG/MODERN and YOUNG/TRADITIONAL (2.70 vs. 2.42) is not significant at the five per cent level (t=1.79). In other words, for the youth informants, it is AGE that counts in connection with ROCK SINGER, rather than DEGREE OF MODERNITY.

Adults place their average ratings at three fairly distinct levels, a relatively high one containing the two YOUNG-combinations, a mid one containing OLD/MODERN, and a low level containing OLD/TRADITIONAL. The cases where adults and youths differ most clearly are their respective ratings of OLD/MODERN and YOUNG/TRADITIONAL, where the adults give significantly higher (t≥2.36) ratings than do the youths. We have already seen, in connection with DISC JOCKEY above, that the adult informants have a slightly unexpected view of YOUNG/TRADITIONAL. Both in the DISC JOCKEY and the ROCK SINGER comparisons, they give higher average ratings of this combinatory subgroup than of YOUNG/MODERN. The youths, however, unlike what was the case in the DISC JOCKEY comparison, are clearly more favourably inclined towards YOUNG/MODERN. It is not easy to understand why this should be, if indeed there is anything in the difference other than random effects. There seems to be something in the confrontation between adults and YOUNG/TRADITIONAL that produces these deviant results, but at this point it is hard to say what it is. One factor which I have already mentioned several times is that the number of observations on which the adult average for YOUNG/TRADITIONAL is based is small (N=2), which might cause undesirable effects.

The discrepancy between adults and youths with regard to OLD/MODERN, i.e. that adults rate this subgroup higher for ROCK SINGER, is more natural within the general framework of expectancy. It seems to show that the adults make finer distinctions, which we have seen on several occasions; it also goes to show that, at least for the adults, it is easier to associate such OLD voices as also exhibit MODERN traits with ROCK SINGER. Probably, these are two sides of the same thing.

It is however not according to the hypothesized structure of this study as a whole that sociolinguistic changes should be more noticeable in the adult ratings than in the youth ratings. It would seem reasonable to expect greater particularity among youths when it comes to such aspects as normally belong to youth culture. The reason why we get an unexpected effect is probably that the two informant groups are not on a par with each other, in that the youths are less sophisticated for lack of experience, whereas the adults are not terribly old (average age 33.4). At least, that is a feasible explanation.

And then again, as we have already noted, the lower level of overall averages in the youth assessment could be looked upon as an indication of particularity when making general distinctions, even if the finer distinctions show unexpected deviations.

GOVERNMENT OFFICIAL.

Hypotheses: As we have already noted, the job label GOVERNMENT OFFICIAL was not a fortunate one because of its lack of semantic exactitude. What we should expect is therefore a more blurred picture. Apart from this, an uprating of TRADITIONAL and OLD, at the expense of MODERN and YOUNG would seem reasonable, since there is a certain amount of authority involved in this job label.

Gov't official	SPEAKER VOICE CATEGORY Non-combinatory subgroups				
	OLD	YOUNG	TRADITIONAL	MODERN	ALL SPEAKERS
Adult inf's M	4.56	4.10	4.84	4.03	4.35
Adult inf's SD	1.36	1.46	1.19	1.47	1.42
Adult inf's N	296	238	215	319	534
Youth inf's M	4.18	3.66	4.28	3.72	3.95
Youth inf's SD	1.59	1.53	1.48	1.62	1.59
Youth inf's N	706	568	517	757	1274
Sp's real age M	45.43	28.64	43.00	34.73	38.04

The overall averages (adults 4.35 [SD 1.42]; youths 3.95 [SD 1.59]) show that our voices are favourably received in connection with GOVERNMENT OFFICIAL. Both adult and youth informants give their highest non-combinatory rating to TRADITIONAL and their second highest to OLD. The difference in rating between these two subgroups is very small in the youth assessment though. The youth informants have a less varied distribution of averages than the adults, that is to say, they do not seem to make quite as clear a distinction between the four voice subgroups.

The difference in overall level between adults and youths (***; t=5.03) calls for some discussion. In fact, no other job label in this section of the investigation has caused such a great overall difference. Why should this be? Why should the adult informants give almost as high ratings here as they did for TEACHER OF ENGLISH, which got the highest ratings of all, and the youths so much lower ratings? I think one explanation could be the vagueness of the job label GOVERNMENT OFFICIAL. Perhaps adult and youth informants have not interpreted the label in quite the same way. The present ratings would seem to indicate that the youth informants look upon GOVERNMENT OFFICIAL as something demanding "higher" linguistic style, and so they downrate (relatively speaking) all four subgroups, particularly YOUNG and MODERN, compared with the adult informants who uprate the voices, possibly because they think that all four subgroups are well equipped linguistically with regard to GOVERNMENT OFFICIAL, a job label they might not assocaite with altogether "high" linguistic style.

Gov't official	SPEAKER VOICE CATEGORY Combinatory subgroups				
	OLD/MOD	OLD/TRAD	YOUNG/MOD	YOUNG/TRAD	ALL SPEAKERS
Adult inf's M	3.97	_4.93_	_4.05_	4.36	_4.35_
Adult inf's SD	1.45	1.17	1.49	1.22	1.42
Adult inf's N	114	182	205	33	534
Youth inf's M	3.92	_4.38_	_3.59_	3.92	_3.95_
Youth inf's SD	1.67	1.50	1.57	1.36	1.59
Youth inf's N	303	403	454	114	1274
Sp's real age M	45.00	45.75	27.89	32.00	38.04

If we look at combinatory subgroups, we see that the chief source of the high adult overall average can be found in their rating of OLD/TRADITIONAL. YOUNG/TRADITIONAL takes an in-between position in the adult assessment, but, mainly owing to the scarcity of adult observations of this subgroup, it is not possible to distinguish with a reasonable degree of statistical significance between YOUNG/TRADITIONAL and the two low-level subgroups OLD/MODERN and YOUNG/MODERN.

The youth informants, on the other hand, have three distinct levels: a relatively high level with OLD/TRADITIONAL (not as high as the adult rating, though); a mid level with OLD/MODERN and YOUNG/TRADITIONAL; and a low level with YOUNG/MODERN. Thus, it seems that OLD/TRADITIONAL stands out the way we have grown used to in many comparisons, among adults and youths alike; but that adults and youths differ in the distribution of the remaining three combinatory subgroups: the adults seem to make a more language-based assessment in not distinguishing between OLD/MODERN and YOUNG/MODERN, while the youths downgrade throughout YOUNG-combinations relative to their respective OLD-combinations.

WORKINGMAN/-WOMAN.

Hypotheses: As was the case with GOVERNMENT OFFICIAL, WORKINGMAN/-WOMAN turned out to be an unsatisfactory job label, since many people do not associate it with a certain social class or certain kind of work, but merely with work in general. This drawback taken into consideration, we might expect ratings to lie close to the non-committal 3.5. If informants had understood the label the way it was intended to be understood, we would have expected lower ratings of TRADITIONAL and OLD, higher ratings of MODERN and YOUNG.

	SPEAKER VOICE CATEGORY				
Workingman	Non-combinatory subgroups				
	OLD	YOUNG	TRADITIONAL	MODERN	ALL SPEAKERS
Adult inf's M	3.24	3.79	3.08	3.76	3.49
Adult inf's SD	1.70	1.54	1.65	1.59	1.65
Adult inf's N	291	235	212	314	526
Youth inf's M	3.33	3.79	3.31	3.69	3.54
Youth inf's SD	1.66	1.57	1.61	1.64	1.63
Youth inf's N	701	566	518	749	1267
Sp's real age M	45.43	28.64	43.00	34.73	38.04

Discussion. Overall values lie very close to 3.5 indeed. The profile made up of the average ratings of the four non-combinatory subgroups follows pretty well the pattern expected originally, with higher ratings of YOUNG and MODERN, lower of OLD and TRADITIONAL. Adults and youths have reacted in very much the same way with one exception: adults give a lower rating of TRADITIONAL than do youths (3.08 [SD 1.65] vs. 3.31 [SD 1.61]). The difference is however not significant at the five per cent level (t=1.74).

Workingman	SPEAKER VOICE CATEGORY Combinatory subgroups				
	OLD/MOD	OLD/TRAD	YOUNG/MOD	YOUNG/TRAD	ALL SPEAKERS
Adult inf's M	3.68	2.98	3.81	3.63	3.49
Adult inf's SD	1.67	1.66	1.55	1.50	1.65
Adult inf's N	111	180	203	32	526
Youth inf's M	3.44	3.25	3.86	3.53	3.54
Youth inf's SD	1.72	1.61	1.56	1.57	1.63
Youth inf's N	298	403	451	115	1267
Sp's real age M	45.00	45.75	27.89	32.00	38.04

The only additional information we get from studying combinatory subgroups is that there is a clear, although not significant, difference between adult and youth ratings of OLD/TRADITIONAL: the adult informants give 2.98 and the youths 3.25 (t=1.85). If there is anything in this difference, it might be either that youths are less fussy about language in this context, or that they have interpreted the label WORKINGMAN/-WOMAN differently from the adults. Since the job label is an unfortunate one, I refrain from further discussion.

FELLOW WORKER/STUDENT.

Hypotheses: This is not a job label in the same sense as the previous labels. The question concerns acceptability in a fellow worker or fellow student, which means that the individual informant is introduced as part of the objective of the assessment. Thus, the informant will no longer be required to give an answer he knows little or nothing about, as he himself is part of the answer.

It can be argued that there exists a will to stress one's identity and one's group membership in various ways, one of which is letting one's speech resemble that of one's peers or that of a group one aspires towards; another, related way, letting one's speech dissociate itself from the speech of such groups as one does not wish to be associated with. In social psychology (cf Brown & Gilman 1960) and of late also within the field of sociolinguistics, the terms *status* and *solidarity* are often used to represent these aspects of interpersonal relations.

I think it can be argued that the pop-song phenomenon discussed above is a condensation of the real situation among the people making up the market for pop songs. That is to say, we shall expect youth informants to be more adverse towards TRADITIONAL than adult informants. The adult informants on the other hand might be expected to give a more blurred picture, as they have not been arranged in social categories. In the light of what we have found when discussing the last few tables, we might also expect the AGE variable to make up a strong distinctive force here, so that youth informants may be more willing than adults to accept YOUNG.

Fellow worker	SPEAKER VOICE CATEGORY Non-combinatory subgroups				
	OLD	YOUNG	TRADITIONAL	MODERN	ALL SPEAKERS
Adult inf's M	*4.07*	*4.39*	*4.07*	*4.31*	*4.21*
Adult inf's SD	1.57	1.42	1.58	1.46	1.51
Adult inf's N	296	239	215	320	535
Youth inf's M	*3.14*	*3.82*	*3.30*	*3.55*	*3.44*
Youth inf's SD	1.66	1.56	1.63	1.66	1.65
Youth inf's N	704	570	520	754	1274
Sp's real age M	45.43	28.64	43.00	34.73	38.04

The first thing to be noticed here is the clear difference in overall rating between adult and youth informants (4.21 [SD 1.51] vs. 3.44 [SD 1.65]; ***; t=9.28). This goes to show that on the whole, the adults are favourably inclined towards these accents in the present context, whereas the youth informants seem to be non-committal.

If we go into the table to scrutinize the ratings of the four non-combinatory subgroups, we find that the adults rate YOUNG highest (4.39 [SD 1.42]) and OLD and TRADITIONAL lowest (4.07). The youths too rate YOUNG highest (3.82 [SD 1.56]), and give their lowest rating to OLD (3.14 [SD 1.66]). That is to say, both adult and youth informants find YOUNG and MODERN more acceptable than OLD and TRADITIONAL, but the adult general level is notably higher.

At first sight it might seem surprising that the adults should present the same pro-YOUNG, pro-MODERN profile as the youths. This state of affairs is however partly explained if we examine the real average age of speakers and informants:

Real average age					
Adult inf's	Youth inf's	OLD	YOUNG	TRAD	MOD
33.4	17.5	45.4	28.6	43.0	34.7

It then turns out that the adult informants on average are of an age very similar to that of MODERN, and reasonably similar to that of YOUNG, which means that we might expect adults to be attracted to these subgroups in accordance with the principle of peer group identification. It also appears that the age averages for OLD and TRADITIONAL, being considerably higher, will probably attract neither adults nor youths in the FELLOW WORKER/ STUDENT comparison.

The widest spread among ratings is the one we find between the youth informants' assessment of OLD and YOUNG. This spread is considerably greater than that between TRADITIONAL and MODERN. This again would seem to indicate that the AGE variable contains an element which is of importance, even though it may be different from DEGREE OF MODERNITY.

Fellow worker	SPEAKER VOICE CATEGORY Combinatory subgroups				
	OLD/MOD	OLD/TRAD	YOUNG/MOD	YOUNG/TRAD	ALL SPEAKERS
Adult inf's M	*4.26*	*3.95*	*4.34*	*4.73*	*4.21*
Adult inf's SD	1.50	1.61	1.44	1.26	1.51
Adult inf's N	114	182	206	33	535
Youth inf's M	*3.10*	*3.17*	*3.84*	*3.74*	*3.44*
Youth inf's SD	1.69	1.65	1.57	1.52	1.65
Youth inf's N	299	405	455	115	1274
Sp's real age M	45.00	45.75	27.89	32.00	38.04

Let us now turn to combinatory subgroups and see how they react with regard to FELLOW WORKER/STUDENT. But first, let us take a look at the real average age of these subgroups (see table above).

The youth informants present a very orderly picture here. They place the subgroups at two levels, a higher level with the two YOUNG-combinations, and a lower level with the two OLD-combinations. It is in other words AGE that plays a part here, not DEGREE OF MODERNITY. This would seem to be a rejection of one of the chief hypotheses of this study: that linguistic modernity could outweigh real age in informant responses.

The adults, on the other hand, give a different, less clearcut set of ratings. For them, it seems that there is one category that stands out from the rest, and in a negative direction, viz. OLD/TRADITIONAL. In other words, it seems that the adults, whose average age as we have seen is 33.4, are more tolerant towards (1) YOUNG-combinations and (2) OLD/MODERN. This might indicate a certain tendency to be attracted to a type of linguistic output that is felt to be similar to one's own. However, it turns out that in terms of AGE *conjecture,* i.e. how old they thought the speakers were, the subgroups that get the highest degree of acceptability in the adult assessment with regard to FELLOW WORKER/STUDENT are all believed to be slightly younger than the adult informants themselves. OLD/TRADITIONAL, which, as we have seen, is the subgroup that stands out negatively (although at a higher than non-committal level) in the adult assessment, is the only subgroup of which the adults give an AGE conjecture that is higher than the age of the adults themselves. Now, why should YOUNG/ TRADITIONAL be more acceptable to the adults than OLD/ TRADITIONAL in this particular context? And why is there virtually no difference at all between YOUNG/MODERN and OLD/MODERN? As for the latter, the AGE discussion above seems to offer a plausible explanation: the adults look upon YOUNG/MODERN and OLD/ MODERN as being of exactly the same age, although there is a real AGE difference between the two subgroups of more than 17 years (if we allow for conservative guessing, we get a difference of 6-7 years between perceived AGE and expected AGE guess). This suggests that linguistic output is of great importance in the area of attitude formation, but that it is "disguised" as something else, viz. physical AGE. This line of argument is blurred when we look at adult responses for OLD/TRADITIONAL and YOUNG/TRADITIONAL. What complicates the matter is that the difference in adult AGE conjecture between the two subgroups is too small to explain the tendency to downgrade OLD/TRADITIONAL and upgrade YOUNG/TRADITIONAL. It seems that there is something in the linguistic output of OLD/TRADITIONAL that causes adult informants to give lower ratings for FELLOW WORKER/STUDENT, and that this cannot be explained in terms of AGE considerations, since there is very little difference in adult AGE conjecture between OLD/TRADITIONAL and YOUNG/TRADITIONAL. What this is, is hard to say at this point. But there seems to be a tendency for OLD/TRADITIONAL to add something to the neutral TRADITIONAL-ness it shares with YOUNG/TRADITIONAL, and that this does not markedly affect the AGE conjecture. The least speculative suggestion for an explanation is of course again that our way of determining DEGREE OF MODERNITY is limited and thus gives only part of the complex which constitutes linguistic modernity.

CHILD/BROTHER/SISTER.

Hypotheses: It would seem that a question on what kind of accent you would accept in your child or brother or sister should give rise to answers that resemble those given in the previous question, on FELLOW WORKER/STUDENT, but as CHILD/BROTHER/SISTER incorporates the informant even more strongly in the judgment, we might expect the tendencies from the CHILD/BROTHER/SISTER comparison to be accentuated here.

Child/br/sis	SPEAKER VOICE CATEGORY Non-combinatory subgroups				
	OLD	YOUNG	TRADITIONAL	MODERN	ALL SPEAKERS
Adult inf's M	*3.51*	*3.69*	*3.57*	*3.60*	*3.59*
Adult inf's SD	1.76	1.67	1.78	1.69	1.72
Adult inf's N	295	236	213	318	531
Youth inf's M	*2.63*	*3.05*	*2.77*	*2.85*	*2.82*
Youth inf's SD	1.65	1.66	1.66	1.66	1.66
Youth inf's N	706	569	518	757	1275
Sp's real age M	45.43	28.64	43.00	34.73	38.04

The overall averages are as we can see considerably lower here than in the previous table. This time the adult ratings are placed around the non-committal 3.5 (3.59), whereas the youth informants give an even lower average (2.89). The overall difference between adults and youths is clearly significant (***; t=8.89).

What is special about the adult assessment is that the four non-combinatory voice subgroups have received very similar average ratings: TRADITIONAL 3.57, OLD 3.51, MODERN 3.60, and YOUNG 3.69, that is, a spread of no more than 0.18. I take this to mean that the adult informants are basically non-committal as to the acceptability of these accents in CHILD/BROTHER/SISTER. Counteracting this is the fact that SD values for the adult ratings of OLD and TRADITIONAL are higher than for YOUNG and MODERN, which would seem to indicate a higher degree of group vacillation in the assessment of these voice subgroups.

The youth informants present a wider spread (2.63-3.05) but interestingly their ratings seem to make up a more pointed version of the adult ratings. It seems that, in this particular case, when we divide the voice material into subgroups according to the principle for estimating DEGREE OF MODERNITY that we have been using, we tend to even out rather than create differences. Our informants do not seem to be particularly concerned about the difference between MODERN and TRADITIONAL in connection with CHILD/BROTHER/SISTER. The little difference there is in this table can be found when comparing YOUNG and OLD. If our method of handling the material is at all reliable, this would seem to mean that here, informants make a non-linguistic distinction, i.e. a distinction based on something other than those probably linguistic factors which have ruled their judgment in several of the previous tables. Maybe it is that when it comes to somebody as close to you as your own near kin, you go for other features in speech than in connection with jobs, features that may have to do with psychological voice quality, warmth, etc.

Child/br/sis	SPEAKER VOICE CATEGORY Combinatory subgroups				
	OLD/MOD	OLD/TRAD	YOUNG/MOD	YOUNG/TRAD	ALL SPEAKERS
Adult inf's M	*3.56*	*3.47*	*3.62*	*4.16*	*3.59*
Adult inf's SD	1.71	1.80	1.68	1.57	1.72
Adult inf's N	114	181	204	32	531
Youth inf's M	*2.54*	*2.70*	*3.05*	*3.03*	*2.82*
Youth inf's SD	1.61	1.67	1.67	1.61	1.66
Youth inf's N	303	403	454	115	1275
Sp's real age M	45.00	45.75	27.89	32.00	38.04

We go on to discuss combinatory subgroups to see if they can add anything. In fact, a quick glance at these figures shows that in the adult ratings, one subgroup stands out markedly from the rest, viz. YOUNG/TRADITIONAL, which gets a favourable adult acceptability average for CHILD/BROTHER/SISTER (4.16). However, owing to the limited number of observations in the subgroup YOUNG/ TRADITIONAL, we do not get statistical support for its outstandingness in more than one case, that between it and OLD/TRADITIONAL (3.47) (*; t=2.04). I would venture to suggest, though, that YOUNG/TRADITIONAL does stand out genuinely; the remaining t-values are sufficiently high to support such a suggestion, considering the smallness of YOUNG/TRADITIONAL (t≥1.70).

Before we go on, let us say a few words about what makes CHILD/BROTHER/SISTER special when compared with the other comparisons. We have already noted that the preceding comparison, on FELLOW WORKER/STUDENT, and the present one, differ from the rest in that they are more personal, less socioeconomic. As for CHILD/BROTHER/SISTER, it is probably also true to say that this comparison seeks to elicit attitudes towards the speech of somebody whom you expect to be able to exert influence on. In that sense it would seem reasonable to expect a more active and prescriptive opinion here.

It is interesting to notice that apart from YOUNG/TRADITIONAL we get very equal ratings from the adult informants in this particular comparison; they all lie pretty close to the non-committal 3.5, whereas YOUNG/TRADITIONAL gets 4.16, i.e. a clearly favourable rating (although, as we have seen, statistics will not always support its outstanding position). It seems that the adults want to prescribe a type of accent which contains certain TRADITIONAL traits, but which lacks certain other traits, present in OLD/TRADITIONAL. We have already noted that the difference in adult AGE conjecture between OLD/TRADITIONAL and YOUNG/TRADITIONAL is not very great, so we are not helped by the AGE aspect. At this point there is not much else to do than leave it at that.

This particular treatment of YOUNG/TRADITIONAL does not happen in the youth assessment. It seems pretty clear from the figures that they tend to go by AGE alone. Again, it might be possible to argue that there is a difference in the outlook on linguistic prescription if we compare youths and adults, so that youths would tend to disregard that aspect more than adults, simply because they have no need for it.

On the other hand, the most conspicuous fact about the CHILD/BROTHER/SISTER comparison is that there is a clear difference in level throughout between adult and youth ratings, the youths rating the voices markedly lower in all subgroups. This is a distribution of ratings which is relatively similar to that of FELLOW WORKER/STUDENT, but at a generally lower level. This might seem to strengthen the suggestion that you are more particular in judging the language of people who are so close to you as to be associated with you and dependent on you. It is also possible that the neutrality which by definition characterizes the voices of this study has an alienating function vis-à-vis young people who to a lesser extent than adults would seem to have been subjected to the status aspect of interpersonal relations. In addition, as we have seen, all but one of the YOUNG speakers are genuinely older than the youth informants.

2.6. Degree of pleasantness.

Hypotheses: In the questionnaire, this question was phrased: "How pleasant do you think this accent is?" and answers were given along a six-step scale as before. A peer group solidarity hypothesis would involve high PLEASANTNESS ratings of accents approximating the informant's own accent; however, as Trudgill (1975a:36-38) has suggested, most people tend to value standard-type accents higher regardless of their own accent. There is also said to exist a tendency to associate accents with the areas in which they are spoken (Giles 1970) so that for example working-class accents spoken in industrialized urban areas are considered less beautiful than those spoken in rural areas. I shall return in greater detail to this discussion in the section on "Regionality and degree of modernity" below.

In the present section, our speakers and informants have not been divided according to social or regional criteria, but according to AGE (in the case of the speakers also according to DEGREE OF MODERNITY). This means that a peer-group solidarity hypothesis would involve higher ratings of YOUNG by the youth informants and vice versa. What we should mainly expect, however, is high ratings of TRADITIONAL throughout, and that the peer-group aspect is provided for by a more flat set of ratings by the youth informants.

Pleasantness	SPEAKER VOICE CATEGORY Non-combinatory subgroups				
	OLD	YOUNG	TRADITIONAL	MODERN	ALL SPEAKERS
Adult inf's M	4.21	4.06	4.30	4.03	4.14
Adult inf's SD	1.33	1.13	1.32	1.19	1.25
Adult inf's N	295	242	217	320	537
Youth inf's M	4.05	3.80	4.22	3.74	3.94
Youth inf's SD	1.31	1.30	1.25	1.31	1.31
Youth inf's N	704	566	520	750	1270
Sp's real age M	45.43	28.64	43.00	34.73	38.04

We see straight away that our accents are on average looked upon as pleasant. There is a significant difference in overall ratings between adults and youths in that the adults rate the voices higher than the youth informants (**; t=3.01). This is a reflection of the subgroup ratings, since the youth informants rate all four non-combinatory subgroups lower than do the adults. Interestingly, though, the subgroups to be considered least pleasant by the youths are YOUNG and MODERN. These two subgroups are also the only subgroups that exhibit significant differences between adult and youth ratings (**; t=2.70 and ***; t=3.41, respectively). The difference both between YOUNG and OLD, and between MODERN and TRADITIONAL in the youth assessment is clearly significant (***; t≥3.39). The adults, on the other hand, present no significant difference between YOUNG and OLD (t=1.39) and a considerably smaller difference between MODERN and TRADITIONAL than the youths (*; t=2.47). The general profile of non-combinatory subgroup ratings is however the same both for adults and youths: TRADITIONAL and OLD are uprated at the expense of MODERN and YOUNG.

This state of affairs is particularly interesting in view of the fact that both adults and youths were more favourably inclined towards YOUNG and MODERN in the CHILD/BROTHER/SISTER comparison above. This goes to show that the aesthetics of an accent is not a unidimensional phenomenon. Both adults and youths, when judging PLEASANTNESS, place TRADITIONAL in the highest position and MODERN in the lowest, the youths more markedly so than the adults. It seems in other words that there is very little correlation between what accent you prefer in your social environment and what you prefer "purely aesthetically", whatever that means. It seems to me that the status-solidarity dichotomy (Brown & Gilman 1960; Andersson 1985:142) cannot account fully for this problem, since it does not treat the aesthetic part of it; or in other words, the coupling between status and aesthetics has not been sufficiently gone into. Trudgill by putting forward the terms "overt" and "covert" prestige (Trudgill 1975b) touches on this problem, but fails to go into the question of *pleasantness* as a function of status/overt prestige.

The ratings in this table also weaken the suggestion that we have made in connection with several of the previous comparisons, that for one reason or other the distinguishing capacity in youth informants might be less developed. On the other hand, the youth PLEASANTNESS rating that we have here could be said to be more conventional, more in accordance with the stereotype, than the adult rating, a suggestion we have made several times before.

Pleasantness	SPEAKER VOICE CATEGORY Combinatory subgroups				
	OLD/MOD	OLD/TRAD	YOUNG/MOD	YOUNG/TRAD	ALL SPEAKERS
Adult inf's M	3.99	4.34	4.06	4.06	4.14
Adult inf's SD	1.23	1.37	1.17	0.92	1.25
Adult inf's N	112	183	208	34	537
Youth inf's M	3.72	4.29	3.75	3.97	3.94
Youth inf's SD	1.34	1.23	1.29	1.29	1.31
Youth inf's N	299	405	451	115	1270
Sp's real age M	45.00	45.75	27.89	32.00	38.04

The really interesting finding appears when we look at combinatory subgroups. It then turns out that it is not OLD *and* TRADITIONAL that stand out from the other subgroups; it is the subgroup OLD/TRADITIONAL that does so on its own, both in the adult and the youth assessment. Furthermore, adults and youths give virtually the same average rating of OLD/TRADITIONAL (4.34 vs. 4.29). The most conspicuous difference between adults and youths is to be found in their respective ratings of YOUNG/ MODERN, where the youths are significantly (**; t=2.95) less favourable than the adults. A similar, but not statistically significant (t=1.86) relationship between ratings can be found in connection with OLD/MODERN (3.99 vs. 3.72). In other words, peer group accent solidarity does not come out naturally in these figures. True, there is greater age similarity between adults and YOUNG and MODERN than between youths, YOUNG and MODERN, but again, the greatest age *dis*similarity of all is of course between youths on the one hand and OLD and TRADITIONAL on the other. As it turns out, youths seem to be more favourably inclined towards such YOUNG speakers who are also TRADITIONAL than towards YOUNG/MODERN, whereas adults do not distinguish between these categories.

The adults place their ratings at two distinct levels, a higher level with OLD/TRADITIONAL, and a lower level with the rest. The youths on the other hand present three levels, a top level with OLD/TRADITIONAL, a mid level with

YOUNG/TRADITIONAL, and a low level with OLD/MODERN and YOUNG/MODERN. However, the mid level is not significantly different from the low level (t≤1.72). If, for the moment, we disregard that, we are facing a situation where youth informants seem to be highly sensitive towards DEGREE OF MODERNITY in a traditional way; so much, in fact, that they make a distinction between YOUNG/MODERN and YOUNG/TRADITIONAL in favour of the latter, something which, as we have seen, the adult informants do not do. And the sufferers are the two MODERN combinations. So again it is the youths who maintain the most traditional view.

2.7. Local/general usualness.

Hypotheses: This question was phrased: "Is this accent heard very often (a) in your part of England? [LOCAL] (b) in England as a whole? [GENERAL]". We should probably not expect a very striking outcome of these comparisons as in the present section the informants are not arranged according to REGIONALITY but according to AGE. We should in other words expect ratings to lie close to the non-committal 3.5.

Local usualness	SPEAKER VOICE CATEGORY Non-combinatory subgroups				
	OLD	YOUNG	TRADITIONAL	MODERN	ALL SPEAKERS
Adult inf's M	*3.67*	*3.79*	*3.86*	*3.63*	*3.72*
Adult inf's SD	1.52	1.49	1.50	1.51	1.50
Adult inf's N	298	240	218	320	538
Youth inf's M	*3.27*	*3.12*	*3.38*	*3.08*	*3.21*
Youth inf's SD	1.52	1.60	1.58	1.53	1.56
Youth inf's N	706	572	524	754	1278
Sp's real age M	45.43	28.64	43.00	34.73	38.04

Gen. usualness	SPEAKER VOICE CATEGORY Non-combinatory subgroups				
	OLD	YOUNG	TRADITIONAL	MODERN	ALL SPEAKERS
Adult inf's M	3.68	3.90	3.77	3.79	3.78
Adult inf's SD	1.24	1.11	1.14	1.22	1.19
Adult inf's N	296	238	217	317	534
Youth inf's M	3.82	3.81	3.91	3.76	3.82
Youth inf's SD	1.18	1.09	1.10	1.17	1.14
Youth inf's N	701	566	518	749	1267
Sp's real age M	45.43	28.64	43.00	34.73	38.04

The overall averages all lie fairly close to 3.5. As for LOCAL USUALNESS, we notice that a majority of adult ratings have values of 4 or more, whereas a majority of youth ratings have 3 or less. The difference in overall ratings between adult and youths is clearly significant (***; t=6.43). In the judgment of GENERAL USUALNESS on the other hand, the majority of both informant groups' ratings have 4 or more. The adults give almost exactly the same overall average rating in both comparisons, indicating that to them there is little difference in USUALNESS between "your part of England" and "England as a whole". The youths on the other hand give a notably higher overall average in the GENERAL USUALNESS table, notably lower for LOCAL USUALNESS.

Keeping in mind that the present subdivision of the informants is not conducive to establishing strong facts about USUALNESS, I would still like to make the following rather tentative suggestions: The overall average figure to stand out most markedly from the rest, the youth figure in the LOCAL table, 3.21 (SD 1.56), could be explained (1) as a result of a certain bias in the regional distribution of informants. REGIONALITY in this investigation is based upon London as the linguistic epicentre having the regional coefficient 1, other areas having higher coefficients roughly proportional to their distance from London. The scale thus obtained goes from 1 to 6. On this scale, the adult informants have 3.24 (SD 1.90), and the youths 3.98 (SD 1.85), which means that the youth informants on average are based significantly (***; t=3.48) farther away from London than are the adults; (2) the figure might also be explained as an exponent of dialect solidarity, i.e. a tendency among young people to mark group solidarity by adopting non-standard features in their speech (cf Labov 1963). It would seem natural if people who adhered to a solidarity principle in their close environment (i.e. LOCAL USUALNESS) also felt that the antithesis of their own dialect, i.e. a neutral, standard-like type of speech of the kind that is represented by definition by the speakers of this sample, is not as usual in their close environment as in their, say, national environment.

Up to now we have been dealing with overall averages. If instead we look into the ratings given of the four non-combinatory subgroups, we notice that in the LOCAL USUALNESS table, both adults and youths give their highest rating to TRADITIONAL and their lowest to MODERN. The difference is clearly significant in the youth assessment (***; t=3.40), but not in the adult assessment (t=1.74). If there had been a strong South-Eastern bias in the informant groups, this would have made up a natural explanation of this problem (provided there is a coupling between the South-East and TRADITIONAL). However, as we have just noted, no such bias exists. Instead we might suggest that a standard-type accent, even if it is alien to a given informant is still more widely heard than any one non-standard accent with the exception of that of the informant himself. In addition, a standard-type accent will naturally be heard in all parts of the country, in the media, and in such environments as traditionally require a standard accent.

In the GENERAL USUALNESS table, as we have already noted, adults give very much the same overall rating as in the LOCAL USUALNESS TABLE. The youth informants on the other hand give a considerably higher overall figure here, a figure almost identical to that of the adults. This is not surprising. It goes to show that the youth informants associate a neutral type of accent not with a certain part of England, but with England as a whole. This is not to say that they consider these accents to be spoken by more people. The question was phrased "heard very often" and no doubt a neutral accent *is* heard often all over the country, not only in the media, but in various situations in which non-standard accents are considered undesirable. Discussing "RP", Trudgill & Hannah (1982:9) suggest that this accent is "used natively by only 3 per cent to 5 per cent of the population of England". Although this does not sound terribly impressive, it must be remembered (cf Wells 1982:297ff) that what is known as "RP" or "Near-RP" is spoken by people who are either considered in some way important and/or whose jobs have a strong oral inclination, which would seem to enhance its subjectively felt usualness. Moreover, if we expand the "RP" concept to mean any basically non-dialectal, non-regional form of British English, we end up with an even greater number of speakers (I will return to the "RP" concept and related problems in greater detail in the section entitled "Regionality and degree of modernity").

We have seen that in the LOCAL USUALNESS table TRADITIONAL was rated highest both by adults and youths, and suggested that this could be explained as a result of a neutral accent normally being the second choice after the informant's own accent. (It is only in the youth assessment that TRADITIONAL is significantly higher than other categories.)

In the GENERAL USUALNESS comparison, the picture is more blurred: the adult informants give their highest rating, 3.90 (SD 1.11) to YOUNG, while the youth informants give theirs, 3.91 (SD 1.10) to TRADITONAL. Before we go any deeper into this, we must be aware that differences between ratings are very small in this table, but that the two top ratings just quoted actually do stand out somewhat. In terms of statistical significance, there is a significant difference between the adult ratings of OLD and YOUNG (*; t=2.30), and between the youth ratings of TRADITIONAL and MODERN (*; t=2.13). Now, why should the adult informants think that YOUNG is heard more often in England as a whole than the other three subgroups? And similarly, why should the youth informants think that TRADITIONAL is heard more often?

One possible explanation has to do with conventionalism. A conventional view would be to upgrade an accent with standard features at the expense of a more non-standard accent, according to principles like the ones we have just been discussing. Another explanation could have to do with expectation, so that informants would tend to expect a high occurrence of standard accents, simply because the prestige attached to the standard might lead informants to believe that it is more widely used than it is.

As for the adult upgrading of YOUNG, we must first remember that the real average age of the adult informants is 33.4, an age not so much higher than that of YOUNG (28.64). In other words, there might be a case of attraction to one's own age group here. I would judge it as more likely, though, that the adult informants for obvious reasons have more experience of life in general, and so their ratings are less conventional, less coloured by expectation. They are more aware that standard-type accents are not spoken by as many people as one might be led to believe, and that certain traits diverging from the traditional norm are getting more and more frequent. The circumstance that many of the adult informants are teachers would also seem to lend probability to the supposition that the adult informants as a group are more aware of such linguistic novelties as are present in pupils.

An interesting detail in this connection is the difference in SD values between the LOCAL and the GENERAL table. SD values are considerably higher in the LOCAL than in the GENERAL comparison. I have suggested earlier on that SD values could be looked upon as markers of group vacillation, so that a group with high SD values would be more vacillating, as a group, than one with lower values. Of course this is a simplification since Standard Deviation really is a marker of the extent to which the individual items in a series of items diverge from the mean. I think a case could be made for interpreting SD values based on informant judgments not only as modifiers of the power of the mean, but also as indicators of group certitude or vacillation.

In this particular case, if my interpretation of SD values is acceptable, both adult and youth informants are less vacillating in their judgment on GENERAL USUALNESS than in that on LOCAL USUALNESS. This can be explained in the following way: Most people are aware of the existence of standard or near-standard accents. They are also aware of dialectal variation. This awareness is easier to handle if it is based on a general situation, since such a situation will probably not involve the informants themselves to a very great extent. A small-scale situation, in which the person himself is involved, will force him to think in terms of personal experience, which will of course vary considerably from person to person.

Paradoxically, in the GENERAL USUALNESS table, adult and youth informants, when low SD values would suggest that they were more certain, give different judgments from one another. The adults seem as a group to be "certain" that YOUNG is the most usual accent, whereas the youth informants go for TRADTIONAL. One explanation of this, which I have hinted at already, could be found in the circumstance that a majority of the tests were carried out in schools, an environment in which youth informants (=pupils) are subjected to some degree of dialectal imperialism, whereas adult informants (=teachers) being exposed to the language of a large number of students all the time, might tend to notice accent development and accent change.

Local usualness	SPEAKER VOICE CATEGORY Combinatory subgroups				
	OLD/MOD	OLD/TRAD	YOUNG/MOD	YOUNG/TRAD	ALL SPEAKERS
Adult inf's M	3.43	*3.82*	*3.74*	*4.12*	*3.72*
Adult inf's SD	1.47	1.53	1.52	1.30	1.50
Adult inf's N	114	184	206	34	538
Youth inf's M	3.15	*3.36*	*3.04*	*3.44*	*3.21*
Youth inf's SD	1.48	1.55	1.56	1.69	1.56
Youth inf's N	299	407	455	117	1278
Sp's real age M	45.00	45.75	27.89	32.00	38.04

Gen. usualness	SPEAKER VOICE CATEGORY Combinatory subgroups				
	OLD/MOD	OLD/TRAD	YOUNG/MOD	YOUNG/TRAD	ALL SPEAKERS
Adult inf's M	3.57	3.75	3.90	3.91	3.78
Adult inf's SD	1.32	1.18	1.14	0.91	1.19
Adult inf's N	112	184	205	33	534
Youth inf's M	3.73	3.90	3.78	3.94	3.82
Youth inf's SD	1.23	1.14	1.12	0.94	1.14
Youth inf's N	299	402	450	116	1267
Sp's real age M	45.00	45.75	27.89	32.00	38.04

Combinatory subgroups do not yield a lot of new information. Rating levels are pretty much the same as in the non-combinatory comparison. In the LOCAL USUALNESS assessment, YOUNG/TRADITIONAL occupies the top position both among adults and youths, in the adult judgment primarily at the expense of OLD/MODERN, in the youth judgment at the expense of YOUNG/MODERN. Even though differences are small, we might speculate that informants are more particular in judging LOCAL USUALNESS subgroups that are close to the informants themselves, whereas subgroups that exhibit neutrality traits are more easily accepted.

As for the GENERAL USUALNESS comparison, the clearest tendency is a certain downgrading of OLD/MODERN, primarily among the adults, the youths giving a weaker reflection of the adults' ratings.

To sum up, the most interesting thing to come out of the LOCAL USUALNESS table is the significantly higher ratings given by the adults than by the youths. This holds throughout. I have already given a number of tentative explanations for this phenomenon, such as an uneven regional distribution of informants. In the GENERAL USUALNESS table, on the other hand, there is very little difference between adults and youths, and, as we have seen, the ratings lie close to the non-committal 3.5.

2.8. Advantage in job interview.

Hypotheses: The question forming the basis of the following discussion was worded: "Do you think the speaker's accent would be a disadvantage or an advantage for him/her in a job interview with an employer?" Answers were given along the same kind of six-step scale as before. This is of course a more specific way of determining whether informants believe accents are socio-economically important. It is well known from a large number of studies with a sociological inclination that informants tend to be overcautious when having to include themselves in the object under scrutiny. It would seem that the present question is well suited to throw light on the general issue, whether people actually think that accents matter and whether there is a change going on from, say, greater to smaller importance being attached to accents. I would hypothesize such a change taking place, showing itself in greater equality between voice categories in the youth assessment than in the adult assessment.

Some criticism could be (and in some of the test sessions actually was) levelled at the fact that I have not specified the type of job or location of job intended in the way that Giles *et al.* (1981) do in asking informants to place the voices along a scale of job labels with *cleaner* at the one extreme and *foreman* at the other. As this question is only one in a battery of many, and as time would not allow any further extension of the test procedure, I decided not to elaborate this point. The informants were not supplied with any additional information, apart from the question as it is phrased here.

Job interview	SPEAKER VOICE CATEGORY Non-combinatory subgroups				
	OLD	YOUNG	TRADITIONAL	MODERN	ALL SPEAKERS
Adult inf's M	4.79	4.41	4.94	4.40	4.62
Adult inf's SD	1.14	1.12	1.05	1.16	1.15
Adult inf's N	296	239	215	320	535
Youth inf's M	4.72	4.24	4.91	4.22	4.50
Youth inf's SD	1.21	1.34	1.05	1.36	1.29
Youth inf's N	706	568	520	754	1274
Sp's real age M	45.43	28.64	43.00	34.73	38.04

Discussion. We first notice that the general level of rating is high for these accents, adults 4.62 (SD 1.15) and youths 4.50 (SD 1.29). We also notice that the difference in overall ratings between adults and youths is small (t=1.86).

If we look at individual non-combinatory subgroups, we can see that there is a striking similarity between the youth and adult ratings of OLD and TRADITIONAL. Both adults and youths clearly give TRADITIONAL their highest average rating, OLD coming in second. In other words, both adults and youths seem to be of the opinion that it is important how you speak, their judgment being clearly in favour of a traditional type of language. Of course, this is not to say that the informants are content with this state of affairs, but the fact that there is virtually no difference between adults and youths goes to show that we are dealing with what seems to be a very stable situation.

YOUNG and MODERN get higher adult than youth ratings, but the difference is significant for MODERN only (*; t=2.07). This would seem to contradict our hypothesis which suggested that youths are more egalitarian in these matters than adults. The adults on the contrary present a less diversified picture than the youths. A few comments must be made about this. First, as we have already noted, the average age of the adult informants is 33.4 and of the youths 17.5, which means that the adults are closer in terms of average age to YOUNG and MODERN than are the youths. Second, there is as usual the aspect of conventionalism to consider, the youths having displayed more conventional views in many of our comparisons up to now. Third, SD values indicate that the greatest degree of group vacillation can be found in the youth ratings of YOUNG and MODERN, which means that both conventionalism and egalitarianism may be present in the youth ratings.

Job interview	SPEAKER VOICE CATEGORY Combinatory subgroups				
	OLD/MOD	OLD/TRAD	YOUNG/MOD	YOUNG/TRAD	ALL SPEAKERS
Adult inf's M	4.41	5.03	4.40	4.45	4.62
Adult inf's SD	1.19	1.04	1.15	0.97	1.15
Adult inf's N	114	182	206	33	535
Youth inf's M	4.37	4.98	4.13	4.68	4.50
Youth inf's SD	1.32	1.04	1.38	1.04	1.29
Youth inf's N	301	405	453	115	1274
Sp's real age M	45.00	45.75	27.89	32.00	38.04

We turn to the combinatory subgroups for further information. Here we get what seems to be a very clear difference between adults and youths: the adults place their ratings at two very distinct levels, a higher level with OLD/TRADITIONAL only (5.03) and a lower level with the remaining subgroups, which lie within 0.05 points from one another. The youths, on the other hand, place their ratings at *four* distinct levels (distinct in the sense that they are all significantly different from one another). Thus we have as number one, OLD/TRADITIONAL, placed at a level virtually identical to that of the adults (4.98); as number two, YOUNG/TRADITIONAL (4.68), higher, but not significantly so (t=1.14), than the adult rating, again marred by smallness in number of observations; number three, OLD/MODERN (4.37), the same level as the adults; and finally, number four, YOUNG/MODERN, which the youths place markedly lower (4.13) than the adults. In other words, we have a situation where the youths seem to make an all-out conventional judgment in which both AGE and DEGREE OF MODERNITY play a part.

What we are discussing is ADVANTAGE IN JOB INTERVIEW. It may be just possible that what we have got here is an honest opinion on that matter given by people who will soon be in that situation themselves; honest in the sense that they could make the judgment without involving themselves directly. We are not asking for their acceptance of this state of affairs, but merely for what they believe would be appropriate in a real situation.

Likewise, it is just possible that the adults, most of whom are beyond the stage where they have to worry about job interviews, put on exactly that acceptance attitude that the youths avoided. This would turn their answer more into an opinion as to how they think things ought to be, rather than how they really are.

This argument could be explained, at least partly, by the circumstance that the youth informants are all secondary school students, whereas a large number of the adults are teachers. It is a commonplace that students find themselves in a situation where they must adapt to values which they do not necessarily agree to. That is part and parcel of the traditional teacher-student relationship. By the same token, a teacher is in a position of authority when it comes to making value judgments.

2.9. Accent similarity personal/friends.

Hypotheses: The question that the informants were required to answer here was: "Do you think that the speaker's accent is like (1) your own accent? (2) the accents of most of your friends?". The reason for having these two parallel questions is that a too personal approach might lead to faulty or at least slightly twisted answers. It is well known that asking a person general questions about his friends is a safer method of gaining information about himself than asking straight questions, not in the sense that he would be prepared to lie about himself, but rather that he would feel uncomfortable about the generality of the question in connection with the detailed knowledge he has of himself. Therefore, we here use both modes of asking, which among other things will enable us to check whether this procedural assumption is correct. It would seem reasonable to expect ratings to lie close to the non-committal 3.5, since the informants have not been arranged according to REGIONALITY in this section. On the other hand, if there exists a tendency for young people to be less TRADITIONAL in their own language output, this ought to be reflected in their ratings, so that they would tend to uprate MODERN and YOUNG relative to TRADITIONAL and OLD to a higher extent than would adult informants.

Simil. personal	SPEAKER VOICE CATEGORY Non-combinatory subgroups				
	OLD	YOUNG	TRADITIONAL	MODERN	ALL SPEAKERS
Adult inf's M	2.78	2.92	2.94	2.78	2.84
Adult inf's SD	1.49	1.45	1.52	1.44	1.47
Adult inf's N	295	243	215	323	538
Youth inf's M	2.52	2.48	2.70	2.37	2.50
Youth inf's SD	1.42	1.40	1.47	1.36	1.41
Youth inf's N	707	571	521	757	1278
Sp's real age M	45.43	28.64	43.00	34.73	38.04

Simil. friends	SPEAKER VOICE CATEGORY Non-combinatory subgroups				
	OLD	YOUNG	TRADITIONAL	MODERN	ALL SPEAKERS
Adult inf's M	*2.92*	*3.10*	*3.08*	*2.94*	*3.00*
Adult inf's SD	1.40	1.33	1.40	1.35	1.37
Adult inf's N	295	242	215	322	537
Youth inf's M	*2.47*	*2.55*	*2.58*	*2.45*	*2.50*
Youth inf's SD	1.33	1.36	1.38	1.32	1.35
Youth inf's N	704	570	518	756	1274
Sp's real age M	45.43	28.64	43.00	34.73	38.04

From the overall averages in both tables we can deduce that on an average both adults and youths regard the accents they have heard as more different than similar both to their own and to their friends' accents. The adults give a higher overall rating in both comparisons, which is not very surprising. The difference between adults' and youths' ratings is significant with regard to overall ratings, and to all subgroup ratings but the ones concerning OLD/TRADITIONAL in the PERSONAL table.

If we examine the four non-combinatory subgroups we find some interesting phenomena. In the PERSONAL table, both adult and youth informants have placed TRADITIONAL in the top position, in the case of the adults a position shared between TRADITIONAL and YOUNG. The youth informants place MODERN last in this table. The four adult ratings lie within a fairly narrow span, so perhaps no strong claims should be made here; but in the case of the youth informants the span is wider, and interestingly the extremes of the youth ratings are made up of TRADITIONAL and MODERN, but in the opposite order from what was hypothesized, so that TRADITIONAL is looked upon as the accent to sound most like the youth informants' own accents, whereas MODERN is judged as being most different from them. Why is this? It may be necessary to recall at this point the regional status of the informant groups that we are now discussing. The adult informants have an average regional coefficient of 3.24 (SD 1.90) and the youths 3.98 (SD 1.85) on the scale going from 1 (London) to 6 (North). If there is a link between TRADITIONAL and the South-East, a higher regional coefficient, as in the case of the youth informants, would seem to make for a lesser degree of similarity with TRADITIONAL, that is, a tendency contrary to what we get here.

In this context I would like to make some suggestions: (1) a standard-like accent is probably more attractive simply by virtue of its being standard-like. This is probably a case parallel to the tendency among many people to claim that their own accent is less regionally coloured, more standard-like than it actually is, so-called over-reporting (cf Trudgill 1975b:93); (2) I think it is also reasonable for a non-standard speaker if comparing his accent with (a) a more standard-like accent and (b) a less standard-like accent, to feel that his own accent is more like the standard. The reason for this has, I believe, to do with markedness: if you have a choice between two options, neither of which you feel fully comfortable with, you tend to go for the one that is less marked. This is what I think the youth informants may have done here.

The FRIENDS table presents figures that are very similar to those of the PERSONAL table both in terms of magnitude and distribution. The biggest single difference is that the spread within the youth ratings is considerably smaller in the FRIENDS table, a situation mainly brought about by a clearly higher rating of TRADITIONAL in the PERSONAL table. This could be seen as an example of the over-reporting tendency mentioned above: that informants tend to upgrade their own accent in relation to their friends' accents.

Another small difference between the tables is, as we have noted, that the adult ratings are all somewhat higher in the FRIENDS table. If indeed this means anything at all, it seems as if the adults are not as prone to over-reporting as the youths. This might perhaps be seen as a sign of social maturity. On the other hand, the reason why we have both a PERSONAL and a FRIENDS comparison in the first place is, as we have already stated, that the FRIENDS comparison is believed to yield a less doctored set of ratings. In that case, the adults' relatively higher FRIENDS ratings may simply be a result of their feeling uncomfortable when having to adapt to somebody else's overgeneralized mould.

Simil. personal	SPEAKER VOICE CATEGORY Combinatory subgroups				
	OLD/MOD	OLD/TRAD	YOUNG/MOD	YOUNG/TRAD	ALL SPEAKERS
Adult inf's M	_2.69_	2.84	_2.82_	_3.50_	_2.84_
Adult inf's SD	1.46	1.51	1.43	1.48	1.47
Adult inf's N	114	181	209	34	538
Youth inf's M	_2.32_	2.67	_2.40_	_2.83_	_2.50_
Youth inf's SD	1.36	1.45	1.36	1.53	1.41
Youth inf's N	302	405	455	116	1278
Sp's real age M	45.00	45.75	27.89	32.00	38.04

| Simil. friends | SPEAKER VOICE CATEGORY Combinatory subgroups | | | | |
	OLD/MOD	OLD/TRAD	YOUNG/MOD	YOUNG/TRAD	ALL SPEAKERS
Adult inf's M	2.87	_2.95_	_2.99_	_3.79_	_3.00_
Adult inf's SD	1.42	1.39	1.32	1.20	1.37
Adult inf's N	114	181	208	34	537
Youth inf's M	2.41	_2.52_	_2.48_	_2.82_	_2.50_
Youth inf's SD	1.31	1.34	1.33	1.48	1.35
Youth inf's N	301	403	455	115	1274
Sp's real age M	45.00	45.75	27.89	32.00	38.04

Combinatory subgroups are more revealing. If we begin with the adults, it seems that it is the subgroup YOUNG/TRADITIONAL that stands out on its own from the remaining three subgroups. In spite of the smallness in number of observations that we have in the adult ratings of this subgroup, YOUNG/TRADITIONAL manages to distinguish itself significantly from the rest, both in the PERSONAL and the FRIENDS table. The averages given to this subgroup (3.50 PERSONAL; 3.79 FRIENDS) are by far the highest in these tables. The remaining three, OLD/TRADITIONAL, OLD/MODERN, and YOUNG/MODERN cannot be significantly distinguished from one another in the adult assessment.

As for the youths, the same holds true as far as SIMILARITY FRIENDS is concerned, although the differences are not as great as in the adult assessment. In the PERSONAL comparison, however, we do not get as clear a picture. It turns out that this comparison does not reveal anything outside what was shown in the non-combinatory tables, i.e. there is a clearly significant (***; t=4.12) difference between the youth average rating of MODERN (2.37) and that of TRADITIONAL (2.70), but not between OLD and YOUNG.

To sum up, both in the SIMILARITY PERSONAL and SIMILARITY FRIENDS comparisons, adults profess greater accent similarity with our samples, on an average, than do the youths. In all comparisons but one, viz. that on OLD/TRADITIONAL in the PERSONAL table, there is a significant difference between adult and youth averages. There can be no doubt that these figures represent a genuine belief. What the figures do not show, however, is the extent to which this belief is true, i.e. do the informants really sound as similar to or as different from the voice samples as they say they do? It does not seem very surprising that adults believe they are more standard than do youths, from a sociological point of view. As we have already pointed out, there is also a more down-to-earth reason for this difference, namely that the adult informants truly are "less regional", in the sense that on an average they have a lower regional coefficient on the scale we are using in this study.

It should be remembered that we are dealing with low ratings throughout in this comparison. The only average ratings to reach even a non-committal level are the adult ratings of YOUNG/TRADITIONAL in both tables. Incidentally, this subgroup is the one that is closest in terms of average age to the adult informants (33.4 vs. 32.0 years of age). This would seem to point in the direction of peer group identification. Whatever the reason, we have to accept that both the adults and the youths place YOUNG/TRADITIONAL highest, and that the difference in level between adults and youths can be found throughout. We also have to accept that the number of individual observations on which the adult average for YOUNG/TRADITIONAL is based is small, which might cause undesirable effects. On the whole, though, it seems that YOUNG/TRADITIONAL is attractive to our informants when it comes to making SIMILARITY judgments, both on a PERSONAL and a FRIENDS basis. If peer group identification is one possible explanation, another may have to do with markedness. It is possible that YOUNG/TRADITIONAL is felt to be less marked than OLD/TRADITIONAL, in a way which we cannot go into at this point, and that this lack of markedness is more easily connected with one's own accent. This may also be true if we compare YOUNG/TRADITIONAL with the two MODERN-combinations.

It is interesting to notice, however, that the relative upgrading of YOUNG/TRADITIONAL in this context would seem to strengthen the case of "self-hatred", since, as we remember, this subgroup was downgraded on several psychological scales, not least by the adults (cf 2.4 above).

The circumstance that the adults give higher ratings throughout in the FRIENDS table than in the PERSONAL table, something which is not the case for the youths, is a little surprising, as it would seem to indicate that the adults look upon the accents of their friends as being "less dialectal" than their own (the accents of the sample are basically neutral/standard-like). This would go against the grain of the idea of "over-reporting" (Labov, Trudgill), i.e. that people tend to idealize their linguistic behaviour somewhat. On the other hand, this might only be an example of the often asserted test tendency to give more pointed answers in connection with one's friends than with oneself.

2.10. Summarizing remarks.

In this section, we have examined how adult and youth (6th Form students) informants react to the 25 voices of our sample grouped according to AGE and DEGREE OF MODERNITY. DEGREE OF MODERNITY was established by checking how the speakers pronounced a set of words that are in the process of changing.

The informants were asked to guess the speakers' age and regional background; to place the speakers on scales for various psychological or related qualities; to assess the acceptability of the voices in connection with a number of job (or group) labels; to judge the accents for pleasantness, usualness, advantage in a job interview, and similarity to the informant's own or his/her friends' accent. All answers except the conjectures on age and regional background, which were open-ended, were given along six-step scales.

The AGE conjecture is complicated by a tendency to make conservative guesses, i.e. avoid extremes, which in this material caused several speakers to be strongly understated in terms of AGE. Among the interesting findings in the AGE comparison is the adult informants' strong understating of the age of those speakers who were placed in the MODERN subgroup. Although the real average age of these speakers was six years higher than the subgroup made up of the YOUNG speakers of our sample, they were in fact believed to be of the same age. Similarly and even more strikingly, the adults guessed about the same low AGE for OLD/MODERN as for YOUNG/MODERN, although there is a 17-year real age difference between the two. There was also a clear tendency among adults to overstate comparatively the AGE of speakers belonging to the TRADITIONAL group, and to combinatory subgroups containing the element TRADITIONAL. The youth informants' conjectures are less clear-cut and hence more difficult to interpret.

When answering the question on regional background, informants could choose between three answer alternatives, depending on the subjective power of their guess: (1) "I am fairly certain he/she comes from..."; (2) "I should think he/she probably comes from..."; (3) "I have no idea". About 50 percent of both adult and youth informants' answers were given in alternative (2); about 35 percent of the adult answers and 21 percent of youth answers were given in alternative (1); 15 percent of adult answers and 28 percent of youth answers were given in alternative (3). This indicates that people's confidence in their ability to make regional judgments based on accent increases over the years. However the relationship between confidence and real ability cannot be determined from this comparison.

All answers were transformed into regional coefficients according to the principle, the farther from London, the higher the coefficient (max. 6). The only truly significant differences to be found in answer alternatives (1) and (2) are those related to the difference between adults and youths. Youths give lower regional ratings throughout, indicating that they place the voices closer to London, on an average, than the adults. Since the youth informants *themselves* have a higher regional coefficient than the adults (3.98 vs. 3.24), it is not possible to ascribe their lower ratings to egocentricity. Instead it might be the case that they feel more alienated from the standard-type accents of the sample, thus giving lower average ratings.

The variation within the youth informants' conjectures is very small, both within alternative (1) and (2). There is a general difference between youths' alternative (1) conjectures and their alternative (2) conjectures in that the level is higher in (2), that is, those youth informants who said they were more confident had a stronger London tendency in their answers than those who professed less confidence.

In the answers given by the adult informants, there is a tendency both in answer alternative (1) and (2) to give more London weight to the OLD and TRADITIONAL subgroups, less to the YOUNG and MODERN subgroups, which can partly, but not entirely, be said to reflect the real average regional spread within the set of subgroups.

The informants were also asked to suggest what they thought the speaker might do for a living. This question was also open-ended. Apart from this, it is obviously related to the job label questions later in the questionnaire.

Both youths and adults on an average seem to look upon these voices as being clearly more "professional" than not. This tendency is stronger among the adults, though. Greater linguistic sensitivity and greater social experience were suggested as possible, although by no means obvious, explanations of this difference between adults and youths.

In terms of the internal profile of ratings, youth informants seem to attach the most weight to the AGE component: relatively old speakers get more "professional", relatively young less "professional" youth ratings. In the adult assessment, it is only the combinatory subgroup OLD/TRADITIONAL that gets a clearly outstanding average rating; all other combinations are fairly equal. I offered a tentative explanation to the effect that youths may associate age and authority to a greater extent than adults, and that this could be a natural consequence of the typical school situation. I also suggested that the wider social and linguistic experience of adults might make for greater powers of linguistic distinction.

The psychological and related qualities dealt with in the next part of the section could be divided up into two categories: (1) socially and (2) individually significant qualities:

(1)	LEADERSHIP	(2)	INTELLIGENCE
	DEPENDABILITY		SELF CONFIDENCE
	HONESTY		AMBITION
	SENSE OF HUMOUR		DETERMINATION
	FRIENDLINESS		-----
			EDUCATION

Among the individually significant qualities could be found EDUCATION, which, although it is not a quality proper, was entered here for convenience. It is also the only item in these lists that can be checked against a real value within the framework of this study.

Our voices get relatively high average ratings for all qualities except LEADERSHIP and SENSE OF HUMOUR. In the case of LEADERSHIP I have suggested that the relatively low rating may be due to the fact that a majority of the speakers are women.

Adults make clearer distinctions between (1) socially and individually significant qualities, and (2) the voice categories TRADITIONAL and MODERN, than do the youths, in the sense that they tend to upgrade TRADITIONAL in the individually significant qualities, apart from SENSE OF HUMOUR, whereas the youth informants seem to take less notice of the difference between OLD and TRADITIONAL, giving both high and relatively equal ratings. One exception here is the quality FRIENDLINESS where, admittedly, TRADITIONAL gets the highest rating, but where YOUNG comes in second, although the differences are small.

From studying combinatory subgroups (OLD/MODERN, OLD/ TRADITIONAL, YOUNG/MODERN, YOUNG/TRADITIONAL), I have proposed that there may be a new phenomenon to take into consideration, viz. harmony or lack of harmony between AGE and DEGREE OF MODERNITY (cf Aboud et al. 1974). This is something which is most noticeable in the adult informants, particularly so in their ratings for LEADERSHIP, DEPENDABILITY, INTELLIGENCE, SELF-CONFIDENCE, AMBITION and DETERMINATION. Here, such combinatory subgroups as do not exhibit age-language harmony (i.e. OLD/MODERN and YOUNG/TRADITIONAL) were downgraded. This is the most remarkable feature of the adult assessment. In connection with SENSE OF HUMOUR, HONESTY and FRIENDLINESS, the adults present a very flat distribution of ratings, which might be attributed to the circumstance that these three qualities are the most closely personal among the socially significant qualities.

I have argued (1) that adults, as a result of greater maturity and life experience, have a greater mastery of linguistic niceties; (2) that the youth informants make more conventional judgments, based upon linguistic and authority-based stereotype. The expected tendency towards a more egalitarian view among youth informants that was hypothesized has not been found in this section.

In the next part of the section, informants were required to assess the acceptability of the voices with regard to the following job (or group) labels: TEACHER OF ENGLISH, ACTOR/ACTRESS, GROCER'S ASSISTANT, BBC NEWS-READER, DISC JOCKEY, BARRISTER, ROCK SINGER, GOVERNMENT OFFICIAL, WORKINGMAN/-WOMAN, FELLOW WORKER/STUDENT, CHILD/BROTHER/SISTER. Answers were given along six-step scales.

In the following table, the *overall* averages of adults and youths are taken up, that is to say, there is no subdivision into different speaker categories.

	TEACH	ACT	GROC	BBC	DJ	BARR	ROCK	GOVT	WORK	FELL	CHILD
A,Y≈same		A 4.07 Y 4.02		A 3.80 Y 3.78	A 2.80 Y 2.72	A 3.72 Y 3.66			A 3.49 Y 3.54		
A higher	A 4.49 Y 4.33 t=2.15						A 4.35 Y 3.95 t=5.03			A 4.21 Y 3.44 t=9.28	
Y lower			A 3.52 Y 3.20 t=3.74			A 2.49 Y 2.32 t=2.31					A 3.59 Y 2.82 t=8.89

Overall average ratings (all speakers) by adult (A) and youth (Y) informants, concerning acceptability of sample accents in TEACHER OF ENGLISH, ACTOR/ACTRESS, GROCER'S ASSISTANT, BBC NEWSREADER, DISC JOCKEY, BARRISTER, ROCK SINGER, GOVERNMENT OFFICIAL, WORKINGMAN/-WOMAN, FELLOW WORKER/STUDENT, CHILD/BROTHER/SISTER. The terms "higher" and "lower" are used to indicate upward or downward deviation from the "non-committal" 3.5 of the six-step scale used here. No values yielding "Y higher" or "A lower" were obtained.

The first thing we notice is that in all cases but one, adults have given higher averages than youths, which would seem to indicate that the general level of acceptance towards these accents is higher among adults. However, we must take into consideration that the ratings forming the basis of these averages were made along six-step scales, which means that in terms of interpretation, a higher average which is placed at the favourable end of the scale should be looked upon as clearly favourable; this is the situation for adults' ratings of TEACHER OF ENGLISH,

191

GOVERNMENT OFFICIAL and FELLOW WORKER/STUDENT. A higher average placed at the lower end of the scale, however, such as the adult rating of GROCER'S ASSISTANT, should rather be looked upon as less unfavourable, i.e. expressing more tolerance.

Secondly, for five of the eleven job (or group) labels, there is no significant difference in level (t<1.96) between adults and youths. Interestingly, among these five labels, we find the three correctness archetypes of our set of job labels, viz. ACTOR/ACTRESS, BBC NEWSREADER, and BARRISTER, which get positive averages throughout. There we also find DISC JOCKEY, a label for which adults and youths agree to place the sample voices at the same low level; and WORKINGMAN/-WOMAN, which ends up in the "non-committal" middle of the scale, possibly because of the semantic inexactitude of that label.

In three cases, adults have given higher overall ratings than youths, at the same time as the latter have stayed closer to the non-committal 3.5, viz. in the case of TEACHER OF ENGLISH, GOVERNMENT OFFICIAL, FELLOW WORKER/STUDENT. These three have a further feature in common: they are the labels that receive the highest adult ratings of all. Youths too rate the sample voices high with regard to these three labels, with the exception of FELLOW WORKER/STUDENT. A possible explanation of this tendency is that TEACHER OF ENGLISH and GOVERNMENT OFFICIAL are less of correctness archetypes, in the sense that they are not looked upon as "ideals", and that this might cause informants to be more liberal in their allotting high ratings to them. In other words, it does not demand as much of an accent to be acceptable in, say, a TEACHER context as in a BARRISTER context.

Finally, we have the three cases where youths have given lower average ratings than adults, the adults having stayed closer to 3.5. They are GROCER'S ASSISTANT, ROCK SINGER and CHILD/BROTHER/ SISTER.

Now we are going to look at subgroup ratings for the eleven job (group) labels, in order to see what are the most conspicuous tendencies with regard to each label.

TEACHER OF ENGLISH: both adults and youths upgrade OLD/ TRADITIONAL and downgrade OLD/MODERN. An interesting difference between adults and youths is that adults rate YOUNG/MODERN significantly higher (**) than do the youths.

ACTOR/ACTRESS: both adults and youths upgrade OLD/TRADITIONAL.

GROCER'S ASSISTANT: adults downgrade OLD/TRADITIONAL. Youths downgrade OLD in general. The only clear upward tendency is the adult upgrading of YOUNG/TRADITIONAL.

BBC NEWSREADER: both adults and youths upgrade OLD/ TRADITIONAL. Youths downgrade YOUNG/MODERN. The greatest difference between adult and youth ratings is that concerning OLD/MODERN, where adults give a significantly lower (*) rating than the youths.

DISC JOCKEY: adults downgrade OLD. Youths maintain a low level throughout, particularly so in connection with OLD/MODERN.

BARRISTER: adults upgrade OLD/TRADITIONAL and downgrade OLD/MODERN. Youths upgrade OLD/TRADITIONAL and downgrade YOUNG/MODERN.

ROCK SINGER: adults give low ratings throughout, particularly of OLD/TRADITIONAL. The main distinction is between OLD and YOUNG, but there is a significant difference (***) between OLD/MODERN and OLD/TRADITIONAL. Youths also give low ratings. They distinguish clearly between OLD and YOUNG.

GOVERNMENT OFFICIAL: adults upgrade OLD/TRADITIONAL. Youths upgrade OLD/TRADITIONAL and downgrade YOUNG/MODERN.

WORKINGMAN/-WOMAN: both adults and youths upgrade YOUNG/MODERN and downgrade OLD/TRADITIONAL.

FELLOW WORKER/STUDENT: both adults and youths upgrade YOUNG, youths more markedly so. There is a very clear difference (***) between adults and youths in every subgroup rating, to the effect that adults give higher ratings.

CHILD/BROTHER/SISTER: adults give a flat, close-to-average profile of ratings with a weak tendency to upgrade YOUNG/TRADITIONAL. Youths distinguish between OLD and YOUNG by downgrading OLD particularly much. Youths are significantly (***) lower in their average ratings of every subgroup than are the adults.

In order to make for a better overview, I shall now present adult and youth ranking-lists for each job (group) label, i.e. indicate which got the highest average rating, second highest, and so on. I will disregard, for the time being, the fact that certain differences are far too small to be looked upon as differences in themselves; in conjunction with other differences going the same way, however, even small differences must be said to contribute to establishing a tendency.

TEACHER OF ENGLISH
Adults: (1) OLD/TRAD (2) YOUNG/TRAD (3) YOUNG/MOD (4) OLD/MOD
Youths: (1) OLD/TRAD (2) YOUNG/TRAD (3) OLD/MOD (4) YOUNG/MOD

ACTOR/ACTRESS
Adults: (1) OLD/TRAD (2) YOUNG/TRAD (3) YOUNG/MOD (4) OLD/MOD
Youths: (1) OLD/TRAD (2) YOUNG/TRAD (3) OLD/MOD (4) YOUNG/MOD

GROCER'S ASSISTANT
Adults: (1) YOUNG/TRAD (2) OLD/MOD (3) YOUNG/MOD (4) OLD/TRAD
Youths: (1) YOUNG/MOD (2) YOUNG/TRAD (3/4) OLD/TRAD OLD/MOD

BBC NEWSREADER
Adults: (1) OLD/TRAD (2) YOUNG/TRAD (3) YOUNG/MOD (4) OLD/MOD
Youths: (1) OLD/TRAD (2) YOUNG/TRAD (3) OLD/MOD (4) YOUNG/MOD

DISC JOCKEY
Adults: (1) YOUNG/TRAD (2) YOUNG/MOD (3) OLD/TRAD (4) OLD/MOD
Youths: (1) YOUNG/TRAD (2) YOUNG/MOD (3) OLD/TRAD (4) OLD/MOD

BARRISTER
Adults: (1) OLD/TRAD (2) YOUNG/TRAD (3) YOUNG/MOD (4) OLD/MOD
Youths: (2) OLD/TRAD (2) OLD/MOD (3) YOUNG/TRAD (4) YOUNG/MOD

ROCK SINGER
Adults: (1) YOUNG/TRAD (2) YOUNG/MOD (3) OLD/MOD (4) OLD/TRAD
Youths: (2) YOUNG/MOD (2) YOUNG/TRAD (3) OLD/TRAD (4) OLD/MOD

GOVERNMENT OFFICIAL
Adults: (1) OLD/TRAD (2) YOUNG/TRAD (3) YOUNG/MOD (4) OLD/MOD
Youths: (1) OLD/TRAD (2/3) OLD/MOD YOUNG/TRAD (4) YOUNG/MOD

WORKINGMAN/-WOMAN
Adults: (1) YOUNG/MOD (2) OLD/MOD (3) YOUNG/TRAD (4) OLD/TRAD
Youths: (1) YOUNG/MOD (2) YOUNG/TRAD (3) OLD/MOD (4) OLD/TRAD

FELLOW WORKER/STUDENT
Adults: (1) YOUNG/TRAD (2) YOUNG/MOD (3) OLD/MOD (4) OLD/TRAD
Youths: (1) YOUNG/MOD (2) YOUNG/TRAD (3) OLD/TRAD (4) OLD/MOD

CHILD/BROTHER/SISTER
Adults: (1) YOUNG/TRAD (2) YOUNG/MOD (3) OLD/MOD (4) OLD/TRAD
Youths: (1) YOUNG/MOD (2) YOUNG/TRAD (3) OLD/TRAD (4) OLD/MOD

There is no doubt that the accents that we have grouped together under the heading OLD/TRADITIONAL do convey socially relevant information both to adult and youth informants. This can be seen in the upgrading of these accents in connection with labels which refer to academic and high-status jobs; and in the corresponding downgrading of them in connection with job labels relating to youth culture, and labels with a more personal touch. In addition to giving higher overall ratings, adults tend to give higher subgroup ratings than youths of OLD/TRADITIONAL in connection with high-status labels. This would seem to indicate that the high-status aspect of certain accent types, even if felt by all, is more strongly felt by adults than by youths.

It is also interesting that in all cases where adults and youths agree as to the top position of OLD/TRADITIONAL, they disagree, in exactly the same way, about the bottom position: adults place OLD/MODERN there, youths YOUNG/MODERN. It may be possible to argue that adults, when making their judgment, go more by purely linguistic factors, as they manage to separate OLD/MODERN and OLD/TRADITIONAL from one another more drastically than do the youths. The youths, on the other hand, may have been more AGE-biassed, in dissociating high-status labels from young age. I have also suggested the possibility of youths being more susceptible to authority considerations based on AGE, and that this can be explained as a result of the traditionally authoritarian school situation, as well as other situations in which non-adults are subjected to the authority of adults.

We also notice that in all the cases with high-status labels, adults rank YOUNG/MODERN higher than do youths. This might seem a little surprising at first, but I have suggested that there may be an element of what is known as "self-hatred" on the part of the youths which could explain this phenomenon; minority groups often develop this type of seemingly counter-intuitive opinion about themselves as a reflection of the way they are (or believe they are) looked upon by the majority.

It is also the case that the adult informants, on an average, are not particularly old: their average age is 33.4, as compared with the 17.5 of the youths. This means that the adults are in fact closer in years to our YOUNG speakers than to our OLD speakers, so there may be an element of peer-group attraction as well, which, in combination with other elements, might cause adults to be more positive towards YOUNG-combinations. In this connection, I have hinted at the possibility of many of my adult informants being particularly prone to linguistic (as well as other kinds of) egalitarianism, because of their age average, which places many of them within reach of the spirit of '68.

Finally, and by no means least likely, there is the element of maturity and the element of conventionalism to consider. It seems reasonable to expect adults to be better equipped when it comes to making fine distinctions between accents, simply because they have had more experience, both from listening to accents, and from learning how to interpret the complex network of social codes involved.

195

Opposed to this stands stereotypical conventionalism, which I have suggested may be more prominent in youths than in adults. This is a methodological drawback in the present study, as it was hypothesized at the outset that linguistic change based on changes in attitude could be detectable in a comparison between adults and youths. Maybe a different age spread among the informants might have brought about a result more in accordance with the original hypothesis.

The two labels which are clearly more personal than the rest, FELLOW WORKER/STUDENT and CHILD/BROTHER/SISTER, both get a sequence of ratings which differs drastically from the high-status labels. In both cases, adults rank YOUNG/TRADITIONAL highest and OLD/TRADITIONAL lowest. Incidentally, this is exactly the same *ranking* as in the ROCK SINGER comparison, although the level differs. It seems that the AGE aspect has been more distinctive than the DEGREE OF MODERNITY aspect here.

The last four questions concerned PLEASANTNESS, USUALNESS, ADVANTAGE IN JOB INTERVIEW, and SIMILARITY, i.e. similarity between the accents of the sample and the accents of the informants and their friends.

Adults on the whole give higher PLEASANTNESS ratings to the accents of the sample than youths (**; t=3.01). In the main, the difference between adults and youths is found in their ratings of MODERN, and more specifically YOUNG/MODERN, where adults give considerably higher ratings than youths. In terms of internal ranking, there is very little difference; the top and bottom position are held by, respectively, OLD/TRADITIONAL and OLD/MODERN, both in the adult and the youth assessment. In other words, we have a ranking for PLEASANTNESS that is reminiscent of the rankings we had for acceptability in high-status professions. This is particularly interesting in view of the fact that we did not get this ranking in the FELLOW WORKER/STUDENT or CHILD/BROTHER/SISTER comparisons. It seems that PLEASANTNESS is one thing, and what you prefer in your near surrounding another. In the one case, we are talking about a detached ideal; in the other about a complex network of considerations, personal and social, which probably defies formalization (cf Trudgill's "overt" and "covert" prestige, Trudgill 1975b).

The fact that the youth informants themselves have a higher regional coefficient, that is more "away-from-London" weight, than the adults, is probably an important reason why they think the accents are heard less often in their part of England than do the adults (***; t=6.43). This could also explain why they rate OLD and particularly TRADITIONAL relatively higher here than do the adults: in a non-standard area, the most widely heard accent apart from that which is normally spoken there is probably a standard-type accent ("the second choice").

When it comes to judging the usualness of the accents in England as a whole, adults and youths present an interesting difference: the adults place YOUNG in the top position, whereas the youths select TRADITIONAL for that position. Linguistic maturity versus linguistic conventionalism is suggested as the probable background to this somewhat surprising phenomenon. I have also hinted at "linguistic imperialism" caused by the school situation (a majority of the tests were carried out in schools) as a possible explanation. A further possibility is the "second choice principle" just mentioned: the youth informants, having a higher regional coefficient, will tend to overrate a standard type accent, since to them it will be the second choice after the vernacular.

If we look at differences between adults and youths with regard to individual subgroups, we first of all notice that there is no significant difference at all in the GENERAL USUALNESS comparison. In the LOCAL USUALNESS comparison, on the other hand, all differences but one are clearly significant. We have already noted that youths give a markedly lower overall average than adults, and argued that the circumstance that the youths themselves on an average live farther away from London is probably a feasible reason for this phenomenon. It is also the case, as we have seen, that in every single subgroup, the youth average rating is lower than the corresponding adult rating. However, this tendency is unduly accentuated in connection with the combinatory subgroup, YOUNG/MODERN. Here, there is a clear youth downrating, even in comparison with the overall difference in level between adults and youths. In other words, youths seem to think that the accents represented by YOUNG/MODERN are less usual in their immediate surrounding than do the adults, and this tendency is stronger than the overall difference between the two informant categories.

This should be compared with the figures we obtained in the discussion on regional background earlier on. It then turns out that the adult informants, who themselves have a regional coefficient of 3.24 (on the 1-to-6 scale with London and the North as extremes), place YOUNG/MODERN very close to themselves in their regional conjecture, giving an average guess of 3.16, as compared with the real YOUNG/MODERN regional average, appr. 3.22. This could be taken as a sign that they feel at home with this particular subgroup. However, there is no strong indication in the LOCAL USUALNESS table that YOUNG/MODERN should be heard more often in the "adult region" than the other three combinatory subgroups. This is something of a paradox, since one might expect a certain amount of concord between LOCAL USUALNESS rating and regional guess, if the regional guess is such that it places the voices in the local region. What the adults are saying about YOUNG/MODERN (on average) is: "It is probably from here, but is not heard so often around here". A possible explanation of this apparent paradox is that the two ways of expressing regionality are not quite parallel. The question on regional background was open-ended, yielding answers that were processed into area codes along our 1-to-6 scale; that is to say, answers such as "Lincoln" and "Birmingham" would get the same code (Midland). Now, answering the question whether a given accent is often heard "in your part of England" (LOCAL USUALNESS) is probably a much more local affair which cannot be satisfactorily represented by our area codes. Since we are dealing with unstable figures here, I shall not attempt to go any further into this.

The youths, on the other hand, who, as we have seen, seem to want to push YOUNG/MODERN away from themselves in the LOCAL USUALNESS table, and to an extent which differs clearly from their treatment of the other three subgroups, show virtually no distinction at all between any of the subgroups in their regional guess. In other words, it seems that the distance between the youth informants themselves and the neutral sample accents creates a situation of linguistic alienation in general terms. The circumstance that YOUNG/MODERN gets a particularly low LOCAL USUALNESS rating, can probably be explained along the following lines: YOUNG/MODERN represents a manner of speaking which is associated with certain modernistic aspirations, but only within certain regional limits. These limits are probably Southern. Outside these limits, deviation from the traditional standard takes on a different shape, becomes "regionally" coloured. A young person from the North who for social reasons wants to maintain a certain amount of non-standardness in his/her speech, will not go for the same non-standardness as a young Southerner in a similar situation. In other words, the present figures do not suggest that a new type of standard, with less obvious class connotations, is emerging at a national level. In fact, it turns out that the youth informants place subgroups which contain TRADITIONAL considerably farther from London on the LOCAL USUALNESS scale than subgroups which do not. I have suggested that what we might have here is a "principle of second choice", i.e. a tendency for speakers of non-standard varieties to give relatively high LOCAL USUALNESS ratings of neutral accents, owing to the fact that a neutral accent is probably the second choice, after the local idiom. This tendency is probably particularly strong in people subjected to education, since the language of education is most of the time more "standard" than not.

When asked whether the accents would be a disadvantage or an advantage in a job interview, adults gave a higher overall rating than youths, the essence of which was that youths downrated YOUNG and MODERN, and more specifically, the combinatory subgroup YOUNG/MODERN, for which there is a significant difference (*; t=2.45) between adults and youths. In the adult judgment, one subgroup only stands out from the rest, viz. OLD/TRADITIONAL. The youths, on the other hand, place the four combinatory subgroups at four significantly distinct levels, with the two TRADITIONAL-combinations at the top, the bottom position being held by YOUNG/MODERN. I have suggested that what we have here is either a more conventional judgment on the part of the youths; or a reflection of the circumstance that the youth informants are themselves more closely and personally involved in the business of job interviews, and that they are therefore more likely to go for what they believe is appropriate. The adults are perhaps more "objective" in giving a judgment which they do not have to worry about in relation to themselves.

Informants were also asked to state whether they thought that the accents were (1) like their own accent, and (2) like the accents of most of their friends. Since the youth informants have a higher regional coefficient, i.e. higher "away-from-London" weight, than the adults, they would be expected to rate these neutral accents lower on both counts. And indeed, this is what happens. Both in the adult and youth assessment, YOUNG/TRADITIONAL is the one combinatory subgroup to stand out positively from the rest, more notably so in the adult judgment. I have suggested two possible explanations of this: (1) particularly in the case of the adults, there might be an element of peer group identification, as YOUNG/ TRADITIONAL is very close in terms of real age to the adult informants; (2) YOUNG/TRADITIONAL may be felt to be less marked than OLD/TRADITIONAL, which in turn might add to its attractiveness in this personally oriented question.

An interesting difference between adult and youth informants can be seen in connection with OLD/TRADITIONAL. Here, adults give a higher rating for FRIENDS than for PERSONAL (2.95 vs. 2.84), whereas the youths act the other way round, giving 2.67 for PERSONAL and 2.52 for FRIENDS. If we assume that in actual fact there is very little difference between one's own accent and that of most of one's friends, which seems reasonable, it is interesting that the same type of stimuli should bring about differently slanted responses in adults and youths. It seems that the adults want to play down whatever it is that makes OLD/TRADITIONAL special in connection with themselves, as compared with their friends, whereas the youths seem to be over-reporting. Sociolinguistic maturity on the part of the adults and conventionalism on the part of the youths are suggested as possible reasons for this.

3. Sex and degree of modernity.

Up to now, our informants have been divided into two categories according to age; we have had an adult group and a youth group. In this section, we shall instead see whether the *sex* variable is in any way related to attitudes to accents of the kind we have been discussing. We shall therefore divide the informants into a male and a female group.

> P.M. Smith (1985, ch 1 & 2) criticizes sociolinguists for using the sex variable as a convenient method of categorization without explaining why they do so, and when they do, for not paying sufficient attention to intra-sex variation. He also suggests that whereas sociolinguists are highly preoccupied with the groups created by sex categorization, they know very little about the principles governing categorization as such.
>
> As for the present project, the reason for using the sex variable at all is partly one of convenience, membership in a sex category being easy for informants to state without a cumbersome interpretational apparatus. It is also the case (cf Labov quotation below) that sex differences in language can be considered interesting from the point of view of language change, women and men traditionally having different responsibilities with regard to the upbringing of children. Furthermore, this project is based upon the principle of viewing the same material from different aspects, the sex aspect being one only. I admit, however, that convenience did play an important part in the selection of variables for this presentation (I had quite a few to choose from). As for Smith's concern about the principles governing categorization, I tend to agree, but again, any researcher has to choose his anchor-point, or else he would be forever wandering the quagmires of indecision.

In order to make for an interesting set of comparisons, a corresponding change will also be made in speaker subgroups, that is to say, there is going to be a MALE and a FEMALE subgroup. However, since it is necessary to maintain a certain "objective" aspect of linguistic significance, these two sexually based subgroups will be linked up with the subdivision of voices according to DEGREE OF MODERNITY that we have used in our previous discussion. This means that there will also be a TRADITIONAL and a MODERN subgroup, i.e. a different categorization of the same speakers.

Most of the time, my discussion will deal with combinatory subgroups, i.e. MALE/MODERN, MALE/TRADITIONAL, FEMALE/MODERN, FEMALE/ TRADITIONAL, and the ratings given of these four subgroups by male and female informants, respectively, with regard to the questions in my material.

In the adult-youth discussion, there were a great many interesting contrasts, although sometimes of a kind that I had not expected, in that youths often took on what seemed to be a more traditional view than adults. This multitude of contrasts yielded a fairly thorough discussion, which is only natural in view of the fact that age differentiation can be looked upon as being highly related to language change.

The question now is: should we expect equally marked contrasts in a comparison based on the two sexes? On the face of it, there seems to be no reason why we should, as women and men would seem to be subjected to very similar types of influence, generally speaking (cf Kramer 1978). However, there are several studies, some of them classic, suggesting that women "[---] consistently produce linguistic forms which more closely approach those of the standard language or have higher prestige than those produced by men [---]" (Trudgill 1975b:89). Labov writes: "[---] it is obvious that this behaviour of women must play an important part in the mechanism of linguistic change. [---] women [...] have a more direct influence during the years when children are forming linguistic rules [...]" (Labov 1972:302f). According to Coates (1986:139), Labov has since "modified his views, and now argues that change is precipitated by linguistic differences between the sexes rather than being associated with one particular sex." Unfortunately, Coates does not offer any formal reference to this in her book.

Trudgill (1986:35) referring to his Norwich research writes:

> [---] even people who were born and brought up in Norwich and who otherwise have perfect local accents do not correctly master [certain distinctions in the Norwich dialect] *if their parents come from somewhere else* [---]. (In some cases, it seems to be necessary for only the mother to have had a non-Norwich accent for the distinction not to be mastered.)

This might of course be interpreted as an empirically-based suggestion that mothers are more influential than fathers with regard to their children's linguistic development. However, Trudgill informs me (personal communication) that the number of informants on which the statement about mothers was based was too small for any real conclusions to be drawn, but that in the Norwich material, there was at any rate no counter-evidence to such a suggestion.

In a project based on his own American (Upper Midwest) linguistic atlas, Allen

(1986) notices a clear tendency among women as compared with men to "accept spelling as a pronunciation guide, to replace old-fashioned spellings with newer ones, and to prefer what is considered standard" (Allen 1986:24).

Kerswill (1987) noted that Durham boys tended to use more vernacular forms than Durham girls.

Labov (1966:489ff) reports that the general "linguistic self hatred" among the New York working class and their attitudinal upgrading of middle-class speech are particularly accentuated among his female informants.

Kramarae (1982) suggests several social explanations of the standard quality of female speech, e.g. the traditional job market for women being more linked up with "proper" linguistic behaviour (teaching, secretarial work), or accommodation theory, according to which "[---] members of subordinate power groups desiring recognition or acknowledging subordination for the purposes of interaction [---]" (Kramarae 1982:98) have to be more adaptable (cf also Trudgill 1974:94). There is also some evidence (Kramer 1977) that women do perceive greater speech differences between the sexes than men.

P.M. Smith (1985:77ff) takes a more cautious stand, warning against over-interpreting scanty evididence (his presentation, although stylistically heavy, is in general very enlightening).

> The idea of females showing a greater tendency towards *conformity* than males is one which has been discussed at great length by psychologists, and which has also found support in several empirical studies (Sistrunk & McDavid 1971:200 and list of references). That this idea is part of a greater, less clearcut complex is however indicated in an empirical study by Sistrunk & McDavid (1971). They show that the degree to which males *and* females conform is dependent on "a number of interrelated determinants, among which are both characteristics of the person and the task he is performing." (p. 206). Thus, females were found to conform more than males on "masculine items", i.e. matters of masculine interest, whereas males conformed more than females on "feminine items". On "[sex-]neutral items", there was no difference.

On the other hand, there are indications that women, particularly in their casual speech, use more advanced forms than men. Certain segmental analyses carried out by Labov and his colleagues (see e.g. Labov 1972:301) have shown that women may lie a whole generation ahead of men in terms of linguistic change. So the problem is twofold: women are said to (1) adapt more closely to the prescribed variety, and (2) be linguistically more advanced. At first sight, it may be difficult to see how the two could be reconciled. However, they both seem to stem from linguistic sensitivity, which might then be the overall quality we are looking for. In our discussion on acceptability in CHILD/BROTHER/SISTER below (pp. 236ff), we shall go more into detail regarding these matters.

For convenience, I shall use as an overall hypothesis in the male-female discussion, that there will be no male-female differences in attitude to my 25 voice specimens.

Partly because there is probably some degree of truth (cf Aronovitch 1976) in this hypothesis (which would seem to argue for analytical brevity), partly because of the circumstance that the reader will by now be familiar with the type of considerations underlying my discussion, I intend to proceed more summarily, less step-by-step, in this section than in the previous one.

One factor which should be kept in mind during the following discussion is the imbalance in number between MALE (N=9) and FEMALE (N=16) speakers. The reason for this imbalance is that in order to avoid circularity, I decided early on not to manipulate the speaker material, which means that with no further doctoring, I use throughout the 25 speakers who volunteered to make recordings. This is not to say that my speakers form a random sample. Far from it. But I have at least tried to minimize such negative sampling effects as might originate in my own interfering with the speaker material.

On the part of the informants, there is better balance: males N=197 (53.24 percent); females N=173 (46.76 percent). Such balance between male and female informants is not always present in sociolinguistic research: Coates (1986:41ff) criticizes dialectologists for their tendency to base far-reaching conclusions on male evidence only.

In brief, then, the following pages will contain a discussion of male and female informants' attitudes towards the accents of MALE and FEMALE speakers, subdivided according to DEGREE OF MODERNITY.

3.1. Overall averages.

Let us first take a look at overall averages to see to what extent our general hypothesis holds true, i.e. that there is no difference between male and female informants' ratings. In doing this, we must of course keep in mind that there may be differences between ratings of individual subgroups, even though the overall averages are equal, and that it is such differences that are linguistically interesting. Checking overall averages gives us a general indication of levels and differences only.

A difference significant at the five per cent level (t≥1.96) will be regarded as a genuine difference.

For the first set of questions, concerning the conjectural age, regional background and occupation of the speakers, there are no significant differences between male and female answers. These particular questions differ from the rest in that they require open-ended answers, whereas the remaining questions are answered along six-step scales.

The second group of questions, the six-step scales on, basically, psychological qualities (LEADERSHIP, DEPENDABILITY, HONESTY, SENSE OF HUMOUR, FRIENDLINESS, INTELLIGENCE, SELF-CONFIDENCE, AMBITION, DETERMINATION, EDUCATION), i.e. to what extent the informants believe the speakers possess them, are more diverse. An interesting observation that we can make straight away is that in all ten comparisons, the female informants give higher overall ratings than the males. This tendency was also found by O'Connell & Rotter (1979) in an experiment on age and sex stereotyping. However, it is only in three of the present comparisons that the difference is significant, viz. DEPENDABILITY, FRIENDLINESS and INTELLIGENCE (***; t=3.61, 4.10, 3.91, respectively). I think that what we have here is a reflection of the male-female distribution among the speakers, i.e. that there are more FEMALE than MALE speakers. Why the three qualities DEPENDABILITY, FRIENDLINESS and INTELLIGENCE give rise to particularly great differences is hard to say at this point. Maybe they represent qualities that are felt to be independent of a stereotypically male outlook, which in turn would enable female informants to upgrade the FEMALE speakers without having to put them in a male context. This is of course less than obvious, but it is undoubtedly intriguing that these three qualities should yield differences that are significant at the 0.1 per cent level, while the remaining differences were not at all significant.

Then follow 11 job labels (group labels): TEACHER OF ENGLISH, ACTOR, GROCER'S ASSISTANT, BBC NEWSREADER, DISC JOCKEY, BARRISTER, ROCK SINGER, GOVERNMENT OFFICIAL, WORKINGMAN, FELLOW WORKER/STUDENT, CHILD/BROTHER/SISTER. The informants were required to state, along a six-step scale, to what extent they thought that the accents would be acceptable in somebody holding the position in question.

Again, the female informants give higher overall average ratings virtually throughout (in 10 out of 11 comparisons). The exception is GOVERNMENT OFFICIAL, but here, the difference is so small as to be negligible. In most of the cases the difference between male and female answers is non-significant, but in the following cases, we get significant differences: TEACHER OF ENGLISH (*; t=2.37), ROCK SINGER (*; t=1.99), WORKINGMAN/-WOMAN (***; t=5.46). As for the very clear male/female difference with regard to WORKINGMAN, it is hard to offer a satisfactory explanation. We have already noted that the label as such is not a good one, as many informants were uncertain about the meaning of it (cf p. 76f). On the other hand, ought not this uncertainty, and any ensuing deficiency of judgment, be distributed equally over males and females alike? I do not believe there is any chance of finding an answer in overall averages, but perhaps an analysis of subgroups will throw further light on the problem.

Finally, there were the questions on PLEASANTNESS, LOCAL/GENERAL USUALNESS, ADVANTAGE IN JOB INTERVIEW and SIMILARITY PERSONAL/FRIENDS (see pp. 77ff for an explanation of these). In all of these, the female informants gave higher ratings than the males (there were in all six six-step questions to be answered). Three male-female differences were significant, viz. PLEASANTNESS (**; t=2.96), GENERAL USUALNESS (**; t=3.13) and ADVANTAGE IN JOB INTERVIEW (**; t=3.24). Thus, there seems to be a certain tendency among female informants for various reasons to attach greater importance to standard-type accents of the kind that the present sample is made up of, as they judge them as being more pleasant, more usual generally, and more advantageous in a job interview than do the male informants. This would seem to fit into the established tradition (Labov, Trudgill and others) discussed above.

Before we go on to look at subgroups, we must remind ourselves that what we have done just now, i.e. studied overall averages, does not yield very much information about language and language change, unless we can be sure that our accent specimens belong to one homogeneous group; in such a case, we might make certain predictions about male-female attitudes to that group.

In the previous section, where the informants were grouped according to age, one complication was the difference in regional background between adult and youth informants. In the present section, because of male and female informants being spread more equally over the investigation places, this would seem to be a less serious problem (the regional coefficient of the male informants is 3.68; of the female informants 3.98; 1-to-6 scale where 1 represents "London" and 6 "North").

We must also keep in mind that the maturity factor, which I claimed played an important part in the previous section, cannot be included in the present discussion other than marginally (male informants: average age 23.4; female informants: 20.7). Here we are primarily dealing with the male-female division. In the case of maturity, we should not expect as great differences between males and females as between adults and youths and this expectation is as we remember accentuated in our general hypothesis: that there are no differences.

3.2. Age conjecture.

Age guess	SPEAKER VOICE CATEGORY Non-combinatory subgroups				
	FEMALE	MALE	TRADITIONAL	MODERN	ALL SPEAKERS
Female inf's M	27.86	32.21	31.48	27.74	29.27
Female inf's SD	7.25	8.39	7.97	7.48	7.89
Female inf's N	544	259	328	475	803
Male inf's M	27.75	32.68	30.93	28.29	29.38
Male inf's SD	7.50	8.90	7.97	8.39	8.32
Male inf's N	611	303	373	536	914
Real age	36.25	41.22	43.00	34.73	38.04
Exp. age guess	28.50	30.38	31.06	27.92	29.18

Age guess	SPEAKER VOICE CATEGORY Combinatory subgroups				
	FEMALE/MOD	FEMALE/TRAD	MALE/MOD	MALE/TRAD	ALL SPEAKERS
Female inf's M	26.41	29.84	30.32	35.32	29.27
Female inf's SD	6.75	7.45	8.15	7.86	7.89
Female inf's N	314	230	161	98	803
Male inf's M	26.45	29.24	31.17	36.05	29.38
Male inf's SD	7.52	7.21	8.89	7.99	8.32
Male inf's N	327	284	209	94	914
Real age	33.2	41.33	37.80	45.50	38.04
Exp. age guess	27.34	30.43	29.08	32.01	29.18

We have already noted that there is no significant difference in overall average AGE conjectures between male and female informants. This turns out to be true about all the individual subgroups as well. This means that the male-female division of informants is of no consequence in this particular comparison (cf Aronovitch 1976) which makes a great difference from the results we had in the AGE comparison. This goes to show that differentiation in perceived AGE is not an effect of sex of informant, but rather of age attraction. We can therefore go on to check how the ratings have been distributed across the subgroups. While doing this, we must remember the effects of conservative guessing (cf p. 98), which will necessitate a certain amount of adjustment of the apparent relationship between real AGE and perceived AGE in order for the comparison to make sense.

The following table is a condensed version of the "combinatory" table above. It shows the relationship between real average AGE, expected conjecture (which is a value based on linear regression analysis, cf p. 100), male conjecture and female conjecture, with regard to the four combinatory voice subgroups:

	MALE/TRAD	FEMALE/TRAD	MALE/MOD	FEMALE/MOD
Real average AGE	45.50	41.33	37.80	33.20
Expected conjecture*)	32.01	30.43	29.08	27.34
Male average conjecture	36.05	29.24	31.17	26.45
Female average conjecture	35.32	29.84	30.32	26.41

*) Based on linear regression analysis of informants' conjectures. r (all speakers)=0.52 (p.100)

I believe that the only claim that can be made on the basis of this table is that there is (or seems to be) a certain tendency among male and female informants alike to give a higher than expected AGE conjecture of MALE/TRADITIONAL. Apart from this, we seem to get average conjectures the levels of which we should expect, on the condition that it is at all possible to make accurate AGE guesses from voice stimuli alone, which seems to be the case, judging by the present results and by several earlier investigations, e.g. Ptacek & Sander (1966), Ryan & Capadano (1978).

Now we might ask: why should MALE/TRADITIONAL be the sole subgroup to be subjected to treatment deviating from the expected pattern? First of all, there is evidence (cf Helfrich 1979) that whereas the male voice decreases in mean fundamental frequency from young through (upper) middle age, the female voice does not present any such systematic changes. This means that there may simply be more physiologically based AGE markers in MALE/TRADITIONAL, since this subgroup has a higher real average AGE than the other groups; similarly, it may be difficult to find such distinctive AGE markers in female speech. In other words, men may be more liable to exhibit higher-AGE speech traits than women. MALE/TRADITIONAL is the only combinatory subgroup which yields what seems to be a clear difference between expected guess and real guess. However, we notice that even though differences are too small for any strong statements to be made, it so happens that both FEMALE-combinations are in fact understated in terms of AGE guess, whereas MALE/MODERN is overstated, although not as much as MALE/TRADITIONAL.

What we seem to have here is a situation in which that (whatever it is) which is conveyed by TRADITIONAL has an AGE-raising effect in males (i.e. attitudes to male voices), but not in females. Maybe this is a phenomenon parallel to one discussed by Elyan et al (1978), concerning the alleged masculinity of non-standard speech (cf Trudgill 1974): this masculinity is said not to be present in *female* non-standard speech. Similarly, it is possible that certain aspects of standardness (if indeed that is what TRADITIONAL stands for) are male-oriented, in this case, perhaps, age authority, etc.

3.3. Regional conjecture.

Area HP	SPEAKER VOICE CATEGORY Non-combinatory subgroups				
	FEMALE	MALE	TRADITIONAL	MODERN	ALL SPEAKERS
Female inf's M	2.53	1.89	2.17	2.42	2.32
Female inf's SD	1.55	1.32	1.28	1.63	1.50
Female inf's N	90	45	54	81	135
Male inf's M	2.50	1.73	2.19	2.29	2.25
Male inf's SD	1.54	1.00	1.26	1.56	1.43
Male inf's N	211	105	139	177	316

Area LP	SPEAKER VOICE CATEGORY Non-combinatory subgroups				
	FEMALE	MALE	TRADITIONAL	MODERN	ALL SPEAKERS
Female inf's M	2.87	_2.06_	2.50	2.67	2.60
Female inf's SD	1.68	1.20	1.54	1.61	1.58
Female inf's N	297	144	177	264	441
Male inf's M	2.79	_2.62_	2.68	2.78	2.74
Male inf's SD	1.64	1.62	1.56	1.68	1.63
Male inf's N	321	159	192	288	480

Area ZP	SPEAKER VOICE CATEGORY Non-combinatory subgroups				
	FEMALE	MALE	TRADITIONAL	MODERN	ALL SPEAKERS
Female inf's M	- -	- -	- -	- -	- -
Female inf's SD	- -	- -	- -	- -	- -
Female inf's N	177	88	114	151	265
Male inf's M	- -	- -	- -	- -	- -
Male inf's SD	- -	- -	- -	- -	- -
Male inf's N	122	57	68	111	179

Area HP	SPEAKER VOICE CATEGORY Combinatory subgroups				
	FEMALE/MOD	FEMALE/TRAD	MALE/MOD	MALE/TRAD	ALL SPEAKERS
Female inf's M	2.56	2.48	2.05	1.74	2.32
Female inf's SD	1.65	1.36	1.56	1.05	1.50
Female inf's N	59	31	22	23	135
Male inf's M	2.56	2.43	1.75	1.71	2.25
Male inf's SD	1.66	1.39	1.17	0.73	1.43
Male inf's N	117	94	60	45	316

Area LP	SPEAKER VOICE CATEGORY Combinatory subgroups				
	FEMALE/MOD	FEMALE/TRAD	MALE/MOD	MALE/TRAD	ALL SPEAKERS
Female inf's M	2.98	2.69	*2.05*	2.09	2.60
Female inf's SD	1.70	1.64	1.19	1.21	1.58
Female inf's N	176	121	88	56	441
Male inf's M	2.82	2.76	*2.71*	2.45	2.74
Male inf's SD	1.67	1.60	1.69	1.46	1.63
Male inf's N	182	139	106	53	480

Area ZP	SPEAKER VOICE CATEGORY Combinatory subgroups				
	FEMALE/MOD	FEMALE/TRAD	MALE/MOD	MALE/TRAD	ALL SPEAKERS
Female inf's M	- -	- -	- -	- -	- -
Female inf's SD	- -	- -	- -	- -	- -
Female inf's N	96	81	55	33	265
Male inf's M	- -	- -	- -	- -	- -
Male inf's SD	- -	- -	- -	- -	- -
Male inf's N	68	54	43	14	179

The regional guess is divided into three optional levels according to how certain the informants were when making the guess: AREA HIGH POWER, AREA LOW POWER, AREA ZERO POWER (cf p. 70). In connection with this division, we can make an interesting observation, more to do with psychology than language, viz. the extent to which males and females chose to answer in AREA HIGH POWER, AREA LOW POWER and AREA ZERO POWER, in relation to the total number of male and female informants (N=370). 53.24 percent of the informants are male and 46.76 percent female. It turns out that 70.07 percent of the answers given in AREA HIGH POWER were male (i.e. considerably more than caused by their number alone); 52.12 percent of AREA LOW POWER answers were male (i.e. the split is just proportional); 40.32 percent of AREA ZERO POWER answers were male (i.e. fewer than their number would motivate). In other words, males seem to be more willing than females to profess certitude. Deaux (1976:342) writes: "One of the most pervasive findings in the literature on sex differences is the lower expectations which females hold for their performance as compared to males." Similar ideas are put forward by Widmark (1980). However, there is no evidence that AREA HIGH POWER answers, male or female, have a higher degree of correctness (regional conjectures can be checked against reality) than AREA LOW POWER answers. If anything, they are worse, which would seem to lend some weight to the prevalent notion that region of speaker is hard to establish from a British standard-like accent.

Now, the one interesting male-female difference in the regional conjecture occurs in connection with AREA LOW POWER ratings regarding MALE versus FEMALE speakers. Here, female informants give a significantly lower (***; t=3.63) rating of MALE than do male informants (low rating—close to London; high rating—far from London). Also, the female rating of MALE is significantly lower (***; t=5.18) than the female rating of FEMALE, a state of affairs which is not present in the male rating. In plain English, this seems to indicate that to the female informants, the MALE voices exhibit more London weight than do the the FEMALE voices; and in addition, this tendency cannot be found in the male ratings (in the AREA HIGH POWER comparisons, however, there is a similar London weighting of MALE both among male and female informants). The question is why this should be.

Let us first look at the real regional coefficients of the speaker and informant groups under scrutiny. As for the speakers, there is a certain difference in regionality to the effect that FEMALE has a higher (i.e. farther from London) regional mean than MALE (MALE 2.78, SD 1.62; FEMALE 3.38, SD 1.80). On the part of the informants there is a similar type of regional differentiation: males have the regional coefficient 3.68, females 3.98.

What we might have here is another instance of the "rebound" effect (cf p. 108), that is to say, a tendency for informants living farther from London to push standard-type accents away from themselves in the direction of London, to a greater extent than informants living nearer to London. The female informants are on an average based farther from London than the males, and they do place MALE (the speaker subgroup genuinely to be based closest to London) closer to London (and farther away from themselves) than do males.

Male informants on the other hand have about the same regional coefficient as the speaker group FEMALE, which might cause them to treat FEMALE more in accordance with a regionally based peer-group principle, that is, to accept FEMALE as being reasonably similar to their own accents, thereby keeping it somewhat closer to themselves.

Let me suggest, tentatively, that there is a blend of rebound and peer-group attraction in the female rating of MALE and FEMALE, so that the circumstance that the female informants on an average are based farther from London causes an alienating effect in their response to standard-type accents, and that, in addition, this effect may be enhanced in the case of MALE, a subgroup which might be felt to represent more strongly the power stereotype that stems from London as the sociopolitical (and thus male) epicentre of England; whereas in the case of FEMALE, this alienation may be hampered by peer-group (sex-group) solidarity.

The male informants on the other hand, by being male themselves, and by having a lower (i.e. closer to London) regional coefficient than the females, may simply associate the MALE accents more with themselves, and thereby avoid a push towards London in their regional conjecture.

The fact that the SD value for the female rating of MALE is markedly lower (1.20) than the corresponding value for any other rating of non-combinatory subgroups (1.68, 1.64, 1.62) in this comparison might be said to support this suggestion: it seems reasonable that stereotyping makes for greater unanimity than guided speculation, as witness several language attitude experiments (cf Introduction).

The complexity of REGIONALITY is of a kind that makes firm, statistically sound judgment virtually impossible. Even though it is necessary for practical reasons to adopt a numerical system to represent REGIONALITY in order for it to be computable and in order for comparisons between regions to be possible, we must always remember that the kind of average-based discussion that we are leading here is dangerously simplistic, in that it treats as homogeneous groups individuals who may be highly different from a factual point of view without making this difference explicit. Interpretational caution is imperative.

3.4. Occupational conjecture.

Occupation	SPEAKER VOICE CATEGORY Non-combinatory subgroups				
	FEMALE	MALE	TRADITIONAL	MODERN	ALL SPEAKERS
Female inf's M	2.59	2.24	2.33	2.57	2.46
Female inf's SD	0.68	0.89	0.71	0.83	0.78
Female inf's N	400	233	284	349	633
Male inf's M	2.58	2.34	2.32	2.60	2.48
Male inf's SD	0.79	1.00	0.71	0.98	0.88
Male inf's N	446	290	312	424	736

Occupation	SPEAKER VOICE CATEGORY Combinatory subgroups				
	FEMALE/MOD	FEMALE/TRAD	MALE/MOD	MALE/TRAD	ALL SPEAKERS
Female inf's M	2.71	2.46	2.35	2.09	2.46
Female inf's SD	0.71	0.62	0.94	0.80	0.78
Female inf's N	214	186	135	98	633
Male inf's M	2.68	2.46	2.51	2.02	2.48
Male inf's SD	0.86	0.69	1.10	0.65	0.88
Male inf's N	235	211	189	101	736

Informants were asked to guess what they thought the speakers did for a living. The question was open-ended, i.e. it required a full answer in writing. The answers obtained were transformed into numerical values according to the system used in this study to group people socio-economically. The scale goes from 1 (professional) to 6 (unskilled). Such answers as would not fit into this system (e.g. "housewife", "student") were discarded from the analysis.

We have already seen that in terms of overall averages, there was no difference between male and female ratings, which means that any subgroup differences that do occur are particularly interesting.

This is the way male and female informants rank the four combinatory subgroups with regard to OCCUPATION, starting from the "professional" end of the scale (average ratings are given in brackets):

```
OCCUPATIONAL RANKING
Male average ratings           Female average ratings
(1) MALE/TRAD (2.02)           (1) MALE/TRAD (2.09)
(2) FEMALE/TRAD (2.46)*)       (2) MALE/MOD (2.35)**)
(3) MALE/MOD (2.51)*) ***)     (3) FEMALE/TRAD (2.45)**)
(4) FEMALE/MOD (2.68)***)      (4) FEMALE/MOD (2.71)

*) Ratings cannot be statistically distinguished at the five per cent
level (t=0.55).
**) Ratings cannot be statistically distinguished at the five per cent
level (t=1.26).
***) Ratings cannot be statistically distinguished at the five per cent
level (t=1.79).
```

The first thing we should notice is that there is very little difference indeed between male and female ratings of the respective subgroups. At no point is the difference significant (t≤1.37). There is however a difference in ranking order which, although it is less than significant, calls for some discussion. The females, in placing MALE/MODERN prior to FEMALE/TRADITIONAL, seem to attach greater occupational importance to SEX than to DEGREE OF MODERNITY. The males on the other hand, present a ranking order in which DEGREE OF MODERNITY seems to have priority over SEX. Within a socio-psychological framework, it is fairly easy to suggest a reason for this difference. Traditionally, the job market used to be an overwhelmingly male affair. Female advancement has often met with resistance and does so still in many areas. For somebody who is in the midst of such a conflict, and on the socially weaker side of it, it is natural to look upon the world in terms of that conflict. On the other hand, somebody who is perhaps not even aware of the magnitude, or indeed existence, of the conflict can probably afford to have a more "objective" world picture. We shall find several opportunities to come back to this type of discussion in the pages to come.

Miller & McReynolds (1973) found that American female listeners rated a male speaker significantly more competent than a female reading the same message. A Swedish replication (Einarsson n.d.) however showed that it was primarily the (Swedish) male listeners who tended to upgrade male speakers for competence.

One cultural factor which might have caused FEMALE-combinations to assume a weaker position than MALE-combinations, even though accent considerations may have pointed in another direction, is of course the open-endedness of the question leading to a traditional choice of jobs to answer it. That is to say, it is simply the case that a vast majority of job labels are looked upon as male. This means that the chance of even finding a typically female job which, in our system of giving numerical values to jobs, would yield, say, 1 ("professional") on the scale is perhaps not terribly great. According to Coates (1986:159), women "constitute less than 10 per cent of those employed in the majority of top professions (architects, barristers, accountants, university professors, top civil servants, etc.)." P.M. Smith (1985:45) claims that most nouns that describe an occupation (e.g. author, plumber, minister) tend to "evoke the image of a man [rather] than of a woman." Thus, there is an obvious risk of ending up in a vicious circle here, something which should be kept in mind. In the light of this, we must perhaps modify our discussion on the ranking somewhat. Maybe the most striking feature among the male ratings is not the relative uprating of FEMALE/ TRADITIONAL, but the downrating of MALE/MODERN (indeed the way the average figures are distributed seems to point in that direction). If so, we may have a situation in which male informants, while being basically untouched by a SEX-structuralist way of thinking, are particularly sensitive to socio-occupational markers in the category to which they themselves would belong. The real average age of the male informants is 23.38, which places them closest to MALE/MODERN (real average age: 37.8), as compared with MALE/TRADITIONAL (real average age: 45.5). The occupational downrating of MALE/MODERN could perhaps therefore be said to contain an element of "self-hatred" (Simpson & Yinger 1972:227; cf p. 120).

It is undoubtedly true that we do get clear distinctions when arranging our voices the way we have done. Now, whether these distinctions are primarily based on SEX, or on DEGREE OF MODERNITY, or indeed on some correlating feature or other is hard to say.

3.5. Psychological qualities.

I shall now examine the ratings by male and female informants with regard to the ten labels concerning psychological qualities and education (cf p. 71f), in order to see in what way the two informant groups distribute their ratings across the four combinatory accent subgroups (FEMALE/MODERN, FEMALE/TRADI-TIONAL, etc.). The discussion will be based on the profile made up of the four average subgroup ratings. The two fundamental aspects here will be *level similarity* (t<1.96) and *level difference* (t≥1.96).

In certain comparisons, it will be impossible to be absolutely consistent with regard to level similarity and level difference, as it sometimes happens that, say, subgroup A is significantly different from subgroup B, but that neither A nor B can be distinguished from subgroup C, etc; or, in the form of an analogy: one football team, say Liverpool, may beat another, say QPR, but this fact does not constitute absolute proof that Liverpool will beat any team that QPR beat. That is the way of life. When these cases occur, I decide on similarity or difference on the basis of which causes the smallest error.

To provide a more detailed reference material, I also include the full tables of comparison of the kind that we had in the previous section. My discussion, however, will be based on level similarity and level difference.

At the outset of the present study (cf p. 72f), I made a suggestion that the ten quality labels could be placed into either of two groups, "socially significant" and "individually significant" labels. An examination of subgroup ratings based on the male-female division gives rise to a more detailed set of groupings, which I shall now go on to discuss.

It turns out that the four labels, LEADERSHIP, AMBITION, SELF-CONFIDENCE, and DETERMINATION are more or less closely related to one another, both in the male and female assessment. Another group is made up of the two labels, INTELLIGENCE and EDUCATION; yet another of HONESTY and FRIENDLINESS; leaving DEPENDABILITY and SENSE OF HUMOUR as odd men out.

SPEAKER VOICE CATEGORY
Leadership — Non-combinatory subgroups

	FEMALE	MALE	TRADITIONAL	MODERN	ALL SPEAKERS
Female inf's M	3.34	4.08	3.77	3.45	3.58
Female inf's SD	1.42	1.42	1.41	1.48	1.46
Female inf's N	570	278	344	504	848
Male inf's M	3.27	3.93	3.68	3.36	3.49
Male inf's SD	1.24	1.40	1.36	1.30	1.33
Male inf's N	650	322	393	579	972

SPEAKER VOICE CATEGORY
Ambition — Non-combinatory subgroups

	FEMALE	MALE	TRADITIONAL	MODERN	ALL SPEAKERS
Female inf's M	3.77	<u>4.53</u>	4.16	3.91	4.02
Female inf's SD	1.30	1.30	1.28	1.39	1.35
Female inf's N	568	274	342	500	842
Male inf's M	3.73	<u>4.31</u>	4.07	3.82	3.92
Male inf's SD	1.23	1.26	1.24	1.27	1.27
Male inf's N	649	318	392	575	967

SPEAKER VOICE CATEGORY
Self-confidence — Non-combinatory subgroups

	FEMALE	MALE	TRADITIONAL	MODERN	ALL SPEAKERS
Female inf's M	3.96	4.54	4.34	4.01	4.14
Female inf's SD	1.46	1.37	1.37	1.49	1.45
Female inf's N	573	276	344	505	849
Male inf's M	3.98	4.38	4.27	4.01	4.11
Male inf's SD	1.31	1.32	1.33	1.31	1.32
Male inf's N	652	322	396	578	974

SPEAKER VOICE CATEGORY
Determination — Non-combinatory subgroups

	FEMALE	MALE	TRADITIONAL	MODERN	ALL SPEAKERS
Female inf's M	3.84	*4.43*	4.16	3.94	4.03
Female inf's SD	1.27	1.21	1.21	1.32	1.28
Female inf's N	569	274	343	500	843
Male inf's M	3.86	*4.14*	4.10	3.85	3.95
Male inf's SD	1.19	1.24	1.17	1.24	1.22
Male inf's N	649	319	393	575	968

SEX AND DEGREE OF MODERNITY

Leadership

SPEAKER VOICE CATEGORY
Combinatory subgroups

	FEMALE/MOD	FEMALE/TRAD	MALE/MOD	MALE/TRAD	ALL SPEAKERS
Female inf's M	3.19	3.50	_4.00_	4.21	3.58
Female inf's SD	1.46	1.33	1.37	1.48	1.46
Female inf's N	338	232	166	112	848
Male inf's M	3.17	3.40	_3.69_	4.40	3.49
Male inf's SD	1.23	1.24	1.34	1.39	1.33
Male inf's N	367	283	212	110	972

Ambition

SPEAKER VOICE CATEGORY
Combinatory subgroups

	FEMALE/MOD	FEMALE/TRAD	MALE/MOD	MALE/TRAD	ALL SPEAKERS
Female inf's M	3.63	3.97	*4.49*	4.58	4.02
Female inf's SD	1.36	1.19	1.26	1.37	1.35
Female inf's N	336	232	164	110	842
Male inf's M	3.64	3.84	*4.11*	4.68	3.92
Male inf's SD	1.27	1.17	1.24	1.24	1.27
Male inf's N	365	284	210	108	967

Self-confidence

SPEAKER VOICE CATEGORY
Combinatory subgroups

	FEMALE/MOD	FEMALE/TRAD	MALE/MOD	MALE/TRAD	ALL SPEAKERS
Female inf's M	3.75	4.25	*4.54*	4.53	4.14
Female inf's SD	1.52	1.31	1.29	1.48	1.45
Female inf's N	340	233	165	111	849
Male inf's M	3.87	4.13	*4.25*	4.64	4.11
Male inf's SD	1.33	1.27	1.23	1.43	1.32
Male inf's N	366	286	212	110	974

Determination

SPEAKER VOICE CATEGORY
Combinatory subgroups

	FEMALE/MOD	FEMALE/TRAD	MALE/MOD	MALE/TRAD	ALL SPEAKERS
Female inf's M	3.70	4.03	_4.43_	4.44	4.03
Female inf's SD	1.35	1.12	1.11	1.35	1.28
Female inf's N	336	233	164	110	843
Male inf's M	3.78	3.96	_3.97_	4.48	3.95
Male inf's SD	1.26	1.10	1.20	1.27	1.22
Male inf's N	365	284	210	109	968

I think it is within the limits of prudence to claim that LEADERSHIP, AMBITION, SELF-CONFIDENCE and DETERMINATION are the labels in this particular selection which stand for stereotypically male virtues (cf Deaux 1976:336; P.M. Smith 1985:108-109). Interestingly, the profiles of ratings for these labels given by the female informants are clearly very much alike. Basically the same, although with slight modifications, goes for the male ratings. In terms of level similarity/difference

216

(cf above), we get the following set-up:

```
LEADERSHIP and AMBITION

Male ratings                    Female ratings
(1) MALE/TRAD                   (1) MALE/TRAD; MALE/MOD
(2) MALE/MOD                    (2) FEMALE/TRAD
(3) FEMALE/TRAD                 (3) FEMALE/MOD
(4) FEMALE/MOD

[A number in brackets, e.g. (1), stands for a level
significantly different from other levels.]
```

```
SELF-CONFIDENCE and DETERMINATION

Male ratings                         Female ratings
(1) MALE/TRAD                        (1) MALE/TRAD; MALE/MOD
(2) MALE/MOD; FEMALE/TRAD            (2) FEMALE/TRAD
(3) FEMALE/MOD*)                     (3) FEMALE/MOD

*) Difference (3)-(2) in DETERMINATION comparison: t≤1.91,
i.e. not significant, but close.
```

It seems that for the female informants, it is the MALE rather than the MODERNITY aspect which determines the highest level, whereas there is a distinction in level between FEMALE/TRADITIONAL and FEMALE/MODERN. This goes for all four labels. The male informants, on the other hand, have a four-level set-up for LEADERSHIP and AMBITION, to the effect that both SEX and DEGREE OF MODERNITY seem to be operative. However, for SELF-CONFIDENCE and DETERMINATION, there is a merger of levels between MALE/MODERN and FEMALE/TRADITIONAL.

A simplified way of explaining what these ranking-lists seem to show would be to say that females very clearly associate accents which they perceive as expressing LEADERSHIP, AMBITION, SELF-CONFIDENCE, DETERMINATION with the male sphere, and that this association is not influenced by a more MODERN or a more TRADITIONAL language output as defined here. If female language production is to fit into whatever it is these four labels stand for, it should, according to the female informants, be more TRADITIONAL than MODERN (cf Elyan *et al*. 1978). The male informants seem to go more by language than by cultural considerations, as they manage to distinguish on the basis of DEGREE OF MODERNITY *within* the categories MALE and FEMALE (LEADERSHIP and AMBITION) and also merge MALE and FEMALE (SELF-CONFIDENCE and DETERMINATION). I would suggest that this is an effect of females being more prone to stereotyping than men in a sex-based voice arrangement, since the undoubtedly strong cultural pressure in favour of male dominance in certain fields is enhanced by the alienation that stems from not being a member of the dominant group (cf Burns 1977). This kind of alienation is not present in the male informants; hence it is only natural if they go more by language as such.

This is what happened to the quality labels that I proposed stood for male stereotypes. Now, let us go on to the next group of labels receiving similar male and similar female treatment.

Intelligence	SPEAKER VOICE CATEGORY Non-combinatory subgroups				
	FEMALE	MALE	TRADITIONAL	MODERN	ALL SPEAKERS
Female inf's M	4.37	4.74	4.64	4.38	4.49
Female inf's SD	1.12	1.13	1.08	1.16	1.14
Female inf's N	567	277	345	499	844
Male inf's M	4.13	4.56	4.47	4.13	4.27
Male inf's SD	1.23	1.21	1.17	1.26	1.24
Male inf's N	649	323	396	576	972

Education	SPEAKER VOICE CATEGORY Non-combinatory subgroups				
	FEMALE	MALE	TRADITIONAL	MODERN	ALL SPEAKERS
Female inf's M	4.39	4.82	4.71	4.40	4.53
Female inf's SD	1.11	1.14	1.05	1.18	1.14
Female inf's N	570	276	345	501	846
Male inf's M	4.30	4.68	4.73	4.22	4.43
Male inf's SD	1.20	1.20	1.10	1.24	1.21
Male inf's N	649	322	395	576	971

Intelligence	SPEAKER VOICE CATEGORY Combinatory subgroups				
	FEMALE/MOD	FEMALE/TRAD	MALE/MOD	MALE/TRAD	ALL SPEAKERS
Female inf's M	4.25	4.53	4.65	4.86	4.49
Female inf's SD	1.15	1.06	1.15	1.10	1.14
Female inf's N	334	233	165	112	844
Male inf's M	3.96	4.34	4.42	4.83	4.27
Male inf's SD	1.27	1.14	1.20	1.17	1.24
Male inf's N	364	285	212	111	972

Education	SPEAKER VOICE CATEGORY Combinatory subgroups				
	FEMALE/MOD	FEMALE/TRAD	MALE/MOD	MALE/TRAD	ALL SPEAKERS
Female inf's M	4.20	4.66	4.81	4.82	4.53
Female inf's SD	1.16	0.98	1.12	1.18	1.14
Female inf's N	337	233	164	112	846
Male inf's M	4.07	4.59	4.48	5.08	4.43
Male inf's SD	1.23	1.09	1.22	1.05	1.21
Male inf's N	364	285	212	110	971

This group is made up of INTELLIGENCE and EDUCATION. On the face of it, it is not very surprising that these two should receive treatment of a similar kind, even though they must be regarded as semantically disparate. This is how male and female informants treated the four combinatory voice subgroups with regard to INTELLIGENCE and EDUCATION (figure in brackets represents distinct level as before):

INTELLIGENCE and EDUCATION

Male ratings
(1) MALE/TRAD
(2) MALE/MOD; FEMALE/TRAD
(3) FEMALE/MOD*)

Female ratings
(1) FEMALE/TRAD; MALE/TRAD; MALE/MOD
(2) FEMALE/MOD*)

*) The female rating of FEMALE/MODERN is significantly higher (**; t=3.15) than the male rating of this subgroup. This comparison deals only with internally distinct levels of rating within male and female ratings, respectively.

.
We notice that the male ratings are distributed in the same way as in the previous comparison, i.e. in a basically male-centred fashion with a merger of MALE/MODERN and FEMALE/TRADITIONAL. The female ratings differ in that FEMALE/TRADITIONAL finishes at about the same level as the two MALE-combinations. In the case of the INTELLIGENCE comparison, this statement should be taken with a grain of salt, as the female rating of MALE/TRADITIONAL is in fact higher than those of FEMALE/TRADITIONAL and MALE/MODERN, even though we do not get statistically significant differences throughout (cf "football team analogy" above p. 214). This means that as far as INTELLIGENCE is concerned, there may not be a great deal of difference between male and female rankings. This possibility will be disregarded in the following discussion.

Even though, in view of prejudice and tradition, there may exist a notional coupling between INTELLIGENCE, EDUCATION and MALE (cf P.M. Smith 1985:151), it would certainly be wrong to regard the two as male stereotypes the way we did the four labels in the previous set of comparisons. And indeed, we do get a different type of response now from the informant group that I suggested was most liable to stereotype in a sex-based comparison, viz. the females. It seems reasonable that we should get less of female stereotyping, more of male/female equivalence, in ratings for the two labels we are now discussing. The apparent male-female difference, i.e. placing or not placing FEMALE/TRADITIONAL at level (1), which, as we have just noted, may not be a very clear difference after all, is probably a phenomenon akin to peer group attraction.

Honesty	SPEAKER VOICE CATEGORY Non-combinatory subgroups				
	FEMALE	MALE	TRADITIONAL	MODERN	ALL SPEAKERS
Female inf's M	4.62	4.35	4.61	4.48	4.53
Female inf's SD	1.00	1.10	1.05	1.03	1.04
Female inf's N	572	277	345	504	849
Male inf's M	4.48	4.36	4.57	4.35	4.44
Male inf's SD	1.02	1.12	1.03	1.07	1.06
Male inf's N	652	322	397	577	974

Friendliness	SPEAKER VOICE CATEGORY Non-combinatory subgroups				
	FEMALE	MALE	TRADITIONAL	MODERN	ALL SPEAKERS
Female inf's M	4.26	3.76	4.13	4.08	4.10
Female inf's SD	1.15	1.18	1.18	1.19	1.19
Female inf's N	575	275	344	506	850
Male inf's M	4.04	3.52	4.01	3.77	3.87
Male inf's SD	1.15	1.22	1.23	1.17	1.20
Male inf's N	653	323	397	579	976

Honesty	SPEAKER VOICE CATEGORY Combinatory subgroups				
	FEMALE/MOD	FEMALE/TRAD	MALE/MOD	MALE/TRAD	ALL SPEAKERS
Female inf's M	4.58	4.68	4.27	4.47	4.53
Female inf's SD	0.97	1.03	1.12	1.07	1.04
Female inf's N	339	233	165	112	849
Male inf's M	4.37	4.62	4.31	4.46	4.44
Male inf's SD	1.05	0.97	1.09	1.16	1.06
Male inf's N	366	286	211	111	974

Friendliness	SPEAKER VOICE CATEGORY Combinatory subgroups				
	FEMALE/MOD	FEMALE/TRAD	MALE/MOD	MALE/TRAD	ALL SPEAKERS
Female inf's M	4.26	4.26	3.72	3.84	4.10
Female inf's SD	1.17	1.13	1.16	1.22	1.19
Female inf's N	341	234	165	110	850
Male inf's M	3.93	4.18	3.51	3.55	3.87
Male inf's SD	1.12	1.18	1.22	1.24	1.20
Male inf's N	366	287	213	110	976

The next pair of labels to be discussed, HONESTY and FRIENDLINESS, is a bit less tidy than the ones we have been dealing with up to now. That is to say, the female ratings of the two labels are very much alike, but in the male ratings there is some deviation. Let us first look at levels:

HONESTY and FRIENDLINESS

Male ratings	Female ratings
(1) FEMALE/TRAD	(1) FEMALE/TRAD; FEMALE/MOD
(2) FEMALE/MOD	(2) MALE/TRAD; MALE/MOD
(MALE/TRAD; MALE/MOD)*)	
(3) (MALE/TRAD; MALE/MOD)*)	

*) In the HONESTY ratings, males place the two MALE-combinations at a level on a par with FEMALE/MODERN, i.e. level (2); in the FRIENDLINESS ratings, the two MALE-combinations make up level (3) on their own.

What strikes us immediately is that both male and female informants place FEMALE-combinations higher than MALE-combinations. As for FRIENDLINESS, this state of affairs is in agreement with the findings of Kramer (1977) and O'Connell & Rotter (1979). The circumstance that FEMALE/MODERN gets higher ratings than both MALE-combinations, by male and female informants alike, seems to be at odds with the findings of Elyan et al. (1978). They write: "RP-accented females in Britain are upgraded in terms of competence and communicative skills but downgraded in terms of social attractiveness and personal integrity relative to regional accented females." True, I have not dealt with the distinction between "RP" and "regional" accents here, but it would seem that the upgrading of FEMALE/TRADITIONAL in this particular comparison shows that a traditional standard-like accent in a female speaker is conducive to social attractiveness, even as compared with less traditional female speakers. Elyan et al. (1978) also found that female listeners tended to polarize their ratings more strongly than male listeners, to the effect that there was a greater difference in terms of female ratings between female RP speakers and female speakers with a Northern accent. In the present comparison, female informants give less polarized ratings of FEMALE than do male informants. (The Giles group has carried out further experiments which modify the original Elyan et al. (1978) study, see Introduction, "Giles and associates 1977-1980: the sexual aspect".)

Of course, it is hard to say to what extent extralinguistic phenomena play a part here. It is possible that what we have is an example of the female friendly speech stereotype (Kramer 1977), in the case of the female informants blended by a certain amount of peer-group attraction. It is interesting that the male informants should be more inclined to make a distinction between FEMALE/MODERN and FEMALE/TRADITIONAL; this would seem in effect to contradict the discussion we had in connection with LEADERSHIP etc above: if FRIENDLINESS (HONESTY?) is a stereotypically female quality, then males would be expected to respond more stereotypically than females, as they are less involved. But they do not seem to. Do women stereotype male accents more than men stereotype female accents? Are men better when it comes to making fine accent distinctions? I would not judge either as particularly likely. Perhaps FRIENDLINESS and HONESTY as conveyed by speech mean one thing between women, another between men, a third between men and women, and so on. Such speculation however goes beyond the scope of the present discussion. Let us leave it at that.

Dependability	SPEAKER VOICE CATEGORY				
	Non-combinatory subgroups				
	FEMALE	MALE	TRADITIONAL	MODERN	ALL SPEAKERS
Female inf's M	4.30	4.27	4.44	4.19	4.29
Female inf's SD	1.09	1.13	1.10	1.10	1.10
Female inf's N	574	275	344	505	849
Male inf's M	4.09	4.12	4.26	3.99	4.10
Male inf's SD	1.10	1.22	1.10	1.16	1.14
Male inf's N	651	321	394	578	972

Sense of humour	SPEAKER VOICE CATEGORY				
	Non-combinatory subgroups				
	FEMALE	MALE	TRADITIONAL	MODERN	ALL SPEAKERS
Female inf's M	3.49	3.37	3.46	3.44	3.45
Female inf's SD	1.27	1.31	1.26	1.30	1.28
Female inf's N	567	276	342	501	843
Male inf's M	3.44	3.18	3.41	3.32	3.36
Male inf's SD	1.23	1.39	1.26	1.31	1.29
Male inf's N	647	322	393	576	969

Dependability	SPEAKER VOICE CATEGORY				
	Combinatory subgroups				
	FEMALE/MOD	FEMALE/TRAD	MALE/MOD	MALE/TRAD	ALL SPEAKERS
Female inf's M	4.24	4.40	4.10	4.51	4.29
Female inf's SD	1.10	1.08	1.10	1.14	1.10
Female inf's N	341	233	164	111	849
Male inf's M	4.00	4.21	3.99	4.39	4.10
Male inf's SD	1.12	1.08	1.23	1.14	1.14
Male inf's N	367	284	211	110	972

Sense of humour	SPEAKER VOICE CATEGORY Combinatory subgroups				
	FEMALE/MOD	FEMALE/TRAD	MALE/MOD	MALE/TRAD	ALL SPEAKERS
Female inf's M	3.47	3.50	3.37	3.37	3.45
Female inf's SD	1.28	1.25	1.33	1.28	1.28
Female inf's N	335	232	166	110	843
Male inf's M	3.42	3.47	3.13	3.28	3.36
Male inf's SD	1.20	1.27	1.46	1.24	1.29
Male inf's N	364	283	212	110	969

We have two quality labels left to discuss, DEPENDABILITY and SENSE OF HUMOUR. These two do not form a pair, nor do they correlate markedly with any of the other eight labels in terms of informant ratings.

As for DEPENDABILITY, male and female informants have parallel profiles of rating. MALE/TRADITIONAL and FEMALE/TRADITIONAL are placed at the top level, MALE/MODERN and FEMALE/MODERN at a slightly lower level. As we noted in our discussion on overall averages above, females have a higher general level in this comparison, most clearly manifested in the ratings of the two FEMALE-combinations, for which there are significant differences between male and female ratings, to the effect that females rate higher, males lower. This is probably a peer-group effect, which it seems reasonable that we should find in a sexually based set of ratings on DEPENDABILITY.

The reader may wonder why we do not get similar rating profiles for DEPENDABILITY and HONESTY, which indeed seem to be semantically related to one another. I cannot explain this, but I would suggest that there is perhaps a greater difference between the two than is apparent: HONESTY is something which stems from the owner of the quality, whereas in the case of DEPENDABILITY, the owner is a recipient of trust, which means that the sentiment of the owner vis-à-vis the listener is not necessarily the same for the two qualities. But again, this does not explain why we get the ratings we get; it merely hints at a possible reason.

According to Kramer (1977) "Sense of humour in speech" is perceived as a typically male characteristic, especially if you ask males. It is therefore interesting that in the present SENSE OF HUMOUR comparison, the only, admittedly weak, tendency is a male downrating of MALE, more specifically MALE/MODERN. Now, this does not necessarily imply a contradiction of Kramer's findings, since she does not discuss listeners' reactions to voices they have actually heard; her study is rather an inventory of what informants believe are male and female speech characteristics, i.e. stereotype *par excellence*.

Apart from this weak tendency, ratings have a rather flat distribution, just under the non-committal 3.5, so it seems that the voice material used here does not give rise to a great deal of sex-differentiating response about SENSE OF HUMOUR.

3.6. Rating of acceptability.

Do men and women differ as to their accepting or not accepting our accents in connection with the eleven job labels used in this study? We have already noted that the female informants place their ratings higher than the males virtually throughout, and that we even get significant overall differences for three of the labels, viz. TEACHER OF ENGLISH, ROCK SINGER, WORKINGMAN/-WOMAN. Now we turn to subgroups instead.

If we look at the eleven job labels (I refer to them as "job labels" for convenience, even though two of them, FELLOW WORKER/STUDENT and CHILD/BROTHER/SISTER, strictly do not fit this description) in terms of statistically distinct levels of rating, the same way we did in the previous discussion, certain groups emerge, which present similarity in the way informants rank their acceptability. Interestingly, it is possible to discern three groups, each containing two job labels, where males and females behave in a certain way with regard to the labels, but where they differ from one another. They are (1) ACTOR/ACTRESS and BBC NEWSREADER ("RP" archetypes); (2) BARRISTER and GOVERNMENT OFFICIAL (professionals); and (3) GROCER'S ASSISTANT and WORKINGMAN/-WOMAN (Working Class). Let us begin by looking at these three groups.

One tendency that is noticeable in all three groups is that male informants seem to be more inclined to distinguish between voice subgroups than females. This is manifested in males placing their mean ratings at three distinct levels, whereas the females place theirs at two. It is also the case that in 7 out of 11 job label comparisons, the numerical distance between the highest and lowest ratings of combinatory subgroups is greater within the male assessment, most of the time markedly so, whereas in 2 out of the 4 comparisons where females have a greater distance between top and bottom ratings, the male-female difference is negligible. It is not altogether easy to adapt these tendencies to either of the two fundamental schools of thought within this field, (1) that there are no male-female differences in evaluative standards (cf Aronovitch 1976); and (2) that females are more discriminating than males (cf Elyan *et al.* 1978, Labov 1972, Trudgill 1974) with regard to standard-type accents (cf also P.M. Smith (1979) for an overview).

Actor

SPEAKER VOICE CATEGORY
Non-combinatory subgroups

	FEMALE	MALE	TRADITIONAL	MODERN	ALL SPEAKERS
Female inf's M	4.02	*4.25*	4.42	3.88	4.10
Female inf's SD	1.52	1.55	1.43	1.56	1.53
Female inf's N	571	279	345	505	850
Male inf's M	4.00	*3.97*	4.37	3.73	3.99
Male inf's SD	1.45	1.60	1.40	1.52	1.50
Male inf's N	654	323	397	580	977

BBC newsreader

SPEAKER VOICE CATEGORY
Non-combinatory subgroups

	FEMALE	MALE	TRADITIONAL	MODERN	ALL SPEAKERS
Female inf's M	3.62	*4.28*	4.36	3.48	3.84
Female inf's SD	1.68	1.58	1.49	1.70	1.67
Female inf's N	575	278	347	506	853
Male inf's M	3.69	*3.84*	4.23	3.40	3.74
Male inf's SD	1.57	1.66	1.54	1.56	1.60
Male inf's N	652	324	397	579	976

Actor

SPEAKER VOICE CATEGORY
Combinatory subgroups

	FEMALE/MOD	FEMALE/TRAD	MALE/MOD	MALE/TRAD	ALL SPEAKERS
Female inf's M	3.71	4.48	*4.22*	4.28	4.10
Female inf's SD	1.54	1.36	1.55	1.57	1.53
Female inf's N	339	232	166	113	850
Male inf's M	3.79	4.26	*3.62*	4.63	3.99
Male inf's SD	1.50	1.35	1.54	1.50	1.50
Male inf's N	367	287	213	110	977

BBC newsreader

SPEAKER VOICE CATEGORY
Combinatory subgroups

	FEMALE/MOD	FEMALE/TRAD	MALE/MOD	MALE/TRAD	ALL SPEAKERS
Female inf's M	3.14	4.32	*4.17*	4.44	3.84
Female inf's SD	1.68	1.41	1.52	1.65	1.67
Female inf's N	341	234	165	113	853
Male inf's M	3.36	4.10	*3.46*	4.58	3.74
Male inf's SD	1.57	1.48	1.53	1.65	1.60
Male inf's N	366	286	213	111	976

The two job labels, ACTOR/ACTRESS and BBC NEWSREADER, make up the first group where male and female informants have responded in a uniform way internally, but different from each other. Ratings were distributed at the following distinct levels:

ACTOR/ACTRESS and BBC NEWSREADER

Male ratings
(1) MALE/TRAD
(2) FEMALE/TRAD
(3) MALE/MOD; FEMALE/MOD

Female ratings
(1) MALE/TRAD; FEMALE/TRAD; MALE/MOD
(2) FEMALE/MOD

It would seem reasonable to expect combinations containing TRADITIONAL to get high ratings and combinations containing MODERN to get low ratings irrespective of sex, since both ACTOR/ACTRESS and BBC NEWSREADER could nowadays be regarded as "unisex" "RP" archetypes. In an American study, Stone (1974) showed that there was no preference for male over female TV newsreaders among a sample of TV viewers. However, as we can see from the table, both male and female informants make certain sexually based distinctions as well. The males distinguish between MALE/TRADITIONAL and FEMALE/TRADITIONAL and the females between MALE/MODERN and FEMALE/MODERN. A somewhat unexpected merger of rating levels is that of MALE/TRADITIONAL, FEMALE/TRADITIONAL and MALE/MODERN in the female assessment. Superficially, it seems that the female informants are less distinguishing, more linguistically egalitarian than the males, in that they allow MALE/MODERN a place at the top level of ratings, together with the two TRADITIONAL-combinations. The males, on the other hand, very clearly equate MALE/MODERN and FEMALE/MODERN in both comparisons.

It is probably the case that both male and female informants exert a certain amount of peer-group promotion in these rankings. From that point of view, we should expect female informants to upgrade, quite realistically it would seem, FEMALE/TRADITIONAL, whereas perhaps this realistic upgrading is more easily forgotten by the males.

The female placing of MALE/MODERN at their top level, together with the two TRADITIONAL-combinations, shows that MALE-ness, probably for traditional reasons, is a strongly decisive factor in the female assessment. We do not find this particular exponent of conventional ranking in the male assessment. Instead, the males, in addition to downgrading MODERN, seem to be carrying out a general downgrading of FEMALE-combinations, relatively speaking, which is also a kind of conventionalism, although differently slanted.

The reason why we get this differentiation between male and female informants' ratings, so that females "generously" upgrade their sexual "adversaries", whereas males take on what seems to be a much less generous attitude towards theirs, in downgrading FEMALE, is probably that this is the way stereotyping works: the closer you are to the matter at issue, the smaller the chance of stereotyping, and vice versa. So men select women and women men for their respective stereotyping activities. Whether we get upgrading or downgrading is determined by the traditional socio-economic forces in society, according to which men are more powerful than women. In this way stereotyping breeds stereotyping. The problem with this interpretation is that it would seem to necessitate a firm association between on the one hand the two job labels under scrutiny, ACTOR/ACTRESS and BBC NEWSREADER, and the idea of maleness on the other, and this association is somehow less than satisfactory from a factual point of view; in neither case would it seem in any way unexpected to have female exponents of these two labels.

Barrister	SPEAKER VOICE CATEGORY Non-combinatory subgroups				
	FEMALE	MALE	TRADITIONAL	MODERN	ALL SPEAKERS
Female inf's M	3.42	4.34	4.20	3.39	3.72
Female inf's SD	1.73	1.66	1.61	1.78	1.76
Female inf's N	570	277	343	504	847
Male inf's M	3.39	4.15	4.06	3.35	3.64
Male inf's SD	1.63	1.64	1.65	1.62	1.67
Male inf's N	650	323	395	578	973

Gov't official	SPEAKER VOICE CATEGORY Non-combinatory subgroups				
	FEMALE	MALE	TRADITIONAL	MODERN	ALL SPEAKERS
Female inf's M	3.78	4.59	4.45	3.78	4.05
Female inf's SD	1.63	1.50	1.47	1.68	1.63
Female inf's N	568	275	339	504	843
Male inf's M	3.87	4.52	4.46	3.83	4.09
Male inf's SD	1.45	1.44	1.38	1.49	1.48
Male inf's N	653	322	397	578	975

Barrister	SPEAKER VOICE CATEGORY Combinatory subgroups				
	FEMALE/MOD	FEMALE/TRAD	MALE/MOD	MALE/TRAD	ALL SPEAKERS
Female inf's M	2.96	*4.08*	*4.26*	*4.45*	3.72
Female inf's SD	1.70	1.54	1.63	1.72	1.76
Female inf's N	339	231	165	112	847
Male inf's M	3.15	*3.71*	*3.71*	*4.99*	3.64
Male inf's SD	1.61	1.61	1.59	1.39	1.67
Male inf's N	365	285	213	110	973

Gov't official	SPEAKER VOICE CATEGORY Combinatory subgroups				
	FEMALE/MOD	FEMALE/TRAD	MALE/MOD	MALE/TRAD	ALL SPEAKERS
Female inf's M	3.43	4.31	4.49	4.74	4.05
Female inf's SD	1.65	1.45	1.50	1.48	1.63
Female inf's N	340	228	164	111	843
Male inf's M	3.66	4.14	4.14	5.27	4.09
Male inf's SD	1.47	1.39	1.49	0.98	1.48
Male inf's N	366	287	212	110	975

Next, we have the group made up of BARRISTER and GOVERNMENT OFFICIAL. I have already suggested that these two job labels together might be referred to as the "professional" group. Here, we get the following levels of rating:

BARRISTER and GOVERNMENT OFFICIAL

Male ratings
(1) MALE/TRAD
(2) FEMALE/TRAD; MALE/MOD
(3) FEMALE/MOD

Female ratings
(1) MALE/TRAD; FEMALE/TRAD; MALE/MOD
(2) FEMALE/MOD

We notice that in terms of levels, female informants have the same arrangement as in the previous comparison. The males, on the other hand, present a slightly modified set-up, in that they have placed MALE/MODERN at the same mid level as FEMALE/TRADITIONAL. I believe it is possible to argue that although BARRISTER and GOVERNMENT OFFICIAL clearly belong to the area of accents normally associated with the "RP" concept, they are not "RP" archetypes, the way that for instance BBC NEWSREADER is such an archetype. This might cause male informants to be more liberal in accepting accents deviating from the archetypical norm. If we accept that, the remaining difference between male and female levels of rating is the female placing of FEMALE/TRADITIONAL at the top level. Probably, this is a peer-group effect on the part of the female informants, as is the male differentiation between MALE/TRADITIONAL and FEMALE/TRADITIONAL.

Grocer's ass.	SPEAKER VOICE CATEGORY Non-combinatory subgroups				
	FEMALE	MALE	TRADITIONAL	MODERN	ALL SPEAKERS
Female inf's M	3.51	2.95	3.07	3.51	3.33
Female inf's SD	1.63	1.66	1.62	1.67	1.66
Female inf's N	571	276	345	502	847
Male inf's M	3.45	2.89	2.96	3.48	3.27
Male inf's SD	1.64	1.68	1.66	1.65	1.67
Male inf's N	650	320	393	577	970

Workingman	SPEAKER VOICE CATEGORY Non-combinatory subgroups				
	FEMALE	MALE	TRADITIONAL	MODERN	ALL SPEAKERS
Female inf's M	*3.91*	3.42	*3.52*	*3.91*	*3.75*
Female inf's SD	1.60	1.61	1.60	1.61	1.62
Female inf's N	564	276	342	498	840
Male inf's M	*3.47*	3.03	*3.02*	*3.54*	*3.33*
Male inf's SD	1.62	1.64	1.61	1.62	1.64
Male inf's N	646	317	392	571	963

Grocer's ass.	SPEAKER VOICE CATEGORY Combinatory subgroups				
	FEMALE/MOD	FEMALE/TRAD	MALE/MOD	MALE/TRAD	ALL SPEAKERS
Female inf's M	3.74	3.19	3.02	2.84	3.33
Female inf's SD	1.63	1.59	1.66	1.67	1.66
Female inf's N	339	232	163	113	847
Male inf's M	3.71	3.12	3.08	2.54	3.27
Male inf's SD	1.58	1.65	1.68	1.61	1.67
Male inf's N	365	285	212	108	970

Workingman	SPEAKER VOICE CATEGORY Combinatory subgroups				
	FEMALE/MOD	FEMALE/TRAD	MALE/MOD	MALE/TRAD	ALL SPEAKERS
Female inf's M	*4.14*	3.57	3.43	*3.41*	*3.75*
Female inf's SD	1.57	1.59	1.60	1.64	1.62
Female inf's N	334	230	164	112	840
Male inf's M	*3.71*	3.17	3.25	*2.61*	*3.33*
Male inf's SD	1.59	1.61	1.64	1.56	1.64
Male inf's N	363	283	208	109	963

Finally we have GROCER'S ASSISTANT and WORKINGMAN/-WOMAN, a group which I have referred to as "Working Class". For this group, levels are distributed in the following way:

```
GROCER'S ASSISTANT and WORKINGMAN/-WOMAN

Male ratings                  Female ratings
(1) FEMALE/MOD                 (1) FEMALE/MOD
(2) FEMALE/TRAD; MALE/MOD      (2) MALE/TRAD; FEMALE/TRAD; MALE/MOD
(3) MALE/TRAD
```

This is, in effect, a reversed version of the rating levels concerning BARRISTER and GOVERNMENT OFFICIAL above. Again we see that male informants distinguish more clearly between voice subgroups than do females. It is of course possible that the female informants are genuinely less concerned with these often testified thesis (Trudgill 1975b, Labov 1972) that women are more conscious of status forms in language. A further possibility, which we have not discussed in this connection, is that there may be a difference between males and females as regards their attitudes to questionnaires. This is something we have touched on briefly earlier (cf p. 209), when we noted that females were less willing than males to profess certitude in regional conjectures. Maybe there is a tendency of this kind in other types of ratings as well, so that female informants are less inclined to accentuate differences which they may very well perceive (Osgood *et al.* 1957:234f, Widmark 1980). There is also the possibility that the questionnaire used in this study, having been constructed by myself, suffers from "androcentricity" (cf Coates 1986:46ff).

The remaining job labels, TEACHER OF ENGLISH, DISC JOCKEY, ROCK SINGER, FELLOW WORKER/STUDENT, CHILD/BROTHER/SISTER, do not fall into groups of the kind that we have been discussing so far, which means that we shall have to discuss them separately.

Teacher of Engl.	SPEAKER VOICE CATEGORY Non-combinatory subgroups				
	FEMALE	MALE	TRADITIONAL	MODERN	ALL SPEAKERS
Female inf's M	4.34	_4.71_	4.95	4.13	_4.46_
Female inf's SD	1.47	1.33	1.18	1.49	1.43
Female inf's N	575	279	347	507	854
Male inf's M	4.31	_4.28_	4.69	4.03	_4.30_
Male inf's SD	1.42	1.52	1.31	1.48	1.45
Male inf's N	652	322	396	578	974

Teacher of Engl.	SPEAKER VOICE CATEGORY Combinatory subgroups				
	FEMALE/MOD	FEMALE/TRAD	MALE/MOD	MALE/TRAD	ALL SPEAKERS
Female inf's M	3.91	4.97	_4.57_	4.90	_4.46_
Female inf's SD	1.50	1.16	1.38	1.23	1.43
Female inf's N	341	234	166	113	854
Male inf's M	4.07	4.62	_3.96_	4.89	_4.30_
Male inf's SD	1.47	1.28	1.50	1.37	1.45
Male inf's N	366	286	212	110	974

We begin by looking at TEACHER OF ENGLISH, for which our informants gave the following levels of rating:

```
TEACHER OF ENGLISH

Male ratings                        Female ratings
(1) FEMALE/TRAD; MALE/TRAD          (1) FEMALE/TRAD; MALE/TRAD
(2) FEMALE MOD; MALE/MOD            (2) MALE/MOD
                                    (3) FEMALE/MOD
```

The only difference in levels between male and female ratings is that females place FEMALE/MODERN at a significantly lower level than MALE/MODERN. Apart from this, we have here what seems to be a reasonably straight case of upgrading TRADITIONAL-combinations at the expense of MODERN-combinations. The reader will remember that most of the test sessions making up the basis of this study were carried out in schools, which would seem to reduce the risk of stereotyping, in that there exists a possibility of checking voices against reality for a great number of informants. This may very well be a reason why TEACHER OF ENGLISH is not treated in a way similar to any other label.

As for the female downgrading of FEMALE/MODERN, we first of all notice that it creates a situation where in fact females do distinguish more clearly between subgroups than do males. In the present job label discussion, this happens only twice: here and in connection with FELLOW WORKER/STUDENT. Now, TEACHER OF ENGLISH and FELLOW WORKER/STUDENT differ from the other job labels in that they are more easily connected with the real life situation of many informants. It is possible, although by no means certain, that the female informants are more willing to differentiate their ratings of such categories as are, at least partly, verifiable on a personal basis.

But the question remains: why is it that the females but not the males afford special treatment to FEMALE/MODERN? In our discussion on BARRISTER and GOVERNMENT OFFICIAL above, I suggested that it would be reasonable to expect informants to be more particular in making judgments that are close to themselves in one way or another. This would apply to females judging FEMALE voices. Now, if there is a downward tendency in terms of attitudes to a given subgroup, it would seem that this tendency would materialize more easily if there is proximity between speaker and listener. This is perhaps part of the reason for the female downgrading of FEMALE/MODERN.

Another possibility has to do with the age distribution among the speakers. In terms of real age, FEMALE/MODERN is on an average younger than MALE/MODERN (33.20 vs. 37.80 years of age). We have also seen that FEMALE/MODERN gets the clearly lowest perceived AGE of the four combinatory subgroups (around 26.5; cf discussion on conservative guesses, pp. 98ff). It is possible that there exists a combination of effects caused by female informants wanting to dissociate

TEACHER from themselves, and effects caused by their being over-particular when judging voices that are close to themselves (cf above). Both these effects could be hampered in the case of the male informants, who do not have to include themselves when judging FEMALE-combinations. The males could in other words disregard things which the females may have been affected by.

On the other hand, if male informants had had the same relative attitude to MALE/MODERN as the females had to FEMALE/MODERN, then it would seem that MALE/MODERN ought to have ended up at the same low level in the male assessment as FEMALE/MODERN did in the female assessment. But as we have seen, this does not happen. The crux of this problem lies in the word "relative" because, as it happens, there is very little difference in absolute figures between these two ratings (3.96 vs. 3.91). The relative difference is created partly by the higher overall level in the female assessment, partly, and most notably, by a female disinclination to downrate MALE/MODERN. It seems therefore that in terms of acceptability in TEACHER OF ENGLISH, females tend to demand more from members of their own sex than do males. This is perhaps one aspect of the often testified idea that women tend to go for the standard more often than men. There may of course also be an element of conventional male-authority thinking in this male-female difference.

Disc jockey	SPEAKER VOICE CATEGORY Non-combinatory subgroups				
	FEMALE	MALE	TRADITIONAL	MODERN	ALL SPEAKERS
Female inf's M	2.77	2.91	2.82	2.81	2.81
Female inf's SD	1.51	1.53	1.50	1.53	1.52
Female inf's N	574	279	345	508	853
Male inf's M	2.74	2.56	2.68	2.68	2.68
Male inf's SD	1.40	1.39	1.41	1.39	1.40
Male inf's N	651	323	395	579	974

Rock singer	SPEAKER VOICE CATEGORY Non-combinatory subgroups				
	FEMALE	MALE	TRADITIONAL	MODERN	ALL SPEAKERS
Female inf's M	2.43	2.50	2.21	2.61	2.45
Female inf's SD	1.48	1.57	1.39	1.57	1.51
Female inf's N	567	276	343	500	843
Male inf's M	2.40	2.13	2.10	2.46	2.31
Male inf's SD	1.48	1.46	1.40	1.51	1.48
Male inf's N	651	322	395	578	973

Disc jockey	SPEAKER VOICE CATEGORY Combinatory subgroups				
	FEMALE/MOD	FEMALE/TRAD	MALE/MOD	MALE/TRAD	ALL SPEAKERS
Female inf's M	2.72	2.84	*3.00*	2.78	2.81
Female inf's SD	1.53	1.47	1.51	1.57	1.52
Female inf's N	342	232	166	113	853
Male inf's M	2.74	2.74	*2.57*	2.53	2.68
Male inf's SD	1.41	1.40	1.37	1.43	1.40
Male inf's N	366	285	213	110	974

Rock singer	SPEAKER VOICE CATEGORY Combinatory subgroups				
	FEMALE/MOD	FEMALE/TRAD	MALE/MOD	MALE/TRAD	ALL SPEAKERS
Female inf's M	2.60	2.17	2.65	2.29	2.45
Female inf's SD	1.57	1.30	1.57	1.56	1.51
Female inf's N	336	231	164	112	843
Male inf's M	2.58	2.19	2.26	1.89	2.31
Male inf's SD	1.50	1.42	1.52	1.32	1.48
Male inf's N	365	286	213	109	973

It may be a little surprising that DISC JOCKEY and ROCK SINGER do not appear as a pair in this set of comparisons. Since they are somehow conceptually related to one another, I shall however discuss them together. This is how they were treated by male and female informants in terms of levels:

DISC JOCKEY	
Male ratings	**Female ratings**
(1) ALL FOUR SUBGROUPS	(1) ALL FOUR SUBGROUPS
- - - - - - - - - -	
ROCK SINGER	
Male ratings	**Female ratings**
(1) FEMALE/MOD	(1) FEMALE/MOD; MALE/MOD
(2) MALE/MOD; FEMALE/TRAD	(2) FEMALE/TRAD; MALE/TRAD
(3) MALE/TRAD	

As we can see, DISC JOCKEY gets the flattest set of mean ratings of all job labels; there are no internal differences that are significant at the 5 per cent level. The closest we get to a significant difference is an upward tendency for MALE/MODERN in the female assessment ($t<1.94$). In the male assessment, there is an interesting, but again not significant ($t=1.89$), difference between ratings of MALE and ratings of FEMALE, to the effect that FEMALE seems to be considered more acceptable in connection with DISC JOCKEY than MALE, regardless of DEGREE OF

MODERNITY.

As for ROCK SINGER, male informants give the same distribution of distinct levels as they did for the two "Working Class" labels (cf above p. 229). The females, on the other hand, present a configuration of levels where it seems that the main influence stems from DEGREE OF MODERNITY, as there are two levels only, separated by the MODERN-TRADITIONAL dividing line.

The circumstance that males have spread their ratings across three levels, as compared with the two levels of the female ratings, does not necessarily mean that their language-based powers of distinction are greater than those of the females; it seems to show, rather, that they take more things into account when making their assessment, things which are, basically, culture-bound. Indeed, if we look at non-combinatory subgroups for a moment, we notice that male informants give a significantly lower (**; t=2.69) ROCK SINGER rating of MALE than of FEMALE. It is far from clear why this should be so. It is probably true to say that the traditional ROCK SINGER stereotype is male rather than female. Now, if that is so, why should male informants make higher acceptability ratings of FEMALE than of MALE, and indeed of FEMALE/MODERN than of MALE/MODERN, and of FEMALE/TRADITIONAL than of MALE/TRADITIONAL in the present ROCK SINGER discussion? Judging by the figures in the ROCK SINGER reference tables above, it is mainly MALE/TRADITIONAL that rejects ROCK SINGER in the male assessment. Since we are dealing with voices that tend to get low ratings for this particular job label, it may be that we should not talk so much about acceptability; they are broadly speaking all unacceptable. Maybe we must instead pay special attention to the subgroup rating that accentuates this unacceptability, in this case MALE/TRADITIONAL in the male assessment. There seems to be something in MALE/TRADITIONAL which causes males, to a greater extent than females, to reject it in connection with ROCK SINGER; and this quality, whatever it may be, does not seem to be as present in FEMALE/TRADITIONAL. Perhaps it is simply a question of males being more sensitive to the maleness of the ROCK SINGER stereotype, which in turn might bring about an increased difficulty in associating with it MALE voices that do not fit this stereotype. FEMALE voices may be felt to be more or less off-side in this discussion. Similarly, there may not exist this strong sensitivity of ROCK SINGER maleness among females, which would tend to flatten their assessment. To put it more simply: males may be more sensitive than females to certain aspects of a TRADITIONAL male accent and their unacceptability in connection with certain male non-standard stereotypes.

Even though DISC JOCKEY and ROCK SINGER must be said to belong partly to the same overall area, we notice that informants treat the two differently. First of all, the general level of ratings is lower for ROCK SINGER (which is not to say that it is high for DISC JOCKEY). Secondly, whereas DISC JOCKEY receives a markedly flat set of ratings by males and females alike, ROCK SINGER manages to differentiate between voice subgroups. What we have here is probably an effect caused by DISC JOCKEY belonging to the broadcasting/public speaking sphere, something which might call for a certain amount of standardness, albeit coloured by certain aspects of the type of non-standardness associated with ROCK SINGER, creating the generally low level of ratings (cf quotation from Howard 1984 above p. 154).

Remaining now are FELLOW WORKER/STUDENT and CHILD/BROTHER/SISTER. These two labels differ from the rest in that they are not job labels (although I have chosen to refer to them as such for convenience). They are also special in that they force the informant to include himself/herself in the assessment. This is particularly true about CHILD/BROTHER/SISTER. In our discussion on AGE, we noted that CHILD/BROTHER/SISTER is special in a different way as well: it would seem that this label might elicit a more prescriptive response from the informants, since they would be in a position to influence the person it refers to.

Fellow worker	SPEAKER VOICE CATEGORY				
	Non-combinatory subgroups				
	FEMALE	MALE	TRADITIONAL	MODERN	ALL SPEAKERS
Female inf's M	3.87	3.50	3.53	3.90	3.75
Female inf's SD	1.63	1.79	1.73	1.66	1.69
Female inf's N	569	276	343	502	845
Male inf's M	3.74	3.34	3.52	3.67	3.61
Male inf's SD	1.57	1.66	1.60	1.62	1.61
Male inf's N	652	322	396	578	974

Fellow worker	SPEAKER VOICE CATEGORY				
	Combinatory subgroups				
	FEMALE/MOD	FEMALE/TRAD	MALE/MOD	MALE/TRAD	ALL SPEAKERS
Female inf's M	3.99	3.69	3.71	3.20	3.75
Female inf's SD	1.64	1.62	1.68	1.90	1.69
Female inf's N	339	230	163	113	845
Male inf's M	3.87	3.57	3.32	3.39	3.61
Male inf's SD	1.55	1.59	1.68	1.61	1.61
Male inf's N	366	286	212	110	974

We have just seen that FELLOW WORKER/STUDENT, together with TEACHER OF ENGLISH, is the only label for which females give a wider distribution of rating levels than males. This is the way ratings were distributed:

```
┌─────────────────────────────────────────────────────────────────┐
│  FELLOW WORKER/STUDENT                                            │
│                                                                   │
│  Male ratings                     Female ratings                  │
│  (1) FEMALE/MOD                   (1) FEMALE/MOD                   │
│  (2) FEMALE/TRAD; MALE/MOD; MALE/TRAD   (2) FEMALE/TRAD; MALE/MOD  │
│                                   (3) MALE/TRAD                    │
└─────────────────────────────────────────────────────────────────┘
```

We notice that level (1), i.e. the highest level, is occupied by FEMALE/MODERN, both in the male and the female assessment. Thus, judging by previous job label rankings, both males and females seem to have a "Working Class" rather than "professional", or indeed ""RP" archetype", inclination in their ratings concerning FELLOW WORKER/STUDENT. The difference between males and females in terms of levels is that females place MALE/TRADITIONAL at their level (3), whereas the males merge FEMALE/TRADITIONAL, MALE/MODERN and MALE/TRADITIONAL within their level (2). Here, it seems reasonable to assume peer-group effects, as females place MALE/TRADITIONAL lower than do males. Another difference, which is not apparent in the table of ranking levels above, is the clear male downrating of MALE/MODERN as compared with the female rating of this subgroup (3.32 vs. 3.71; *; t=2.23). Perhaps this is again caused by male informants being more particular when it comes to making judgments about MALE voices, i.e. the kind of effect that I suggested in connection with ROCK SINGER above. It is like a moderately good impersonation: it amuses only those who are but vaguely familiar with the object, whereas insiders are unimpressed.

Child/br/sis	SPEAKER VOICE CATEGORY Non-combinatory subgroups				
	FEMALE	MALE	TRADITIONAL	MODERN	ALL SPEAKERS
Female inf's M	3.13	3.02	2.97	3.18	3.09
Female inf's SD	1.75	1.82	1.80	1.75	1.77
Female inf's N	569	275	340	504	844
Male inf's M	3.12	2.77	3.04	2.98	3.01
Male inf's SD	1.67	1.67	1.68	1.67	1.67
Male inf's N	649	323	395	577	972

Child/br/sis	SPEAKER VOICE CATEGORY Combinatory subgroups				
	FEMALE/MOD	FEMALE/TRAD	MALE/MOD	MALE/TRAD	ALL SPEAKERS
Female inf's M	3.16	3.08	*3.21*	2.75	3.09
Female inf's SD	1.72	1.79	1.80	1.82	1.77
Female inf's N	340	229	164	111	844
Male inf's M	3.19	3.04	*2.63*	3.05	3.01
Male inf's SD	1.67	1.66	1.61	1.75	1.67
Male inf's N	364	285	213	110	972

For CHILD/BROTHER/SISTER, we get the following levels of rating:

CHILD/BROTHER/SISTER	
Male ratings	**Female ratings**
(1) FEMALE/MOD; MALE/TRAD; FEMALE/TRAD	(1) FEMALE/MOD; FEMALE/TRAD; MALE/MOD
(2) MALE/MOD	(2) MALE/TRAD

Here we see that FEMALE/MODERN does not stand out the way it did in the previous comparison. Thus, it seems that the informants do not have the same "Working Class" inclination here as they had in the judgment for FELLOW WORKER/STUDENT. What happens is instead that males and females choose to sort out one subgroup each which they rate as being the *least* acceptable in CHILD/BROTHER/SISTER. The males choose MALE/MODERN and the females MALE/TRADITIONAL. If we compare subgroup ratings, we also see that the most dramatic difference is to be found between male and female ratings of MALE/MODERN, which was also the case in the FELLOW WORKER/STUDENT comparison. Judging by the figures, it is the male informants who *downrate* MALE/MODERN; it is not an uprating by the females. The difference between male and female ratings of MALE/MODERN is clearly significant (***; t=3.29), which means that we seem to have here a stronger version of the tendency that existed in the FELLOW WORKER/STUDENT comparison. Doubtless, this is a somewhat confusing phenomenon. The female downrating of MALE/TRADITIONAL might be explained as a (reversed) peer-group effect, in that females might be expected to dissociate CHILD/BROTHER/SISTER from a type of accent which is different from their own in terms of SEX and, possibly, DEGREE OF MODERNITY. Or we might say that it feels intuitively right somehow that females should dissociate the accent to be used by their own CHILD or BROTHER or SISTER from the accents represented by MALE/TRADITIONAL. Gleason (1979:155) found that "mothers' utterances were more closely attuned to the children's than fathers' were". But if that is so, why is there not a similar tendency among the males? If there is something in MALE/MODERN that repels CHILD/BROTHER/SISTER in the male assessment, why does not the same thing happen in the female assessment? It seems that the males and the females may be sensitive, negatively, to different things; males to MALE/MODERN, which is perhaps felt to contain too much of a certain kind of non-standardness which the males are more aware of than the females; females to MALE/TRADITIONAL, which may be regarded as too standard from the point of view of female awareness.

Perhaps we should look for the answer in a slightly different field, viz. male and female attitudes to the upbringing of children; after all, we are dealing with informants' accepting or not the sample accents in their own CHILD (or BROTHER/SISTER). It may be the case that when making judgments as to what would be acceptable in such near relations as they would be expected to exert influence on, males tend to stress authority markers and status markers, and, consequently, to reject varieties where such markers are absent. Females, on the other hand, might feel that other, less status-minded, perhaps more personal, aspects are what matters, which might make them turn their backs on varieties which lack, or even actively oppose, such aspects.

Now, if this is true, and indeed if the Labovian suggestion about the strong female influence on children's linguistic development is acceptable (Labov 1972:301ff; cf Coates 1986:149 for an opposed view), there is perhaps an indication here that prestige forms might change according to the following model:

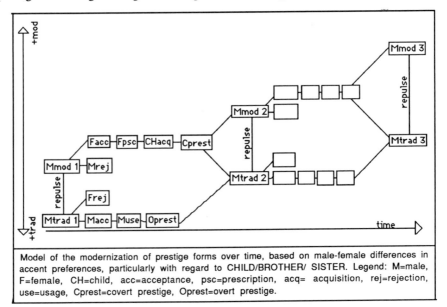

Model of the modernization of prestige forms over time, based on male-female differences in accent preferences, particularly with regard to CHILD/BROTHER/ SISTER. Legend: M=male, F=female, CH=child, acc=acceptance, psc=prescription, acq= acquisition, rej=rejection, use=usage, Cprest=covert prestige, Oprest=overt prestige.

Peter Trudgill (1975b) distinguishes between "overt" and "covert" prestige. Overt prestige pertains to a form which the speaker favours explicitly. Covert prestige, on the other hand, can be determined by checking to what extent speakers overstate and/or understate their use of certain forms. In his Norwich research, Trudgill found that males tended to overstate their use of non-prestigious forms, whereas females understated theirs; that is to say, males, when asked, said that they were more non-prestigious in terms of language use than they actually were, whereas for females, it was the other way round. Trudgill interprets this as meaning that among males non-prestigious forms enjoy relative prestige of a kind different from ordinary "overt" prestige. This different kind of prestige is known as "covert".

I have assumed here that MALE/TRADITIONAL represents the language type which at any given time within the cultural tradition that we are in today enjoys overt prestige in certain areas and among certain people. As we have already noted, there is in the present material a clear downrating of MALE/MODERN by male informants and a downrating of MALE/TRADITIONAL by female informants for CHILD/BROTHER/SISTER. FEMALE-combinations get a very flat set of ratings throughout. It seems reasonable to assume that since the question concerned acceptability in CHILD or BROTHER or SISTER, informants would respond to MALE voices as representing "SON" and BROTHER, FEMALE voices as "DAUGHTER" and SISTER, respectively (I am grateful to Lars-Gunnar Andersson for making a suggestion to this effect). If this is correct, the downratings mentioned above are really indications of what males and females think boys/young men over whom they have some degree of close educational influence should be like linguistically.

What the model says, then, is that the "modernization" of prestige forms may be an effect of female educators (in the widest possible sense) promoting a type of language which has certain close-group qualities, so that by virtue of the strong female influence on children's linguistic development, this type of language gets a stronger position in the next linguistic generation.

This tendency is counteracted by male influence which works in the other direction, in that (1) males, according to the present results, reject that very type of language (MALE/MODERN) which the females rate highest; (2) males, owing to socio-economic and other cultural factors, exert stronger influence in terms of large-scale social prestige than do females. Cultural changes in society will probably change this situation too.

It seems reasonable to assume that a "second-generation" prestige form based on these two tendencies would contain features which lie in between the MODERN and the TRADITIONAL of the first generation. However, if MODERN did not modernize over time in a way similar to TRADITIONAL, the two would gradually come closer to one another, and ultimately merge. I believe such a development is counteracted by MODERN and TRADITIONAL repelling each other, more or less inherently, at any given time; normally, I would imagine, by TRADITIONAL pushing MODERN away from itself in a modern direction.

Obviously, this model, just like any other model, is a simplification. Many components in the very complex aggregate which governs language change have not been taken into consideration. My attempt has been to reconcile some rather puzzling ratings in my own material with the prevalent sociolinguistic tradition. The trouble is that this tradition, naturally, is less than clearcut. The combination of alleged conservativeness and alleged advanced-ness in female language is not altogether easy to handle, something which has also been observed by Coates (1986:41ff). I believe however that I have managed to show, admittedly on the basis of scanty evidence, how female influence can cause prestige forms to move in a modern direction. A topic for further research might be that of trying to prove or disprove this model.

As for the perpetual question Why? (e.g. Labov 1972:302: "Why do women do this?"), I would suggest that one possible answer is that females are more socially sensitive than males. Now, whether this is due to innate, neuroendocrinological factors, or to social pressure, or indeed to both, is as we know hard to say. (It is in fact hard even to find examples of modern research with a non-environmental approach to sex differences, something which makes it even more difficult to form an opinion. For exceptions, see e.g. Hamburg & Lunde (1966), Goldberg (1979).)

Gun Widmark (1980:86) points out that it is

> [---] natural if in the close little world of women, emotional links between people would play a more important part than in the world of men. Their [the women's] language became emotionally coloured in a way which reflects important human relations. [My translation]

This, according to Widmark, also explains why female language often takes on certain "working class" traits, such as formal simplicity and a personal rather than impersonal style, something which has been shown by comparing male and female essays in a major investigation into Swedish upper secondary school students' composition and essay writing (Hultman & Westman 1977); the decisive factor is the limitations of the social environment of the speaker. What causes such limitations is a different matter.

Widmark's article also presents implicitly a suggestion as to the seemingly difficult problem of reconciling the existence of this kind of "working class" features with the prevalent idea of females being inclined to go for the correct, prestigious forms: they are not at the same level; one is a stylistic necessity brought about by the traditionally close female environment, presenting itself as greater simplicity, etc.; the other an adaptation to large-scale social norms, i.e. the forms that are used, however simple, are correctly dressed. But both suggest social sensitivity.

To sum up this rather extended discussion, which, as we remember, was triggered by (1) a clear male downrating of MALE/MODERN, and (2) a certain female downrating of MALE/TRADITIONAL, with regard to CHILD/BROTHER/ SISTER:

(1) Females are linguistically advanced because they bring up children. Thus, their language will be a major influence on generation II (which of course does not necessarily mean that their language output at a given time is particularly strange or modernistic; being advanced merely means that one is ahead; the others will follow).

(2) Women's language is often marked by certain traits that can be associated with a close social environment (cf working class).

(3) There is also a tendency among women to adapt to certain occupational and social pressures by using "correct" forms. This tendency is probably enhanced by the circumstance that women have a stronger instructional responsibility vis-à-vis their children; teachers normally speak "correctly".

> Coates (1986), in reporting the findings of Lesley Milroy and Jenny Cheshire, offers a further possibility to explain why women seem to go for "correctness" to a greater extent than men: people's language is governed by the tightness of the social network of the speakers (cf Milroy 1983). A "tight-knit" network exerts greater pressure on its members than a loose network, and in the studies referred to by Coates, there were signs that males tended to form tighter networks than females, which would explain why males wanted to emphasize their belonging to a group by using more non-standard language forms. Women's more standard-like language, according to Coates, is not a function of social aspirations, but rather of the circumstance that they "belong to relatively loose-knit networks which have less capacity to enforce focused linguistic norms [---]" (Coates 1986:93).

> The problem with Coates's discussion is that it is based on working-class material, which makes it rather difficult to incorporate it in the present study. However, if we look upon MALE/TRADITIONAL as an exponent of the same kind of "tight-knit" social structure as that which was reported to exist in certain working-class environments, but this time with a middle-class setting, then we might get a reflection of the results reported by Coates even in the present results. In that case, MALE/TRADITIONAL is a marker of network control, and as such it is inaccessible to people outside the network, which ought to be conducive to a lesser degree of acceptability among such outsiders. So that if females downrate MALE/TRADITIONAL in connection with CHILD/BROTHER/SISTER, they would in fact seem to perform the same type of act as they do when seemingly downgrading non-standard forms: it is an act of not belonging to a certain group, and, possibly, of

emphasizing the feelings of inappropriateness that they have with regard to MALE/TRADITIONAL in such a connection. What this means is in fact that women's alleged linguistic correctness *and* linguistic advancedness could be looked upon as two sides of one and the same thing, depending on whether the network structure they are implicitly reacting against is working class or middle class.

We have already noted that it was only the two MALE-combinations that were subjected to deviant treatment by either male or female informants in the CHILD/BROTHER/SISTER comparison. Both FEMALE/MODERN and FEMALE/TRADITIONAL receive ratings exhibiting no male-female differentiation, and very little (certainly not significant) differentiation between them (FEMALE/MODERN is rated slightly higher than FEMALE/TRADITIONAL by both males and females). We are therefore confronted with the rather disturbing question: Why is it that the strange pattern of downrating discussed above affects MALE-combinations only, and not FEMALE-combinations? I have already suggested that informants, when listening to my accent samples, would probably associate MALE voices with SON/BROTHER, FEMALE voices with DAUGHTER/SISTER; it is unlikely that they would listen to the samples as sexless accent prototypes. This would seem to mean that it is mainly in connection with SON/BROTHER, rather than DAUGHTER/SISTER that differentiating ratings occur.

Within the field of social psychology, there is an extensive literature about sex differences in the rearing of children. It turns out that there exists a strong scientific school of thought within which the role of the father is accentuated, in relation both to sons and to daughters, but interestingly, in different ways. We recall that the strongest single tendency in the present CHILD/BROTHER/SISTER comparison was the male downrating of MALE/MODERN. This was also superficially the most surprising rating, as it seemed to indicate a certain amount of self-rejection on the part of the male informants, whose average age, as we remember, is low (23.38 years of age), a consequence of a majority of the informants being sixth form students. However, several scholars have suggested that males (i.e. fathers) differ in their relationship to sons and daughters, respectively. Bronfenbrenner (1961) writes: "[---] boys are subjected to more achievement demands and physical punishment (from fathers only)." (p. 248); "With sons, socialization seems to focus primarily on directing and constraining the boy's impact on environment. With daughters, the aim is rather to protect the girl from the impact of environment." (p. 260); "Fathers show greater individual differences in parental behavior than do mothers and thus account for more of the variation in the behavior of their children." (p. 268). Similar thoughts are put forward by Johnson (1963:331): "Boys would make a sharp distinction between the parents because the father is more controlling toward them than the mother whose degree of nurturance-control is roughly the same toward both sexes." Heilbrun (1972) investigates the personality profile (based on self-characterization by means of an adjective check list) of males and females who identify with, respectively, their fathers and mothers. On the basis of the investigation, he suggests that "identification with (role-modeling after) the instrumental father is associated with enhanced masculinity in the son and femininity in the daughter   [---] (p. 57). Gleason (1979:155) discusses studies by herself and others which suggest that fathers "are the primary agents for maintaining and enforcing sex role distinctions." Maccoby (1980) reports on studies in which it was shown that fathers are particularly sensitive to deviations from established sex norms in children: "Clearly, it is the fathers who are the most concerned about the sex-appropriateness of their children's play. Furthermore, fathers react more negatively to their sons' than their daughters' sex-inappropriate play." (p. 240). An excellent critical overview of this field of research can be found in Block (1976).

A great deal of this discussion rests on the "instrumental"-"expressive" dichotomy introduced by Parsons & Bales (1955), in which the male and female roles (particularly within the nuclear family) are regarded as variations along an instrumental-expressive axis (cf also Leik 1972). According to the typical, but by no means uncontroversial, theory, the male is instrumentally superior, whereas the female is expressively superior. What this means, superficially, is that the male is believed to be more task-oriented, whereas the female is believed to be more emotional. In the words of Talcott Parsons himself (1958:333):

> The feminine role is primarily focused on the maternal function. The crux of this is, through the *combination* of instrumental child care and love, to provide a suitable object for the child's earliest identification, and subsequently for the child's autonomous object-cathexis [concentration of psychic energy on an object; my comment]. The agent of these functions must be anchored in an organizational unit of the larger society, otherwise the leverage for socialization beyond the earliest stage would not be adequate.

> The masculine role, on the other hand, is not primarily focused on socialization, but on the performance of function in the wider society - economic, political, or otherwise. If boys are to achieve in this arena, they must make the proper set of transitions between the intrafamilial context of early socialization and the larger societal context. The coalition of the *two* parents in the family leadership

243

structure is the main sociological mechanism which makes this possible. Clearly, also, the relation of girls to their fathers, and hence to men in general, is just as important as that of boys to their mothers in balancing these forces as they are involved in the functioning of human society.

Now, I am not claiming that this is the ultimate truth; I merely want to illustrate the kind of thought underlying one major set of theories regarding certain types of sexual differences. I believe it is fair to say that on the whole, this kind of thinking is reasonably common in many societies, past and present (cf Barry *et al.* (1957) for a cross-cultural survey). True, it has been accused of being biassed or stereotypical, but as Block (1976:295) puts it:

> [---] while stereotypes may only embody "myths", they may have encoded also certain culturally discerned and repeatedly validated truths. Rather than automatically giving precedence to one kind of data and devaluing another, the quality and inferential adequacy of *all* kinds of data must be evaluated closely in the weighting and integrating of findings. So, too, with stereotypes: they should neither be rejected reflexively nor accepted uncritically as we pursue the scientific task of evaluating sex differences.

For an even stronger defence of the reality-basis of stereotypes, see Goldberg (1979:120).

Let me suggest, then, that the answer to my own question as to why MALE-combinations are treated deviantly, MALE/MODERN as we remember being downrated by male informants, MALE/ TRADITIONAL by female informants, in connection with acceptability in CHILD/BROTHER/SISTER, is to be found in genuine male-female differences, stereotypical or not, in the outlook on the upbringing of children. If it is true that females are more expressive/emotional, more concerned with the relationship between the actors within a given group than with the group's achievement, then it would seem natural to expect females not to differ in their various judgments of acceptability in CHILD/BROTHER/SISTER, unless they sense a risk of that relationship being destroyed by one of the actors; in that case, they might react negatively towards that actor. And indeed, this could be said to happen in the female downrating of MALE/TRADITIONAL: the tendency towards social elevation that is likely to be present in MALE/TRADITIONAL is perhaps looked upon as less than acceptable in SON/BROTHER if group cohesion is what is primarily desired.

Males, on the other hand, if they are more "instrumental" or task-oriented, may tend to downgrade such features in SON/BROTHER as are not conducive to economic (in a wide sense) success, which might explain their downrating of MALE/MODERN in the present comparison.

3.7. Pleasantness, usualness, job interview, similarity.

We now turn to the final set of questions in this section, concerning DEGREE OF PLEASANTNESS, GENERAL and LOCAL USUALNESS, ADVANTAGE IN JOB INTERVIEW, and ACCENT SIMILARITY (PERSONAL/FRIENDS). The meaning of these labels will be clarified as we go along.

DEGREE OF PLEASANTNESS.

Pleasantness	SPEAKER VOICE CATEGORY Non-combinatory subgroups				
	FEMALE	MALE	TRADITIONAL	MODERN	ALL SPEAKERS
Female inf's M	4.10	*4.08*	4.29	*3.96*	4.09
Female inf's SD	1.23	1.21	1.19	1.23	1.22
Female inf's N	570	274	345	499	844
Male inf's M	4.04	*3.67*	4.21	*3.71*	3.91
Male inf's SD	1.31	1.37	1.34	1.31	1.35
Male inf's N	649	324	396	577	973

Pleasantness	SPEAKER VOICE CATEGORY Combinatory subgroups				
	FEMALE/MOD	FEMALE/TRAD	MALE/MOD	MALE/TRAD	ALL SPEAKERS
Female inf's M	3.95	4.33	*3.99*	4.21	4.09
Female inf's SD	1.24	1.18	1.22	1.20	1.22
Female inf's N	337	233	162	112	844
Male inf's M	3.85	4.28	*3.46*	4.05	3.91
Male inf's SD	1.30	1.30	1.30	1.43	1.35
Male inf's N	365	284	212	112	973

Here the informants were asked to state how pleasant they thought the accents they heard were and to indicate this along the same type of six-step scale as before. An interesting observation that we can make straight away is that males, but not females, show a distinct upgrading of FEMALE as compared to MALE. Among the ratings concerning psychological qualities, which are of course related to the present rating, we found this configuration on one occasion only: in connection with SENSE OF HUMOUR. It may be that the PLEASANTNESS of FEMALE is seen as a stereotype by the male informants (cf O'Connell & Rotter 1979) which tends to colour ratings on SENSE OF HUMOUR, which is, as we recall, not seen as a typical female stereotype (cf Kramer 1977).

In terms of levels, the following result was obtained:

```
DEGREE OF PLEASANTNESS

Male  ratings                      Female  ratings
(1) FEMALE/TRAD; MALE/TRAD         (1)  FEMALE/TRAD; MALE/TRAD*)
(2) FEMALE/MOD                     (2)  FEMALE/MOD; MALE/MOD
(3) MALE/MOD

*) Strictly statistically, MALE/TRADITIONAL cannot be separated
fully from either FEMALE/MODERN (t=1.94) or MALE/MODERN (t=1.48).
However, the present set-up is clearly the closest we can get within the
framework of distinct levels. The alternative would have been to merge
MALE/TRADITIONAL with FEMALE/MODERN and MALE/MODERN, which
would have created the greater error of not considering the clear
similarity in levels FEMALE/TRADITIONAL and MALE/TRADITIONAL (t=0.88).
```

The only subgroup for which there is a significant difference between male and female average ratings is MALE/MODERN (***; t=4.01), and it is clearly a case of a male downgrading (rather than a female upgrading) of this subgroup. This particular downgrading seems to be reminiscent of the one we had in connection with CHILD/BROTHER/SISTER above. It seems that the female ratings reflect a tendency to distinguish mainly on the basis of linguistic considerations, as it is only DEGREE OF MODERNITY, and not SEX, which separates levels in the female judgment. The males on the other hand include SEX in their distinguishing between the two MODERN-combinations.

I believe that a great deal of my discussion on acceptability in CHILD/BROTHER/SISTER is applicable here as well, albeit with some modification. It is interesting that the female informants should reverse, virtually, their ratings for CHILD/BROTHER/SISTER in the present comparison. This would seem to indicate that they recognize certain traits in the two TRADITIONAL-combinations which signal PLEASANTNESS, but that these traits are not altogether agreeable in connection with CHILD/BROTHER/SISTER. Now, if we place an instrumental-expressive hypothesis (cf p. 243 above) of the Parsons type at the bottom of our discussion, it would seem reasonable to expect such an apparently anomalous result in the assessment by a group in which group solidarity and closeness are accentuated at the expense of group achievement, i.e. an "expressive" group, i.e. females. This is the kind of result we get here.

It is also interesting to notice that the male informants retain the tendency to downrate MALE/MODERN that they showed in the CHILD/BROTHER/SISTER comparison,

SEX AND DEGREE OF MODERNITY

which I subjected to a fairly thorough investigation in that connection. Thus, it seems that there is greater harmony between the acceptability rating for CHILD/BROTHER/SISTER and the PLEASANTNESS rating in the male than in the female assessment, which, again, might be expected from the point of view of a Parsons-type hypothesis. Parsons, as we remember, suggests that the male is more "instrumental" or task-oriented.

Now, it could be argued that there is nothing which necessarily links up the "expressive" aspect with the existence of *dis*-harmony between CHILD/BROTHER/SISTER and PLEASANTNESS ratings; or the "instrumental" aspect with the existence of harmony between the two; it could be argued that we might just as well expect the reverse. In other words, it could be argued that there is nothing particularly "expressive" about *not* wanting CHILD/BROTHER/SISTER to speak as PLEASANTLY as possible; and that there is nothing terribly "instrumental" about wanting it. Undoubtedly, it is hard to offer a water-tight causal description of this kind of relationship. The key lies, I believe, in the interpretation of the concept PLEASANTNESS.

When we talk about PLEASANTNESS, we are really talking about something which is very closely related to aesthetic quality, i.e. beauty. The apparent paradox that we found when comparing ratings for CHILD/BROTHER/SISTER with those for PLEASANTNESS could perhaps be elucidated in an analogy: A says: "These roses are beautiful, and so I would like to have them in my own garden." B, on the other hand, says: "These roses are beautiful, but I wouldn't like to have them in my own garden". Now, it seems that A's opinion is really this: "These roses, beautiful as they are, would turn my old garden into a virtual Eden; I might even have a chance in next year's flower show". B's opinion is different: "If I were to plant those roses, beautiful as they may be, in my old garden, they would destroy the harmony that exists there; nobody would look at the more humble flowers any more; my garden would be ruined". Perhaps it is fair to say that what we have is a contrast between on the one hand progression and movement, and on the other, conservation and harmony. One need not be better than the other. It seems to me that this analogy fits reasonably well into the expressive-instrumental dichotomy discussed above.

LOCAL AND GENERAL USUALNESS.

Local usualness	SPEAKER VOICE CATEGORY Non-combinatory subgroups				
	FEMALE	MALE	TRADITIONAL	MODERN	ALL SPEAKERS
Female inf's M	3.30	3.49	3.47	3.29	3.36
Female inf's SD	1.54	1.61	1.55	1.58	1.57
Female inf's N	574	277	348	503	851
Male inf's M	3.37	3.32	3.57	3.20	3.35
Male inf's SD	1.51	1.64	1.59	1.52	1.56
Male inf's N	651	324	398	577	975

Gen. usualness	SPEAKER VOICE CATEGORY Non-combinatory subgroups				
	FEMALE	MALE	TRADITIONAL	MODERN	ALL SPEAKERS
Female inf's M	3.84	_4.04_	_3.98_	_3.85_	3.90
Female inf's SD	1.12	1.16	1.09	1.16	1.13
Female inf's N	571	273	342	502	844
Male inf's M	3.76	_3.65_	_3.77_	_3.70_	3.73
Male inf's SD	1.15	1.21	1.12	1.20	1.17
Male inf's N	647	320	397	570	967

Local usualness	SPEAKER VOICE CATEGORY Combinatory subgroups				
	FEMALE/MOD	FEMALE/TRAD	MALE/MOD	MALE/TRAD	ALL SPEAKERS
Female inf's M	3.19	3.46	3.50	3.49	3.36
Female inf's SD	1.55	1.53	1.62	1.59	1.57
Female inf's N	339	235	164	113	851
Male inf's M	3.21	3.58	3.20	3.55	3.35
Male inf's SD	1.46	1.56	1.61	1.68	1.56
Male inf's N	365	286	212	112	975

Gen. usualness	SPEAKER VOICE CATEGORY Combinatory subgroups				
	FEMALE/MOD	FEMALE/TRAD	MALE/MOD	MALE/TRAD	ALL SPEAKERS
Female inf's M	3.77	3.94	_4.01_	4.07	3.90
Female inf's SD	1.17	1.03	1.12	1.21	1.13
Female inf's N	339	232	163	110	844
Male inf's M	3.76	3.77	_3.59_	3.76	3.73
Male inf's SD	1.19	1.10	1.22	1.19	1.17
Male inf's N	362	285	208	112	967

The question we are going to deal with now was phrased: "Do you think this accent is heard very often (a) in your part of England [LOCAL]? (b) in England as a whole [GENERAL]?" Before we go on to discuss this question with regard to male-female differences, we should recall the *real* regional status of the various parties involved.

The four combinatory speaker subgroups, MALE/TRADITIONAL, FEMALE/ TRADITIONAL, MALE/MODERN, FEMALE/ MODERN show a distribution of average regional coefficients from 2.75 to 3.50 (1-to-6 scale, 1=London, 6=North; average values are not altogether fortunate in this context, as they conceal the values they are calculated from; in the present discussion, however, this will not be gone into any deeper). As for the informants, there is a certain, although less than significant (t=1.55), difference in regionality between males and females, to the effect that females have a higher regional coefficient than males (3.98 vs 3.68).

In terms of distinct levels, we get the following results:

LOCAL USUALNESS

Male ratings	Female ratings
(1) FEMALE/TRAD; MALE/TRAD*)	(1) FEMALE/TRAD; MALE/TRAD; MALE/MOD
(2) FEMALE/MOD; MALE/MOD	(2) FEMALE/MOD

*) The difference between MALE/TRAD and MALE/MOD is not quite significant at the five per cent level (t=1.83).

GENERAL USUALNESS

Male ratings	Female ratings
(1) ALL SUBGROUPS SAME*)	(1) FEMALE/TRAD; MALE/TRAD; MALE/MOD
	(2) FEMALE/MOD**)

*) There is a less than significant (t≤1.71) downward tendency for MALE/MOD.
**) The difference between FEMALE/MOD and FEMALE/TRAD is not quite significant at the five per cent level (t=1.79).

Among the LOCAL USUALNESS ratings, there are no significant differences between male and female ratings. We also remember that the overall averages for *all* speakers were virtually identical when we compared male and female ratings. In the GENERAL USUALNESS comparison, there is one clearly significant difference (***; t=3.41) between male and female subgroup ratings, viz. that concerning MALE/MODERN. Here, there is a slight upward tendency in the female assessment (4.01), and a downward tendency in the male assessment (3.59). In fact, MALE/MODERN is the only subgroup that comes anywhere close to showing a significant male-female difference in the LOCAL USUALNESS table as well (t=1.79). Even though differences may be small, it is undoubtedly intriguing that MALE/MODERN should end up at the top of the female USUALNESS ratings, but at the bottom of the male ones, both in the LOCAL and in the GENERAL comparisons (see reference tables p. 248).

Similarly, it is interesting that there is a clear downward tendency in the female ratings concerning FEMALE/MODERN, though this is not matched by a corresponding uprating by the males.

I think that a reasonable way of explaining this phenomenon has to do with the kind of self-idealization that has been described by Trudgill and others ("over-reporting" of prestige forms, etc.; see for example Trudgill 1975b). The closer you get to your own group, or indeed your own person, the more particular, the less inclined to generalize, you will be. If this is true, it would seem to explain why males (a majority of whom are relatively young) tend to downrate MALE/MODERN, and females (who are even younger) FEMALE/MODERN. In the present USUALNESS context, this would mean that informants, when confronted with voices that bear some sort of resemblance to themselves, want to accentuate the difference, rather than the likeness, for reasons of integrity.

The picture is less clear in the male assessment. In the LOCAL table, the males seem to go by DEGREE OF MODERNITY, to the effect that they uprate TRADITIONAL-combinations and downrate MODERN-combinations. In the GENERAL table, on the other hand, ratings are not statistically distinguishable in terms of distinct levels, though there is, as we have seen, a certain downrating of MALE/MODERN. Now, why should males, but not females, feel that TRADITIONAL is such an important distinguisher at the LOCAL level? In a way, the question is wrongly put. I think it is rather a question of females *not* downgrading MALE/MODERN. This would fit rather well into a sociological analysis with a certain feminist inclination: females uprate TRADITIONAL-combinations in the same way that males do, probably because of the "second choice" principle (cf p. 196f), according to which a standard-type accent will be regarded as USUAL if there exists no local alternative that is right on target (which, if it existed, would be the first choice). The reason for this can probably be found in the great cultural influence (in a wide sense) that pertains to the standard. And, as we have already suggested in the previous section, standard-type accents *are* USUAL, passively, all over England, simply by virtue of their being standard-type. In addition to this (expected) uprating of TRADITIONAL-combinations, female informants also place MALE/MODERN (but not FEMALE/MODERN) at their highest level. A feminist would, no doubt, argue that there is such a strong traditional connection between maleness, social authority and language correctness that an observer from the outside, a woman, might find it difficult to distinguish maleness from the other aspects. Maybe this is what confronts us here: a merger on the part of the female informants of maleness and TRADITIONAL.

Basically, male informants do the same thing, but without an uprating of MALE/MODERN; according to the type of discussion above, they do not feel the same overwhelming cultural impact of maleness as do the females, and so they are free to go by linguistic considerations to a greater extent.

FEMALE/MODERN, finally, loses both ways: it lacks whatever it is that makes TRADITIONAL attractive, and, in addition, it cannot be helped by its SEX in terms of cultural impact.

There is one complication in this set of comparisons: whereas the female informants give very much the same ranking in the LOCAL and GENERAL tables, apart from the overall level, which is higher in the GENERAL table, the males are less tidy. We have already seen how the males in the LOCAL table uprate TRADITIONAL-combinations and downrate MODERN-combinations, according to the "expected" pattern. In the GENERAL table, however, average ratings are distributed flatly, at one and the same statistical level, with nothing but a slight, non-significant ($t \leq 1.71$), downward tendency for MALE/MODERN. On the face of it, this is a little surprising, since it would seem to be more in accordance with the expected pattern to have this flatness at the LOCAL level, where one would expect all standard-type accents to sound about equally "foreign".

However, if we scrutinize SD (Standard Deviation) values in the two tables, we notice straight away that the LOCAL table has considerably higher (males average 1.56; females average 1.57) SD values than in the GENERAL table (males 1.17; females 1.13). This indicates that the GENERAL assessment has been made with a lower degree of variation of judgment, which could point in one out of two directions: either there is a genuine sense of certitude in favour of the given average level; or there is a sense of incertitude leading to ratings in the area of the "non-committal" 3.5. I would suggest that the latter is a reasonable explanation of the flatness of male ratings in the GENERAL table. Within this framework, the circumstance that male LOCAL ratings are more diverse, both in terms of the average ratings themselves and the corresponding SD values, seems to be a function of variations in regional background among the informants.

ADVANTAGE IN JOB INTERVIEW.
The informants were asked to state whether they thought that the accents they heard would be advantageous or disadvantageous in a job interview with an employer and to indicate this along the same type of six-step scale as before (1 being the negative, "disadvantageous" pole). For a brief discussion about deficiencies in this particular question, see p. 180.

Job Interview	SPEAKER VOICE CATEGORY Non-combinatory subgroups				
	FEMALE	MALE	TRADITIONAL	MODERN	ALL SPEAKERS
Female inf's M	4.49	*4.94*	4.98	*4.41*	*4.64*
Female inf's SD	1.21	1.05	0.99	1.24	1.18
Female inf's N	569	274	342	501	843
Male inf's M	4.47	*4.42*	4.88	*4.17*	*4.45*
Male inf's SD	1.25	1.39	1.10	1.35	1.30
Male inf's N	651	325	397	579	976

Job Interview	SPEAKER VOICE CATEGORY Combinatory subgroups				
	FEMALE/MOD	FEMALE/TRAD	MALE/MOD	MALE/TRAD	ALL SPEAKERS
Female inf's M	4.20	4.91	*4.82*	5.12	*4.64*
Female inf's SD	1.26	0.99	1.09	0.96	1.18
Female inf's N	337	232	164	110	843
Male inf's M	4.19	4.83	*4.13*	4.99	*4.45*
Male inf's SD	1.34	1.03	1.38	1.24	1.30
Male inf's N	366	285	213	112	976

We have already noted that in terms of overall averages, disregarding any subgroup ratings, female informants have a significantly higher (**; t=3.24) average than males with regard to this question, and I have suggested that this might indicate a certain tendency among females to pay greater attention to the social importance of standard-type accents; all our voice specimens are, as we remember, standard-type. Such a tendency would be in agreement with the mainstream of sociolinguistic theory (cf above p. 201ff).

In terms of distinct statistical levels, we get the following configuration:

ADVANTAGE IN JOB INTERVIEW	
Male ratings	**Female ratings**
(1) FEMALE/TRAD; MALE/TRAD	(1) MALE/TRAD
(2) FEMALE/MOD; MALE/MOD	(2) FEMALE/TRAD; MALE/MOD
	(3) FEMALE/MOD

Before discussing this table, we should note that we are now dealing with average ratings that are markedly higher than in our previous comparisons. Averages span from 4.13 to 5.12.

To put it briefly, what female informants seem to be saying here is that in order to gain advantages in a job interview (linguistically), one should either be a man

(MODERN or TRADITIONAL), or a TRADITIONAL woman.

The male informants again go by DEGREE OF MODERNITY alone, it seems. One is more likely to stand a good chance in a job interview if one has a TRADITIONAL accent, regardless of SEX; less so if one has a MODERN accent.

A possible explanation of this male-female difference is that females, as a result of being subjected to the workings of a male-centred society, think (1) that a TRADITIONAL MALE stands a better chance than a TRADITIONAL FEMALE; and that a MODERN FEMALE is worse off than a MODERN MALE. "So a girl is damned if she does, damned if she doesn't." (Lakoff 1973:48). The males on the other hand being in the insensitive midst of maleness themselves, can afford to be more objectively aloof in saying that SEX does not matter.

SIMILARITY PERSONAL/FRIENDS.

Simil. personal	SPEAKER VOICE CATEGORY Non-combinatory subgroups				
	FEMALE	MALE	TRADITIONAL	MODERN	ALL SPEAKERS
Female inf's M	2.64	2.68	2.82	2.55	2.65
Female inf's SD	1.51	1.44	1.53	1.45	1.49
Female inf's N	572	276	342	506	848
Male inf's M	2.57	2.57	2.75	2.44	2.57
Male inf's SD	1.37	1.46	1.45	1.35	1.40
Male inf's N	653	325	398	580	978

Simil. friends	SPEAKER VOICE CATEGORY Non-combinatory subgroups				
	FEMALE	MALE	TRADITIONAL	MODERN	ALL SPEAKERS
Female inf's M	2.64	2.67	2.74	2.59	2.65
Female inf's SD	1.44	1.42	1.48	1.40	1.43
Female inf's N	572	273	340	505	845
Male inf's M	2.67	2.59	2.71	2.60	2.64
Male inf's SD	1.31	1.33	1.34	1.30	1.32
Male inf's N	652	324	397	579	976

Simil. personal	SPEAKER VOICE CATEGORY Combinatory subgroups				
	FEMALE/MOD	FEMALE/TRAD	MALE/MOD	MALE/TRAD	ALL SPEAKERS
Female inf's M	2.44	2.95	2.77	2.54	2.65
Female inf's SD	1.43	1.58	1.46	1.41	1.49
Female inf's N	341	231	165	111	848
Male inf's M	2.43	2.75	2.47	2.76	2.57
Male inf's SD	1.32	1.41	1.41	1.55	1.40
Male inf's N	367	286	213	112	978

Simil. friends	SPEAKER VOICE CATEGORY Combinatory subgroups				
	FEMALE/MOD	FEMALE/TRAD	MALE/MOD	MALE/TRAD	ALL SPEAKERS
Female inf's M	2.49	2.87	2.81	2.47	2.65
Female inf's SD	1.38	1.50	1.44	1.38	1.43
Female inf's N	340	232	165	108	845
Male inf's M	2.62	2.74	2.56	2.63	2.64
Male inf's SD	1.30	1.33	1.32	1.36	1.32
Male inf's N	367	285	212	112	976

Behind these rather cryptic labels lies the question: "Do you think the speaker's accent is like (a) your own accent [PERSONAL]? (b) the accents of most of your friends [FRIENDS]?" and in terms of distinct levels we get the following set-up of average ratings:

SIMILARITY PERSONAL	
Male ratings	**Female ratings**
(1) FEMALE/TRAD; MALE/TRAD	(1) FEMALE/TRAD; MALE/MOD
(2) FEMALE/MOD; MALE/MOD	(2) FEMALE/MOD; MALE/TRAD

SIMILARITY FRIENDS	
Male ratings	**Female ratings**
(1) ALL SUBGROUPS SAME	(1) FEMALE/TRAD; MALE/MOD
	(2) FEMALE/MOD; MALE/TRAD

There is a clear likeness between the distribution of levels here and in the above discussion on LOCAL/GENERAL USUALNESS, apart from the fact that the general level of ratings is considerably lower now (in the area of 2.6 on the six-step scale, as compared with the 3.3-3.9 of the USUALNESS comparisons). There is one difference in subgroup levels, however: in the present comparison, the female informants have placed MALE/TRADITIONAL at level (2), together with FEMALE/MODERN; in the USUALNESS comparisons, MALE/TRADITIONAL ended up at the highest (1) level, leaving FEMALE/MODERN as the sole occupant of level (2).

In the USUALNESS discussion, I suggested that the female downgrading of FEMALE/MODERN, the subgroup which would seem to be closest to the female informants (female informants' average age: 20.7), was due to the same kind of phenomenon as the overreporting of prestige forms described by Trudgill (1975b), but, as it were, the other way round. This suggestion is, I believe, equally valid in the present context. The question then is: why have the female informants downrated MALE/TRADITIONAL in the SIMILARITY comparisons, as compared with those concerning USUALNESS? I think the answer must be that as opposed to the USUALNESS discussion, there is no way in the present discussion in which the informants can avoid including themselves in the assessment; in fact, including oneself is what this question is all about. And it seems to be in accordance with expectations that the female informants might want to dissociate themselves from the subgroup which would seem to be farthest from themselves in terms of SEX as well as (probably) MODERNITY (and, as it happens, *real* regionality). In other words, the female informants, I suggest, have made a relative downgrading of FEMALE/MODERN and MALE/TRADITIONAL for two diametrically opposed reasons: (1) they feel too close to FEMALE/MODERN and so they tend to be overcritical towards this subgroup; (2) they recognize the genuine distance between themselves and MALE/TRADITIONAL.

As for MALE/MODERN, it seems to be the case that male and female informants maintain a (relatively speaking) negative and positive standpoint, respectively. It seems that we can use the same explanation as we did in connection with USUALNESS above. Males are critical because they feel that MALE/MODERN is close, but not quite accurate, in comparison with themselves (cf females on FEMALE/MODERN). Females, on the other hand, while having to exclude themselves in terms of SEX from a direct comparison, can still recognize a certain fellowship with MALE/MODERN, owing to various cultural (in a wide sense) considerations, without being threatened by the uncomfortable closeness that ensues from SEX sameness.

Let us go on by comparing male and female ratings with regard to SIMILARITY PERSONAL and SIMILARITY FRIENDS, respectively. If we start by looking at the female informants, it turns out that the overall average (i.e. disregarding subgroups) is exactly the same for both sets of comparison, which means that any deviations in subgroup ratings are particularly interesting. The females have chosen to upgrade TRADITIONAL-combinations somewhat in the PERSONAL table as compared with the FRIENDS table, and to downgrade MODERN-combinations somewhat in the same way. Thus, the female informants seem to add TRADITIONAL-ness to themselves, and to remove MODERN-ness from themselves. The males do the same apart from FEMALE/TRADITIONAL which assumes a top position both in the PERSONAL and the FRIENDS comparison.

However, if we scrutinize the figures involved, we find that in fact it is the males who make the strongest distinctions between the PERSONAL and the FRIENDS ratings, viz. in connection with FEMALE/MODERN and MALE/TRADITIONAL. As for FEMALE/ MODERN, the males clearly downrate this subgroup with regard to PERSONAL at the expense of FRIENDS, whereas they uprate MALE/TRADITIONAL correspondingly. In other words, the males, more markedly than the females, seem to want to associate the SEX-appropriate TRADITIONAL-combination with themselves, and, likewise, dissociate the SEX-inappropriate MODERN-combinations from themselves. Taking into consideration that we are dealing with rather small numerical differences, we still find ourselves at odds with Trudgill's (e.g. 1975b) Norwich findings, according to which it is the females who tend to "over-report" the degree to which they use prestige forms.

Now, if we assume, the same way we have done earlier, that MALE-combinations and FEMALE-combinations, when seen in relation to the informants themselves, are not sexless accent prototypes, but that MALE-combinations are primarily looked upon as *male*, FEMALE-combinations as *female*, we might be able to throw some further light on the figures and the way they are distributed. It turns out that in the SIMILARITY PERSONAL comparison, the female informants give their clearly highest subgroup rating to FEMALE/TRADITIONAL (2.95); in fact, this is the highest subgroup rating in both SIMILARITY tables. This rating is significantly higher (*; t=2.32) than the female rating of MALE/TRADITIONAL (2.54). Interestingly, though, we do not get the same tendency in the male ratings: they give almost exactly the same average rating to both TRADITIONAL-combinations (FEMALE/TRADITIONAL 2.75; MALE/TRADITIONAL 2.76). This would seem to imply one of two things: (1) either females are more SEX-biassed in their assessment, i.e more inclined to associate FEMALE accents, if otherwise acceptable, with themselves, and, consequently, males less so; (2) or there is some sort of feature, or set of features, in FEMALE/TRADITIONAL which is especially attractive, in that it manages to attract not only female informants, which could be seen as natural, but also males, just as much as does MALE/TRADITIONAL (alternatively, it could be a question of MALE/TRADITIONAL being especially unattractive).

If we check the FRIENDS table in the same way, we find the same tendencies in the female ratings, although somewhat weaker throughout. The males, too, give pretty much the same profile of ratings, but there is an interesting, admittedly weak, downrating of MALE/TRADITIONAL as compared with the rating in the PERSONAL table, which in fact causes the male rating of FEMALE/TRADITIONAL to stand out positively from the rest (there are no significant differences between subgroup ratings in the male FRIENDS assessment, however).

On the basis of these findings, it seems that SEX-appropriate ratings are more likely to occur in the PERSONAL than in the FRIENDS assessment. This tendency seems to be more strongly marked in the male ratings. Maybe it is difficult for certain males to disregard maleness in connection with themselves, even though the MALE-combination in question may have features which are less than fully agreeable. In connection with their FRIENDS, on the other hand, their judgment can be more de-SEXed, which would seem to lend some further attractiveness to FEMALE/TRADITIONAL, since this subgroup manages to attain the top position among both male and female informants in the PERSONAL as well as the FRIENDS comparison.

So FEMALE/TRADITIONAL stands out as the most attractive, or least unattractive—ratings are generally low—subgroup in our sample, with regard to informants' willingness to associate it with themselves or their friends. The reason for this cannot be established within the present framework, but I would suggest, in the same way I did in the AGE discussion earlier on (cf p. 187), that it may have to do with markedness: it is probably easier to associate with oneself something which is less, rather than more, marked. Maybe the voices making up the subgroup MALE/TRADITIONAL, to a greater extent than the voices of any other subgroup, carry with them social connotations that are not altogether agreeable to many informants (cf also discussion on networks above p. 241f).

4. Regionality and degree of modernity.

4.1. Introduction.

The aspect of accents and dialects that is most obvious to people is probably the regional aspect. In this section, I shall try to elucidate various ways in which REGIONALITY may play a part in a set of attitudinal assessments similar to the ones we have already studied.

In order to achieve speaker and informant units that will serve this purpose, I decided to split the group of 25 speakers making up the accent sample of this study into a Northern and a Southern subgroup. The two subgroups will be referred to as NORTH and SOUTH, respectively. NORTH consists of 11 speakers, SOUTH of 14. The inequality in number between the two subgroups is of course not entirely fortunate from the point of view of comparability, but it was not felt to be possible within the limited scope of this investigation to carry out an overall matching procedure. Also, I think that it is preferable to keep manipulation at the lowest possible level in order to avoid circularity. Thus, for better or worse, I use in all comparisons all of the 25 speakers who volunteered to record passages, regardless of the internal structure of the speaker group.

In terms of the major English dialect areas, plus London, we get the following distribution in the two regional subgroups:

NORTH
10 speakers from the Midlands
1 speaker from the North

SOUTH
5 speakers from (Greater) London
9 speakers from the South East (excluding London)

The condition that had to be satisfied in order for a speaker to qualify as a member in one of these regional groups is that he/she spent the major part of his/her first 20 years there (or, more exactly, that it was in that particular region that he/she lived longest during those 20 years). By chance, it so happened that none of the 25 speakers of my sample came from regions 3 (South West) and 4 (East) on the 1-to-6 scale I use to indicate regionality, where 1 represents London and 6 the North. In addition to this, there was also the coincidence that very few of my informants as well (14 in all) came from regions 3 and 4. This naturally led to a decision to discard altogether these two regions from the REGIONALITY comparison, a decision which furthermore would seem to promote that kind of clarity which stems from polarization.

In order for an *informant* to qualify as a member of the Northern or Southern group, I decided that he/she had to have spent the major part of his/her life from age 10 onwards (youths)/the major part of his/her first 20 years (adults) in the Northern or Southern area. This had as a result that in addition to the 14 discarded informants from areas 3 and 4 mentioned above, another 12 informants dropped out because they did not meet this particular requirement; hence, the somewhat lower values for N in this section of the report.

The total number of Southern informants is 146; and of Northern informants, 195.

In exactly the same way as in the AGE and SEX discussions above, DEGREE OF MODERNITY (as defined on pp. 83ff) will be used as a basis for subdivision in order to maintain an "objective" language-based categorization that will be combined with the subdivision founded on REGIONALITY. Thus, most of my discussion will deal with combinatory subgroups, i.e. NORTH/MODERN (N=7), NORTH/TRADITIONAL (N=4), SOUTH/MODERN (N=8), SOUTH/ TRADITIONAL (N=6).

In our discussions on the AGE and SEX variables, we could see how these two variables tended to produce interesting differences which could be taken as indications of mechanisms underlying language change. As for AGE, this would seem to be natural, since language change necessarily happens over time. The SEX differentiation, too, might be seen as an integrated part of such a change in view of the circumstance that women and men traditionally have different responsibilities with regard to the next generation and with regard to large-scale vs. small-scale social and economic activity.

Is it likely that a subdivision of speakers and informants based upon REGIONALITY will lead to equally interesting differences? Let us begin answering that question by looking at what is at stake in the present comparison. We have 25 speakers who, when making their recordings, were asked to speak in a "natural" voice, not to "put on an accent", and to use the "voice that you would consider proper when discussing a serious matter with a stranger, i.e a fairly neutral, basically non-dialectal, voice" (cf p. 61f). On the basis of their domicile during their first 20 years, we have placed them in the subgroup NORTH or the subgroup SOUTH. We have also determined the DEGREE OF MODERNITY in their language output, so that they can be referred to either as TRADITIONAL or MODERN (cf p. 83ff). These voice specimens were then confronted with informants, i.e. listeners, who were also subdivided regionally in basically the same way as the speakers, i.e. into a Northern and a Southern group. Now, should we expect informants' attitudes to differ according to the REGIONALITY of the speaker combined with the speaker's DEGREE OF MODERNITY although this REGIONALITY is concealed by the "neutral" quality of his/her speech? If attitudes differ, this is of course first of all an indication that the variable, REGIONALITY, is at all noticed by the informants; but it is only after we have checked their responses for tendencies that we can see whether the differentiation has any kind of regional bias—either in the sense that one REGIONALITY label generally assumes a high-status position at the expense of another, or that such status is dependent upon the REGIONALITY of the informant. There is also, of course, the possibility that there may be additional differentiation depending on the content of the question. If one REGIONALITY label should get high ratings by a majority of informants with regard to such questions as could be judged as being positively related to, say, socio-economic status, then it would seem reasonable to suggest that accent features exhibited by speakers belonging to that region are high-status features. If, on the other hand, we get a blurred picture where high-status ratings are spread in a way which does not correlate to one or the other of our REGIONALITY labels, then it would seem as if REGIONALITY, at least the way we use the term here, is not related to accent prestige.

It is perhaps necessary to say a few words about the "RP" concept at this point, although, as the reader will have noticed, I have wherever possible refrained from using the term and the type of discussion often connected with it, in order to avoid begging the question. It seems to me that a great deal of what is written about "RP" suffers more or less badly from circularity, in that authors, when attempting to explain the nature of "RP", use the concept, or at least substantial parts of it, as part of their explanation.

"RP" is sometimes referred to as a "regionless accent" (Wells 1970:240; Trudgill 1979:10; cf also Abercrombie 1956), i.e. an accent which does not reveal the regional origin of its speakers. At the same time, it is said to be possible to identify a "regional base" (Gimson 1984:46f) for this type of pronunciation. He writes (1984:47): "[RP's] characteristic features have always been those of the south-eastern region of England." Wells (1970) partly disagrees, claiming that "RP" has certain traits in common with Southern accents, whereas other Southern traits, e.g. [i:] in *happy* and vocoid allophones of /l/ do not occur in "RP" (Wells has since partly changed his mind; in his excellent *magnum opus*, *Accents of English* (1982), he placed the former in his category "mainstream RP", the latter in "near-RP").

However, as early as in 1967, S.S. Eustace carried out a small-scale investigation in which he compared his own accent with those of a small sample of Eton schoolboys (Eustace himself is an ex-Etonian). It then turned out that in this epicentre of "RP", which the public school *par excellence* must be said to be, Southern features (including vocoid allophones of /l/, glottalization, etc.) seemed to be gaining ground considerably. This phenomenon is recognized by Gimson (1984) who claims that it is no longer possible to define "RP" in terms of a sociologically relevant sample of speakers because as often as not they do not speak "RP" (cf also Cheshire 1984). Gimson goes on to say (1984:46): "It is clear [...] that there still exists a widely held notion, albeit ill-defined, of a standard pronunciation and that this standard is identified as having the features of RP." Undoubtedly, there is an element of circularity in this type of discussion. The problem with trying to define the "RP" concept is that "RP" is the *name* of an accent in much the same way that "zebra" is the name of an animal (I am grateful to Aimo Seppänen for putting me on the right track here; cf Seppänen 1974:210ff). Names do not allow definition; they cannot be explained in terms of external criteria, unless we resort to a proliferation of detail which in the end amounts to very much the same as the thing itself. It is probably true to say that "RP" exists somehow as an accent prototype and that it is possible to argue that a given accent resembles this prototype to a greater or lesser extent. Within an individual speaker or hearer, there is probably also a fairly strict sense of delimitation, so that he/she will be prepared to claim that a given accent belongs or does not belong to the category governed by the prototype. Whether such delimitation is based on segmental or suprasegmental phenomena is a matter of debate. Gimson (1984) recommends that the phonological system of middle-of-the-road "RP speakers" be used as a "basis for our definition of present-day RP". J. Windsor Lewis (1985:244) takes an opposing view: "[---] such [prestigious] varieties are marked least of all by the distribution of phonemes within individual words, mostly by background voice quality, segment quality and prosody features."

Since we are talking about prestige accents, it seems to me that rather than putting in an enormous effort trying to define something which defies definition, we should explore those areas in which prestige operates, viz. the areas of contact between individuals and groups. Nothing is prestigious in its own right; it is only if it experienced as such that it can get that type of recognition. Or as Spencer (1958:21) puts it: "[---] accent is in the hearer, not in the speaker." The present study is an attempt to explore the speaker/hearer area with regard to the formal register of a group of speakers by using an "objectively" definable set of criteria, "RP" consequently not being one of them.

We now go on to see in what way the REGIONALITY variable adds to our understanding of the problem.

4.2. Overall averages.

In order to get some overview, we shall begin by looking at the overall average ratings made by Southern and Northern informants, respectively, with regard to the questions in our material. Doing this, we must of course keep in mind, as we did in the SEX discussion above, that overall averages are based on *all* speakers, regardless of REGIONALITY, which means that subgroup ratings are concealed. We will, however, get some indication as to the possible variation with which our informants, Northern and Southern, regard the 25 voices making up the sample of this study.

The first few questions deal with AGE, AREA and OCCUPATION. The AREA question is divided into three optional subquestions, AREA HIGH POWER, AREA LOW POWER and AREA ZERO POWER, according to how strongly the informants believe in their own conjectures (cf p. 70).

In the AGE question, there is a slight, although less than significant (t=1.88), overall difference between Northern and Southern ratings, to the effect that Southerners rate the voices as being on an average somewhat older than do Northerners. We shall see later on that this tendency is mainly caused by Northerners downrating MODERN comparatively strongly.

The area questions offer some interesting results, even at the overall level. First, it is interesting to notice to what extent Northern and Southern informants have chosen to answer according to AREA HIGH POWER, AREA LOW POWER and AREA ZERO POWER, respectively, as this choice would seem to be an indication of their subjectively felt regional familiarity with the voices. It turns out that the Southerners have chosen the HIGH POWER alternative to a greater extent than their number would motivate; that there is balance in the LOW POWER alternative; and that Northerners have chosen the ZERO POWER alternative more often than expected from their number. In other words, it seems as if the Southerners subjectively feel more confident about their ability to place these voices regionally. I would offer as a provisional explanation of this tendency that the neutral quality of the voices, partly brought about by the speakers genuinely having a neutral accent, partly by the speakers adjusting their accents in accordance with the recording instructions (cf p. 62), is felt to be indigenous to the South. Whether this is primarily a linguistic or a socio-economic statement is hard to say at this point.

There is a significant difference in overall averages between Northern and Southern ratings in the AREA LOW POWER comparison (*; t=2.07). It turns out that Southerners give a lower, Northerners a higher, overall rating, i.e. Northerners on an average place the voices somewhat more to the north, Southerners to the south. It will be seen later on that this tendency is due to a certain difference in the subgroup ratings concerning SOUTH, which, in turn, is possibly due to self-attraction on the part of the Northern informants.

As for the question on OCCUPATION, there is no overall difference between the ratings of Northern and Southern informants.

Then come the ten questions on psychological qualities (LEADERSHIP, DEPENDABILITY, HONESTY, SENSE OF HUMOUR, FRIENDLINESS, INTELLIGENCE, SELF-CONFIDENCE, AMBITION, DETERMINATION, EDUCATION) that the informants were required to answer by rating the extent to which they thought the speakers possessed the respective qualities (EDUCATION, not being a quality, was entered here for convenience). A six-step scale was used for this purpose. For two of the qualities, there are clearly significant differences between Northern and Southern overall averages, viz. INTELLIGENCE and EDUCATION. In both cases, the Northern informants give higher ratings than do the Southern. It is possible that what we have here is an effect of two ways of experiencing the formal type of speech which our speakers produce: (1) to Northern listeners, this kind of accent not being indigenous to the North, the voices of the sample signal intellectual or socio-economic prestige; (2) to Southern listeners, this is the way people talk. As usual the "truth" is most probably less pointed both as regards Northern and Southern listeners; both categories give clearly favourable averages for INTELLIGENCE and EDUCATION, but I would suggest that the difference between the two could be accounted for this way.

The eleven job (or group) labels (TEACHER OF ENGLISH, ACTOR, GROCER'S ASSISTANT, BBC NEWSREADER, DISC JOCKEY, BARRISTER, ROCK SINGER, GOVERNMENT OFFICIAL, WORKINGMAN, FELLOW WORKER/STUDENT, CHILD/BROTHER/SISTER, cf p. 75f) give rise to significant differences in overall average ratings in three cases, viz. ACTOR, GOVERNMENT OFFICIAL, FELLOW WORKER/STUDENT.

As for ACTOR, it is the Northern informants who give the higher overall average. This upgrading is probably a function of such generalization as follows from not being close to the matter at issue: to a Southerner, there is probably less of conspicuous prestige-markers in the rather neutral voices of the present sample, since they are felt to be pretty ordinary voices; a Northern listener, on the other hand, will probably be less critical to fine distinctions; to him, the formal neutrality of the voices indicates more of a standard.

The two labels, GOVERNMENT OFFICIAL and FELLOW WORKER/ STUDENT, get significantly higher overall ratings by the Southern than by the Northern informants. I have pointed out elsewhere (cf p. 76) that GOVERNMENT OFFICIAL was not an altogether fortunate label, as it suffers from a certain amount of semantic inexactitude. Maybe this is a reason why we get this difference in overall average ratings: Southern informants may primarily associate GOVERNMENT OFFICIAL with the national government, or at least more so than Northern informants, because of their proximity to London (Southern informants have an average regional coefficient of 1.78, as compared with the 5.45 of the Northern informants; 1-to-6 scale with London and North as extremes). It would seem reasonable for Northerners to expect local government officials to be more "regional" in their speech, which might partly explain the difference. We shall come back to this in greater detail in our discussion on subgroups below.

As for FELLOW WORKER/STUDENT, the relative upgrading by the Southern informants is, on the face of it, quite natural, provided the neutral speech of the sample speakers is regarded as being more Southern than Northern.

The last batch of questions, concerning DEGREE OF PLEASANTNESS, LOCAL and GENERAL USUALNESS, ADVANTAGE IN JOB INTERVIEW, SIMILARITY PERSONAL, and SIMILARITY FRIENDS, is perhaps more interesting than the previous ones from the point of view of REGIONALITY-based comparison. With the exception of ADVANTAGE IN JOB INTERVIEW, the questions all give rise to significant differences in overall averages when comparing Northern and Southern ratings. In some (i.e. the obvious) cases, the difference is extremely great.

In the PLEASANTNESS assessment, there is a significant (**; t=2.65) relative uprating of our voices on the part of the Northern informants. We shall see in detail later on that the chief source of this overall uprating is to be found among the ratings of NORTH-combinations.

The overall answers to the two USUALNESS questions, LOCAL USUALNESS and GENERAL USUALNESS, i.e. informants' indications as to how often the accents were felt to be heard locally and generally, are clearly illuminating: there is a tremendous difference in rating levels between Northern and Southern overall ratings in the LOCAL comparison (***; t=16.96), to the effect that Southerners uprate, and Northerners downrate the accents for LOCAL USUALNESS. There is a great deal more to be said about this, but that will have to wait until we get to the detailed discussion later on.

The difference in the GENERAL USUALNESS comparison is considerably smaller, but still significant (**; t=2.81). Here, however, the difference goes in the other direction; it is the Northern informants who give the higher level of rating this time. I believe it could be argued that it is distance-based generalization and closeness-based particularity that are operative here; if a neutral mode of speech is not indigenous to one, then one is likely to believe that it is usual by virtue of its neutrality; if, on the other hand, there is a certain amount of familiarity in one's relationship to a speech mode, then one might be inclined to go for minute details, in which case one's sense of neutrality and usualness may be lost.

As might be expected, the two SIMILARITY questions, concerning the degree to which informants believed the sample accents were like their own accents (SIMILARITY PERSONAL), and like most of their friends' accents (SIMILARITY FRIENDS), produce answers that are very similar in terms of overall level to the answers concerning LOCAL USUALNESS. Thus, we get a highly significant difference (***; t≥11.21) brought about by Northerners downrating the voices for SIMILARITY more strongly than do Southerners (who, in fact, also place them towards the negative end of the six-step SIMILARITY scale).

4.3. Age conjecture.

We have already noted that in terms of overall averages, there is a near-significant difference (t=1.88) between Northern and Southern informants' age conjectures, to the effect that Southerners rate the voices as being on an average 0.77 years older than do the Northerners. Partly, this could be explained as a consequence of the fact that Southern informants, again on an average, are slightly older than Northern informants (22.30 vs. 21.86), that is to say, it might be the case that we have a certain amount of egocentricity in the ratings.

| Age guess | SPEAKER VOICE CATEGORY Non-combinatory subgroups | | | | |
	NORTH	SOUTH	TRADITIONAL	MODERN	ALL SPEAKERS
South'n inf's M	27.63	30.95	31.10	28.77	29.72
South'n inf's SD	6.38	8.69	7.95	8.01	8.07
South'n inf's N	246	418	271	393	664
North'n inf's M	26.70	30.53	31.07	27.46	28.95
North'n inf's SD	6.97	8.38	7.84	7.87	8.05
North'n inf's N	378	541	380	539	919
Real age	34.91	40.43	43.00	34.73	38.04
Exp. age guess	27.99	30.08	31.06	27.92	29.18

Age guess	SPEAKER VOICE CATEGORY Combinatory subgroups				
	NORTH/MOD	NORTH/TRAD	SOUTH/MOD	SOUTH/TRAD	ALL SPEAKERS
South'n inf's M	26.18	29.56	30.20	32.09	29.72
South'n inf's SD	6.50	5.70	8.41	8.99	8.07
South'n inf's N	140	106	253	165	664
North'n inf's M	24.94	29.25	29.25	32.31	28.95
North'n inf's SD	7.03	6.05	7.96	8.65	8.05
North'n inf's N	224	154	315	226	919
Real age	32.57	39.00	36.50	45.66	38.04
Exp. age guess	27.10	29.54	28.59	32.07	29.18

However, if we look at subgroup ratings, which of course are central to the present discussion, we notice that the difference between Northern and Southern ratings is primarily brought about by a relative downrating on the part of the Northern informants of MODERN-combinations, particularly NORTH/ MODERN. There is in fact a clearly significant difference (*; t=2.49) between Northern and Southern average ratings of MODERN. How do we explain this? Let us first of all remind ourselves that the real average age of the MODERN speakers is 34.67, which goes to show that both Northern and Southern informants carry out a considerable downrating. However, as we have seen on several occasions, we must also take into account the conservative guess phenomenon (cf p. 98), according to which informants' guesses tend away from extremes. This is the most likely general cause of the downrating. Having adjusted for conservative guesses, we see that Northern informants place their average AGE conjecture of MODERN (27.46) just under the expected value (27.89), whereas Southern informants place theirs (28.77) notably higher than the expected value (the expected value is obtained by means of linear regression analysis, cf p. 100). On the other hand, if we look at the combinatory subgroup NORTH/ MODERN, which, as we have seen, is the chief source of the significant difference concerning MODERN, but which does not itself produce a significant difference between Northern and Southern ratings, partly because the N values of NORTH/MODERN are (naturally) smaller, we see that both Northern (24.94) and Southern (26.18) informants place their average ratings of this subgroup lower than the expected value (27.10), the Northerners markedly so. We might perhaps speculate that MODERN does not have as strong an AGE-lowering effect on Southern listeners because of the voices in SOUTH/MODERN (which of course constitute part of MODERN) not being sufficiently marked for young age from the point of view of the Southern informants, who are themselves quite young (average age 22.30) and therefore in a sense experts when it comes to modernity; indeed we do get an upward tendency in the Southern AGE guess concerning SOUTH/MODERN. On the other hand, NORTH/MODERN, as we have seen, is downgraded in terms of conjectural AGE by both informant groups, most clearly so by the Northerners. It seems therefore that NORTH/MODERN has a general marker of relatively low AGE attached to it; alternatively, in view of the fact that the informants on an average are young (Southerners 22.30, Northerners 21.86), that it is attractive to young people, more so than NORTH/TRADITIONAL and the two SOUTH-combinations, in that informants seem to want to pull it closer to themselves in terms of AGE. The circumstance that this tendency is more marked among the Northern informants is probably explicable in terms of a genuine feeling of resemblance, that is, not only preference in general, among the Northerners.

There are several indications suggesting that Northern features are gaining ground in the sound systems of non-Northern speakers, e.g. the open articulation of the vowel in *back*, which is heard very often among young Southerners today (cf Wells 1982:291f; Eustace 1967). Such tendencies would in turn seem to fit into the idea of various aspects of Northern culture gaining ground nationally; or as Anthony Burgess (1983) puts it when discussing the Sixties: "The popular culture of Liverpool invaded the capital, and young people brought up on East Midlands English considered it smart to speak in Liverpudlian." At this point, however, interpretative caution is imperative; differences are small and tendencies weak. It is only together with other results pointing in the same direction that we can put forward a reliable statement.

4.4. Regional conjecture.

This question deals with the informants' ability to place the speakers regionally. About a quarter of the answers to the regional questions were given in the AREA HIGH POWER answer alternative, i.e. the alternative in which informants professed relatively great certitude when making their guess.

Area HP	SPEAKER VOICE CATEGORY Non-combinatory subgroups				
	NORTH	SOUTH	TRADITIONAL	MODERN	ALL SPEAKERS
South'n inf's M	2.67	1.91	2.07	2.26	2.18
South'n inf's SD	1.55	1.03	0.92	1.50	1.29
South'n inf's N	76	140	92	124	216
North'n inf's M	3.34	1.92	2.33	2.36	2.34
North'n inf's SD	1.85	1.23	1.53	1.62	1.58
North'n inf's N	62	144	89	117	206

Area HP	SPEAKER VOICE CATEGORY Combinatory subgroups				
	NORTH/MOD	NORTH/TRAD	SOUTH/MOD	SOUTH/TRAD	ALL SPEAKERS
South'n inf's M	3.00	_2.17_	1.82	2.02	2.18
South'n inf's SD	1.74	1.05	1.15	0.86	1.29
South'n inf's N	46	30	78	62	216
North'n inf's M	3.18	_3.58_	1.96	1.86	2.34
North'n inf's SD	1.81	1.91	1.36	1.04	1.58
North'n inf's N	38	24	79	65	206

In one of the combinatory subgroup comparisons within the AREA HIGH POWER conjecture, we get a clearly significant difference (***; t=3.45) between Northern and Southern informants' regional guess. This is in connection with the combinatory subgroup NORTH/ TRADITIONAL. Interestingly, the Northern informants place this subgroup significantly farther from London than do the Southerners. Thus, it seems that there are features of some regional significance in this subgroup but that these features are hidden to the Southern informants (who, as it happens, give very similar ratings of NORTH/TRADITIONAL and SOUTH/TRADITIONAL: 2.17 vs. 2.02; t=0.73). Or, to put it slightly differently, it seems that DEGREE OF MODERNITY is a more decisive factor than REGIONALITY in the Southern AREA HIGH POWER guess, whereas the opposite seems to hold true in the Northern guess. The explanation of this phenomenon may simply be that standard-type Northern accents are looked upon as neutral standard-type accents, unless the listener has regionally based knowledge of minute details of such accents. Obviously, we do not get the opposite effect, i.e. Southern informants placing SOUTH considerably closer to themselves, since there is probably a clear association between Southern accents and accent neutrality among all listeners.

Having said this, we must of course make it clear that Southern informants, too, give a higher (i.e. farther from London) regional rating of NORTH-combinations than of SOUTH-combinations, but that this tendency is primarily restricted to NORTH/MODERN. REGIONALITY does play a part for both informant categories, but, as it seems, less markedly so for the Southerners.

About 50 percent of the answers on AREA were given in the AREA LOW POWER alternative, i.e. an answer alternative in which informants were less confident about the factual status of their conjecture.

Area LP	SPEAKER VOICE CATEGORY Non-combinatory subgroups				
	NORTH	SOUTH	TRADITIONAL	MODERN	ALL SPEAKERS
South'n inf's M	3.25	*2.10*	<u>2.41</u>	2.67	<u>2.56</u>
South'n inf's SD	1.70	1.09	1.33	1.57	1.48
South'n inf's N	150	222	157	215	372
North'n inf's M	3.22	*2.46*	<u>2.83</u>	2.76	<u>2.79</u>
North'n inf's SD	1.74	1.60	1.72	1.69	1.70
North'n inf's N	204	271	185	290	475

Area LP	SPEAKER VOICE CATEGORY Combinatory subgroups				
	NORTH/MOD	NORTH/TRAD	SOUTH/MOD	SOUTH/TRAD	ALL SPEAKERS
South'n inf's M	3.39	3.02	2.13	<u>2.07</u>	<u>2.56</u>
South'n inf's SD	1.76	1.59	1.15	1.02	1.48
South'n inf's N	93	57	122	100	372
North'n inf's M	3.20	3.25	2.39	<u>2.56</u>	<u>2.79</u>
North'n inf's SD	1.76	1.70	1.53	1.69	1.70
North'n inf's N	131	73	159	112	475

Contrary to what was the case in the AREA HIGH POWER assessment, we now get the greatest differences between Northerners' and Southerners' ratings in the answers concerning SOUTH-combinations, notably SOUTH/TRADITIONAL. It turns out that the Northern informants place SOUTH-combinations farther from London than do Southern informants.

The explanation nearest to hand for this state of affairs is, I believe, self-attraction. It makes sense that if one is not fully confident about one's guess, one tends to avoid extremes, extremes in this case being regions felt to be too remote from one's own region. Indeed, in three out of four subgroup comparisons, the fourth being that on NORTH/MODERN, there seems to be a certain amount of self-attraction, in Northern informants giving higher (i.e. farther from London) regional conjectures than Southerners. But it is only in the SOUTH/TRADITIONAL comparison that the difference between Southern and Northern conjectures is statistically significant (*; $t=2.52$). In other words, it is in connection with this subgroup that we get what seems to be the highest degree of self-attraction. Now, why should this be? If we assume that SOUTH/TRADITIONAL represents a type of accent (types of accent) which could be said to be more prestigious than those represented by the other three subgroups, then it would seem natural if this type exerted more attraction in accordance with the theory of idealizing one's own accent, discussed both in the present study (cf p. 255f) and elsewhere (Trudgill 1975b, Labov 1966).

Even though the difference is not significant ($t=0.80$), we should perhaps say a few words about the comparison concerning the subgroup NORTH/MODERN, since this subgroup, as we have seen, deviates from the other three combinatory subgroups in terms of self-attraction; here, Southern informants actually place NORTH/MODERN farther north than do the Northerners. Keeping in mind that we are talking about a non-significant difference, which thus may be strongly affected by random factors, we might argue that NORTH/MODERN, in being non-neutral both in terms of REGIONALITY and DEGREE OF MODERNITY, elicits an exaggerated response from those informants to whom this non-neutrality is most conspicuous, in this case the Southerners, so that they tend to push it away from themselves rather than attract it. The Northerners, on the other hand, who themselves have an average regional coefficient of 5.45 on the six-step regional scale, will probably tend to go more by the neutrality feature which is of course part of all our voices by definition, since all speakers were required to speak in a neutral voice when making their recordings.

Let us also compare the AREA LOW POWER comparisons with the AREA HIGH POWER ones to see if any interesting similarities or differences occur. As we have already seen, NORTH/TRADITIONAL is a subgroup which elicits different responses when comparing HIGH POWER and LOW POWER answers. It is the Southern informants who, when they are more confident, place NORTH/TRADITIONAL closer to London. On the other hand, when they are less confident, they push it away from themselves in a Northern direction. In other words, it seems as if certitude and factual accuracy do not walk hand in hand here.

Let us scrutinize the situation in somewhat more detail. We have speakers with a Northern regional background who speak in a traditional (according to our way of using that term) type of accent. Northern informants who profess certitude place these voices (as always, on average) closer to themselves than Northern informants who are less certain. In doing so, they actually exhibit greater factual accuracy, which would suggest that their subjective certitude is justified.

However, the Southern informants, from their point of view, behave in the same way with regard to NORTH/TRADITIONAL: they place it closer to themselves when they claim to be more certain, farther away from themselves when less certain, which, as we have seen, disturbs the picture.

It could be argued that this phenomenon is simply a function of certitude as such; that certitude will always be more closely linked up with the person who professes it. However, as we have seen in connection with SOUTH-combinations, primarily SOUTH/TRADITIONAL, we do not always get this configuration. Both SOUTH-combinations are placed closer to London by Northern informants who profess certitude, than by those who are less sure. This would seem to indicate that Northern informants who answer the regional question in the AREA HIGH POWER alternative are in fact better guessers, at least as far as REGIONALITY is concerned.

Perhaps this is not altogether strange. If SOUTH is associated with the standard, which there is every reason to believe it is, then it is natural if, say, a Northerner's knowledge of it is better than a Southerner's knowledge of, say, NORTH, which, then, is not associated with the standard. Accurate knowledge of accent variation *within a neutral spectrum of accents* would, according to this idea, be better in people who are at a distance from the standard, since they will at least know the standard and their own accent, whereas for standard-accent speakers, the two amount to very much the same.

Another difference between AREA HIGH POWER guess and AREA LOW POWER guess can be found in connection with SOUTH/TRADITIONAL, as we have already indicated. In the HIGH POWER comparison, there is first of all very little difference between Northern and Southern conjectures (t=0.94), whereas the difference in the LOW POWER comparison, as we have seen, is clearly significant (*; t=2.52). Furthermore, the differences are slanted differently in that it is the Northern informants who give the lower (i.e. closer to London) rating in the HIGH POWER comparison, whereas it is the other way round in the LOW POWER comparison. In other words, when certain, Northerners place SOUTH/TRADITIONAL somewhat closer to London than do Southerners; when less certain, they place SOUTH/TRADITIONAL farther from London than do Southerners.

Two questions should be asked here: (1) why does this happen? and (2) why does this happen here? I would suggest that the answer is to be found in the status of SOUTH/TRADITIONAL as compared with the other three combinatory subgroups: SOUTH/TRADITIONAL is the subgroup in which there is harmony between REGIONALITY and DEGREE OF MODERNITY from the point of view of traditional spoken standard English; it is Southern, and it is traditional. In other words, it is *neutrally marked*. Answering in the HIGH POWER alternative means that the informant is, perhaps, more sophisticated when it comes to making regional assessment; at least that would make some kind of sense. Thus, a Southern informant giving a HIGH POWER answer is perhaps more sensitive to certain finely tuned regional aspects in SOUTH/TRADITIONAL, whereas for a Northerner, it is probably much easier to answer "London" when listening to a neutral type of Southern voice, London being the epicentre of everything connected with the notion of "standard", culturally as well as linguistically. This, if it is true, creates a situation where the apparently distinct answer "London" given by a Northerner is in fact based upon less distinct linguistic knowledge, whereas a less distinct answer, e.g. "South" given by a Southerner is actually founded on better knowledge. In order for a Southerner to answer "London", there would probably have to be more obvious London features in the accent in question, which, as we know, is not the case here.

Answering in the LOW POWER alternative probably reflects a lesser degree of such sophistication. It is only natural, then, that an answer made by such a less certain informant should be coloured by the informant's own regionality, which is what seems to have happened here.

Incidentally, the other combinatory subgroup which exhibits a kind of harmony between REGIONALITY and DEGREE OF MODERNITY, although not from a standard point of view, viz. NORTH/MODERN, also gets ratings which are differently slanted, but in the opposite direction: when more certain, Southerners place NORTH/MODERN closer to London than do Northerners; when less certain, they place NORTH/MODERN farther from London than do Northerners. In fact, Northerners present very little difference between HIGH POWER and LOW POWER ratings of NORTH/MODERN. I think it is fair to assume that there is a connection between London and the absence of regional markedness (or presence of neutral markedness), so that informants who are at all inclined to give a pointed verdict will lean towards London, unless they possess expertise which would make them move in a different direction.

In the present case, Southerners, who would seem to lack regionally based expertise about NORTH/MODERN, might be said to go for the neutral aspect of NORTH/MODERN, placing it closer to London than Northerners. Northerners, on the other hand, who are probably less regionally familiar with SOUTH/TRADITIONAL, place that subgroup closer to London than do Southerners. Both these assessments are made in the HIGH POWER answer alternative, indicating that the informants are more active in their assessment than would otherwise be the case.

As for the LOW POWER assessments, it could be argued that they are placed farther away from London, but it is just as likely that there is a tendency among LOW POWER informants either to spread their assessments across the regional spectrum, and indeed, SD values are higher in the LOW POWER comparison, or to avoid regional extremes. The idea of regional extremes is however not altogether clearcut in a country where the cultural epicentre is not even close to the geographical centre.

Area ZP	SPEAKER VOICE CATEGORY Non-combinatory subgroups				
	NORTH	SOUTH	TRADITIONAL	MODERN	ALL SPEAKERS
South'n inf's M	- -	- -	- -	- -	- -
South'n inf's SD	- -	- -	- -	- -	- -
South'n inf's N	48	74	42	80	122
North'n inf's M	- -	- -	- -	- -	- -
North'n inf's SD	- -	- -	- -	- -	- -
North'n inf's N	140	137	120	157	277

Area ZP	SPEAKER VOICE CATEGORY Combinatory subgroups				
	NORTH/MOD	NORTH/TRAD	SOUTH/MOD	SOUTH/TRAD	ALL SPEAKERS
South'n inf's M	- -	- -	- -	- -	- -
South'n inf's SD	- -	- -	- -	- -	- -
South'n inf's N	31	17	49	25	122
North'n inf's M	- -	- -	- -	- -	- -
North'n inf's SD	- -	- -	- -	- -	- -
North'n inf's N	83	57	74	63	277

We have already seen that there is a certain amount of imbalance in the way Northerners and Southerners choose to answer in the HIGH POWER and ZERO POWER answer alternatives, respectively. The tendency was, as we remember, for Southerners to profess greater certitude, Northerners less so. If we look at ZERO POWER subgroup ratings, we see straightaway that more Northerners choose to answer in this answer category in every single subgroup comparison, than would be motivated by their number in relation to the whole, with the exception of the SOUTH/MODERN rating, in which we get about the same distribution of Northerners and Southerners as in the total informant group.

This seems to indicate that there is felt to be a Southern bias in our voices, in that we should expect a greater amount of incertitude among people who experience a higher degree of regional alienation to the voices they hear. Now, if our voices were totally void of any regional information (something which is often said about "RP"), then there would seem to be no reason why this non-regionality should be more strongly felt by Northerners than by Southerners. But as we have seen, it is only the combinatory subgroup SOUTH/MODERN that gets a non-biassed kind of treatment in the ZERO POWER comparison, indicating, perhaps, that this particular subgroup possesses a generic quality which is not shared by the remaining three.

4.5. Occupational conjecture.

The informants were asked to guess what they thought the speakers did for a living. The question was open-ended, that is to say, no guidelines or instructions were supplied. Informant answers were then translated into numerical values according to a system based upon the *Classification of Occupations* (1980). In this six-step system, 1 represents "professional etc." and 6 "unskilled" (cf p. 57).

Occupation	SPEAKER VOICE CATEGORY Non-combinatory subgroups				
	NORTH	SOUTH	TRADITIONAL	MODERN	ALL SPEAKERS
South'n inf's M	2.57	2.45	2.39	2.58	2.49
South'n inf's SD	0.75	0.91	0.72	0.94	0.86
South'n inf's N	202	338	236	304	540
North'n inf's M	2.56	2.37	2.28	2.58	2.45
North'n inf's SD	0.70	0.88	0.71	0.88	0.82
North'n inf's N	280	443	318	405	723

Occupation	SPEAKER VOICE CATEGORY Combinatory subgroups				
	NORTH/MOD	NORTH/TRAD	SOUTH/MOD	SOUTH/TRAD	ALL SPEAKERS
South'n inf's M	2.55	2.59	2.59	2.27	2.49
South'n inf's SD	0.83	0.64	1.01	0.74	0.86
South'n inf's N	116	86	188	150	540
North'n inf's M	2.62	2.48	2.55	2.16	2.45
North'n inf's SD	0.74	0.62	0.96	0.73	0.82
North'n inf's N	160	120	245	198	723

We have already noted that in terms of overall averages, i.e. disregarding any subgroups, there is no difference between the ratings made by Northern informants and those made by Southern informants. Both categories place their averages close to 2.5, i.e. towards the "professional" end of the scale.

Furthermore, in none of the subgroups is there a significant difference in ratings between Northerners and Southerners. This goes to show that there exists a great deal of regional unanimity in the occupational interpretation of voice/accent data.

Since we shall henceforth be discussing ratings placed along six-step scales, it is illuminating and economical to present differences between subgroup ratings in terms of differences in levels, the same way we did in the SEX discussion above. What this means is simply that I check whether the difference between, say, Northerners' ratings of SOUTH/MODERN and SOUTH/TRADITIONAL is statistically significant at the five per cent level (t≥1.96). If it is, I shall regard these two ratings as belonging to two separate and distinct levels. If, on the other hand, the difference is less than significant, the two ratings will be looked upon as belonging to one and the same level. Obviously, it will not be possible to maintain a clearcut system of this kind throughout, since there are four combinatory subgroups involved in each comparison (NORTH/ MODERN, NORTH/TRADITIONAL, SOUTH/MODERN, SOUTH/TRADITIONAL), and one of these may very well be significantly distinguished from, say, two of the remaining ones, but not the third one, although these three are not distinguishable between them. In such cases it is necessary to resort to rational judgment.

The full tables of comparison will also be included for reference.

This is the way Northern and Southern informants rank the four combinatory subgroups with regard to OCCUPATION (average ratings given in brackets):

OCCUPATIONAL RANKING

Southern ratings
(1) SOUTH/TRAD (2.27)
(2) NORTH/MOD (2.55); NORTH/TRAD (2.59); SOUTH/MOD (2.59)

Northern ratings
(1) SOUTH/TRAD (2.16)
(2) NORTH/TRAD (2.48); SOUTH/MOD (2.55); NORTH/MOD (2.62)

As we can see, it is only SOUTH/TRADITIONAL that distinguishes itself according to a system of significantly distinguished levels. This happens both in Northerners' and Southerners' ratings. In the Northerners' ranking, there seems to be a certain tendency to regard NORTH/TRADITIONAL as leaning more towards the "professional" end of the scale. However, this tendency is not statistically verifiable. If there is something in this tendency, it would seem to indicate that Northerners are more capable of distinguishing socially between different varieties of Northern neutral English than Southerners, or indeed more used to doing so. This seems to make sense.

One factor which may reduce the predictive power of these suggestions is the SEX distribution in the combinatory subgroups. Since we are dealing with subgroups made up of relatively few speakers, it is impossible to control for all conceivable imbalances. Even trying to do so would involve reducing group sizes far beyond usability.

In the present case, there is balance between male and female speakers in SOUTH/TRADITIONAL (3xM, 3xF), whereas in the other three subgroups, there is a certain female majority. It may well be the case (cf the discussion on SEX-based differences above) that traditional values with regard to professional labels affect conjectures. We asked an open question in order to receive open answers and such a method obviously leans heavily on traditional values among informants: in labels such as "doctor", "lawyer" there is probably a strong sense of maleness, even today (cf P.M. Smith 1985:45). As usual, interpretative caution is imperative.

> Loman (1973) reports on related experiments performed by the Loman group in Sweden. Recorded spontaneous speech (interviews) from a southern, a western and a northern area of Sweden was played to informants from Stockholm, the South and the far North. One of the informants' tasks was to combine job labels from a list with the voices they heard, the job labels having been chosen so as to represent the three "social groups" often referred to in Swedish socio-economic analysis. The job labels were then translated into "social indices" (cf the present study). Other tasks included the judgment of "articulation", "pronunciation" and "expression". It turned out that the informants were very successful in their selection of job labels for the western voices (the speaker category to be most closely associated with the Swedish "standard" accent in this material). By checking the corresponding ratings on articulation, pronunciation and expression, it was also possible to see which of these had the greatest impact on the job label selection. Interestingly, articulation and expression showed a clearly higher correlation than did pronunciation. By comparison, the northern variety of Swedish did not give rise to accurate job label selection; instead, the informants had rated the voices on the basis of pronunciation, creating a social downgrading of speakers with a Finnish accent (the working class immigrant stereotype in Sweden), that particular part of the North being characterized by Swedish-Finnish bilingualism.

4.6. Psychological qualities.

We now enter into the next section of the questionnaire, which is made up of the questions on psychological qualities. The informants were asked to rate the voices they heard along a six-step scale going from "very little" to "very much" with regard to ten psychological, or related, qualities (LEADERSHIP, DEPENDABILITY, HONESTY, SENSE OF HUMOUR, FRIENDLINESS, INTELLIGENCE, SELF-CONFIDENCE, AMBITION, DETERMINATION, EDUCATION).

We have noted on several occasions that it is possible to claim that among these quality labels, there are some that are related to one another by virtue of their semantic content. It is of course possible, and interesting, to check to what extent there exist patterns in the way speaker subgroups are graded by, in this case, Northern and Southern informants. Going about the matter in such a way means that we do not have to get too involved with each individual quality, but rather employ a more structural method of investigation. Practically, this can be done by checking the ratings of the qualities in terms of statistically significant levels, the same way we did when discussing the OCCUPATIONAL guess above. Qualities for which the voices are ranked similarly can then be discussed together.

SPEAKER VOICE CATEGORY

Ambition — Non-combinatory subgroups

	NORTH	SOUTH	TRADITIONAL	MODERN	ALL SPEAKERS
South'n inf's M	3.76	4.03	4.04	3.85	3.92
South'n inf's SD	1.22	1.28	1.24	1.27	1.26
South'n inf's N	277	431	286	422	708
North'n inf's M	3.88	4.14	4.21	3.90	4.03
North'n inf's SD	1.36	1.32	1.27	1.38	1.35
North'n inf's N	402	550	389	563	952

SPEAKER VOICE CATEGORY

Ambition — Combinatory subgroups

	NORTH/MOD	NORTH/TRAD	SOUTH/MOD	SOUTH/TRAD	ALL SPEAKERS
South'n inf's M	3.81	3.67	3.87	4.25	3.92
South'n inf's SD	1.27	1.12	1.27	1.26	1.26
South'n inf's N	173	104	249	182	708
North'n inf's M	3.86	3.93	3.94	4.39	4.03
North'n inf's SD	1.42	1.26	1.35	1.25	1.35
North'n inf's N	249	153	314	236	952

SPEAKER VOICE CATEGORY

Determination — Non-combinatory subgroups

	NORTH	SOUTH	TRADITIONAL	MODERN	ALL SPEAKERS
South'n inf's M	3.84	4.05	4.05	3.91	3.97
South'n inf's SD	1.17	1.19	1.16	1.20	1.19
South'n inf's N	277	434	288	423	711
North'n inf's M	3.90	4.12	4.21	3.90	4.03
North'n inf's SD	1.30	1.29	1.21	1.34	1.30
North'n inf's N	401	550	389	562	951

Determination	SPEAKER VOICE CATEGORY Combinatory subgroups				
	NORTH/MOD	NORTH/TRAD	SOUTH/MOD	SOUTH/TRAD	ALL SPEAKERS
South'n inf's M	3.90	3.75	3.92	4.22	3.97
South'n inf's SD	1.19	1.13	1.21	1.14	1.19
South'n inf's N	173	104	250	184	711
North'n inf's M	3.88	3.93	3.92	4.39	4.03
North'n inf's SD	1.39	1.16	1.31	1.21	1.30
North'n inf's N	248	153	314	236	951

Let us first of all note that two qualities, AMBITION and DETERMINATION, receive identical relative ratings of subgroups by Northern and Southern informants:

DETERMINATION and AMBITION	
Southern ratings	Northern ratings
(1) SOUTH/TRAD	(1) SOUTH/TRAD
(2) THE REST	(2) THE REST

In fact, what we get here is the same ranking as in the OCCUPATIONAL comparison above. SOUTH/TRADITIONAL stands out as the speaker subgroup possessing most of these qualities, which indeed would seem to be associated with good professional prospects. The fact that these two qualities get similar ratings is not surprising: they are obviously strongly linked semantically.

Leadership	SPEAKER VOICE CATEGORY Non-combinatory subgroups				
	NORTH	SOUTH	TRADITIONAL	MODERN	ALL SPEAKERS
South'n inf's M	3.31	3.63	3.61	3.44	3.50
South'n inf's SD	1.37	1.38	1.39	1.38	1.39
South'n inf's N	277	436	286	427	713
North'n inf's M	3.42	3.67	3.82	3.39	3.56
North'n inf's SD	1.39	1.41	1.38	1.40	1.41
North'n inf's N	406	551	391	566	957

Leadership	SPEAKER VOICE CATEGORY Combinatory subgroups				
	NORTH/MOD	NORTH/TRAD	SOUTH/MOD	SOUTH/TRAD	ALL SPEAKERS
South'n inf's M	3.35	3.23	3.49	3.82	3.50
South'n inf's SD	1.42	1.29	1.36	1.40	1.39
South'n inf's N	173	104	254	182	713
North'n inf's M	3.31	3.60	3.45	3.96	3.56
North'n inf's SD	1.48	1.21	1.34	1.46	1.41
North'n inf's N	252	154	314	237	957

Education	SPEAKER VOICE CATEGORY Non-combinatory subgroups				
	NORTH	SOUTH	TRADITIONAL	MODERN	ALL SPEAKERS
South'n inf's M	4.41	4.39	4.63	4.24	4.40
South'n inf's SD	1.04	1.28	1.08	1.24	1.19
South'n inf's N	280	435	290	425	715
North'n inf's M	4.45	4.61	4.80	4.36	4.54
North'n inf's SD	1.11	1.23	1.08	1.22	1.18
North'n inf's N	401	552	390	563	953

Education	SPEAKER VOICE CATEGORY Combinatory subgroups				
	NORTH/MOD	NORTH/TRAD	SOUTH/MOD	SOUTH/TRAD	ALL SPEAKERS
South'n inf's M	4.39	4.44	4.13	4.73	4.40
South'n inf's SD	1.02	1.06	1.35	1.08	1.19
South'n inf's N	174	106	251	184	715
North'n inf's M	4.37	4.57	4.35	4.95	4.54
North'n inf's SD	1.15	1.03	1.28	1.08	1.18
North'n inf's N	248	153	315	237	953

Very much the same tendencies, albeit slightly modified, can be found in connection with two of the other quality labels, viz. LEADERSHIP and EDUCATION. As for LEADERSHIP, the only difference is that there exists a certain downgrading of NORTH/MODERN in the Northern assessment. EDUCATION on the other hand differs from AMBITION and DETERMINATION by a downgrading of SOUTH/ MODERN by Southern informants. That is to say, in both cases the deviation is one brought about by the informants' downgrading their own regional compatriots when MODERN. The circumstance that SOUTH/TRADITIONAL gets the highest ranking from both informant groups is perhaps not so strange: LEADERSHIP and EDUCATION are notionally linked with each other and with the career-promoting qualities we have just been discussing. It seems that whatever features are operational in SOUTH/TRADITIONAL do have a strong bearing on such qualities.

It is interesting though that there should be an element of "self-hatred" in the way informants rate the subgroups to which they, or at least most of them, would probably belong themselves. In the case of the Southerners, they seem to feel that the accents most closely linked with their own accents are lacking in EDUCATION, as compared with the rest. A possible reason for this is that these informants, being from the South themselves, are particular enough in their judgment of the Southern voices to be able to hear either that SOUTH/MODERN sounds familiar, which might cause them to want to dissociate this voice category (which they might thus associate with themselves) from the traditional quality of EDUCATION; or that it is genuinely lacking in this quality from their point of view (we shall see later on that Southern informants, when asked, in fact associate themselves with SOUTH/TRADITIONAL, cf below p. 328f). That Northerners do not react in the same way vis-à-vis SOUTH/MODERN, even though for social reasons they might be expected to, is probably due to their not being able to make such fine distinctions in SOUTH.

The Northern downgrading of NORTH/MODERN with regard to LEADERSHIP, on the other hand, is perhaps a reflection of socio-politically founded "self-hatred". It is undoubtedly the case that whereas one might very well be educated without this having a necessary link with the South, LEADERSHIP to all British people would seem to be somehow associated with that region; that is the way cultural dominance works. However that does not answer the question why NORTH/TRADITIONAL does not receive the same treatment. Either there is less of whatever forms that particular attitude in NORTH/TRADITIONAL, or we are seeing a certain amount of social bias based on DEGREE OF MODERNITY: in order for somebody from the North to express LEADERSHIP in her voice, she should at least have a TRADITIONAL output.

In this context, it should be noted that there is a significant difference (*; t=2.35) between Northerners' and Southerners' ratings of NORTH/TRADITIONAL, apparently created in the main by the Southerners downgrading this subgroup. This is worth considering, since among the quality scales, we do not get very many significant differences between Northerners' and Southerners' ratings of combinatory subgroups. In my opinion, the most likely explanation is that certain LEADERSHIP markers in NORTH/ TRADITIONAL are lost upon the Southerners. Perhaps this happens particularly easily when there is social or cultural pressure working in the opposite direction, as in the present case, the pressure caused by a majority of the speakers in NORTH/TRADITIONAL being women.

The two SOUTH-combinations give rise to significant differences between Northerners' and Southerners' ratings for EDUCATION: it turns out that the Northern informants upgrade these two subgroups relative to Southerners. This is a tendency which, expectedly, resembles that which occurs in connection with INTELLIGENCE below. Thus, it would seem that Southern neutral accents are marked for such traits when perceived by non-Southerners; whereas to regional peers, they are unmarked.

Self-confidence	SPEAKER VOICE CATEGORY Non-combinatory subgroups				
	NORTH	SOUTH	TRADITIONAL	MODERN	ALL SPEAKERS
South'n inf's M	4.02	4.18	4.25	4.03	4.12
South'n inf's SD	1.37	1.35	1.38	1.34	1.36
South'n inf's N	278	439	290	427	717
North'n inf's M	3.95	4.31	4.38	4.00	4.16
North'n inf's SD	1.47	1.35	1.32	1.45	1.41
North'n inf's N	403	553	390	566	956

Self-confidence	SPEAKER VOICE CATEGORY Combinatory subgroups				
	NORTH/MOD	NORTH/TRAD	SOUTH/MOD	SOUTH/TRAD	ALL SPEAKERS
South'n inf's M	3.92	4.19	4.11	4.29	4.12
South'n inf's SD	1.44	1.24	1.26	1.46	1.36
South'n inf's N	173	105	254	185	717
North'n inf's M	3.80	4.19	4.17	4.51	4.16
North'n inf's SD	1.56	1.28	1.34	1.34	1.41
North'n inf's N	250	153	316	237	956

LEADERSHIP appears in another set of qualities as well, viz. together with SELF-CONFIDENCE. It is the Northern informants who give parallel ratings with respect to these two qualities:

```
LEADERSHIP and SELF-CONFIDENCE

Northern ratings
(1) SOUTH/TRAD
(2) NORTH/TRAD; SOUTH/MOD
(3) NORTH/MOD
```

The most interesting thing about this ranking is that Northerners downgrade NORTH/MODERN. Incidentally, Southerners, too, do this, but the difference between NORTH/MODERN and the remaining subgroups is not fully significant in the Southern assessment. As for LEADERSHIP, Southerners agree with Northerners in upgrading SOUTH/TRADITIONAL, but not in downgrading NORTH/MODERN. In other words, both informant categories seem to link SOUTH/TRADITIONAL specifically with a relatively high degree of LEADER-SHIP, whereas they seem to think that NORTH/MODERN is low on SELF-CONFIDENCE. On the other hand, Southerners do not seem to feel that SOUTH/TRADITIONAL is so much more marked by SELF-CONFIDENCE than the remaining subgroups (there is a slight tendency to that effect, but the difference is less than significant; $t \leq 1.38$), and they obviously do not seem willing to claim that NORTH/MODERN is typically lacking in LEADERSHIP.

Even though LEADERSHIP and SELF-CONFIDENCE would seem to belong to the same general semantic area, there is undoubtedly a clear difference between them: LEADERSHIP is a quality which requires a social situation for its manifestation; SELF-CONFIDENCE, on the other hand, while normally appearing in social situations, would not seem to require, necessarily, such a situation; we have claimed elsewhere that SELF-CONFIDENCE is an individually significant trait. Now, people clearly generalize more about things that are far away from them. Thus, it is perhaps not so strange that Northerners experience more SELF-CONFIDENCE in SOUTH/TRADITIONAL than do Southerners: they are aware of the typical directions of power in their society and regard it as natural that SELF-CONFIDENCE is an ingredient in the LEADERSHIP they are subjected to. Southerners being regionally close to SOUTH/ TRADITIONAL are perhaps not as likely to connect on an equal basis the individual quality, SELF-CONFIDENCE, with the social quality, LEADERSHIP, even though they, too, are aware of the LEADERSHIP signals conveyed by SOUTH/TRADITI0NAL. They use a finer measurement, it seems.

The downgrading of NORTH/MODERN for SELF-CONFIDENCE by Northern and Southern informants alike (the tendency is stronger among the Northerners) is more difficult to explain. There may be a variety of reasons for the lack of SELF-CONFIDENCE signalled by NORTH/MODERN: listeners who can to some extent pinpoint NORTH/MODERN geographically might make a sociopolitically based judgment from knowing that NORTH/MODERN is located far from the sociopolitical epicentre. Such a judgment might spill over into psychological judgments, e.g. regarding SELF-CONFIDENCE. It might also be the case that the sheer absence of certain Southern prestige markers causes such a reaction to take place. And then again we have the idea of "self-hatred". However, if self-hatred is the cause of the downgrading of NORTH/MODERN by both informant groups, then it would seem that both informant groups associate themselves with NORTH/MODERN. In the case of the Northern informants, this is perhaps within reason, but what about the Southerners? One interesting circumstance in this connection, which we shall deal with more thoroughly later on, is Northerners' and Southerners' respective ratings for LOCAL USUALNESS and SIMILARITY PERSONAL/FRIENDS. It turns out that for all three, Southerners give a higher rating of NORTH/MODERN than do Northerners, even though NORTH/MODERN assumes a low relative position *within* both the Northern and the Southern assessment. In other words, there seem to be certain signs that Southern informants experience as great affinity to NORTH/MODERN as do Northerners. Now, this affinity could very well cause ratings to become more similar than would otherwise be the case. Thus, in theory, it would seem possible that "self-hatred" was operative in all informants' ratings of NORTH/MODERN. Alternatively, there could be factors working here that are too individual to be handled within the present (average-based) framework.

Dependability	SPEAKER VOICE CATEGORY Non-combinatory subgroups				
	NORTH	**SOUTH**	**TRADITIONAL**	**MODERN**	**ALL SPEAKERS**
South'n inf's M	4.23	4.12	4.27	4.09	4.16
South'n inf's SD	1.15	1.15	1.15	1.14	1.15
South'n inf's N	277	437	288	426	714
North'n inf's M	4.32	4.16	4.41	4.09	4.22
North'n inf's SD	1.04	1.17	1.07	1.13	1.12
North'n inf's N	405	553	391	567	958

Dependability	SPEAKER VOICE CATEGORY Combinatory subgroups				
	NORTH/MOD	**NORTH/TRAD**	**SOUTH/MOD**	**SOUTH/TRAD**	**ALL SPEAKERS**
South'n inf's M	4.24	4.21	3.98	4.30	4.16
South'n inf's SD	1.13	1.19	1.15	1.13	1.15
South'n inf's N	174	103	252	185	714
North'n inf's M	4.26	4.41	3.96	4.42	4.22
North'n inf's SD	1.08	0.96	1.16	1.14	1.12
North'n inf's N	251	154	316	237	958

Honesty	SPEAKER VOICE CATEGORY Non-combinatory subgroups				
	NORTH	**SOUTH**	**TRADITIONAL**	**MODERN**	**ALL SPEAKERS**
South'n inf's M	4.58	4.34	4.56	4.35	4.43
South'n inf's SD	1.04	1.10	1.05	1.09	1.08
South'n inf's N	279	438	290	427	717
North'n inf's M	4.70	4.41	4.64	4.46	4.53
North'n inf's SD	0.97	1.06	1.02	1.03	1.03
North'n inf's N	404	552	392	564	956

Honesty	SPEAKER VOICE CATEGORY Combinatory subgroups				
	NORTH/MOD	**NORTH/TRAD**	**SOUTH/MOD**	**SOUTH/TRAD**	**ALL SPEAKERS**
South'n inf's M	4.51	4.71	4.24	4.48	4.43
South'n inf's SD	1.04	1.04	1.12	1.05	1.08
South'n inf's N	174	105	253	185	717
North'n inf's M	4.65	4.79	4.31	4.55	4.53
North'n inf's SD	0.98	0.95	1.04	1.06	1.03
North'n inf's N	250	154	314	238	956

Friendliness — SPEAKER VOICE CATEGORY — Non-combinatory subgroups

	NORTH	SOUTH	TRADITIONAL	MODERN	ALL SPEAKERS
South'n inf's M	4.21	3.77	4.05	3.86	3.94
South'n inf's SD	1.15	1.19	1.16	1.21	1.20
South'n inf's N	278	438	289	427	716
North'n inf's M	4.32	3.73	4.04	3.94	3.98
North'n inf's SD	1.12	1.23	1.24	1.21	1.22
North'n inf's N	406	554	392	568	960

Friendliness — SPEAKER VOICE CATEGORY — Combinatory subgroups

	NORTH/MOD	NORTH/TRAD	SOUTH/MOD	SOUTH/TRAD	ALL SPEAKERS
South'n inf's M	4.15	4.30	3.67	3.90	3.94
South'n inf's SD	1.19	1.09	1.20	1.18	1.20
South'n inf's N	173	105	254	184	716
North'n inf's M	4.25	4.43	3.69	3.79	3.98
North'n inf's SD	1.10	1.15	1.23	1.23	1.22
North'n inf's N	252	154	316	238	960

Intelligence — SPEAKER VOICE CATEGORY — Non-combinatory subgroups

	NORTH	SOUTH	TRADITIONAL	MODERN	ALL SPEAKERS
South'n inf's M	4.30	4.24	4.40	4.17	4.27
South'n inf's SD	1.09	1.25	1.14	1.21	1.19
South'n inf's N	280	435	290	425	715
North'n inf's M	4.47	4.49	4.68	4.34	4.48
North'n inf's SD	1.12	1.23	1.11	1.22	1.19
North'n inf's N	401	551	391	561	952

Intelligence — SPEAKER VOICE CATEGORY — Combinatory subgroups

	NORTH/MOD	NORTH/TRAD	SOUTH/MOD	SOUTH/TRAD	ALL SPEAKERS
South'n inf's M	4.29	4.31	4.09	4.46	4.27
South'n inf's SD	1.07	1.12	1.30	1.15	1.19
South'n inf's N	174	106	251	184	715
North'n inf's M	4.40	4.58	4.30	4.74	4.48
North'n inf's SD	1.19	1.00	1.25	1.17	1.19
North'n inf's N	248	153	313	238	952

Among the qualities that we have discussed so far, AMBITION, DETERMINATION, LEADERSHIP, EDUCATION, all seem to be associated with a large-scale, career outlook on life, rather than a close, inter-personal relationship. We shall now turn to five qualities which also receive partly similar treatment by the informants, but which are more personal in terms of semantic content. These qualities are: DEPENDABILITY, HONESTY, FRIENDLINESS, INTELLIGENCE and EDUCATION.

Before we enter into the discussion on combinatory subgroups, we should note that non-combinatory subgroups give rise to a distribution of average ratings which, for the first three of these qualities, is very different from what we found in connection with the career-type qualities above: NORTH gets higher average ratings throughout, and apart from the Southerners' DEPENDABILITY ratings (t=1.25), differences are clearly significant (t values range from 2.19 to 7.62). There is a peer-group effect in that Northerners more emphatically upgrade NORTH, but the general tendency is the same for both informant groups. This finding, i.e. a relative upgrading of regionally accented speech with regard to traits which represent solidarity (in a wide sense), is in agreement with several earlier studies (e.g. Strongman & Woosley 1967, Cheyne 1970, Giles 1971b). More recent studies (Creber & Giles 1983, Brown *et al.* 1985, cf Introduction: Howard Giles) have yielded results deviating from this idea, probably owing to the fact that they have disregarded the peer-group effect by having any group of regional informants judge any group of regionally accented speakers. There are probably restrictions as to what accents are solidarity-promoting to whom. The present figures seem to support the idea of the North-South dimension in England as a productive dimension for certain realizations of accent-based solidarity.

From these figures, it could be argued that INTELLIGENCE and EDUCATION should rather belong to a career-type category, but the distribution of ratings of combinatory subgroups indicates that they may be partly parallel to DEPENDABILITY, HONESTY and FRIENDLINESS. What these five qualities have in common in terms of informant ratings of combinatory subgroups is that for all five qualities, Southern informants downgrade the voice subgroup SOUTH/MODERN. In terms of statistically distinguishable levels, we get the following ranking:

DEPENDABILITY, HONESTY, FRIENDLINESS*), INTELLIGENCE, EDUCATION**)
Southern ratings***)
(1) NORTH/MOD; NORTH/TRAD; SOUTH/TRAD*)**)
(2) SOUTH/MOD*)

*) In the FRIENDLINESS assessment, there is in fact an even stronger tendency among Southern informants to downgrade SOUTH/MODERN, and indeed SOUTH/TRADITIONAL: SOUTH/MODERN really should have a third level on its own, SOUTH/TRADITIONAL occupying the second level. From the point of view of tendencies, I think this can be disregarded in the present discussion.

**) In their assessment on EDUCATION, Southern informants place SOUTH/TRADITIONAL at a significantly higher level than NORTH/MODERN and NORTH/TRADITIONAL. This too can be disregarded in the present discussion.

***) In terms of downgrading SOUTH/MODERN, Northern informants agree on all these traits. Apart from details, they differ from Southern informants mainly in not distinguishing between the two SOUTH-combinations on FRIENDLINESS, but placing both at the same low level; and in not distinguishing between NORTH-combinations and SOUTH/MODERN on EDUCATION, but placing all three at the same low level. Cf tables.

There is no doubt that these figures are somewhat puzzling. It would have been natural, one would have thought, if "peer-group" ratings had been more favourable. We have already noted on several occasions that the voice subgroups which are closest to the informants themselves in terms of age are the ones comprising MODERN. This is of course not very surprising. The strange thing is that these relatively young, and hence probably modern, informants should choose to downrate that very subgroup to which they would probably belong themselves, had they been included in the voice sample. We should remember that we are now dealing with qualities for which small-scale relationships would seem to play a highly important part, which ought to bring about a certain peer-group effect. But this does not happen.

Before we go on to speculate as to the reason for this, we should remind ourselves that we are talking about average figures which are generally above the middle of the six-step scale; that is to say, in absolute figures, most subgroups get favourable ratings. As for the four qualities we are discussing now, DEPENDABILITY, HONESTY, FRIENDLINESS, INTELLIGENCE, they all yield subgroup ratings above the "non-committal" 3.5, the lowest being the 3.67 that the Southern informants give of SOUTH/MODERN for FRIENDLINESS. However, in all comparative discussions, difference is what matters, and there is no doubt that there is a clear relative downrating of SOUTH/MODERN in the assessment made by Southern informants with regard to these four qualities.

Now, why is this? As for one of the qualities, INTELLIGENCE, I think it could be argued that the link between it and TRADITIONAL is so strong that other considerations will have to take second place. But otherwise? DEPENDABILITY, HONESTY, FRIENDLINESS all seem to belong to that close, small-scale sphere in which peer-group solidarity is more important than prestige. Drawing on Brown's & Gilman's (1960) power/solidarity dichotomy, Andersson (1985:142) writes:

> The status principle tells us that we should appreciate and try to acquire that linguistic form which is used by people of high social status. If we follow this principle in our thinking, we should rank standard language high and dialect low. The solidarity principle tells us that we should appreciate and seek to acquire that linguistic form which is used by the people who are close to us. If we follow this principle, we should rank our own dialect high and the standard language low. It seems reasonable to assume that these two principles are in conflict with each other in many people's minds. Which principle will be victorious in an individual is probably dependent on a number of social, psychological and political factors. Considerations to do with the structure of the competing linguistic forms are probably not of very great importance in this choice (or struggle). [My translation]

Thus, we should expect relatively young (and hence relatively modern) Southern informants to be more favourably inclined towards SOUTH/MODERN than towards other subgroups. On the other hand, small-scale group solidarity probably operates within a clearly limited environment, that is to say, in order for it to operate at all in an accent assessment of the present kind, the accent must be right on target. If it is not, we may well end up in a situation, also described by Andersson (1985:140f), in which people are said to judge their own accent/dialect positively (or negatively, if they take a prestige view); the nearest surrounding accents/dialects negatively, because they sound different and people often come into contact with them; accents/dialects from farther away positively, because they combine difference and that kind of positive, romantic myth which stems from distance and the absence of everyday contact. I shall suggest that the main reason for Southern informants to downgrade SOUTH/MODERN is that it is close, but not close enough, to them. It assumes a "neighbour" rather than a peer position.

An interesting detail in the INTELLIGENCE rating is the general difference in rating levels between Northern and Southern informants. We have already seen that there is a clearly significant difference in terms of overall average ratings (***; t=3.57), and it turns out that this overall difference is paralleled in almost all the subgroup ratings as well. As it is, the Northern informants who give the higher ratings throughout, we can conclude that the neutral kind of voices we use in this study signal INTELLIGENCE particularly strongly to Northerners, probably because Southerners feel more at home with standard-like accents in general (cf EDUCATION above). Interestingly, the Northerners' tendency to upgrade is weakened in connection with NORTH/MODERN, i.e. the Northern informants' most likely peer category in terms of accent.

Sense of humour	SPEAKER VOICE CATEGORY Non-combinatory subgroups				
	NORTH	SOUTH	TRADITIONAL	MODERN	ALL SPEAKERS
South'n inf's M	3.51	3.35	3.44	3.40	3.41
South'n inf's SD	1.28	1.35	1.25	1.37	1.32
South'n inf's N	275	434	285	424	709
North'n inf's M	3.63	3.21	3.43	3.35	3.38
North'n inf's SD	1.20	1.29	1.28	1.27	1.27
North'n inf's N	403	551	391	563	954

Sense of humour	SPEAKER VOICE CATEGORY Combinatory subgroups				
	NORTH/MOD	NORTH/TRAD	SOUTH/MOD	SOUTH/TRAD	ALL SPEAKERS
South'n inf's M	3.52	3.49	3.32	3.40	3.41
South'n inf's SD	1.32	1.21	1.40	1.28	1.32
South'n inf's N	171	104	253	181	709
North'n inf's M	3.58	3.72	3.17	3.25	3.38
North'n inf's SD	1.17	1.25	1.32	1.26	1.27
North'n inf's N	250	153	313	238	954

The third group of qualities that I shall discuss is made up of SENSE OF HUMOUR and FRIENDLINESS. These two qualities undoubtedly belong to the close, personal sphere. The thing they have in common in terms of informant rating is that for both of them, Northern informants upgrade NORTH-combinations and downgrade SOUTH-combinations. Within NORTH and SOUTH, however, they make no significant distinctions. In terms of levels, there is the difference between SENSE OF HUMOUR and FRIENDLINESS ratings that in the latter, the distance between Northerners' ratings of NORTH and SOUTH is considerably greater ($t \geq 4.37$). That is to say, Northern informants distinguish more drastically between NORTH-combinations and SOUTH-combinations with regard to FRIENDLINESS than to SENSE OF HUMOUR. (As it happens, Southern informants give a rather flat set of average ratings for all four subgroups re SENSE OF HUMOUR—small ups, small downs; all ratings between 3.3 and 3.5.)

The questions that should be answered in this context are: (1) why is it that Northerners behave this way towards NORTH-combinations and SOUTH-combinations? and (2) why do we not get a strong reflection of this in the Southerners' ratings?

It seems obvious that Northern informants are exhibiting some kind of peer-group preference here. It also seems natural that such preference should occur in connection with SENSE OF HUMOUR and FRIENDLINESS, as they are qualities in which closeness plays an important part. But what about the Southerners? Ought not they to give the same type of response, albeit in the opposite direction? Is peer-group preference more of a Northern than a Southern feature?

Before we go deeper into this, let us scrutinize the figures we are discussing (cf reference tables above). If we do, it turns out that in the FRIENDLINESS comparison, we get very much the same general tendency in the Southerners' ratings as in those of the Northerners, the difference being that the Southerners distinguish between SOUTH/MODERN and SOUTH/TRADITIONAL to the effect that the latter receives a significantly higher rating (*; t=1.99). We have just noted that Southerners give a flat set of ratings for SENSE OF HUMOUR, in the sense that there are no significantly different levels. However, the (less than significant) tendency in the Southerners' ratings is for them to do exactly the same as the Northerners: upgrade NORTH at the expense of SOUTH. In other words, we do get a reflection of the Northerners' ratings in those of the Southerners, but not a reversed image, as might have been expected. Both Northerners and Southerners seem to rank NORTH higher with regard to SENSE OF HUMOUR, and they certainly do so with regard to FRIENDLINESS (cf Pear quotation p. 330).

So our next question must be: (3) why should NORTH-combinations receive this favourable treatment, not only from Northerners, but also from Southerners? Since there is very little difference in terms of average ratings between Northerners and Southerners, we can perhaps conclude that they have responded in much the same way here, according to much the same principles. That means that we can discard what would otherwise have been a possibility, that Southerners might have judged NORTH according to the principle mentioned above, according to which dialects/accents from afar are said to be judged more favourably. NORTH and SOUTH cannot very well be similarly alien to Northerners and Southerners alike, and at the same time.

Giles (1971b) found that informants responded more favourably to regional accents than to "RP" if ratings concerned "integrity" (cf "solidarity" principle, Andersson quotation above), whereas ratings along "competence" scales (cf "status" principle) were generally higher for "RP". However, "sense of humour", which was one of the personality traits used by Giles, did not follow this pattern: when assessing recordings with regard to this trait, informants tended to exhibit "accent loyalty".

289

Getting different results when judging accents for SENSE OF HUMOUR as compared with FRIENDLINESS would seem to fit into the categorization of personality traits used by Lambert (1967), in which FRIENDLINESS would probably fall within the category referred to as "Personal Integrity", whereas SENSE OF HUMOUR would be regarded as belonging to "Social Attractiveness". It is not altogether clear to me what constitutes the demarkation line between these two categories. And indeed, as we have seen, in the present investigation, we get ratings pointing in the same direction for both these qualities, although Southerners' ratings for SENSE OF HUMOUR do not display significant tendencies.

Basically, however, my results tally with those of Giles (1971b), who interprets his results as indicating

> [...] that the more prestigious "standard" accented voice in Britain is stereotyped as commensurate with highly favourable personality traits of competence - a finding seemingly independent of listeners' regional membership. Nevertheless, "non-standard" regional accented speakers would seem to be stereotyped more favourably than R.P. speakers with respect to personal integrity and social attractiveness.

The difference, of course, is that whereas Giles (and most other researchers that I have studied) concentrates on attitudinal distribution across a wide spectrum of speech modes, going from standard to regional accents (dialects), I have concentrated on the standard area itself. It is interesting to notice that even so, REGIONALITY seems to play much the same part here as it does when regional accent is what is primarily at stake.

But let us return to question (3) concerning the reason for NORTH-combinations receiving favourable treatment from Northerners and Southerners alike. Giles refers to "stereotyping", but of course what is really interesting is why we get the effect at all. This seems to be particularly interesting in the present case, accent differences being by definition small. In other words, what is it in NORTH that promotes FRIENDLINESS and SENSE OF HUMOUR? I think it can be argued that primarily it is the *absence* of certain rhetorical prestige-markers that exist in SOUTH, these prestige-markers being caused by "social connotations" (Trudgill 1983:216ff) which in turn have their origin in the social, political, economic power structure of British society.

Let me elaborate a little on this. If the voices belonging to NORTH had been clearly accented or dialectal, then it would have been natural to look upon informants' responses to them as being brought about by associating them with the regions they come from, which, according to research reported in Trudgill (1983:219f), would enhance positive reactions to accents spoken in "pleasant" regions. In the present study, however, *all* speakers were instructed to speak "neutrally" when making their recordings (cf p. 62). It would seem less than probable that such "neutral" pronunciations would give rise to reactions that are highly regional. On the other hand, there is no doubt that informants do sense a regional difference between NORTH and SOUTH, something that we could demonstrate in our discussion on regional assessment above. Still, I believe that there is a case for referring the relative upgrading of NORTH with respect to FRIENDLINESS and SENSE OF HUMOUR to its lack of certain SOUTH features. The circumstance that in the SENSE OF HUMOUR discussion we are dealing with the downgrading of SOUTH as much as the upgrading of NORTH (judging by subgroup ratings in relation to the non-committal 3.5) would seem to add further weight to this argument.

A less spectacular interpretation would be to say that even though speakers speak "neutrally", there is enough of REGIONALITY in their speech for informants to carry out a region-based assessment, in which case rating levels would be a matter of degree rather than type.

4.7. Rating of acceptability.

This section deals with informants' responses with regard to the 11 job (or group) labels of the questionnaire. They were asked to assess the acceptability of the voices they heard by rating them along six-step scales. The labels were: TEACHER OF ENGLISH, ACTOR/ACTRESS, GROCER'S ASSISTANT, BBC NEWSREADER, DISC JOCKEY, BARRISTER, ROCK SINGER, GOVERNMENT OFFICIAL, WORKINGMAN/-WOMAN, FELLOW WORKER/STUDENT, CHILD/BROTHER/SISTER. The last two labels are not job labels, but were entered here for convenience.

I shall discuss Northerners' and Southerners' ratings of these labels from the point of view of significant differences in rating levels, in much the same way that I have done before, that is, if a voice subgroup gets a significantly higher average rating than another subgroup by one group of informants, then I will look upon the two voices as occupying two distinctly different levels in terms of rating; if not, I will judge them as belonging to one and the same level. As I have pointed out before, it is not possible to maintain this principle at all costs; when it is not, I shall have to make a reasonable judgment of levels.

A quick glance at the ratings given by Northern and Southern informants with regard to the four combinatory voice subgroups, NORTH/MODERN, NORTH/TRADITIONAL, SOUTH/MODERN, SOUTH/TRADITIONAL, and their relation to the 11 job labels, shows that we tend to get two basic groups of labels.

One of these is characterized by an upgrading of TRADITIONAL, particularly SOUTH/TRADITIONAL. To this group belong TEACHER OF ENGLISH, ACTOR/ACTRESS, BBC NEWSREADER, GOVERNMENT OFFICIAL and BARRISTER. The other is marked primarily by a downgrading of SOUTH/TRADITIONAL and, in several cases, an upgrading of NORTH/MODERN. Here we get the following labels: GROCER'S ASSISTANT, ROCK SINGER, WORKINGMAN/-WOMAN, FELLOW WORKER/STUDENT and CHILD/BROTHER/SISTER. The odd man out is DISC JOCKEY which does not present any significant differentiation in levels.

This state of affairs is perhaps not all that surprising. It would seem to fit well into a traditional sociolinguistic structure, possibly with the exception of the two personal labels. However, this grouping is very general. In order to find interesting deviations, we shall have to go deeper into the material.

I am now going to discuss the job labels in such sets as are naturally filtered out by informants' ratings. The greater the unanimity between Northerners' and Southerners' ratings, the stronger the sociolinguistic link between job label and voice subgroup. This would seem to be a reasonable way of looking at things. Also, if there is a difference between Northern and Southern ratings with respect to a certain label, or set of labels, this could be interesting from the point of view of regionally based language change.

Teacher of Engl.	SPEAKER VOICE CATEGORY Non-combinatory subgroups				
	NORTH	SOUTH	TRADITIONAL	MODERN	ALL SPEAKERS
South'n inf's M	4.36	4.27	4.75	4.00	4.31
South'n inf's SD	1.36	1.51	1.33	1.46	1.45
South'n inf's N	280	442	293	429	722
North'n inf's M	4.41	4.40	4.83	4.12	4.41
North'n inf's SD	1.44	1.44	1.22	1.51	1.44
North'n inf's N	405	551	390	566	956

Teacher of Engl.	SPEAKER VOICE CATEGORY Combinatory subgroups				
	NORTH/MOD	NORTH/TRAD	SOUTH/MOD	SOUTH/TRAD	ALL SPEAKERS
South'n inf's M	4.17	4.66	3.89	4.80	4.31
South'n inf's SD	1.31	1.40	1.54	1.29	1.45
South'n inf's N	174	106	255	187	722
North'n inf's M	4.19	4.78	4.06	4.86	4.41
North'n inf's SD	1.54	1.18	1.49	1.24	1.44
North'n inf's N	251	154	315	236	956

Actor	SPEAKER VOICE CATEGORY Non-combinatory subgroups				
	NORTH	SOUTH	TRADITIONAL	MODERN	ALL SPEAKERS
South'n inf's M	4.00	3.90	4.30	3.70	3.94
South'n inf's SD	1.46	1.56	1.42	1.54	1.52
South'n inf's N	279	442	293	428	721
North'n inf's M	4.15	4.08	4.43	3.89	4.11
North'n inf's SD	1.52	1.49	1.40	1.54	1.50
North'n inf's N	405	551	389	567	956

Actor	SPEAKER VOICE CATEGORY Combinatory subgroups				
	NORTH/MOD	NORTH/TRAD	SOUTH/MOD	SOUTH/TRAD	ALL SPEAKERS
South'n inf's M	3.84	4.25	3.60	4.33	3.94
South'n inf's SD	1.44	1.45	1.60	1.41	1.52
South'n inf's N	173	106	255	187	721
North'n inf's M	4.00	4.39	3.79	4.46	4.11
North'n inf's SD	1.59	1.37	1.48	1.42	1.50
North'n inf's N	252	153	315	236	956

BBC newsreader	SPEAKER VOICE CATEGORY Non-combinatory subgroups				
	NORTH	SOUTH	TRADITIONAL	MODERN	ALL SPEAKERS
South'n inf's M	3.65	3.87	4.30	3.44	3.79
South'n inf's SD	1.57	1.61	1.50	1.56	1.59
South'n inf's N	279	442	292	429	721
North'n inf's M	3.66	3.89	4.30	3.45	3.80
North'n inf's SD	1.63	1.69	1.54	1.67	1.67
North'n inf's N	406	552	392	566	958

BBC newsreader	SPEAKER VOICE CATEGORY Combinatory subgroups				
	NORTH/MOD	NORTH/TRAD	SOUTH/MOD	SOUTH/TRAD	ALL SPEAKERS
South'n inf's M	3.41	4.05	3.45	4.45	3.79
South'n inf's SD	1.53	1.55	1.59	1.46	1.59
South'n inf's N	174	105	255	187	721
North'n inf's M	3.48	3.96	3.42	4.51	3.80
North'n inf's SD	1.69	1.49	1.65	1.54	1.67
North'n inf's N	252	154	314	238	958

Among the job labels for which SOUTH/TRADITIONAL receives a favourable rating, three labels stand out as being treated very similarly by Northerners and Southerners, viz. TEACHER OF ENGLISH, ACTOR/ACTRESS and BBC NEWSREADER. The only difference in terms of distinct levels is that there is a tendency for SOUTH/TRADITIONAL to form its own higher level sometimes, whereas sometimes it shares the same level with NORTH/ TRADITIONAL:

TEACHER OF ENGLISH

Northern ratings	Southern ratings
(1) NORTH/TRAD; SOUTH/TRAD	(1) NORTH/TRAD; SOUTH/TRAD
(2) NORTH/MOD; SOUTH/MOD	(2) NORTH/MOD
	(3) SOUTH/MOD

ACTOR/ACTRESS

Northern ratings	Southern ratings
(1) NORTH/TRAD; SOUTH/TRAD	(1) NORTH/TRAD; SOUTH/TRAD
(2) NORTH/MOD; SOUTH/MOD	(2) NORTH/MOD; SOUTH/MOD

BBC NEWSREADER

Northern ratings	Southern ratings
(1) SOUTH/TRAD	(1) SOUTH/TRAD
(2) NORTH/TRAD	(2) NORTH/TRAD
(3) NORTH/MOD; SOUTH/MOD	(3) NORTH/MOD; SOUTH/TRAD

These tables show that in terms of distinct levels of rating, there is full agreement between Northerners and Southerners both for ACTOR/ACTRESS and for BBC NEWSREADER. The levels given for ACTOR/ACTRESS seem to be primarily based on DEGREE OF MODERNITY, less so on REGIONALITY. When judging the voices with regard to BBC NEWSREADER on the other hand, both informant groups place SOUTH/TRADITIONAL significantly higher than any other voice subgroup. As for TEACHER OF ENGLISH, Southerners interestingly downgrade SOUTH/MODERN, while showing the same preferences as the Northerners at the top of the ranking-list.

I think it is interesting that we get these particular similarities and differences when comparing Northern and Southern ratings. They show first of all that the voices that according to the system of categorization used in this study fall within MODERN are generally thought to be less acceptable, and similarly so, with regard to job labels which would seem to have a traditional link with language "correctness". Consequently, TRADITIONAL receives favourable treatment here. We have referred to BBC NEWSREADER earlier on as a "correctness archetype", that is, a model of language correctness and neutrality. According to the present results, there seems to be a certain amount of REGIONALITY built into that ideal.

The difference between Northern and Southern ratings with respect to TEACHER OF ENGLISH seems to indicate greater particularity on the part of the Southerners in accepting voice differences in teachers, as they select one particular combinatory subgroup, SOUTH/MODERN, for particularly negative treatment. We recall that this subgroup is the one to which a large proportion of the Southern informants would belong themselves, viz. the sixth-formers, who are a majority among the informants of this study. This would seem either to indicate unwillingness on the part of Southerners to associate the idea of TEACHER with themselves—but there seems to be no good reason why such a sentiment should not be shared by the Northerners—or to suggest that the accents represented by SOUTH/MODERN are somehow stigmatized in the opinion of Southerners in connection with TEACHER. A couple of pages back, I discussed the perceived ranking of subgroups on the traits HONESTY, FRIENDLINESS, DEPENDABILITY, INTELLIGENCE and EDUCATION. We recall that what these traits had in common in that context was the significant downgrading of SOUTH/MODERN by the Southern informants. It might be possible to argue that there is some kind of parallelism between the Southerners' rating for TEACHER and that for these five traits: the Southerners feel (1) that the traits are highly valued in a TEACHER; and (2) that the low ratings of SOUTH/MODERN for the traits make this subgroup linguistically unsuitable for that job label. From a student's viewpoint, such a parallelism would not seem to be entirely at fault. Again, we see that the greater expertise on the part of the Southerners towards SOUTH naturally leads to greater particularity.

Barrister	SPEAKER VOICE CATEGORY Non-combinatory subgroups				
	NORTH	SOUTH	TRADITIONAL	MODERN	ALL SPEAKERS
South'n inf's M	3.43	3.88	4.18	3.38	3.71
South'n inf's SD	1.64	1.69	1.60	1.66	1.68
South'n inf's N	277	438	290	425	715
North'n inf's M	3.42	3.86	4.09	3.39	3.67
North'n inf's SD	1.71	1.74	1.67	1.73	1.74
North'n inf's N	404	552	389	567	956

Barrister	SPEAKER VOICE CATEGORY Combinatory subgroups				
	NORTH/MOD	NORTH/TRAD	SOUTH/MOD	SOUTH/TRAD	ALL SPEAKERS
South'n inf's M	3.32	3.61	3.42	4.51	3.71
South'n inf's SD	1.62	1.66	1.69	1.46	1.68
South'n inf's N	172	105	253	185	715
North'n inf's M	3.29	3.62	3.46	4.40	3.67
North'n inf's SD	1.75	1.61	1.72	1.64	1.74
North'n inf's N	252	152	315	237	956

Gov't official	SPEAKER VOICE CATEGORY Non-combinatory subgroups				
	NORTH	SOUTH	TRADITIONAL	MODERN	ALL SPEAKERS
South'n inf's M	4.01	4.28	*4.60*	3.89	4.18
South'n inf's SD	1.42	1.50	1.30	1.52	1.48
South'n inf's N	278	436	289	425	714
North'n inf's M	3.82	4.11	*4.31*	3.77	3.99
North'n inf's SD	1.55	1.62	1.50	1.62	1.59
North'n inf's N	403	551	387	567	954

Gov't official	SPEAKER VOICE CATEGORY Combinatory subgroups				
	NORTH/MOD	NORTH/TRAD	SOUTH/MOD	SOUTH/TRAD	ALL SPEAKERS
South'n inf's M	3.86	4.26	3.91	4.79	4.18
South'n inf's SD	1.43	1.39	1.59	1.20	1.48
South'n inf's N	173	105	252	184	714
North'n inf's M	3.73	3.99	3.81	4.52	3.99
North'n inf's SD	1.61	1.44	1.64	1.50	1.59
North'n inf's N	251	152	316	235	954

Of the job labels for which SOUTH/TRADITIONAL seems to be favoured, two labels remain to be discussed, viz. BARRISTER and GOVERNMENT OFFICIAL. They get the following treatment in terms of distinct levels:

BARRISTER

Northern ratings
(1) SOUTH/TRAD
(2) THE REST

Southern ratings
(1) SOUTH/TRAD
(2) THE REST

GOVERNMENT OFFICIAL

Northern ratings
(1) SOUTH/TRAD
(2) THE REST

Southern ratings
(1) SOUTH/TRAD
(2) NORTH/TRAD
(3) NORTH/MOD; SOUTH/MOD

First, I would like to comment on the difference between BARRISTER and BBC NEWSREADER (cf above). In both cases, there seems to be full agreement between Northerners and Southerners. However, whereas both informant groups give a three-level set of ratings for BBC NEWSREADER, it is only SOUTH/TRADITIONAL that stands out positively in the BARRISTER assessment. I would suggest that the reason for this is that although both BBC NEWSREADER and BARRISTER might be looked upon as correctness archetypes, there is the difference that whereas people stare newsreaders straight in the eye every night, most of them have never had the opportunity to meet a barrister at all, apart from film barristers. In other words, stereotyping is probably much stronger in the BARRISTER assessment than in the BBC NEWSREADER assessment.

As for GOVERNMENT OFFICIAL, we have already noted that the job label as such is not an entirely satisfactory one because of semantic inexactitude. Looking at the ratings, it would seem as if Northern informants made a more stereotypical judgment in elevating SOUTH/TRADITIONAL at the expense of the remaining subgroups, whereas Southerners would rather seem to be more detailed in their judgment in distinguishing between NORTH/TRADITIONAL and SOUTH/TRADITIONAL as well as the remaining two subgroups. When at the beginning of this section I discussed briefly overall averages (cf p. 297), I noted that there was in fact a significant difference (*; t=2.49) between Northerners' and Southerners' overall ratings regarding GOVERNMENT OFFICIAL: the Southerners' overall rating is higher than that of the Northerners. It turns out that the subgroup to affect the overall average most strongly is SOUTH/TRADITIONAL; here Southern informants give a significantly higher rating (*; t=1.99) than do the Northerners. Also, Southerners seem to favour NORTH/TRADITIONAL more strongly than do Northerners in this connection.

One possible way of approaching this problem is to say that Southerners, by virtue of their regional location, experience greater proximity to the business of government, which might bring about a less stereotyped judgment. There is also the problem of the label itself to be considered. "Government" can mean different things, e.g. national and local government. If Northerners because of their distance from London are more likely to associate GOVERNMENT OFFICIAL with local government, then we might expect greater equality between their ratings of the four subgroups; they would in that case exhibit a blend of national and local viewpoints. For the Southerners, on the other hand, national and local viewpoints might perhaps walk hand in hand, thus enhancing the acceptability rating of SOUTH/TRADITIONAL. But this discussion is clearly speculative.

Grocer's ass. — SPEAKER VOICE CATEGORY — Non-combinatory subgroups

Grocer's ass.	NORTH	SOUTH	TRADITIONAL	MODERN	ALL SPEAKERS
South'n inf's M	3.48	3.08	2.94	3.44	3.24
South'n inf's SD	1.64	1.66	1.62	1.66	1.66
South'n inf's N	277	436	289	424	713
North'n inf's M	3.37	3.19	3.01	3.44	3.26
North'n inf's SD	1.62	1.70	1.66	1.65	1.67
North'n inf's N	404	550	389	565	954

Grocer's ass. — SPEAKER VOICE CATEGORY — Combinatory subgroups

Grocer's ass.	NORTH/MOD	NORTH/TRAD	SOUTH/MOD	SOUTH/TRAD	ALL SPEAKERS
South'n inf's M	3.57	3.34	3.36	2.71	3.24
South'n inf's SD	1.63	1.66	1.69	1.55	1.66
South'n inf's N	173	104	251	185	713
North'n inf's M	3.45	3.23	3.43	2.86	3.26
North'n inf's SD	1.59	1.66	1.70	1.64	1.67
North'n inf's N	251	153	314	236	954

Rock singer — SPEAKER VOICE CATEGORY — Non-combinatory subgroups

Rock singer	NORTH	SOUTH	TRADITIONAL	MODERN	ALL SPEAKERS
South'n inf's M	2.53	2.28	2.11	2.56	2.38
South'n inf's SD	1.54	1.43	1.34	1.54	1.48
South'n inf's N	277	434	289	422	711
North'n inf's M	2.36	2.37	2.19	2.49	2.37
North'n inf's SD	1.42	1.55	1.42	1.53	1.49
North'n inf's N	405	551	390	566	956

Rock singer — SPEAKER VOICE CATEGORY — Combinatory subgroups

Rock singer	NORTH/MOD	NORTH/TRAD	SOUTH/MOD	SOUTH/TRAD	ALL SPEAKERS
South'n inf's M	2.63	2.36	2.52	1.97	2.38
South'n inf's SD	1.59	1.46	1.51	1.24	1.48
South'n inf's N	172	105	250	184	711
North'n inf's M	2.41	2.27	2.55	2.13	2.37
North'n inf's SD	1.43	1.40	1.61	1.43	1.49
North'n inf's N	251	154	315	236	956

Workingman	SPEAKER VOICE CATEGORY Non-combinatory subgroups				
	NORTH	SOUTH	TRADITIONAL	MODERN	ALL SPEAKERS
South'n inf's M	3.77	3.31	3.13	3.74	3.49
South'n inf's SD	1.63	1.67	1.67	1.63	1.67
South'n inf's N	276	429	286	419	705
North'n inf's M	3.62	3.46	3.32	3.68	3.53
North'n inf's SD	1.57	1.65	1.59	1.63	1.62
North'n inf's N	400	550	388	562	950

Workingman	SPEAKER VOICE CATEGORY Combinatory subgroups				
	NORTH/MOD	NORTH/TRAD	SOUTH/MOD	SOUTH/TRAD	ALL SPEAKERS
South'n inf's M	3.97	3.45	3.57	2.94	3.49
South'n inf's SD	1.57	1.69	1.65	1.63	1.67
South'n inf's N	170	106	249	180	705
North'n inf's M	3.62	3.62	3.72	3.12	3.53
North'n inf's SD	1.59	1.55	1.66	1.58	1.62
North'n inf's N	247	153	315	235	950

We now turn to the second of the two basic groups that we created to begin with, viz. the one made up of GROCER'S ASSISTANT, ROCK SINGER, WORKINGMAN/-WOMAN, FELLOW WORKER/STUDENT, CHILD/ BROTHER/SISTER. I shall discuss the first three together and then go on to the last two; there seem to be good reasons to make that kind of subdivision, partly owing to the semantics of the labels, and partly to the way ratings were made.

GROCER'S ASSISTANT

Northern ratings	Southern ratings
(1) NORTH/MOD; NORTH/TRAD; SOUTH/MOD	(1) NORTH/MOD; NORTH/TRAD; SOUTH/MOD
(2) SOUTH/TRAD	(2) SOUTH/TRAD

ROCK SINGER

Northern ratings	Southern ratings
(1) NORTH/MOD; SOUTH/MOD	(1) NORTH/MOD; NORTH/TRAD; SOUTH/MOD
(2) NORTH/TRAD; SOUTH/TRAD	(2) SOUTH/TRAD

WORKINGMAN/-WOMAN

Northern ratings	Southern ratings
(1) NORTH/MOD; NORTH/TRAD; SOUTH/MOD	(1) NORTH/MOD
(2) SOUTH/TRAD	(2) NORTH/TRAD; SOUTH/MOD
	(3) SOUTH/TRAD

It is clear from these tables that SOUTH/TRADITIONAL is regarded as incompatible with these job labels, and there is no regional variation in this particular judgment. Another thing that should be noticed straightaway is that in four of the ranking-lists above, we get exactly the same relative ranking: SOUTH/TRADITIONAL stands out negatively, whereas the remaining three subgroups occupy one and the same level. Since this kind of configuration has a strong sense of stereotypicality about it, I shall start by dealing with the two ranking-lists that exhibit a deviant pattern.

It seems that Northerners differ from Southerners in their judgment of ROCK SINGER, the difference being that NORTH/TRADITIONAL is regarded as equally unacceptable as SOUTH/ TRADITIONAL in connection with this particular job label. The figures underlying these ranking-lists show that the difference in this respect is not as great as the lists suggest. However, it seems reasonable that Northerners, by having a keener ear for nuances in NORTH, should feel that NORTH/TRADITIONAL is as inappropriate as anything in a ROCK SINGER. The greatest difference in subgroup ratings when comparing Northern and Southern informants' assessments regarding ROCK SINGER is the one we find for the subgroup NORTH/MODERN. Without being significant (t=1.48), the difference might indicate that Southern informants feel that NORTH/MODERN is less inappropriate (we are still at the negative end of the scale on the whole) in a ROCK SINGER than do Northerners. It can probably be argued that in the same way as they seemed less willing to accept NORTH/TRADITIONAL in connection with ROCK SINGER, Northern informants are perhaps too particular when making a judgment of NORTH/MODERN to be able to accept this variety in that connection. To Southerners, it is probably easier to go by whatever "foreign" sounds they hear in NORTH/MODERN and link them up with the age factor, which obviously plays a part here. It is a commonplace that in Britain since The Beatles, there is a strong notional link between the North and pop culture. For somebody who is a member of the Northern community, more requirements probably have to be fulfilled in order for a Northern voice to earn that kind of recognition.

Because of the way subgroup ratings are distributed, differences being small, this discussion is inevitably of a speculative nature. However, what seems to be beyond doubt is that whereas Northern and Southern informants agree as to the relative inappropriateness in a ROCK SINGER of TRADITIONAL as compared with MODERN (relative, since we are talking about values which are clearly at the negative end of the scale), Southerners apparently feel that NORTH is less inappropriate than SOUTH in this connection (*; t=2.21). This is not the case in the assessment made by the Northerners, who in fact give exactly the same rating of NORTH as of SOUTH (2.36 vs. 2.37).

Quite apart from the matter at issue, this discussion shows how tricky it is to attain interpretative clarity when several levels of subdivision are involved. A tendency which is reasonably strong at one level (such as the difference between Northerners' and Southerners' ratings of NORTH mentioned in the preceding paragraph), will often be broken up into much weaker tendencies when dealt with at a lower, subgroup, level. In the present case, it is the Southern informants' ratings of NORTH/MODERN (2.63, relatively high) and SOUTH/TRADITIONAL (1.97, relatively low) which make up the basis for the significant difference between the Southern ratings of the superordinate groups, NORTH and SOUTH. It is here that the difference between Northerners' and Southerners' ratings is created. The Southerners give a wider scope of ratings, and of course this is something which is easily concealed in averages of a higher level.

To sum up, ROCK SINGER, as might have been expected, yields low ratings throughout when considered in relation to the neutral voices we have here. Northern and Southern informants have exactly the same overall average (2.37 and 2.38, respectively). The main difference between Northerners' and Southerners' subgroup ratings is that Southerners give a relatively higher rating of NORTH/MODERN and a relatively lower rating of SOUTH/ TRADITIONAL. As for the higher rating of NORTH/MODERN, it is probably an effect of a cultural stereotype strengthened by distance. The lower rating of SOUTH/TRADITIONAL could perhaps be explained in terms of Southerners being more conscious of certain subtle prestige markers in SOUTH/TRADITIONAL which might add to its inappropriateness with regard to ROCK SINGER. Although subgroup differences are often small here, I believe it is safe to regard this particular difference between Southerners' and Northerners' ratings as genuine.

The second job label of the ones we are discussing now for which a deviant pattern of ratings is given is WORKINGMAN/-WOMAN. The label as such suffers from semantic inexactitude, which might cause certain questionable results. That I shall disregard for the time being. The deviation from the majority of the ranking-lists that we can notice with respect to WORKINGMAN/-WOMAN is in many ways similar to what we found regarding ROCK SINGER. If anything, it is more clearcut.

The most conspicuous thing about the WORKINGMAN/-WOMAN ratings, and indeed what makes up the deviation from the other ranking-lists, is the way Southern informants elevate NORTH/ MODERN with respect to this job label. The difference between Southerners' and Northerners' ratings of this job label is one of the few differences in the entire job label comparison to attain statistical significance (*; t=2.22). Thus, there seems to be little doubt that to the Southern informants, NORTH/MODERN signals features which have a bearing on WORKINGMAN/-WOMAN, or rather, what this label stands for, which, as we have seen, is not

301

altogether clear.

Another interesting thing to notice is the total lack of differentiation in the Northern assessment between NORTH/MODERN and NORTH/TRADITIONAL. Both subgroups get the rating 3.62 from the Northern informants, that is to say, their ratings are centred around the "non-committal" 3.5. This non-differentiation should be compared with the clearly significant difference that the Northerners make between SOUTH/MODERN and SOUTH/TRADITIONAL (***; t=4.28). This difference is primarily caused by a downgrading of SOUTH/TRADITIONAL, but also a slight upgrading of SOUTH/MODERN with regard to WORKINGMAN/-WOMAN (3.72 vs. 3.12).

The Southern informants, as we have seen, distinguish markedly between NORTH/MODERN and NORTH/TRADITIONAL (**; t=2.60). In addition to this, they distinguish between SOUTH/MODERN and SOUTH/TRADITIONAL (***; t=3.92).

As was the case in the ROCK SINGER discussion above, these ratings create a situation in which Southern informants seem to make a significant regional distinction between NORTH and SOUTH (***; t=3.60), whereas there is no such distinction in the assessment made by the Northern informants (t=1.51). But again, as we have seen, it is essential to bear in mind that this situation is one brought about by the upgrading/downgrading of combinatory subgroups, rather than of non-combinatory regional groups. In other words, there seem to be features in NORTH/MODERN which to people who themselves do not belong to that region give rise to certain "working-class" responses, whereas people who do belong to that region do not seem to make that kind of response. On the other hand, SOUTH/TRADITIONAL seems to elicit a non-working class response from all informants.

I believe it could be argued that SOUTH/TRADITIONAL is the linguistic antithesis of what is often referred to as "working class", and that this situation is general all over England. This comes as no great surprise; it is well in keeping with prevailing ideas about "RP". The Southern upgrading of NORTH/MODERN in this connection is probably a stereotype whose origin can be traced back to the historical structure of British industry, coupled with, perhaps, a certain amount of influence from pop culture, not least in the sense that pop culture (in a wide sense, of course) gave access to cultural phenomena that were previously outside the scope of general concern. The circumstance that Northern informants do not isolate NORTH/MODERN this way is, I believe, ascribable to their greater involvement, which would seem to reduce the risk of generalization. It is probably significant that Northerners' ratings of NORTH are very close to the non-committal 3.5, as for that matter are all the ratings within the WORKINGMAN/-WOMAN comparison except those concerning SOUTH/ TRADITIONAL and, as we have noted, Southerners' ratings of NORTH/ MODERN. To the Northern informants, there is probably no "working class" quality in these voices; they are simply neutral voices with little or no markedness about them. The same seems to be the case with SOUTH/MODERN: both Northern and Southern informants place their ratings of this subgroup fairly close to 3.5. If there is a tendency—less than significant—it is for Northern informants to give a slightly higher WORKINGMAN/-WOMAN rating of SOUTH/MODERN. Since differences are small here, I shall not go any deeper into this. Suffice it to say that the MODERN-ness of SOUTH/MODERN, in addition to its foreignness in relation to Northern informants, might produce such an effect.

At the outset of my discussion of GROCER'S ASSISTANT, ROCK SINGER and WORKINGMAN/-WOMAN, I said that four out of six ranking-lists regarding these job labels exhibited identical ranking: SOUTH/TRADITIONAL occupying a low level on its own, the remaining three subgroups sharing a higher level. Now, this configuration certainly has a stereotypical touch to it, similar to what we found in connection with BARRISTER above, but the other way round, of course. When dealing with BARRISTER, I suggested that the circumstance that most people have never been in touch with such a person might lead to their making a stereotypical judgment. Similarly, strange as it may seem at first sight, people's relationship with WORKINGMAN/-WOMAN (in the strict sense of the word, cf p. 76) is probably equally prone to stereotypicality, primarily because the label has no typical oral expression. Such stereotypicality is probably reinforced by the semantic looseness of the WORKINGMAN/-WOMAN label.

GROCER'S ASSISTANT is a job label chosen because of its presumed oral expression linked up with a, shall we say, humble social position. Both informant groups react in a stereotypical way when confronted with this label: the only significant difference between subgroups is that brought about by the downgrading of SOUTH/TRADITIONAL. Furthermore, there is very little difference between Southern and Northern ratings. However, if we conflate combinatory subgroups into purely regional categories, NORTH and SOUTH, we get an interesting difference between Northern and Southern informants' ratings. It turns out that whereas Northerners present no significant differences between their ratings of NORTH and SOUTH (t=1.65), Southerners distinguish very clearly (**; t=3.15) between these two groups: SOUTH gets a lower rating for GROCER'S ASSISTANT. If, despite their non-significant differentiation, we look at subgroups to see how they have contributed to this difference, we notice that again it is probably the Southerners' relative upgrading of NORTH/MODERN and downgrading of SOUTH/ TRADITIONAL that have caused this effect. We also notice, interestingly, that in terms of exact rating levels, Northern informants give (non-significantly) lower ratings than Southerners of both NORTH-combinations, whereas they give (non-significantly) higher ratings of both SOUTH-combinations; that is to say, it seems that there is a certain tendency for informants to stress more strongly the inappropriateness of their "own" category with regard to GROCER'S ASSISTANT. It should be noticed, finally, that apart from SOUTH/TRADITIONAL, all subgroups get average ratings that lie fairly close to the non-committal 3.5, which might be said to point towards a certain inability among informants to connect these voices with the label GROCER'S ASSISTANT.

Disc jockey	SPEAKER VOICE CATEGORY Non-combinatory subgroups				
	NORTH	SOUTH	TRADITIONAL	MODERN	ALL SPEAKERS
South'n inf's M	2.80	2.65	2.64	2.75	2.70
South'n inf's SD	1.56	1.45	1.47	1.51	1.49
South'n inf's N	279	439	289	429	718
North'n inf's M	2.79	2.75	2.80	2.74	2.77
North'n inf's SD	1.43	1.44	1.42	1.44	1.43
North'n inf's N	406	553	391	568	959

Disc jockey	SPEAKER VOICE CATEGORY Combinatory subgroups				
	NORTH/MOD	NORTH/TRAD	SOUTH/MOD	SOUTH/TRAD	ALL SPEAKERS
South'n inf's M	2.85	2.70	2.67	2.61	2.70
South'n inf's SD	1.57	1.54	1.47	1.43	1.49
South'n inf's N	174	105	255	184	718
North'n inf's M	2.72	2.92	2.77	2.72	2.77
North'n inf's SD	1.43	1.42	1.45	1.42	1.43
North'n inf's N	252	154	316	237	959

The label DISC JOCKEY receives a remarkably flat set of ratings by Northerners and Southerners alike, which, together with the low absolute level of the ratings (2.61-2.92), indicates that the informants find it difficult to associate these voices with that label, and to differentiate between voices on a NORTH-SOUTH basis. This goes to show that the regional aspect of the typical DISC JOCKEY voice is probably not linked to any British geographical region, but rather with the non-geographical, imaginary region of the media (cf Howard quotation above p. 154).

The last two labels to be discussed are FELLOW WORKER/STUDENT and CHILD/BROTHER/SISTER. The questions underlying these labels were phrased, "How acceptable would you consider this accent to be in a fellow worker/student of yours?" and "in your child (or brother/sister)?". Obviously these labels are not job labels, but rather group labels, or something to that effect. They were, however, answered by the informants together with the job labels and will be discussed together with them here, because they belong to the social sphere and give rise to very much the same kind of discussion as the job labels.

Fellow worker	SPEAKER VOICE CATEGORY Non-combinatory subgroups				
	NORTH	SOUTH	TRADITIONAL	MODERN	ALL SPEAKERS
South'n inf's M	4.01	3.56	3.55	3.87	3.74
South'n inf's SD	1.53	1.68	1.67	1.60	1.64
South'n inf's N	278	435	290	423	713
North'n inf's M	3.79	3.33	3.38	3.62	3.53
North'n inf's SD	1.62	1.68	1.65	1.67	1.67
North'n inf's N	405	551	389	567	956

Fellow worker	SPEAKER VOICE CATEGORY Combinatory subgroups				
	NORTH/MOD	NORTH/TRAD	SOUTH/MOD	SOUTH/TRAD	ALL SPEAKERS
South'n inf's M	4.17	3.76	3.66	3.43	3.74
South'n inf's SD	1.48	1.58	1.65	1.71	1.64
South'n inf's N	173	105	250	185	713
North'n inf's M	3.84	3.69	3.45	3.18	3.53
North'n inf's SD	1.61	1.64	1.70	1.64	1.67
North'n inf's N	252	153	315	236	956

Child/br/sis	SPEAKER VOICE CATEGORY Non-combinatory subgroups				
	NORTH	SOUTH	TRADITIONAL	MODERN	ALL SPEAKERS
South'n inf's M	3.29	2.93	3.03	3.10	3.07
South'n inf's SD	1.69	1.72	1.72	1.71	1.72
South'n inf's N	277	433	286	424	710
North'n inf's M	3.23	2.76	2.88	3.01	2.96
North'n inf's SD	1.71	1.70	1.72	1.72	1.72
North'n inf's N	405	551	389	567	956

Child/br/sis	SPEAKER VOICE CATEGORY Combinatory subgroups				
	NORTH/MOD	NORTH/TRAD	SOUTH/MOD	SOUTH/TRAD	ALL SPEAKERS
South'n inf's M	3.41	3.10	2.88	3.00	3.07
South'n inf's SD	1.67	1.72	1.71	1.73	1.72
South'n inf's N	174	103	250	183	710
North'n inf's M	3.24	3.22	2.82	2.67	2.96
North'n inf's SD	1.72	1.71	1.70	1.70	1.72
North'n inf's N	252	153	315	236	956

In terms of answers in general, both FELLOW WORKER/STUDENT and CHILD/BROTHER/SISTER fall within the same category as the job labels we have just been discussing, i.e. the labels which seem to elicit low level ratings for SOUTH/TRADITIONAL and often relatively high levels for NORTH/MODERN. Let us look at these two labels in somewhat more detail.

FELLOW WORKER/STUDENT and CHILD/BROTHER/SISTER

Northern ratings	Southern ratings
(1) NORTH/MOD; NORTH/TRAD	(1) NORTH/MOD
(2) SOUTH/MOD; SOUTH/TRAD	(2) THE REST

This is the way ratings are distributed onto distinct levels. We see straightaway that Northern informants seem to go by REGIONALITY in giving ratings according to what seems to be a solidarity or closeness principle. In the case of Southerners, things are more confusing. They in fact elevate NORTH/MODERN at the expense of the remaining three subgroups with regard to FELLOW WORKER/STUDENT and CHILD/BROTHER/SISTER. In other words, they seem to perform a reversed closeness activity in rating the voices.

However, there are deviations from these rather clearcut levels if we look at subgroup ratings more closely, even if we do not always get statistical significance. If we start by looking into the ratings concerning FELLOW WORKER/STUDENT, we immediately notice two things: (1) as compared with the other subgroups, there is a clear upgrading of NORTH/MODERN in the Southern assessment. There is no doubt about this. (2) There is a clear downgrading of SOUTH/ TRADITIONAL in the Northern assessment; in fact, we very nearly get a third level in the Northern ranking-list above, made up by SOUTH/TRADITIONAL alone (it is significantly lower than NORTH/ TRADITIONAL (**; t=3.00) but the difference is just short of significance (t=1.87) when compared with SOUTH/MODERN). Now, as for Northerners downgrading SOUTH/TRADITIONAL, it would seem to be in accordance with expectations, but why should Southerners *and* Northerners give their highest rating to NORTH/MODERN? Self-hatred does not seem to be able to explain it, as such an emotion ought reasonably to be working in both informant groups, and it is only the Southerners who have given a reversed closeness answer here. In addition to the strangeness of this situation, we even get a significant difference (*; t=2.14) between Northerners' and Southerners' ratings of NORTH/MODERN, to the effect that Southerners give a higher rating in terms of absolute rating level too.

A couple of pages back, when we were discussing FRIENDLINESS and SENSE OF HUMOUR (cf pp 288ff), we obtained results that had certain, but not all, traits in common with the present ones. This means first of all that we may be dealing with voices which, for reasons beyond the horizon of the present method of investigation, possess a number of positive qualities, which of course would make the speakers agreeable as fellow workers. That possibility I shall not pursue any further. In that earlier context, however, I referred to a paper by Giles (1971b) in which he claims that people who speak non-standard regional accents get more favourable ratings in general for "personal integrity and social attractiveness". On the other hand, Hudson (1980:204) reports a study by Greg Smith, in which working-class secondary school pupils of Newham, London, evaluated accented speech similar to their own negatively, even for qualities such as friendliness, kindness, and honesty. These two examples from the field of sociolinguistic research show at any rate that interpretation of attitudinal data is far from clearcut.

The model I can offer on the basis of my own results and of course within the framework of my own method is that a neutral type of Northern English (1) signals sociability to English listeners in general, regardless of the regionality of the listeners; (2) is perceived as containing more sociability traits by listeners who are not themselves Northern (cf Pear quotation p. 330).

In his very fine book, *On Dialect* (1983), Peter Trudgill refers to the so-called "mental map" theory devised by geographers in order to elucidate people's regional preferences, i.e. where they would like to live, had they a free choice. Geographers use this theory to explain, or add structure to, migrational trends in society, etc. Informative writing on mental maps can be found in Gould & White (1968), Gould & White (1974, new ed. 1986), Gould (1975).

Gould and his colleagues found that British school leavers exhibited a great deal of unanimity in their regional preferences: if we exclude the obvious egocentricity aspect, which causes people to state that they would prefer to stay where they are, it turns out that the region along the English south coast, from Cornwall to Kent, constitutes the area of residential top preference for British school leavers in general. We can also see that the London metropolitan area gets considerably lower ratings than immediately surrounding areas; London is a "sinkhole", in the topographical metaphor of Gould. Broadly speaking, residential preference ratings drop the farther north we go in Britain, but there are certain exceptions to this tendency, such as the area in the North West of England (Cumberland, Westmoreland) known for its scenic beauty and the attraction it has for tourists. As far as England proper is concerned, the least attractive area seems to be one delimited by the Scottish border in the north and a line from roughly Liverpool to the Humber in the south, excluding the "Lake District Dome" (Gould)—in other words, what is generally referred to as the North. However, as Gould and his colleagues point out, the most interesting thing about a mental map is where there are "high gradients" (Gould's metaphor again), i.e. great differences in perception over a limited distance. Such a high gradient can be seen to enclose the "Midland Mental Cirque", i.e. an area south of the Liverpool-Humber line, between the Border on Wales and East Anglia, which receives considerably lower preference ratings than the areas immediately surrounding it.

Trudgill (1983:219) draws on this information, saying that "it is probable that there would be widespread agreement in England that the most unattractive accents in the country are those of the West Midlands in general and Birmingham in particular." Trudgill's idea is that people associate accents with the areas where they are spoken, to the effect that pleasant areas are said to have nice-sounding accents, and vice versa (cf Introduction, Giles 1970).

However, from my point of view, at least two things could be said about this: (1) it seems as if Trudgill has partly misread Gould's and White's "national perception surface" of Britain (Gould & White 1986:43), because according to that presentation, as we have just noted, the area north of the "Midland Mental Cirque" (*ib.*) gets even lower residential preference ratings, although the "gradient" between Midland and North is not as high as between South and Midland; and according to Trudgill's own logic, this situation ought to be reflected in accents as well, which, in Trudgill's opinion, is not the case. Trudgill's pessimistic view of the way people perceive Birmingham is however corroborated by Dicken & Lloyd (1981:298, cf below), so we must be careful when making judgments here. (2) At any rate, my own results with regard to FELLOW WORKER/STUDENT and CHILD/BROTHER/SISTER do not fit into this pattern. I am aware that what we are discussing is acceptability in FELLOW WORKER/STUDENT, not pleasantness in general (that will come later).

So it seems to be reasonably clear that a neutral type of spoken English with a possible regional touch to it cannot be socio-linguistically graded on the basis of a Gould & White national perception surface, at least not where acceptability in FELLOW WORKER/STUDENT is concerned. The average regional coefficient of the speaker subgroup NORTH/MODERN (the subgroup which receives the highest ratings for FELLOW WORKER/STUDENT) is 5.00 on a scale going from 1 to 6, where 1 is "London" and 6 is "North". This goes to show that we in fact get ratings which are reversed from what we might have expected going by Trudgill's speculation.

If I may speculate a little myself, I think that a crucial point lies in the very label, FELLOW WORKER/STUDENT. What is it you want to find in a person you are working together with? Probably various kinds of socially attractive traits contribute to forming such an ideal person. But it should be noted that what we probably do not want *a priori* is too much self-consciousness, or other ego-promoting qualities. We have seen on several occasions that there is a notional link between SOUTH/TRADITIONAL and such qualities, judging by informants' ratings. Now, maybe NORTH/MODERN, rather than explicitly representing something in its own right, functions as a notional antithesis of SOUTH/TRADITIONAL; or, to put it more simply, maybe the chief attraction in NORTH/MODERN is that it lacks some of the prestige markers that exist in SOUTH/TRADITIONAL. It is also possible that this lack is more obvious to people who are not themselves Northern; Northern informants will probably be less inclined to take notice of certain traits in NORTH/MODERN that are obvious to Southern informants, simply because they do not stand out as being very special to them. On the other hand, they will probably be more likely than Southerners to notice certain features in SOUTH/TRADITIONAL, which, in the present context, ought to show itself in a downgrading of SOUTH/TRADITIONAL by Northerners. And indeed, that is the result we get in the FELLOW WORKER/STUDENT comparison.

We should notice here that what seems on the surface to be a case of contradiction—I have on several occasions claimed that *proximity* promotes expertise—is really a function of two entirely different things. It is quite possible for, say, a Northerner with little knowledge of subtle accent distinctions in SOUTH to be more observant than a Southerner of certain social prestige markers in SOUTH, and vice versa.

If we turn to CHILD/BROTHER/SISTER, we see straightaway that in terms of relative levels, we get the same distribution as for FELLOW WORKER/STUDENT. But there are differences between the two comparisons. One interesting difference is that NORTH/MODERN, while being the highest-rating subgroup in the assessment of both informant groups, does not stand out as markedly as it did in connection with FELLOW WORKER/STUDENT. We should also remember that we are now talking about considerably lower overall levels of rating (around 3.00).

As for the NORTH-SOUTH division, it seems absolutely clear that there is a preference in favour of NORTH, both among Northerners and Southerners. The NORTH-SOUTH difference is significant all over (Southern assessment **; t=2.74; Northern assessment ***; t=4.21). Contrary to what was the case for FELLOW WORKER/STUDENT, we do not get significant differences between MODERN and TRADITIONAL; that is to say, it seems to be REGIONALITY only, however it may be conveyed, that manages to distinguish between levels of preference in CHILD/BROTHER/SISTER.

The only combinatory subgroup for which there is a significant difference between Northerners' and Southerners' ratings is SOUTH/ TRADITIONAL (*; t=1.96), Northern informants giving a lower rating.

It is undoubtedly intriguing that Southerners should be as favourably inclined (in the case of NORTH/MODERN more so) to NORTH as Northerners in the CHILD/BROTHER/SISTER connection. In fact, Southerners' rating of NORTH/MODERN (3.41) is the only rating in the present comparison that comes close to the "non-committal" 3.5 of our six-step scale. Other ratings are considerably lower.

A great deal of what I said when discussing FELLOW WORKER/ STUDENT above is, I believe, valid here too. We might again ask the question: what kind of language, or accent, do we prefer in people who are so close to us as to be directly associated with us? Looking at subgroup ratings, it seems clear that preferences do not always follow a regionally predictable pattern. The Southern low water mark is the rating concerning SOUTH/MODERN. This result seems to be the reverse of what would be expected, considering the fact that SOUTH/MODERN ought to be the accent nearest to the Southern informants themselves, a majority of whom are relatively young.

I believe it can be argued that "self-hatred" is a possible explanation of this result, which might tally with the results reported by Hudson (1980; cf above p. 307) concerning the downgrading of their own accent by secondary school pupils in Newham, London.

It would have been interesting to find out to what extent such downgrading is supported, implicitly, by the Gould & White mental map theory: whether London informants in any way deviate from other informants in not giving high residential preference to their home territory. Unfortunately, however, we do not get any information about Londoners' mental map ratings, in spite of the fact that there were London informants in Gould's and White's investigation (1968). The authors chose to select a limited number of locations for their presentation, and the metropolis is not one of them. So Gould and White do not offer an answer to the obvious question whether London is a "sinkhole" even as perceived by the Londoners themselves (Gould (1975) fails to answer the same question about the Stockholm "sinkhole" in a similar investigation about Swedish mental maps).

Now, suppose "self-hatred" is more of a capital city phenomenon, owing to the circumstance that in the metropolis, there is a more obvious clash between the correctness principle of the cultural and socio-economic epicentre on the one hand, and the popular vernacular on the other; then we would expect London working-class school children to downgrade Cockney or near-Cockney speech the way they do according to Hudson's report (1980); we might perhaps also expect the Southern informants of the present study to be more prone to self-hatred than the Northerners and to show this by downgrading SOUTH/MODERN and upgrading (relatively speaking) SOUTH/TRADITIONAL. This is the result we get here.

Also, suppose people who are more directly subjected to linguistic imperialism by living close to a linguistic power centre, such as London, are in addition more sensitive to the attractiveness caused by its lack of metropolitan prestige features that can be found in NORTH/MODERN. This, in conjunction with general distance-based romanticism, and a certain amount of post-Beatle pop cultural influence, might be the factor underlying the present upgrading by Southern informants of NORTH/MODERN in CHILD/BROTHER/SISTER.

The circumstance that there seems to be such preference also indicates the direction in which the standard language is moving with regard to accent, since the CHILD/BROTHER/SISTER question deals with the language of people you are in a position to influence, one way or another. This is something rather more than simply stating what you prefer on some kind of aesthetic grounds.

The Northern informants, as we have seen, give very much the same ratings in terms of general tendencies, but their differentiation mainly takes place within SOUTH: the two NORTH subgroups get virtually identical ratings.

I believe there is a case here for the metropolitan "sinkhole" idea put forward by Gould & White. Gould (1975:62) writes about the sinkhole in the mental map of residential preference constituted by Stockholm, the capital of Sweden: "We can only speculate that the Stockholm region is also condemned as the seat of government—*any* government—whose bureaucrats push paper around, but do little but mess up the situation in the North." Gould goes on to say that there exists a similar situation in Britain, giving as an example the "disparaging views" Scottish informants have of London. (Judging by the findings of Romaine 1980:223, these disparaging views also spill over into the field of accent: "RP" is "emphatically rejected" by Scottish listeners, both with regard to personal similarity and preference for personal use.)

This explanation, then, is purely socio-political in that it associates language with the power position of its speakers. I would like to stress though, that even if this kind of explanation has its advantages, not least by being neat and reasonably easy to handle, I do not think that it can account for all the variation that is normally ascribed to it within the field of sociolinguistics. For one thing, it necessitates, as far as I can see, a certain amount of foreknowledge on the part of the hearer; how else could she possibly know what to associate with what? Do we know for sure that all hearers have this foreknowledge always? Probably not. I shall not go deeper into this matter here.

I would, however, like to go a little deeper into the arguments offered by social and economic geographers which seem to have a bearing on the present issue.

There is no doubt that Gould's mental map theory has its advantages as a point of reference when carrying out attitudinal investigations of other kinds, e.g. about language, so long as there is some kind of regional aspect involved. A mental map in fact is a map of attitudes.

Similar to mental maps are investigations such as the one reported by Dicken & Lloyd (1981:298), in which respondents were asked to "rank up to six [urban] areas in which they would most like to live and six in which they would least like to live." Among the twenty or so most-preferred areas, we find typical tourist places, such as Keswick, York, Tunbridge Wells, Stratford-upon-Avon; in fact, they are all to some extent examples of smallish, well-known resorts, often of historical interest, The least-preferred urban areas, on the other hand, are, not unexpectedly, the large industrial towns and cities, such as Birmingham, Liverpool, Manchester, Leeds, Cardiff. One city which gets a very high ranking for both preference and non-preference is London, which might be taken as an indication of London's highly special status among British cities: nowhere in Britain is there such glaring social contrast as in the metropolis. On the one hand, London is virtually the only place for a large and growing number of career opportunities in the higher social tiers (D.M. Smith 1979:132); on the other, it is the site of the most turbulent changes in lower-level socio-economic life in the UK recently (Hudson & Williams 1986:105ff).

As a contrast to mental maps, there are also investigations whose aim is to present "objective" facts about different regions, based on official statistics. An example of such an investigation can be found in D.M. Smith (1979:122ff). Ten British regions were given a value representing their status with regard to 25 objective measures of life quality, e.g. Gross Domestic Product, unemployment rate, infant mortality. These measures were then subjectively weighted by informants for relative importance, and then the original values were transformed into "weighted quality-of-life indicators" for the ten regions, respectively. The results of this investigation were condensed in the form of a map of Britain with the ten regions indicated. For each of these regions, there was a figure representing "quality of life", the basic division being between regions above and regions below the average quality of life, according to the method used. This division turns out to be extremely clearcut when rendered graphically on a map of Britain: above average are the areas of England proper south of a line going from just south of Liverpool to the Wash, that is to say, West Midlands, East Midlands, East Anglia, the South West and the South East, the South East getting by far the highest rating for quality of life; below average is the rest, i.e. Wales, England north of the Midlands, and Scotland, Scotland getting a considerably lower rating than the other low scorers.

Now, it is interesting to see to what extent an objectively based account such as D.M. Smith's correlates with a subjective, purely attitudinal one, for instance Gould's mental map. There is a formal difficulty involved when attempting a comparison of this kind: whereas the objective investigation has been carried out within defined areas, what will look like areas on a mental map will to a very great extent be governed by the instruction supplied to the person making up such a map.

In the case of Gould's & White's British investigation (1968, 1974, 1986), informants were asked to rank the 92 counties of Britain (in 1965) with regard to residential preference. Informants were given a map with all the counties indicated. As we noted when discussing Dicken's & Lloyd's investigation above, there is a strong tendency for informants to let their preferences be governed by knowledge or prejudice of whatever happens to be well-known in the area/county under scrutiny. That is to say, rather than covering the area, a mental map informant expands that which symbolizes the area into a full mental area. Liverpool is expanded to become the mental picture of all Lancashire; Brighton, perhaps, or the Downs, of all Sussex.

In very broad terms, the Gould mental map does seem to correlate with Smith's objective map, particularly with respect to the North-South-Wales-Scotland division. One type of deviation is obvious, though, viz. that which is created by archetypical tourist areas, such as the Lake District, or the South West, which are elevated on the mental maps as compared with the objective ones. Another deviation is probably London, which forms a "sinkhole" in Gould's presentation, whereas in Smith's presentation it is not even treated separately, but merely as a part of the South East, which of course reduces comparability a great deal.

Before we turn back to the language discussion, we should also notice that there is a third aspect of the problem of regional preference, viz. the satisfaction felt by people who actually live in a given area. This is discussed by Knox (1982:303f). He writes:

> [...] people in Northern Ireland are strikingly—and understandably—less satisfied with life than is the 'average' UK or EEC resident; but the greatest overall levels of satisfaction are in Yorkshire and Humberside, the East Midlands, and Scotland and not in the 'objectively' more prosperous London and South-East.

Knox's own explanation of this phenomenon is that the level of expectation is higher in the more "prosperous" areas, hence a lower level of subjectively felt fulfilment of these expectations.

Now, this might form a clue as to why distance-based romanticism does not work both ways in our FELLOW WORKER/STUDENT and CHILD/BROTHER/ SISTER discussion, in addition to what we have suggested regarding socio-economic reasons of various kinds: maybe satisfaction is greater, relatively speaking, even as regards accent, among people who live relatively far away from the epicentre of a prestige accent (cf Introduction, p. 49f: "Melchers 1985"). This would tally with suggestions I have made earlier, that the degree of conflict between a prestigious language variety and a "deviant" accent will probably be greater the closer one gets to the home base of the prestigious variety.

4.8. Pleasantness, usualness, job interview, similarity.

And now for the last group of questions in the questionnaire. The content of the questions will be explained as we go along.

DEGREE OF PLEASANTNESS.
Here, the informants were asked to state how pleasant they thought the accents they heard were. Answers were given along a six-step scale. Of course, it is highly interesting to see to what extent the scores obtained here harmonize with the ones we got for FELLOW WORKER/STUDENT and CHILD/BROTHER/ SISTER; in other words, to see if there is a difference between aesthetics with an explicit social base and aesthetics without such a base in the judgment of accent preference.

Pleasantness	SPEAKER VOICE CATEGORY Non-combinatory subgroups				
	NORTH	SOUTH	TRADITIONAL	MODERN	ALL SPEAKERS
South'n inf's M	4.12	3.76	4.15	3.73	3.90
South'n inf's SD	1.20	1.32	1.31	1.25	1.29
South'n inf's N	278	430	290	418	708
North'n inf's M	4.38	3.84	4.30	3.90	4.07
North'n inf's SD	1.16	1.34	1.25	1.30	1.30
North'n inf's N	408	552	392	568	960

Pleasantness	SPEAKER VOICE CATEGORY Combinatory subgroups				
	NORTH/MOD	NORTH/TRAD	SOUTH/MOD	SOUTH/TRAD	ALL SPEAKERS
South'n inf's M	4.03	4.26	3.52	4.08	3.90
South'n inf's SD	1.20	1.21	1.24	1.36	1.29
South'n inf's N	172	106	246	184	708
North'n inf's M	4.27	4.55	3.61	4.14	4.07
North'n inf's SD	1.18	1.12	1.32	1.31	1.30
North'n inf's N	253	155	315	237	960

One difference is obvious from the start: overall averages (i.e. disregarding subgroup ratings) are higher here than in the previous comparisons, so it seems as if there is something in the type of voices we are dealing with that promotes "purely aesthetic" appreciation.

In terms of distinct levels of rating, we get the following result:

```
DEGREE OF PLEASANTNESS

Northern  ratings                 Southern  ratings
(1) NORTH/TRAD                    (1) NORTH/MOD; NORTH/TRAD; SOUTH/TRAD
(2) NORTH/MOD; SOUTH/TRAD         (2) SOUTH/MOD
(3) SOUTH/MOD
```

As usual, these levels are based on statistical significance to as great an extent as possible. It should be noticed, however, that in terms of (less than significant) tendencies, we get very much the same ranking in the Southerners' assessment as in the Northerners'.

Two combinatory subgroups give rise to significant differences between Northerners' and Southerners' ratings, viz. NORTH/ MODERN and NORTH/TRADITIONAL. For both of these, Northern informants give significantly higher ratings than do Southerners (*; t=2.04, t=1.99). The explanation closest at hand is of course that the judgment has been made according to a principle of closeness.

More interesting, however, is to see how ratings differ within Northerners' and Southerners' assessments. As we have just noted, there are great similarities in the way the two informant groups distribute their ratings from a relative aspect. Both groups agree that NORTH/TRADITIONAL should be placed highest and that SOUTH/MODERN ought to end up lowest. Furthermore, both groups place NORTH/MODERN and SOUTH/TRADITIONAL at very much the same internal in-between level. Let us discuss the subgroups placed at the extremes by both informant groups, NORTH/TRADITIONAL and SOUTH/MODERN.

It could be argued of course that the very circumstance that Northerners and Southerners give a similarly shaped distribution of ratings might point in the direction of there not being a regional basis for their ratings, but that underlying factors must be looked for elsewhere. This is obviously a strong possibility. I shall however try to suggest explanations within the framework of the present study, much the same way as I have been doing all the time. The reader, just like myself, will have to keep in mind that this discussion is limited by the boundaries of my own method, and to the extent that this method is unsatisfactory, my explanations will suffer. This is a matter of course, and need not be gone into any further.

Why should both Northern and Southern informants agree that SOUTH/MODERN is the least PLEASANT subgroup; and NORTH/ TRADITIONAL the most PLEASANT one? And why is it that SOUTH/ TRADITIONAL, which as we remember got very favourable ratings in many of the questions concerning psychological qualities and job labels, does not reach a peak position here? A possible explanation is *social markedness*. SOUTH/TRADITIONAL is in a sense the more marked of the two TRADITIONAL-combinations; and SOUTH/MODERN is the more marked of the two MODERN-combinations. It is reasonably easy to offer evidence of the markedness of SOUTH/TRADITIONAL: this variety exhibits a strong combination of on the one hand regional power markers (SOUTH) and on the other cultural/educational prestige markers (TRADITIONAL). This combination will probably be associated by many people with the national (chiefly London-based) establishment, and hence, whatever dislikes people have of such an establishment will affect the language variety linked up with it. It is like being both old and ugly (or young and good-looking): these qualities add up to something rather more than either of them represents—markedness.

> The reader will notice that I use the word "markedness", not as a technical term, once and for all defined, but as a term to be supplied with various modifiers in order to make sense in a variety of contexts. Thus, I have talked about "neutral markedness" (p. 271), "regional markedness" (p. 272), and now, "social markedness". There are probably connections between the various kinds of markedness, but the relationship is likely to be a multidimensional one which does not allow a simple explanatory model.

> Honey (1985:248) distinguishes between "*marked* and *unmarked* RP, where 'unmarked' suggests the mainstream—and arguably socially neutral—form, and 'markings' are linguistic signals of certain forms of social privilege or pretension." This would seem to be an idea closely related to the one presented here.

The markedness of SOUTH/MODERN is less easy to motivate. I believe we have to resort to a concept we have used on several occasions earlier on: self-hatred, and all that is connected with it. As for the Southern informants and their downgrading of SOUTH/MODERN, self-hatred would seem to make up a reasonable explanation, according to the same kind of arguments as the ones I used when discussing FELLOW WORKER/STUDENT and CHILD/ BROTHER/SISTER above. Now, is it at all possible that such self-hatred might be transmittable to people farther away from the core of a conflict, so that they too adopt this disparaging view of the "self-haters"? Or to use a pointed example, the self hatred reported to be present in working-class London school children's language evaluations (cf Hudson 1980:204), which I suggest is created, or at least enhanced, by these children's proximity to London as a centre of prestigious English, can that self-hatred be transmitted so that for instance Northerners also experience a certain downgradedness in their judgment of such working-class London English? I shall not pretend that I am capable of answering that question in an unequivocal way. But if the answer is yes, that might explain Northerners' and Southerners' unanimous relative downgrading of SOUTH/MODERN. A circumstance supporting such a view is, I believe, the outstanding status of Cockney as compared with other English accents and dialects. The reason why Cockney is so much more of a recognized phenomenon than most other accents is not only Eliza Doolittle and other mythical heroes and heroines; as Wells (1982:301) points out, "[London's] working-class accent is today the most influential source of phonological innovation in England and perhaps in the whole English-speaking world." By being so influential, it is only natural if Cockney is recognized as a symbol of substandard, or working-class, language, much the same way that SOUTH/TRADITIONAL is a symbol of the language of the upper tiers of society. Provisional support for this suggestion is offered by Giles & Sassoon (1983), who found that listeners in a matched-guise experiment tended to downgrade Cockney socially relative to "RP" even after learning that the Cockney speaker was middle class. Even though I may be accused of stretching things too far, I suggest that there is resemblance between our subgroup SOUTH/MODERN on the one hand, and Cockney (or near-Cockney) on the other. An amusing illustration of this suggestion can be found in Cleave (1982), which is an interview with the seventy-eight-year-old historian, writer, ex-Etonian and expatriate, Sir Harold Acton. Sir Harold "feels himself [...] entangled in the past, and his semi-isolation from changing times has preserved him *en gelée* and lent him the interest of an historical personage." Having lived most of his life abroad, he objects to the remark that "[h]e doesn't sound completely English":

> 'The English one hears nowadays seems strange to my ears. I went to Eton not long ago to see a play of Anouilh and they were all talking cockney. They acted with enthusiasm, but their accents defeated me.'

If there is a link between Cockney and modern Southern neutral accents, SOUTH/MODERN may well attain enough markedness to make it relatively un-PLEASANT at a national level. I have of course no intention of downgrading any accent; all I am trying to do is interpret the present results.

317

The idea of "contagious self-hatred" seems to find support in the United States: Labov (1966:482ff) reports on the negative prestige of New York City speech which is very much recognized by the New Yorkers themselves. He even suggests (p. 488) that the oft-reported dislike of the New York accent by outsiders is a projection of the New Yorkers' own linguistic self-hatred. However that may be, Labov offers several accounts of New Yorkers claiming to have been ridiculed by outsiders because of their accent. As for the reason for this negative prestige, Labov does not attempt an explanation, but refers the matter to other disciplines than linguistics.

It may also be a question of expectations (I am grateful to my colleague David Wright for making a comment to this effect). Maybe people who are not themselves Southern expect Southerners to "speak proper"; and if they do not, they will be more stigmatized than Northern substandard speakers would be in a reversed situation, because for them, there is no such expectation.

To sum up this rather speculative discussion: I have suggested that SOUTH/TRADITIONAL and SOUTH/MODERN, which both receive relatively low ratings from Northern and Southern informants alike, are *socially marked*, SOUTH/TRADITIONAL owing to its "upper-crust" (Wells 1982) implications, SOUTH/MODERN owing to its popular Southern, possibly Cockney-like, qualities, which make it function as a substandard symbol. I have also suggested that it is this markedness which causes informants, when dealing with DEGREE OF PLEASANTNESS, (1) to place NORTH/TRADITIONAL, rather than SOUTH/TRADITIONAL, in the top position; (2) to place SOUTH/MODERN in the bottom position.

Here a question could be raised: why should markedness be unattractive from the point of view of DEGREE OF PLEASANTNESS? To answer that question, we must recall what our figures represent and also in what sort of situations ratings were given. All the ratings that I have been discussing are average ratings calculated from individual informants' ratings. Furthermore, these individual ratings concerned individual voices. It would seem natural that a set-up of this kind might promote a distribution of average ratings which avoids extremes, since in order for informants to want to choose an extreme variety for their preference, this variety must probably be right on target from the point of view of the informant. Since it is unlikely that a large group of informants would exhibit exactly the same kind of preference pattern, it seems probable that, as a group, they go for whatever is less, rather than more, marked. That such an idea is not just the result of speculation but is very much in existence in the "real world" becomes obvious if we study a related phenomenon, viz. the decision-making process which guides what TV shows to put on at a given time within a commercial, advertisement-financed TV system (cf Gottlieb 1986): you never choose somebody's first choice, because that will probably be too special to attract a big audience; rather, you choose something that can be *accepted* by everybody. "Nobody likes it very much but they still watch it." You won't get an Emmy, but you'll get the dollars (cf also the Ford Edsel discussion, Introduction p. 87).

There is, of course, also the possibility of individual informants wanting to avoid extremes, to play it safe somehow. This tendency is common in guessing, as we have noted on several occasions (cf for example p. 98), and it does not seem totally out of the question to expect something of the same kind in an open judgment of preference.

I suggest that the present figures indicate that it is clearly insufficient to draw strong conclusions about accent preferences from comparisons between "RP" and "regional accents" alone, since we find within a neutral range of accents, such as the one studied here, clear internal differentiation which, at any rate, does not place SOUTH/TRADITIONAL highest, even though SOUTH/ TRADITIONAL gets generally high ratings for "competence".

If we compare the general profile of ratings that we obtained for DEGREE OF PLEASANTNESS with those obtained for acceptability in FELLOW WORKER/STUDENT and CHILD/BROTHER/SISTER, we see that the main shift seems to take place between NORTH/MODERN and NORTH/TRADITIONAL, NORTH/MODERN being preferred generally in connection with FELLOW WORKER/STUDENT and CHILD/BROTHER/ SISTER, NORTH/TRADITIONAL in connection with DEGREE OF PLEASANTNESS. In principle, this goes for Southern as well as Northern informants. Thus, it seems that at any rate neutral accents/voices displaying the features NORTH, whatever the substance of that feature, exert some kind of positive attraction on listeners. I would like to offer as a tentative explanation that it is NORTH's dialectic quality of being non-SOUTH that causes this preference. As for the shift between NORTH/MODERN and NORTH/ TRADITIONAL, it only goes to show that preference is a complex matter. I believe a crucial factor is whether the listener in any way has to involve himself in the judgment he is making, because as soon as he is, he will be part of a power structure which will tend to promote other opinions than purely "objective" ones. That is not to say that such other opinions are less real or true: they are simply different.

LOCAL AND GENERAL USUALNESS.
We now turn to the questions on LOCAL and GENERAL USUALNESS. The informants were asked the question, "Do you think this accent is heard very often (a) in your part of England [LOCAL]? (b) in England as a whole [GENERAL]?" and were required to answer along six-step scales.

Obviously, these questions are crucial to this investigation, particularly when discussing REGIONALITY, since they will show to what extent informants can actually place neutral accents like the ones used here regionally.

| Local usualness | SPEAKER VOICE CATEGORY Non-combinatory subgroups | | | | |
	NORTH	SOUTH	TRADITIONAL	MODERN	ALL SPEAKERS
South'n inf's M	3.76	4.17	4.27	3.82	4.01
South'n inf's SD	1.46	1.43	1.35	1.50	1.45
South'n inf's N	279	436	293	422	715
North'n inf's M	3.12	2.56	2.87	2.75	2.80
North'n inf's SD	1.39	1.43	1.48	1.42	1.44
North'n inf's N	409	552	393	568	961

| Local usualness | SPEAKER VOICE CATEGORY Combinatory subgroups | | | | |
	NORTH/MOD	NORTH/TRAD	SOUTH/MOD	SOUTH/TRAD	ALL SPEAKERS
South'n inf's M	3.58	4.06	3.99	4.40	4.01
South'n inf's SD	1.47	1.39	1.49	1.31	1.45
South'n inf's N	172	107	250	186	715
North'n inf's M	3.05	3.25	2.51	2.63	2.80
North'n inf's SD	1.39	1.40	1.40	1.47	1.44
North'n inf's N	254	155	314	238	961

Let us start with the LOCAL USUALNESS comparison. A quick glance at the figures makes it clear that we get very obvious differences between Northerners' and Southerners' ratings throughout (***; t≥3.77). These differences are all slanted towards the South, so the broadest possible analysis is that Southern informants feel more at home with these accents than Northern informants, generally speaking.

However, it is only when we check the way ratings are distributed internally by Northerners and Southerners that we get at the really interesting differences. This is the way informants place the four subgroups in terms of distinct levels:

LOCAL USUALNESS

Northern ratings
(1) NORTH/MOD; NORTH/TRAD
(2) SOUTH/MOD; SOUTH/TRAD

Southern ratings
(1) SOUTH/TRAD
(2) NORTH/TRAD; SOUTH/MOD
(3) NORTH/MOD

It seems obvious that Northern informants recognize the accents somehow, and that their judgment is a reflection of this. The Southerners' assessment is somewhat less clearcut, but here too we find certain amount of "correctness" in REGIONALITY, although there is a merger between NORTH/TRADITIONAL and SOUTH/MODERN in terms of levels.

It is interesting to notice that the relative attractiveness of NORTH/ MODERN that we found in Southerners' (and Northerners') acceptability ratings for FELLOW WORKER/STUDENT and CHILD/ BROTHER/SISTER is not reflected in a high relative LOCAL USUALNESS rating. In other words, it seems that Southerners are attracted by NORTH/MODERN somehow, even though they are certain as to its "foreignness".

SOUTH/TRADITIONAL gets the highest rating by far of all the ratings in this comparison, viz. Southern informants' 4.40 on a six-step scale. The difference between this rating and the remaining three ratings by Southern informants is clearly significant (t≥2.09). Particularly interesting is the difference (**; t=2.99) between Southerners' rating of SOUTH/TRADITIONAL (4.40) and that of SOUTH/MODERN (3.99), since this indicates that people from the South believe that SOUTH/TRADITIONAL is in fact more frequently heard in the South than SOUTH/MODERN, which, although this can be neither verified nor falsified here, does not appear likely from a strictly factual point of view.

In this context, it should be remembered that a majority of the informants of this study are sixth-formers, which means that they are subjected to spoken English produced by teachers five days a week. It is probable that in the South at least, a "SOUTH/TRADITIONAL ideal" prevails in that particular situation (cf Trudgill 1983:186ff). To some extent the same goes for several unequal social contact situations in which these sixth-formers, as well as other Southerners, participate, because the very situation of being *subjected* to language, rather than acting in a spontaneous speech role, is one which promotes "correctness" ideals (cf Freire 1970, *passim*).

Some more weight is added to this idea by the Northern informants' rating of NORTH/TRADITIONAL, which, although differences are less than significant at the five per cent level (t=1.41), is the highest average rating given by the Northerners. Thus, it seems that a locally coloured TRADITIONAL delivery is felt to be "often heard" both by Northerners and Southerners. I believe that the school situation is responsible for a large part of this result. The reason for SOUTH/TRADITIONAL receiving an outstandingly high average rating by Southern informants, apart from the school situation, can probably be found in the rather special status of SOUTH/TRADITIONAL in connection with various aspects of official life in the South, and nationally; it would seem natural for such status to colour informants' views, even though the present question is supposed to deal with LOCAL USUALNESS.

Gen. usualness	SPEAKER VOICE CATEGORY Non-combinatory subgroups				
	NORTH	SOUTH	TRADITIONAL	MODERN	ALL SPEAKERS
South'n inf's M	3.70	3.71	3.73	3.69	3.71
South'n inf's SD	1.13	1.18	1.16	1.15	1.16
South'n inf's N	274	436	288	422	710
North'n inf's M	3.90	3.85	3.94	3.82	3.87
North'n inf's SD	1.13	1.15	1.07	1.18	1.14
North'n inf's N	405	548	392	561	953

Gen. usualness	SPEAKER VOICE CATEGORY Combinatory subgroups				
	NORTH/MOD	NORTH/TRAD	SOUTH/MOD	SOUTH/TRAD	ALL SPEAKERS
South'n inf's M	3.74	3.63	3.67	3.78	3.71
South'n inf's SD	1.14	1.11	1.16	1.19	1.16
South'n inf's N	171	103	251	185	710
North'n inf's M	3.91	3.89	3.75	3.98	3.87
North'n inf's SD	1.20	1.02	1.17	1.11	1.14
North'n inf's N	251	154	310	238	953

The GENERAL USUALNESS comparison is in many ways different from the LOCAL USUALNESS comparison, which is reassuring from the point of view of this study and the method employed in it, since it indicates that informants respond, not arbitrarily, but in what seems to be an honest way.

For instance, in terms of overall levels, Northern informants this time give higher ratings throughout, that is, they consider the accents of this study more common in England as a whole than do the Southerners. However, most of the time, these differences are less than significant. On three occasions, we do get significant differences between Northerners' and Southerners' average ratings: (1) Northerners give a higher GENERAL USUALNESS rating of NORTH, as compared with SOUTH (*; t=2.26), which perhaps is not terribly surprising; (2) Northerners rate TRADITIONAL higher than Southerners (*; t=2.44); (3) Northerners (as a consequence, of course) rate ALL voices higher (**; t=2.81) than Southerners. No combinatory subgroup manages to attain a significant difference in rating, but NORTH/TRADITIONAL is close (t=1.93) in Northerners upgrading this subgroup, relatively speaking.

There seems in other words to be a tendency among Northern informants to consider TRADITIONAL more often heard "in England as a whole", as compared with Southerners. In fact, the highest subgroup rating of all in this particular comparison is Northern informants' rating of SOUTH/TRADITIONAL (3.98). I believe there is a case for interpreting this as an overgeneralization caused by SOUTH/TRADITIONAL's very strong position in the media and other official or power-related social networks; if an accent is regionally alien to a listener, but at the same time widely heard, for instance on television, then this listener will probably tend to allot greater quantitative importance to that accent than would somebody to whom the accent was more familiar, provided the latter had some good reason not to believe that the accent was so widely heard. Such a reason might be personal knowledge of the accent distribution in one's own region.

Contrary to what was the case when discussing LOCAL USUALNESS, there is no dramatic internal spread of average ratings within Southerners' and Northerners' assessment. This is how they distribute their average ratings in terms of distinct levels:

```
+---------------------------------------------------------------+
|                                                               |
|  GENERAL  USUALNESS                                           |
|                                                               |
|  Northern  ratings                     Southern  ratings      |
|  (1) NORTH/MOD; NORTH/TRAD; SOUTH/TRAD  (1) ALL SUBGROUPS SAME |
|  (2) SOUTH/MOD                                                 |
|                                                               |
+---------------------------------------------------------------+
```

It is striking how close to one another Southerners place their ratings in terms of average values. Their entire spread is contained within the 3.63-3.78 area, i.e. just above the non-committal 3.5.

Northerners, as we have already noted, give generally higher ratings, with the exception of their rating of SOUTH/MODERN (3.75).

I believe what we are seeing here is in fact a twofold phenomenon on the part of Northerners' ratings: (1) they naturally overrate the importance of NORTH-combinations, such accents being familiar to them in their everyday life, which, as we have seen, is mainly school life; (2) in addition, they overrate the importance of the nationally prestigious SOUTH/TRADITIONAL, this accent being frequently heard in the media and other places of importance.

For the Southern informants, the situation is different: they partly feel regionally alienated from NORTH-combinations; partly they know that SOUTH/TRADITIONAL, although nationally well-known, is not as common as people might believe; and as for SOUTH/MODERN, which in terms of speaker AGE and REGIONALITY would seem to be closest to the Southern informants themselves, it perhaps misses the target of GENERAL USUALNESS by being too special, or indeed too far from the conventional correctness ideal.

We might add that the very idea of GENERAL USUALNESS is not altogether unproblematic. If we exclude people with a special interest in language, or perhaps people with a very extensive experience from various regions, there is really no other way for a person to come to grips with GENERAL USUALNESS than by generalizing from the language of *general sources*, which in a centralized society is equivalent to what is known as the standard.

ADVANTAGE IN JOB INTERVIEW.

The next question was phrased "Do you think the speaker's accent would be a disadvantage or an advantage for him/her in a job interview with an employer?". Answers were given along a six-step scale. Here we should expect answers to reflect informants' subjectively felt attitudes concerning the socio-economic status of the accents, which is also a type of aesthetics, although different.

Job Interview	SPEAKER VOICE CATEGORY Non-combinatory subgroups				
	NORTH	SOUTH	TRADITIONAL	MODERN	ALL SPEAKERS
South'n inf's M	4.49	4.51	4.90	4.23	4.50
South'n inf's SD	1.13	1.34	1.08	1.30	1.26
South'n inf's N	280	430	290	420	710
North'n inf's M	4.67	4.52	4.93	4.35	4.58
North'n inf's SD	1.11	1.29	1.03	1.28	1.22
North'n inf's N	409	551	390	570	960

Job interview	SPEAKER VOICE CATEGORY Combinatory subgroups				
	NORTH/MOD	NORTH/TRAD	SOUTH/MOD	SOUTH/TRAD	ALL SPEAKERS
South'n inf's M	4.36	4.70	4.14	5.01	4.50
South'n inf's SD	1.14	1.08	1.40	1.06	1.26
South'n inf's N	173	107	247	183	710
North'n inf's M	4.57	4.83	4.17	4.99	4.58
North'n inf's SD	1.17	0.96	1.34	1.06	1.22
North'n inf's N	255	154	315	236	960

Generally speaking, there is no great difference between Northerners' and Southerners' ratings. An indication of this is their respective overall averages (i.e. disregarding any subgroups): Northerners 4.58; Southerners 4.50. This shows that at any rate our accents are regarded as conducive to success in a job interview, on an average.

There is one (non-combinatory) subgroup of which Northerners and Southerners do give significantly different ratings, viz. NORTH (*; t=2.08). It is the Northern informants who upgrade this subgroup (4.67). There is also a combinatory subgroup (NORTH/MODERN) which gets an all but significant (t=1.84) difference in rating: Southerners seem to downgrade it somewhat. Apart from this, differences between Northerners' and Southerners' average ratings are clearly non-significant, in some cases extremely small (SOUTH, SOUTH/MODERN,

SOUTH/TRADITIONAL, TRADITIONAL).

We shall now look at the way in which ratings were distributed onto distinct levels by Northern and Southern informants:

```
┌─────────────────────────────────────────────────────────────────┐
│ ADVANTAGE IN JOB INTERVIEW                                        │
│                                                                   │
│ Northern  ratings              Southern  ratings                 │
│ (1) NORTH/TRAD; SOUTH/TRAD     (1) SOUTH/TRAD                     │
│ (2) NORTH/MOD                  (2) NORTH/TRAD                     │
│ (3) SOUTH/MOD                  (3) NORTH/MOD; SOUTH/MOD           │
└─────────────────────────────────────────────────────────────────┘
```

Looking at these ranking lists, it seems as if Southerners are more particular at the upper end of the scale, in elevating SOUTH/ TRADITIONAL and SOUTH/TRADITIONAL alone, whereas Northerners rather seem to go for the lower end of the scale, in giving special treatment to SOUTH/MODERN. Another way of interpreting the lists is to say that TRADITIONAL, regardless of REGIONALITY, has a high standing among Northern informants, whereas Southerners stress the disadvantage of MODERN, regardless of REGIONALITY. The question that should be answered here is: why do Southerners make a point of treating positively SOUTH/TRADITIONAL; and Northerners negatively SOUTH/MODERN, with respect to ADVANTAGE IN JOB INTERVIEW?

It can probably be argued that informants' answers are to some extent a function of their relative knowledge of accent subtleties, which in turn is a function of their distance from the accent in question. That SOUTH/TRADITIONAL is regarded as significantly (*; t=2.39) more advantageous in a job interview than NORTH/ TRADITIONAL by Southern informants is, I suggest, an effect of Southerners being more aware of those fine nuances of SOUTH/ TRADITIONAL which make it special, rather than simply one category of neutral accents among many. To the Northern informants, TRADITIONAL seems to be a sufficiently clear marker of socio-economic advantage; they seem not to attach such great importance to its NORTH-SOUTH difference (they do give a higher rating of SOUTH/TRADITIONAL, though, but the difference is not significant (t=1.51)).

The situation gets rather more complex when we try to explain why Northerners feel that SOUTH/MODERN is the least advantageous accent in this connection. However, if we scrutinize the figures, we see that in terms of absolute values, there is no difference between Northerners' and Southerners' average ratings of SOUTH/MODERN. The difference lies rather in the Northerners' relative upgrading of NORTH/MODERN. This might serve as an indication that a phenomenon akin to "self-hatred" is operative to a higher degree in the judgment of the Southerners. This is something I have already discussed at length above (pp. 310ff). It may be that the circumstance that Southerners live in the linguistic area which is marked both by upper-crust correctness ideals and fierce social turbulence increases their tendency to project correctness ideals on themselves; whereas Northerners are perhaps more content linguistically because they do not have to face as severe a linguistic conflict at so close a distance. This might explain why they too choose to downgrade SOUTH/MODERN. To explain this, we shall have to resort to a speculative idea that I discussed in connection with FELLOW WORKER/STUDENT and CHILD/BROTHER/SISTER above, viz. that self-hatred may be "contagious" in the sense that people other than the self-haters themselves are secondarily affected by whatever causes self-hatred in the first place, so that they are made to agree as to the relative badness of the self-haters' accent. This is of course merely a suggestion. What is quite clear, however, is that SOUTH/MODERN does end up in the bottom position, significantly so in the Northerners' assessment; somewhat less markedly in the Southern judgment. We recall that this was the position it occupied in the FELLOW WORKER/STUDENT and CHILD/BROTHER/SISTER, as well as DEGREE OF PLEASANTNESS, comparisons above. We also recall that, although scoring lower than SOUTH/TRADITIONAL for LOCAL USUALNESS in the Southerners' assessment, SOUTH/MODERN was clearly distinguished from NORTH/MODERN. All this adds up to rather strong support for the suggestion of linguistic self-hatred among certain categories of people, in the present case Southerners, as compared with Northerners. If you want a good job, whatever you do, do not speak SOUTH/MODERN.

SIMILARITY PERSONAL/FRIENDS.
The last two questions concern SIMILARITY PERSONAL and SIMILARITY FRIENDS, respectively. Informants were asked whether they thought "the speaker's accent is like (a) your own accent [PERSONAL]; (b) the accents of most of your friends [FRIENDS]" and to answer along six-step scales the same way as before. Obviously, this question is related to the one concerning LOCAL USUALNESS, and a quick glance at the two SIMILARITY comparisons shows that ratings are distributed according to the same basic pattern as we had for LOCAL USUALNESS.

The reason for having two questions about SIMILARITY, one for PERSONAL and one for FRIENDS, is of course that whatever difference comes out of such an arrangement is highly interesting, since it pinpoints informants' less than fully explicit preference, there being no reason to believe that there exists a genuine difference, on the whole, between the accent of a given informant and that of his friends.

Siml. personal	SPEAKER VOICE CATEGORY Non-combinatory subgroups				
	NORTH	SOUTH	TRADITIONAL	MODERN	ALL SPEAKERS
South'n inf's M	2.91	*3.16*	*3.33*	*2.88*	*3.06*
South'n inf's SD	1.38	1.46	1.45	1.39	1.43
South'n inf's N	280	437	292	425	717
North'n inf's M	2.62	*1.97*	*2.34*	*2.18*	*2.24*
North'n inf's SD	1.38	1.20	1.35	1.29	1.32
North'n inf's N	408	552	389	571	960

Siml. friends	SPEAKER VOICE CATEGORY Non-combinatory subgroups				
	NORTH	SOUTH	TRADITIONAL	MODERN	ALL SPEAKERS
South'n inf's M	*2.92*	*3.11*	*3.16*	*2.95*	*3.04*
South'n inf's SD	1.28	1.37	1.35	1.32	1.34
South'n inf's N	279	434	289	424	713
North'n inf's M	*2.66*	*2.05*	*2.34*	*2.28*	*2.31*
North'n inf's SD	1.35	1.19	1.32	1.28	1.30
North'n inf's N	408	551	389	570	959

Siml. personal	SPEAKER VOICE CATEGORY Combinatory subgroups				
	NORTH/MOD	NORTH/TRAD	SOUTH/MOD	SOUTH/TRAD	ALL SPEAKERS
South'n inf's M	2.78	3.13	*2.95*	*3.45*	*3.06*
South'n inf's SD	1.34	1.41	1.43	1.47	1.43
South'n inf's N	173	107	252	185	717
North'n inf's M	2.58	2.68	*1.85*	*2.11*	*2.24*
North'n inf's SD	1.39	1.37	1.11	1.30	1.32
North'n inf's N	255	153	316	236	960

Siml. friends	SPEAKER VOICE CATEGORY Combinatory subgroups				
	NORTH/MOD	NORTH/TRAD	SOUTH/MOD	SOUTH/TRAD	ALL SPEAKERS
South'n inf's M	2.88	*3.00*	*3.00*	*3.26*	*3.04*
South'n inf's SD	1.26	1.30	1.36	1.37	1.34
South'n inf's N	173	106	251	183	713
North'n inf's M	2.66	*2.66*	*1.98*	*2.14*	*2.31*
North'n inf's SD	1.33	1.38	1.15	1.24	1.30
North'n inf's N	255	153	315	236	959

If we compare ratings in the PERSONAL and FRIENDS tables, we notice that differences are generally very small. There are however a couple of exceptions, which are perhaps worth some consideration. Statistical significance cannot be used as a tool here, since the PERSONAL and FRIENDS questions are strictly speaking two different questions. However, if for the sake of argument we assume that the two questions are really two different facets of the same thing and carry out a fake check of significance, we do not find any significant differences. Apart from this, it seems that Southern informants tend to give higher ratings of SOUTH/ TRADITIONAL in the PERSONAL than in the FRIENDS table. The same tendency holds for TRADITIONAL in general. Northern informants, on the other hand, give a lower rating of SOUTH/ MODERN in the PERSONAL than in the FRIENDS table. I believe it can be argued that these findings correlate with those of Labov (1966) and Trudgill (1975b), which suggest that informants tend to "overreport", i.e. claim that their own personal way of speaking is more standard, less non-standard, than is actually the case (this is a simplification of Trudgill's Norwich findings in which there was a clear difference between men and women in this respect; cf p. 238f). If we regard SOUTH/TRADITIONAL as a correctness prototype and SOUTH/MODERN as something of an antithesis of SOUTH/TRADITIONAL, which in a sense it is, then we get a reasonably neat picture of the way overreporting works.

In terms of overall levels of rating, there is virtually no difference at all between the two sets of comparison. Average ratings are generally placed well below the non-committal 3.5 (range PERSONAL 1.85-3.45; range FRIENDS 1.15-3.26). For both SIMILARITY PERSONAL and SIMILARITY FRIENDS, there is a clearly (***; t≥11.21) significant difference between Northerners' and Southerners' overall averages (disregarding subgroups), so that Northerners profess a lesser degree of SIMILARITY than do Southerners.

All subgroups but one present clearly significant differences between Northerners' and Southerners' average ratings. The exception is NORTH/MODERN, which is placed at about the same level by both informant groups, the difference being that whereas the Southern rating of NORTH/MODERN is a downrating, relatively speaking, the Northern rating is an uprating, but the effect of this is a merger.

Now let us look at the way informants distribute their ratings onto distinct levels with regard to SIMILARITY PERSONAL and SIMILARITY FRIENDS:

SIMILARITY PERSONAL

Northern ratings
(1) NORTH/MOD; NORTH/TRAD
(2) SOUTH/TRAD
(3) SOUTH/MOD

Southern ratings
(1) SOUTH/TRAD
(2) NORTH/TRAD; SOUTH/MOD
(3) NORTH/MOD

SIMILARITY FRIENDS

Northern ratings
(1) NORTH/MOD; NORTH/TRAD
(2) SOUTH/MOD; SOUTH/TRAD

Southern ratings
(1) SOUTH/TRAD
(2) THE REST

It seems that the Northern informants make an assessment in which pure REGIONALITY plays a more important part than in the Southerners' assessment, since they do not merge subgroups of different REGIONALITY at one and the same level of rating. It also seems as if the correctness ideal of SOUTH/TRADITIONAL, if indeed that is what SOUTH/TRADITIONAL stands for, is distinctly attractive to Southern informants. We also notice that both informant groups select the MODERN variety of the other rather than their own REGION for the bottom position in the PERSONAL judgment, but that this specific selection is not reflected in their FRIENDS judgment. Probably MODERN-ness promotes a feeling of foreignness in an accent which exhibits certain other foreign traits; and consequently, TRADITIONAL-ness reduces feelings of foreignness by virtue of its adapting to a conventional standard.

The circumstance that Southerners, but not Northerners, merge subgroups of different REGIONALITY at the same level might be an indication of a higher degree of acceptance of NORTH among Southerners, which would be in accordance with many of the (rather loose but still) ideas put forward since the Sixties about changes in the way neutral English is pronounced. Many of these ideas are in fact presented in the shape of rather ferocious attacks by believers in language conservatism on modern features of pronunciation:

> As it is, young players are not even being taught how to use the correct vowel sounds when a part demands it—though they could easily revert to the more fashionable subcultural tones in private speech, should they want to. However, such is the inverted snobbery of the BBC that its presenters and reporters, especially the young women (the quack-quack girls I have heard them called, their a's being particularly non-euphonious), seem actually to be encouraged to speak in this awful way. [From a letter to the editor, *The Sunday Telegraph*, January 15, 1984.]

Now, obviously, this particular correspondent does not have a high degree of acceptance of NORTH, or anything short of "RP", in a neutral, national context. Whatever we choose to think about such ideas, there is no doubt that a change has taken place, and is taking place, in the pronunciation of neutral English, and it is of course reasonable to assume that speakers who prefer to use "fashionable subcultural tones" do this because they want to (cf Ryan 1979:147). That is where acceptance comes in.

The present figures, however, seem to show that the position of SOUTH/TRADITIONAL is strong, at least among Southerners, since they all seem willing to associate this accent with themselves or their friends. It is also very interesting to note that this association does not entirely harmonize with the way informants regard the accents from a PLEASANTNESS point of view.

It is undoubtedly the case that Southerners feel more at home with the accents of this investigation, although there is a wide regional spread within the selection of speakers. It is even clearer, though, that Northern informants experience a more dramatic split between NORTH and SOUTH than do Southerners. The form this takes here might be seen as an indication of a higher degree of linguistic openness among Southerners, as their aversion to NORTH is considerably smaller than Northerners' aversion to SOUTH. Maybe holding one's own is something we should expect of people who are at the losing end of a socio-economic continuum. And maybe influence from the post-1960 pop culture, as well as a traditional longing for the pleasures of country life, make for linguistic openness among Southerners.

Let me close this discussion, and the study as a whole, by quoting a suggestion made by the pioneer of the study of language attitudes, T.H. Pear (1931:92, footnote):

> Most Northerners strongly dislike Cockney—this is fairly evident whenever the 'North v. South' problem is discussed in the newspapers. This may be due to a distrust of its 'slickness.' On the other hand, Southerners appear to enjoy the Lancashire and Yorkshire accents, which give them unconsciously or semi-consciously an impression of slow thinking, homeliness, etc. All this may result from the attitude of the Londoner to the provincial, and *vice versa*. Note the extraordinary popularity of the Lancashire comedians in the London halls, and the similar popularity of Provençal and Southern French comedians in Paris. The popularity of the Yorkshire comedian, 'Stainless Stephen,' with Southern listeners probably far outweighs the popularity of Mabel Constanduros (Cockney) with Northern listeners.

5. Summary.

Several previous experiments, notably by the Giles group, have shown that the British English accent known as "RP" enjoys more prestige than any other British accent. What these studies have in common is a tendency to treat accents as definitionally unproblematic entities: "RP" as well as other accents are often taken for granted without any discussion about their characteristics and variability.

There are several signs that the standard area of British English accents is moving away from its rather strict class- and education-based delimitations. Windsor Lewis (1985) even suggests a new name, "General British", for a basically neutral, non-dialectal, type of spoken British English.

Sociolinguists have put a lot of effort into attempts to define "RP". These attempts are probably futile, since "RP", being the *name* of an accent, cannot be defined (cf p. 261). A more interesting project, therefore, would be to investigate the speaker-listener area using "objective" methods of categorizing speech modes in order to see how various types of prestige operate.

The present study is an attempt at such an investigation. Its general framework is the same as in several previous studies: recordings of speech are played to listener-informants who are required to rate the speech samples in various ways. It differs, however, from its predecessors in two fundamental ways: (1) its object of study is the standard, "General British" area itself, not a wide spectrum ranging from standard to regional accent; (2) within this area, speakers are subcategorized for "DEGREE OF MODERNITY" by means of a word pronunciation test including words that are objectively known to be in a process of phonetic change. On the basis of this test, speakers are placed in a TRADITIONAL or a MODERN group. In addition, there are also subcategorizations based on AGE, SEX and REGIONALITY, all of which are binary. The subgroups used in the analysis are (1) 8 non-combinatory ones (i.e. TRADITIONAL, MODERN, and each of the binary subdivisions of the AGE, SEX and REGIONALITY variables); (2) 12 combinatory ones (i.e. intersections between TRADITIONAL and MODERN on the one hand, and each of the binary subdivisions of AGE, SEX and REGIONALITY on the other, e.g. YOUNG/MODERN, MALE/TRADITIONAL). All of these subgroups can be subjected to attitude-based analysis, the most interesting ones being the combinatory ones.

There are three report sections in the present study, "Age and degree of modernity", "Sex and degree of modernity, "Regionality and degree of modernity". Both speakers and listeners are subdivided according to AGE, SEX and REGIONALITY, respectively, while the speakers (not the listeners) are also categorized according to

DEGREE OF MODERNITY. Thus, the AGE section deals with young and adult listeners' attitudes to YOUNG and OLD speakers subdivided according to DEGREE OF MODERNITY; the SEX section deals with male and female listeners' attitudes to MALE and FEMALE speakers subdivided according to DEGREE OF MODERNITY; the REGIONALITY section deals with Northern and Southern listeners' attitudes to NORTHern and SOUTHern speakers subdivided according to DEGREE OF MODERNITY. The principle, therefore, is one of variable subdivision: the same speaker and listener groups are subdivided in different ways.

The total number of speakers is 25. They are all English in the strict sense and there is a certain middle-class bias in the speaker sample. The recordings consist of free descriptions of a cartoon, each with a duration of about one and a half minutes. When making the recording, the speakers were asked to speak in a neutral voice without putting on an accent. They were also asked to supply some written information about themselves.

The 25 speech samples were grouped together in sets of 5 in each. These 5-voice sets were later used in the listening sessions in England. This means that all listeners did not listen to all voices. However, since the analysis is one of group averages where speakers and listeners who answer a certain description are treated jointly, no major disadvantage should result from this.

There were in all 370 informants who listened to the voice programmes. In order to achieve a certain spread in AGE and REGIONALITY, schools and places of work in the South, the Midlands and the North of England were selected as test locations.

At a test session, the listeners would first supply background information about themselves. Then they would listen to a 5-voice programme, answering a set of questions about the voices. The questions concerned: perceived age, occupation, psychological qualities, job suitability, social significance, etc.

The post-test analysis included subdivision of speakers and listeners on the basis of the information obtained. The discussion in the three report sections of the present study tries to explain the various group differences that arise.

The most general statement that could be made about the results is that even though we have not used voices with marked regional accents, and even though we have grouped our accent samples according to other criteria than are normally used in investigations into accent attitudes, we still get a very clear pattern of differentiation between our "objectively" defined accent groups.

In the first question, the listeners were required to guess the age of the speakers. It is only when the subdivision of speakers and listeners is itself based on age that we get significant differences in the age guess, which indicates that informants, when making age conjectures, are attracted by their own age. One factor which has to be taken into account when assessing the answers to this question is a tendency to guess conservatively, i.e. avoid extremes, which has nothing particular to do with the present project, but rather with guessing in general. Guesses must therefore be compared not primarily with the speakers' real age but with an "expected" age guess. If this is done, the following tendencies emerge: adults seem to be influenced by the DEGREE OF MODERNITY in the speakers. This is shown by their giving higher age guesses to TRADITIONAL accent groups than to MODERN ones. For young listeners ("youths" for short), DEGREE OF MODERNITY does not seem to have this influence. In the SEX-based comparison there is a tendency for the accent group MALE/TRADITIONAL to be overstated in terms of age, whereas in the REGIONALITY-based comparison the tendency is for the group NORTH/MODERN to be understated, particularly when judged by Northern listeners.

In the next question, the informants were asked to guess where the speakers came from. Their answers were translated into numerical regional coefficients based on a 6-point scale where 1 represents "London" and 6 "North". This question is probably the question least suited for the present type of average-based analysis, since areas such as "North" or "Midland" are too heterogeneous from the point of view of accent differentiation, and so what seems to be a neat mean value may conceal a great deal of incongruous variation. Hence, the regional conjecture is probably the most difficult one to interpret in this study. An interesting observation is, however, that adults, males and Southerners were more confident of their own ability to guess the speakers' regionality than, respectively, youths, females and Northerners, even though this confidence was not always matched by a similar degree of accuracy. Since all our accents belong to the neutral area, this might be seen as an indication as to who feels most at home with neutral accents. In terms of conjectural accuracy, we notice that in all three comparisons, all subgroup ratings lie closer to London than the real regional averages of our voices. Thus, it seems as if the often testified non-regionality of English neutral pronunciations is not perceived as such by listeners. London is obviously associated with accent neutrality. However, in the REGIONALITY comparison we do get a clear differentiation between ratings of NORTHern and SOUTHern voices, which indicates that at any rate informants notice a difference between them.

The occupational conjecture was also an open-ended question the answers to which had to be transformed into numerical expressions (1 - "professional"; 6 - "unskilled"). It is only in the AGE comparison that we find significant differences between the ratings of the two informant categories: adult informants seem to be more sensitive to the "professional" implications of the accent type OLD/TRADITIONAL than youths. The youths on the other hand seem to go more by age as such, giving more "professional" ratings to OLD than to YOUNG voices. In the SEX comparison, MALE/TRADITIONAL receives the most "professional" ratings. There is however a certain tendency for female informants to upgrade MALE accent groups in general at the expense of FEMALE ones, which might be taken as a reflection of "self-hatred" caused by male-centred society, i.e. a tendency among members of a "minority" to look upon themselves through what is believed to be the eyes of the "majority". The REGIONAL comparison gave rise to one strong tendency only: an upgrading of the accent group SOUTH/TRADITIONAL by Northern and Southern informants alike.

The next section of the questionnaire concerned 10 "psychological qualities", one of which, EDUCATION, is not really such a quality, but was entered here for convenience. For the sake of brevity and clarity, we can simplify this discussion by grouping the 10 qualities in 3 semantically homogeneous groups: (1) "career" qualities (LEADERSHIP, SELF-CONFIDENCE, AMBITION, DETERMINATION); (2) "closeness" qualities (DEPENDABILITY, HONESTY, SENSE OF HUMOUR, FRIENDLINESS); (3) "IQ" qualities (INTELLIGENCE, EDUCATION).

In the AGE-based comparison, the "career" qualities all seem to promote the voice subgroup OLD/TRADITIONAL. This goes for adult as well as youth informants. The adults however exhibit a special preference pattern in downgrading the two subgroups in which age and modernity do not harmonize (OLD/MODERN, YOUNG/TRADITIONAL). The "closeness" qualities give rise to less varied adult ratings, whereas the youths continue to upgrade OLD/TRADITIONAL. The two "IQ" qualities also produce high ratings of OLD/TRADITIONAL. The most interesting tendency is the downrating of YOUNG/MODERN by the youth informants, which again seems like an exponent of "self-hatred". Thus, we do not get the peer-group solidarity effect that might have been expected.

The SEX-based comparison gives rise to slightly different tendencies. For the "career" and "IQ" qualities, female informants upgrade MALE voices in general, irrespective of whether they are MODERN or TRADITIONAL. The male informants are more specific in upgrading MALE/TRADITIONAL only. Males and females, however, agree that FEMALE/MODERN should be downgraded for "career" and "IQ" qualities. The "closeness" qualities seem primarily to promote FEMALE voice groups at the expense of MALE ones, both as judged by male and female informants.

The chief tendency in the REGIONALITY-based judgment of "career" qualities is an upgrading of SOUTH/TRADITIONAL. The same goes for the "IQ" qualities but here there is also a corresponding downgrading of SOUTH/MODERN by Northerners and Southerners alike. The "closeness" qualities, finally, tend to promote NORTHern accents at the expense of SOUTHern ones. The subgroup SOUTH/ MODERN seems to be particularly incompatible with such qualities regardless of whether the informant is Northern or Southern.

In the occupational conjecture (cf above) the informants had been asked to guess the occupation of the speakers as an answer to an open-ended question. The next item in the questionnaire is a related question. This time the informants were asked to rate the voices they heard with regard to 11 job (or group) labels. We can facilitate summarizing by regarding the 11 labels as belonging to one of 4 sociosemantic categories: (1) the "correctness" category (TEACHER OF ENGLISH, ACTOR/ACTRESS, BBC NEWSREADER, BARRISTER, GOVERNMENT OFFICIAL); (2) the "youth culture" category (DISC JOCKEY, ROCK SINGER); (3) the "working class" category (GROCER'S ASSISTANT, WORKINGMAN/ -WOMAN); (4) the "closeness" category (FELLOW WORKER/STUDENT, CHILD/BROTHER/ SISTER).

Beginning with the AGE-based comparison, we notice that for the "correctness" labels the adults upgrade OLD/TRADITIONAL and downgrade MODERN, especially OLD/MODERN, i.e. one of the "disharmonious" subgroups (cf above). The youths, too, upgrade OLD/TRADITIONAL, but where they downgrade, they seem more prone to "self-hatred" by being especially negative toward YOUNG/MODERN. As for the "youth culture" labels, the main result is the markedly low level of ratings both among adults and youths. The strongest tendency for individual subgroups is the adult downgrading of OLD/TRADITIONAL for ROCK SINGER. The youths by comparison seem to go more by AGE as such, downgrading OLD in general. The two "working class" labels are characterized by the downgrading of OLD/TRADITIONAL by adults and youths alike. The youths in addition make a certain upgrading of YOUNG/MODERN. The two "closeness" labels give rise to a relative upgrading by the adults of YOUNG/ TRADITIONAL, whereas the youths seem to go by AGE alone, upgrading YOUNG, downgrading OLD.

In the SEX-based comparison the chief tendency with respect to the "correctness" labels is a downgrading of FEMALE/MODERN, which is particularly marked among the female informants. The males accentuate the upgrading of TRADITIONAL, especially MALE/ TRADITIONAL. The "youth culture" labels are primarily marked by low and relatively unvaried ratings, an indication that our neutral accents do not fit into a youth culture paradigm. As for the "working class" labels, male and female informants agree in upgrading FEMALE/MODERN (the females markedly so) and downgrading MALE/TRADITIONAL. The "closeness" labels produce ratings that are very similar to the "working class" ones, but there is one interesting point of differentiation between males and females, which is subjected to some scrutiny in the text: in the CHILD/BROTHER/SISTER comparison, females accentuate the inappropriateness of MALE/TRADITIONAL, whereas males choose MALE/MODERN for their downgrading. Thus, we get an indication that males and females differ with regard to "status" and "solidarity" in their linguistic relationship with their near kin.

The "career" labels in the REGIONALITY-based comparison give rise to an upgrading of TRADITIONAL in general or, in some cases, of SOUTH/TRADITIONAL alone. Likewise, it is primarily MODERN as a whole that is downgraded with regard to these labels, with a certain tendency toward downgrading SOUTH/MODERN particularly strongly among Northern and Southern informants alike. Of the two "youth culture" labels, DISC JOCKEY produces flat sets of rating with a slight tendency for Southern informants to upgrade NORTH/ MODERN. ROCK SINGER, apart from producing low ratings in general, mainly distinguishes between MODERN and TRADITIONAL, Southern informants accentuating the inappropriateness of SOUTH/ TRADITIONAL. The "working class" labels are associated with the accent group NORTH/MODERN by Southern informants. The Northerners tend rather to upgrade MODERN as a whole. Both informant categories however downgrade SOUTH/TRADITIONAL in this connection. The two "closeness" labels cause both Northerners and Southerners to upgrade NORTHern accents, the Southerners mainly NORTH/MODERN. Thus, Northerners seem to act more in accordance with expectations, whereas Southerners seem somehow to be attracted by "foreign" sounds, even in connection with their own near kin.

The last set of questions concerned DEGREE OF PLEASANTNESS, LOCAL USUALNESS, GENERAL USUALNESS (i.e. whether informants thought the accents heard were usual in "your part of England" and in "England as a whole"), ADVANTAGE IN JOB INTERVIEW, and SIMILARITY PERSONAL/FRIENDS (i.e. whether informants thought the accents heard were similar to their own and their friends' accents, respectively).

In the PLEASANTNESS question, adults and youths agreed in upgrading OLD/TRADITIONAL. Adults in addition downgraded the "disharmonious" subgroup OLD/MODERN, whereas youths down-graded MODERN as a whole. In the SEX-based comparison, female informants upgraded TRADITIONAL, especially FEMALE/TRADITIONAL, and downgraded MODERN. Males chose to upgrade FEMALE/TRADITIONAL and downgrade MALE/MODERN. In the REGIONALITY-based comparison, both Northern and Southern informants downgraded the subgroup SOUTH/MODERN for PLEASANTNESS. The Northerners in addition upgraded NORTH/TRADITIONAL.

It is of course primarily in the REGIONALITY-based comparison that we should expect marked regional tendencies in connection with the question on LOCAL

USUALNESS. The ratings made by the Northern informants seem to be more clearly governed by the REGIONALITY of the accents than those made by the Southerners: they upgrade NORTH and downgrade SOUTH. The Southerners do not distinguish between NORTH/TRADITIONAL and SOUTH/MODERN, placing both at a position between their top-ranking subgroup, SOUTH/TRADITIONAL, and their bottom one, NORTH/MODERN.

As for GENERAL USUALNESS, both Northerners and Southerners give flat sets of rating, Northerners downgrading SOUTH/MODERN somewhat.

In the AGE-based comparisons on USUALNESS, the main tendency is for adult informants to downgrade OLD/MODERN. There is also a tendency for adults to upgrade YOUNG accents for USUALNESS, whereas youths go for TRADITIONAL.

FEMALE/MODERN is downgraded by the female informants both in the LOCAL and in the GENERAL USUALNESS rating. This is the only marked tendency in the SEX-based comparison.

Both adults and youths think that OLD/TRADITIONAL is the most advantageous accent in a job interview. The youths in addition downgrade the accent closest to themselves, YOUNG/MODERN. In the SEX-based comparison, females upgrade MALE/TRADITIONAL and downgrade FEMALE/MODERN, i.e., there is clearly a SEX aspect to their rating. The males seem to go by DEGREE OF MODERNITY alone, upgrading TRADITIONAL and downgrading MODERN. Southern informants mark SOUTH/TRADITIONAL as being the most advantageous accent in the REGIONALITY-based comparison, whereas Northerners do not distinguish between SOUTH/TRADITIONAL and NORTH/TRADITIONAL. Instead, Northerners seem to distinguish more at the lower end of the scale in downgrading SOUTH/MODERN particularly strongly.

By comparing the ratings given as answers to the two SIMILARITY questions we get an indication of the overt/covert attitudinal relationship of the informants vis-à-vis the various accent subgroups. It turns out that the youth informants tend to associate TRADITIONAL with themselves, but YOUNG/TRADITIONAL with their friends. Similarly, male informants upgrade TRADITIONAL and downgrade MODERN in connection with themselves, whereas they give no pointed ratings in connection with their friends. The female informants seem particularly keen that FEMALE/MODERN should not be associated with themselves. In the REGIONALITY-based comparison, the informants mainly follow the expected pattern of upgrading the accents of their respective regions. The Southerners however accentuate SOUTH/TRADITIONAL both in connection with themselves and with their friends.

SUMMARY

Among the explanatory models used, we find *self-hatred*, i.e. a tendency for mainly youths, or women, to downgrade their peer category. *Maturity* could be seen as the reason for adult informants being more favourably inclined toward MODERN than youths; similarly, *conventionalism* caused by lack of experience and by subjection to "linguistic imperialism", as in the case of school pupils, might explain the more marked upgrading of TRADITIONAL among young informants. A related explanatory model is that of *age authority*, which is seen to cause young informants to upgrade relatively old speakers, regardless of linguistic status. *Closeness* between accent and listener may explain greater expertise, whereas *distance* may be the reason why informants sometimes tend to over-generalize. Certain results can probably be ascribed to *sociopolitical projection*, for instance the downgrading of certain subgroups, which have earlier been recognized as prestigious, for closeness and pleasantness qualities. In the AGE section, we also found indications of sensitivity among informants toward *"harmony/disharmony"* between who you are in terms of age and how you speak, which might be related to the notion of "cognitive consonance/dissonance".

Bibliography.

Legend: In the case of several items published by the same author in one year, the sequence is chronological. If the first name in a group of authors occurs individually as well, the group of authors and the individual are listed in the same chronological sequence. Example: Smith, A. (1910) precedes Smith, A. & Jones, B. (1911), which in turn precedes Smith A. (1912).

In the text, the expression *"et al."* is normally used where the name of the first author is followed by *more than one name*. It may also be used for two authors working together, *if there is no risk of misunderstanding* (i.e. if, say, a 2-person and a 3-person group headed by the same name have *not* published quoted material in the same year). Normally, however, the names of two people working together are quoted in full.

A letter after the year is used in the orthodox way to separate items by the same author (with or without *et al.*) which were written in the same year.

An asterisk (*) before the author's name indicates direct reference in the text.

*Abercrombie, David   1956   "English accents"
Chapter 4 in *Problems and Principles: Studies in the Teaching of English as a Second Language*
London
Longmans, Green and Co.
41-56

*Aboud, Frances E., Clement, Richard & Taylor, Donald M.   1974   "Evaluational reactions to discrepancies between social class and language"
Sociometry, vol 37, no 2
239-250

*Allen, Harold B.   1986   "Sex-linked variation in the responses of dialect informants. Part 2: Pronunciation"
Journal of English Linguistics, vol 19.1
Whitewater
4-24

*Allport, G.W. & Cantril, H.   1934   "Judging personality from voice"
Journal of Social Psychology 5
37-55

*Amis, Martin   1983   "The war according to supersoap"
The Observer, September 18 (Television and radio guide)
London

*Andersson, Lars-Gunnar   1985   *Fult språk. Svordomar, dialekter och annat ont*
('Ugly Language. Curses, Dialects and other Evils')
Stockholm
Carlsson Bokförlag

*Anisfeld, E. & Lambert, W.E.,   1964   "Evaluational reactions of bilingual and monolingual children to spoken languages"
Journal of Abnormal and Social Psychology, vol 69, no 1
89-97

*Anisfeld, M., Bogo, N. & Lambert, W.E.   1962   "Evaluational reactions to accented English speech"
Journal of Abnormal and Social Psychology, vol. 65, no. 4
223-231

*Apple, W., Streeter, L.A. & Krauss, R.M. 1979   "Effects of pitch and speech rate on personal attributions"
Journal of Personality and Social Psychology, vol 37, no 5
715-727

*Argyle, M., Salter, V., Nicholson, H., Williams, M. & Burgess, P.
1970   "The communication of inferior and superior attitudes by verbal and non-verbal signals"
British Journal of Social and Clinical Psychology, 9
222-231

*Aronovitch, Charles D.   1976   "The voice of personality: stereotyped judgments and their relation to voice quality and sex of speaker"
Journal of Social Psychology, vol 99
207-220

*Ball, P., Byrne, J., Giles, H., Berechree, P., Griffiths, J., MacDonald, H. & McKendrick, I.
1982   "The retrospective speech halo effect: some Australian Data"
Language & Communication, vol 2, no 3
277-284

*Ball, Peter   1983   "Stereotypes of Anglo-Saxon and non-Anglo-Saxon accents: Some exploratory Australian studies with the matched guise technique"
Language Sciences, vol 5, no 2
163-183

*Baroni, Maria Rosa & D'Urso, Valentina   1984   "Some experimental findings about the question of politeness and women's speech (research note)"
Language in Society, 13
67-72

*Barry III, H., Bacon, M.K. & Child, I.L.   1957   "A cross-cultural survey of some sex differences in socialization"
Journal of Abnormal and Social Psychology, vol 55
327-332

*Barton, A.H.   1958   "Asking the embarassing question"
Public Opinion Quarterly 22
67-68

Beardsley, M.C.   1958   "The instrumentalist theory of aesthetic value"
(Reprinted from Beardsley, *Aesthetics*, 1958)
Hospers (ed.), *Introductory Readings in Aesthetics*
1969 (ch. 19)

*Beebe, Leslie M. & Giles, Howard   1984   "Speech accommodation theories: a discussion in terms of second-language acquisition"
International Journal of the Sociology of Language, 46
Amsterdam
5-32

*Bell, Allan   1983   "Broadcast news as a language standard"
International Journal of the Sociology of Language, 40
Amsterdam
29-42

*Block, Jeanne H.   1976   "Issues, problems, and pitfalls in assessing sex differences: a critical review of *The Psychology of Sex Differences*"
Merrill-Palmer Quarterly, vol 22, no 4
283-308

*Bogart, L.   1967   "No opinion, don't know, and maybe no answer"
Public Opinion Quarterly 31:3

*Bolinger, Dwight   1975   *Aspects of Language* (2nd ed.)
New York
Harcourt Brace Jovanovich, Inc.

*Bonaventura, Maria   1935   "Ausdruck der Persönlichkeit in der Sprechstimme und im Photogramm"
Archiv für die gesamte Psychologie, 94
501-570

Bonjean, C.M., Hill, R.J. & McLemore, S.D. 1967   *Sociological Measurement. An Inventory of Scales and Indices*
San Francisco

*Bourhis, R.Y., Giles, H. & Lambert, W.E. 1975   "Social consequences of accommodating one's style of speech: a cross-national investigation"
International Journal of the Sociology of Language 6
55-71

*Bronfenbrenner, Urie   1961   "Some familial antecedents of responsibility in adolescents"
Petrullo, L. & Bass, B.M. (eds.), *Leadership and Interpersonal Behavior*
New York
Holt, Rinehart and Winston, Inc.
239-271

Broverman, I., Vogel, S., Broverman, D., Clarkson, F. & Rosenkrantz, P. 1972   "Sex-role stereotypes: a current appraisal"
Journal of Social Issues 28 (2)
59-78

Brown, B.L., Strong, W.J. & Rencher, A.C. 1975   "Acoustic determinants of perceptions of personality from speech"
International Journal of the Sociology of Language 6

*Brown, B.L. & Bradshaw, J.M.   1985   "Towards a social psychology of voice variations"
Giles, H. & St Clair, R.N. (eds.), *Recent Advances in Language, Communication, and Social Psychology*
London
Lawrence Erlbaum Associates Ltd
144-181

*Brown, B.L., Giles, H. & Thakerar, J.N. 1985   "Speaker evaluations as a function of speech rate, accent and context"
Language & Communication, vol 5, no 3
207-220

*Brown, R. & Gilman, A   1960   "The pronouns of power and solidarity"
Sebeok, T.A. (ed.), *Style in Language*
New York
John Wiley & Sons
253-276

*Burchfield, Robert   1981   *The Spoken Word. A BBC Guide*
London
British Broadcasting Corporation

*Burgess, Anthony   1983   "Decline of actor's English"
The Observer, September 18
London

*Burns, Robert B.   1977   "Male and female perceptions of their own and the other sex"
British Journal of Social and Clinical Psychology, 16
213-220

*Butler, Christopher   1985 *Statistics in Linguistics*
                                    Oxford
                                    Basil Blackwell

Chambers, J.K. & Trudgill, P. 1980 *Dialectology*
                                    Cambridge
                                    Cambridge University Press

*Cheshire, Jenny   1984 "Indigenous nonstandard English varieties and
                                    education"
                                    Trudgill, P. (ed.), *Language in the British Isles*
                                    Cambridge
                                    Cambridge University Press

*Cheyne, William M.   1970 "Stereotyped reactions to speakers with Scottish
                                    and English regional accents"
                                    British Journal of Social and Clinical Psychology, 9
                                    77-79

*Classification of Occupations 1980 London
                                    Her Majesty's Stationery Office

*Cleave, Maureen   1982 "Acton in aspic"
                                    The Observer, February 21
                                    London

*Coates, Jennifer   1986 *Women, Men and Language: A Sociolinguistic
                                    Account of Sex Differences in Language*
                                    London
                                    Longman

*Creber, Clare & Giles, Howard 1983 "Social context and language attitudes: the role of
                                    formality-informality of the setting"
                                    Language Sciences, vol 5, no 2
                                    155-161

*Davies, Alan   1984 "Idealization in sociolinguistics: the choice of the
                                    standard dialect"
                                    *Georgetown University Round Table on Languages
                                    and Linguistics 1984* (ed. Deborah Schiffrin)
                                    Washington D.C.
                                    Georgetown University Press
                                    229-239

*Davis, Lawrence M.   1986 "Sampling and statistical inference in dialectology"
                                    Journal of English Linguistics, vol 19.1
                                    Whitewater
                                    42-48

Day, Richard R.   1982 "Children's attitudes toward language"
                                    Ryan, E.B. & Giles, H. (eds.), *Attitudes towards
                                    Language Variation: Social and Applied Contexts*
                                    London
                                    Edward Arnold
                                    116-131

*Deaux, Kay   1976 "Sex: A perspective on the attribution process"
                                    Harvey, J.H., Ickes, W.J. & Kidd, R.F. (eds.), *New
                                    Directions in Attribution Research*, vol 1
                                    Hillsdale New Jersey
                                    Lawrence Erlbaum Associates
                                    335-352

*Dicken, Peter & Lloyd, Peter E. 1981 *Modern Western Society: A Geographical
                                    Perspective on Work, Home and Well-Being*
                                    London
                                    Harper & Row

Dickie, G.	1971	*Aesthetics. An Introduction* New York Pegasus
Ducasse, C.J.	1929	"The subjectivity of aesthetic value" Ch. 15 in Ducasse, *The Philosophy of Art*; reprinted in Hospers (ed.), *Introductory Readings in Aesthetics*, 1969
*Edwards, John R.	1982	"Language attitudes and their implications among English speakers" Ryan, E.B. & Giles, H. (eds.), *Attitudes towards Language Variation: Social and Applied Contexts* London Edward Arnold 20-33
Edwards, V.K.	1978	"Language attitudes and underperformance in West Indian children" *Educational Review*, vol 30, no 1
*Einarsson, Jan	n.d.	"Två roller söker sina egenskaper. En pilotstudie" ('Two roles trying to find their content. A pilot study') Mimeo
*Eisenberg, Philip & Zalowitz, Eleanor	1938	"Judging expressive movement: III. Judgments of dominance-feeling from the phonograph records of voice" *Journal of Applied Psychology*, 22 620-631
Ekman, R.	1972	*Estetiska problem* ('Aesthetical Problems') Lund Gleerups
El-Dash, L. & Tucker, G.R.	1975	"Subjective reactions to various speech styles in Egypt" *International Journal of the Sociology of Language*, 6
Ellis, Alexander J.	1869	*On Early English Pronunciation 1+2* London
*Elyan, O., Smith, P., Giles, H. & Bourhis, R.		
	1978	"RP-accented female speech: The voice of perceived androgyny" Trudgill (ed.), *Sociolinguistic Patterns in British English* London Edward Arnold
*Eustace, S.S.	1967	"Present changes in English pronunciation" *Proceedings of the Sixth International Congress of Phonetic Sciences* Prague Academia 303-306
*Fay, Paul J. & Middleton, Warren C.	1939a	"Judgment of Spranger personality types from the voice as transmitted over a public address system" *Character and Personality*, 8 144-155
*Fay, Paul J. & Middleton, Warren C.	1939b	"Judgment of occupation from the voice as trans- mitted over a public address system and over a radio" *Journal of Applied Psychology*, 23 586-601

343

*Fay, Paul J. & Middleton, Warren C.	1940a	"Judgment of intelligence from the voice as transmitted over a public address system" *Sociometry*, vol III, no 2 186-191
*Fay, Paul J. & Middleton, Warren C.	1940b	"Judgment of Kretschmerian body types from the voice as transmitted over a public address system" *Journal of Social Psychology*, 12 151-162
*Fay, Paul J. & Middleton, Warren C.	1940c	"The ability to judge the rested or tired condition of a speaker from his voice as transmitted over a public address system" *Journal of Applied psychology*, 24 645-650
*Fay, Paul J. & Middleton, Warren C.	1941a	"The ability to judge sociability from the voice as transmitted over a public address system" *Journal of Social Psychology*, 13 303-309
*Fay, Paul J. & Middleton, Warren C.	1941b	"The ability to judge truth-telling, or lying, from the voice as transmitted over a public address system" *Journal of General Psychology*, 24 211-215
*Fay, Paul J. & Middleton, Warren C.	1941c	"Judgment of emotional balance from the transmitted voice" *Character and Personality*, 10 109-113
*Fay, Paul J. & Middleton, Warren C.	1942a	"Judgment of introversion from the transcribed voice" *Quarterly Journal of Speech*, 28 226-228
*Fay, Paul J. & Middleton, Warren C.	1942b	"Measurement of the persuasiveness of the transcribed voice" *Journal of Psychology*, 14 259-267
*Fay, Paul J. & Middleton, Warren C.	1943a	"Judgment of leadership from the transmitted voice" *Journal of Social Psychology*, 17 99-102
*Fay, Paul J. & Middleton, Warren C.	1943b	"Judgment of the effect of Benzedrine sulphate from the transmitted voice" *Journal of General Psychology*, 29 319-323
*Fay, Paul J. & Middleton, Warren C.	1944	"Judgment of confidence from voice" *Journal of General Psychology*, 30 93-95
*Fraser, Bruce	1973	"Some 'unexpected' reactions to various American-English dialects" Shuy, R.W. & Fasold, R.W., *Language Attitudes: Current Trends and Prospects* Washington D.C. Georgetown University Press
*Freire, Paulo	1970	*Pedagogy of the Oppressed* (Swedish translation *'Pedagogik för förtryckta'*, Stockholm, Gummessons, 1973) New York Herder and Herder

*Frender, R., Brown, B. & Lambert, W.E. 1970 "The role of speech characteristics in scholastic success"
Canadian Journal of Behavioural Science, 2

Frodi, A., Macauly, J. & Thome, P.R. 1977 "Are women always less aggressive than men? A review of the experimental literature"
Psychological Bulletin, vol 84, no 4
634-660

Garcia, Gilbert Narro & Frosch, Susan F. 1978 "Sex, color, and money; who's perceiving what? Or where did all the differences go (to?)?"
International Journal of the Sociology of Language, 17
83-90

*Giles, Howard 1970 "Evaluational reactions to accents"
Educational Review, vol 22, no 3
211-227

*Giles, Howard 1971a "Ethnocentrism and the evaluation of accented speech"
British Journal of Social and Clinical Psychology, 10
187-188

*Giles, Howard 1971b "Patterns of evaluation to R.P., South Welsh and Somerset accented speech"
British Journal of Social and Clinical Psychology, 10
280-281

*Giles, Howard 1972a "Evaluation of personality content from accented speech as a function of listeners' social attitudes"
Perceptual and Motor Skills, 34
168-170

*Giles, Howard 1972b "The effect of stimulus mildness-broadness in the evaluation of accents"
Language and Speech, vol 15
262-269

*Giles, Howard & Bourhis, Richard Y. 1973 "Dialect perception revisited"
The Quarterly Journal of Speech, vol 59
337-342

*Giles, H., Bourhis, R., Trudgill, P. & Lewis, A.
1974 "The imposed norm hypothesis: A validation"
The Quarterly Journal of Speech, vol 60, no 4
405-410

*Giles, H., Baker, S. & Fielding, G. 1975 "Communication length as a behavioral index of accent prejudice"
International Journal of the Sociology of Language, 6
73-81

*Giles H. & Powesland, P.F. 1975 *Speech Style and Social Evaluation*
European Monographs in Social Psychology 7
London
Academic Press

*Giles, Howard 1979 "Sociolinguistics and social psychology: an introductory essay"
Giles H. & St Clair R.N. (eds.) *Language and Social Psychology*
Oxford
Basil Blackwell
1-20

*Giles, H., Bourhis, R. & Davis, A. 1979 "Prestige speech styles: the imposed norm and inherent value hypotheses"
McCormack, W.C. & Wurm, S.A. (eds.), *Language and Society: Anthropological Issues*
The Hague
Mouton
589-596
(Originally published in 1975 in the editors'
Language in Anthropology IV: Language in Many Ways, same publisher)

*Giles, Howard, & Farrar, Kathryn 1979 "Some behavioural consequences of speech and dress styles"
British Journal of Social and Clinical Psychology, 18
209-210

*Giles, Howard & Marsh, Patricia 1979 "Perceived masculinity, androgyny and accented speech"
Language Sciences, vol 1, no 2
301-315

Giles, Howard & St Clair, Robert N. (eds.) 1979 *Language and Social Psychology*
Oxford
Basil Blackwell

*Giles, H., Smith, P.M., Browne, C., Whiteman, S. & Williams, J.
    1980a "Women's speech: the voice of feminism"
McConnell-Ginet, S., Borker, R. & Furman, N. (eds.)
Women and Language in Literature and Society
New York
Praeger
150-156

*Giles, H., Smith, P.M., Ford, B., Condor, S. & Thakerar, J.N.
    1980b "Speech style and the fluctuating salience of sex"
Language Sciences, vol 2, no 2
260-282

*Giles, H., Wilson, P. & Conway, A. 1981 "Accent and lexical diversity as determinants of impression formation and perceived employment suitability"
Language Sciences, vol 3, no 1
Tokyo
91-103

*Giles, H., Harrison, C., Creber, C., Smith, P.M. & Freeman, N.H.
    1983 "Development and contextual aspects of children's language attitudes"
Language & Communication, vol 3, no 2
141-146

*Giles, Howard & Sassoon, Caroline 1983 "The effect of speaker's accent, social class background and message style on British listeners' social judgements"
Language & Communication, vol 3, no 3
305-313

*Giles, Howard & Fitzpatrick, Mary Anne 1984 "Personal, group, and couple identities: Towards a relational context for the study of language attitudes and linguistic forms"
Georgetown University Round Table on Languages and Linguistics 1984 (ed. Deborah Schiffrin)
Washington D.C.
Georgetown University Press
253-277

*Gimson, A.C.   1984   "The RP accent"
Trudgill, P. (ed.), *Language in the British Isles*
Cambridge
Cambridge University Press
45-54

*Gleason, Jean Berko   1979   "Sex differences in the language of children and parents"
Garnica, O.K. & King, M.L. (eds.), *Language, Children and Society. The Effect of Social Factors on Children Learning to Communicate*
(International Series on Psychobiology and Learning)
Oxford
Pergamon
149-157

*Gleason, J.B. & Perlmann, R.Y.   1985   "Acquiring social variation in speech"
Giles, H. & St Clair, R.N. (eds.), *Recent Advances in Language, Communication, and Social Psychology*
London
Lawrence Erlbaum Associates Ltd
86-111

*Goldberg, Steven   1979   *Male Dominance: The Inevitability of Patriarchy*
(First published in the US in 1973 under the title, *The Inevitability of Patriarchy*; revised edition first published in the UK in 1977 under the same title)
London
Abacus

*Gottlieb, Anthony   1986   "Television: The daydream machine. A survey"
The Economist, December 20
London

*Gould, P.R. & White, R.R.   1968   "The mental maps of British school leavers"
Regional Studies, vol 2
Oxford
Pergamon
161-182

*Gould, Peter & White, Rodney   1974   *Mental Maps*
Harmondsworth
Penguin
(2nd ed., Boston: Allen & Unwin, 1986)

*Gould, Peter   1975   *People in Information Space: The Mental Maps and Information Surfaces of Sweden*
Lund
Lund Studies in Geography, Gleerup

*Graff, D., Labov, W. & Harris, W.A.   1986   "Testing listeners' reactions to phonological markers of ethnic identity: A new method for sociolinguistic research"
Sankoff, D. (ed.), *Diversity and Diachrony*
(Amsterdam studies in the theory and history of linguistic science, series IV: Current issues in linguistic theory, vol 53)
Amsterdam/Philadelphia
John Benjamins Publishing Company
45-58

Gumperz, J.J.   1958   "Dialect Differences and Social Stratification in a North Indian Village"
American Anthropologist, vol 60
Menasha Wisconsin
668-682

*Hamburg, David A. & Lunde, Donald T. 1966 "Sex hormones in the development of sex differences in human behavior"
Maccoby, Eleanor E. (ed.), *The Development of Sex Differences*
Stanford
Stanford University Press
1-24

*Harris, Frank 1916 *Oscar Wilde: His Life and Confessions* 2 vols
(Quoted from Bendz, E., *Oscar Wilde: A Retrospect* Vienna: Alfred Hölder, 1921)
New York
Privately published

*Heilbrun, Jr, Alfred B. 1972 "An empirical test of the modeling theory of sex-role learning"
Reiss, I.L. (ed.), *Readings on the Family System* (reprinted from *Child Development*, vol 36, no 3, September 1965)
51-60

*Helfrich, Hede 1979 "Age markers in speech"
Scherer, K. & Giles, H. (eds.), *Social Markers in Speech*
Cambridge
Cambridge University Press
63-107

*Herzog, Herta 1933 "Stimme und Persönlichkeit"
Zeitschrift für Psychologie, Bd 130, Heft 3 bis 5
300-369

*Hollingworth, H.L. 1910 "The central tendency of judgment"
The Journal of Philosophy, Psychology and Scientific Methods, 7
New York
461-469

*Honey, John 1985 "Acrolect and hyperlect: the redifinition of English RP"
English Studies, 3
241-257

*Hopper, Robert & Williams, Frederick 1973 "Speech characteristics and employability"
Speech Monographs, vol 40
296-302

*Howard, Philip 1984 *The State of the Language. English Observed*
London
Hamish Hamilton

*Hudson, R.A. 1980 *Sociolinguistics*
Cambridge
Cambridge Textbooks in Linguistics
Cambridge University Press

*Hudson, Ray & Williams, Allan 1986 *The United Kingdom*
Western Europe: Economic and Social Studies
London
Harper & Row

*Hultman, Tor G. & Westman, Margareta 1977 *Gymnasistsvenska* ('Upper Secondary School Swedish')
Skrifter utgivna av Svensklärarföreningen 167
Lund
Liber Läromedel

Jessop, T.E.	1932 -33	"The definition of beauty" *Proceedings of the Aristotelian Society*, vol 33 (also in Hospers (ed.), *Introductory Readings in Aesthetics*, New York, 1969, ch. 17)
*Johnson, Miriam M.	1963	"Sex role learning in the nuclear family" *Child Development*, 34 319-333
*Jones, Daniel	1924	*Everyman's English Pronouncing Dictionary*, 2nd ed. London J.M. Dent & Sons Ltd
*Jones, Daniel	1963	*Everyman's English Pronouncing Dictionary*, 12th ed. (reprint of 11th ed. of 1956) London J.M. Dent & Sons Ltd
*Jones, Daniel	1977	*Everyman's English Pronouncing Dictionary*, 14th ed. (ed. A. C. Gimson) London J.M. Dent & Sons Ltd
Kant, Immanuel	1963	"The Basis of Aesthetic Judgment" Levich, M. (ed.), *Aesthetics and the Philosophy of Criticism* New York Random House 501-519
*Kenyon, J.S. & Knott, T.A.	1953	*A Pronouncing Dictionary of American English* Springfield, Massachusetts G. & C. Merriam Company, Publishers
*Kerswill, Paul E.	1987	"Levels of linguistic variation in Durham" *Journal of Linguistics*, 23 25-49
*Knox, Paul L.	1982	"Living in the United Kingdom" Johnston, R.J. & Doornkamp, J.C. (eds.), *The Changing Geography of the United Kingdom* London Methuen
*Kramarae, Cheris	1982	"Gender: how she speaks" Ryan. E.B. & Giles, H. (eds.), *Attitudes towards Language Variation: Social and Applied Contexts* London Edward Arnold 84-98
*Kramer, Cheris	1977	"Perceptions of female and male speech" *Language and Speech*, vol 20 Hampton Hill Kingston Press Services
*Kramer, Cheris	1978	"Women's and men's ratings of their own and ideal speech" *Communication Quarterly*, vol 26, no 2 2-11
*Kramer, Ernest	1964	"Personality stereotypes in voice: a reconsideration of the data" *Journal of Social Psychology*, 62 247-251
*Labov, William	1963	"The social motivation of sound change" *Word*, 19 (also in Labov 1972) 273-309

*Labov, William   1966   *The Social Stratification of English in New York City*
Washington D.C.
Center for Applied Linguistics

*Labov, William   1972   *Sociolinguistic Patterns*
Oxford
Basil Blackwell

Labov, William   1980   "The social origins of sound change"
Labov, W. (ed.), *Locating Language in Time and Space*
New York
Academic Press
251-266

*Lakoff, Robin   1973   "Language and woman's place"
Language in Society, vol 2
Cambridge University Press

*Lambert, W.E., Hodgson, R.C., Gardner, R.C. & Fillenbaum, S.
    1960   "Evaluational reactions to spoken languages"
Journal of Abnormal and Social Psychology, vol 60, no 1
44-51

*Lambert, W.E., Frankel, H. & Tucker, G.R.
    1966   "Judging personality through speech: a French-Canadian example"
Journal of Communication, 4
Philadelphia
305-321

*Lambert, W.E.   1967   "A social psychology of bilingualism"
Journal of Social Issues, 23
91-109

*Lambert, W.E.   1972   *Language, Psychology and Culture: Essays by Wallace E. Lambert* (ed. A.S. Dil)
Stanford

Lambert, W.E., Giles, H. & Picard, O.   1975   "Language attitudes in a French-American community"
International Journal of the Sociology of Language, 4
127-152

*Langlet, P. & Wärneryd, B.   1983   *Att fråga. Om frågekonstruktion vid intervju- och enkätundersökningar* ('To Ask. On Question Formation in Interviews and Questionnaires')
Stockholm
SCB/Liber

*Laver, John D.M.   1968   "Voice quality and indexical information"
British Journal of Disorders of Communication, 3
43-54

*Leik, Robert K.   1972   "Instrumentality and emotionality in family interaction"
Reiss, I.L. (ed.), *Readings on the Family System*
(reprinted from *Sociometry*, 26, no 2)
Holt, Rinehart and Winston
257-269

*Leitner, G.   1980   "BBC English and Deutsche Rundfunksprache: A comparative and historical analysis of the language on the radio"
International Journal of the Sociology of Language, 26
75-100

Licklider, J.C.R. & Miller, G.A.   1951   "The perception of speech"
                                                  Stevens, S.S. (ed.), *Handbook of Experimental*
                                                  Psychology
                                                  New York
                                                  John Wiley & Sons Inc.

*Lieberson, Stanley   1980   "Procedures for improving sociolinguistic surveys
                                                  of language maintenance and language shift"
                                                  International Journal of the Sociology of Language,
                                                  25
                                                  The Hague
                                                  11-27

*Lloyd James, A.   1935   *Broadcast English*, 3rd ed. (1st ed. 1928)
                                                  London
                                                  British Broadcasting Corporation

*Loman, Bengt   1973   "Miljö och språkförmåga" ('Environment and
                                                  linguistic ability')
                                                  Svensklärarföreningens årsskrift
                                                  Lund
                                                  Gleerups
                                                  34-60

*Macaulay, Ronald K.S.   1976   "Social class and language in Glasgow"
                                                  Language in Society, 5
                                                  173-188

*McConnell-Ginet, S., Borker, R. & Furman, N. (eds.)
                                           1980   *Women and Language in Literature and Society*
                                                  New York
                                                  Praeger

*Maccoby, Eleanor E.   1980   *Social Development*
                                                  New York

*Markel, N.N. & Meisels, M.   1964   "Judging personality from voice quality"
                                                  Journal of Abnormal and Social Psychology, vol 69,
                                                  no 4
                                                  458-463

*Markel, N.N. & Roblin, G.L.   1965   "The effect of content and sex-of-judge on
                                                  judgments of personality from voice"
                                                  International Journal of Social Psychiatry, XI, no 4
                                                  London

*Markel, N.N., Eisler, R.M. & Reese, H.W. 1967   "Judging personality from dialect"
                                                  Journal of Verbal Learning and Verbal Behaviour, 6
                                                  33-35

*Melchers, Gunnel   1985   "'Knappin', 'Proper English', 'Modified Scottish'.
                                                  Some language attitudes in the Shetland Isles"
                                                  Görlach, Manfred (ed.), *Focus on: Scotland*
                                                  (Varieties of English around the World. General
                                                  Series, vol 5)
                                                  Amsterdam/Philadelphia
                                                  John Benjamins Publishing Company
                                                  87-100

*Miller, G.R. & McReynolds, M.   1973   "Male chauvinism and source competence: a
                                                  research note"
                                                  Speech Monographs, vol 40
                                                  New York

*Milroy, Lesley   1983   Comment article on L.B. Breitborde's Focus article
                                                  International Journal of the Sociology of Language,
                                                  39
                                                  Amsterdam
                                                  103-110

Nilsen, Don & Nilsen, Alleen 1987 "Humor, language, and sex roles in American culture"
International Journal of the Sociology of Language, 65
Amsterdam
67-78

*O'Connell, Agnes N. & Rotter, Naomi G. 1979 "The influence of stimulus age and sex on person perception"
Journal of Gerontology, vol 34, no 2
220-228

*Osgood, C.E., Suci, G.J. & Tannenbaum, P.H.
1957 *The Measurement of Meaning*
Urbana
University of Illinois Press

*Påhlsson, Christer 1972 *The Northumbrian Burr. A Sociolinguistic Study*
Lund
Gleerup

*Påhlsson, Christer 1982 "On linguistic attitudes in a northern English village"
Vetenskap och företagsledning. Studier i ekonomi och ledarskap tillägnade Lars Wahlbeck
Helsinki
Publications of the Swedish School of Economics and Business Administration, 31

*Påhlsson, Christer. forthc. *Work Status and English Accents: Studies on Linguistic Attitudes in a Northern Village*
(Based on *A Sociolinguistic Study on Linguistic Attitudes, Report No 2, The Social Position of Eight English Accents*, 1974, Dept of English, Swedish School of Economics and Business Administration, Helsinki, Finland)
Mimeo

*Parsons, Talcott & Bales, Robert F. 1955 *Family, Socialization and Interaction Process*
Glencoe Illinois
The Free Press

*Parsons, Talcott 1958 "Social structure and the development of personality. Freud's contribution to the integration of psychology and sociology"
Psychiatry, 21
321-340

*Pear, T.H. 1931 *Voice and Personality*
London
Chapman & Hall

Pickford, Glenna Ruth 1956 "American linguistic geography: a sociological appraisal"
Word, vol 12, no 2
211-233

*Polanyi, Michael 1967 *The Tacit Dimension*
London
Routledge & Keegan Paul

*Preston, M.S. 1963 *Evaluational Reactions to English, Canadian French and European French Voices*
Unpublished M.A. thesis
McGill University, Redpath Library
(reported in Lambert 1967)

*Ptacek, P.H. & Sander, E.K.   1966   "Age recognition from voice"
Journal of Speech and Hearing Research, 9
273-277

Ramsay, R.W.   1968   "Speech patterns and personality"
Language and Speech, vol 11
54-63

Reiss, Ira L. (ed.)   1972   *Readings on the Family System*
New York
Holt, Rinehart and Winston

*Romaine, Suzanne   1980   "Stylistic variation and evaluative reactions to speech: Problems in the investigation of linguistic attitudes in Scotland"
Language and Speech, vol 23, part 3
213-232

*Ryan, Ellen Bouchard   1973   "Subjective reactions toward accented speech"
Shuy, R.W. & Fasold, R.W., *Language Attitudes: Current Trends and Prospects*
Washington D.C.
Georgetown University Press

*Ryan, E.B. & Capadano, H.L.   1978   "Age perceptions and evaluative reactions toward adult speakers"
Journal of Gerontology, vol 33, no 1
98-102

*Ryan, Ellen Bouchard   1979   "Why do low-prestige language varieties persist?"
Giles, H. & St Clair, R.N. (eds.), *Language and Social Psychology*
Oxford
Basil Blackwell
145-157

*Ryan, E.B. & Sebastian, R.   1980   "The effects of speech style and social class background on social judgments of speakers"
British Journal of Social and Clinical Psychology, 19
229-233

*Ryan, E.B. & Giles, H. (eds.)   1982   *Attitudes towards Language Variation: Social and Applied Contexts*
London
Edward Arnold

*Ryan, E.B., Giles, H. & Sebastian, R.J.   1982   "An integrative perspective for the study of attitudes toward language variation"
Ryan, E.B. & Giles, H. (eds.), *Attitudes towards Language Variation: Social and Applied Contexts*
London
Edward Arnold
1-19

*Safire, W.   1986   "On surgical strike"
New York Times Magazine, May 4
New York
(In the column, On Language)

*Sanford, Fillmore H.   1942   "Speech and personality"
Psychological Bulletin, vol 39, no 10
811-845

*Sapir, Edward   1927   "Speech as a personality trait"
American Journal of Sociology, 32
892-905

Scherer, K. & Giles, H. (eds.)   1979   *Social Markers in Speech*
Cambridge
Cambridge University Press

*Scholes, Robert   1974   *Structuralism in Literature. An Introduction*
New Haven
Yale University Press

*Schuman, H. & Presser, S.   1981   *Questions and Answers in Attitude Surveys. Experiments on Question Form, Wording, and Context*
New York
Academic Press, Inc.

*Sebastian, R.J. & Ryan, E.B.   1985   "Speech cues and social evaluation: Markers of ethnicity, social class, and age"
Giles, H. & St Clair, R.N. (eds.), *Recent Advances in Language, Communication, and Social Psychology*
London
Lawrence Erlbaum Associates Ltd
112-143

*Seligman, C.R., Tucker, G.R. & Lambert, W.E.
    1972   "The effects of speech style and other attributes on teachers' attitudes toward pupils"
Language in Society, 1
131-142

*Seppänen, Aimo   1974   *Proper Names in English: a Study in Semantics and Syntax* vols 1-2
Tampere
Publications of the Department of English Philology, University of Tampere, no. 1

*Shosteck, Herschel   1974   "Factors influencing appeal of TV news personalities"
Journal of Broadcasting, 18:1, winter 1973-74
63-71

*Shryock, Henry S., Siegel, Jacob S. & associates
    1980   *The Methods and Materials of Demography*
US Department of Commerce. Bureau of the Census.
Fourth printing (rev.)
Washington D.C.
US Government Printing Office

*Shuy, Roger & Williams, Frederick   1973   "Stereotyped attitudes of selected English dialect communities"
Shuy, R. & Fasold, R. (eds.), *Language Attitudes: Current Trends and Prospects*
Washington D.C.
Georgetown University Press
85-96

*Simpson, G.E. & Yinger, J.M.   1972   *Racial and Cultural Minorities: An Analysis of Prejudice and Discrimination*, 4th ed.
New York
Harper & Row

*Sistrunk, Frank & McDavid, John W.   1971   "Sex variable in conforming behavior"
Journal of Personality and Social Psychology, vol 17, no 2
200-207

*Smith, B.L., Brown, B.L., Strong, W.J., Rencher, A.C.
    1975   "Effects of speech rate on personality perception"
Language and Speech, 18
145-152

*Smith, David M.   1979   *Where the Grass is Greener: Living in an Unequal World*
                                                 Harmondsworth
                                                 Penguin

*Smith, Philip M.   1979   "Sex markers in speech"
                                                 Scherer, K.R. & Giles, H. (eds.), *Social Markers in Speech*
                                                 Cambridge
                                                 Cambridge University Press
                                                 109-146

*Smith, Philip M.   1985   *Language, the Sexes and Society*
                                                 Oxford
                                                 Basil Blackwell

Smith, Riley B. & Lance, Donald M.   1979   "Standard and disparate varieties of English in the United States: Educational and sociopolitical implications"
                                                 International Journal of the Sociology of Language, 21
                                                 127-140

*Spencer, J.   1958   "Received pronunciation: some problems of interpretation"
                                                 Lingua, VII, 1957-58
                                                 7-29

*Stagner, Ross   1936   "Judgments of voice and personality"
                                                 Journal of Social Psychology, 27
                                                 1936
                                                 272-277

*Stewart, M.A. & Ryan, E.B.   1982   "Attitudes toward younger and older adult speakers: effects of varying speech rates"
                                                 Journal of Language and Social Psychology, vol 1, no 2
                                                 91-109

*Stewart, M.A., Ryan, E.B. & Giles, H.   1985   "Accent and social class effects on status and solidarity evaluations"
                                                 Personality and Social Psychology Bulletin, vol 11, no 1
                                                 98-105

*Stone, Vernon A.   1974   "Attitudes toward television newswomen"
                                                 Journal of Broadcasting, 18:1, winter 1973-74
                                                 49-62

*Strongman, K.T. & Woosley, J.   1967   "Stereotyped reactions to regional accents"
                                                 British Journal of Social and Clinical Psychology, 6
                                                 164-167

Sunday Telegraph   1984   January 15: Letter to the editor by Kathleen Humphreys
                                                 London

Swacker, M.   1975   "The sex of the speaker as a sociolinguistic variable"
                                                 Thorne, B. & Henley, N. (eds.), *Language and Sex: Difference and Dominance*
                                                 Rowley Massachusetts
                                                 Newbury House Publishers Inc.

Swacker, M.E.   1977   *Attitudes of Native and Nonnative Speakers toward Varieties of American English*
                                                 Texas A&M University

*Taylor, Harold C.   1934   "Social agreement on personality traits as judged from speech"
Journal of Social Psychology, 5
244-248

*Thakerar, Jitendra N. & Giles, Howard   1981   "They are - so they spoke: noncontent speech stereotypes"
Language & Communication, vol 1, no 2/3
255-261

Thorne, Barrie & Henley, Nancy   1975   "Difference and dominance: an overview of language, gender and society"
Thorne, B. & Henley, N. (eds.), *Language and Sex: Difference and Dominance*
Rowley Massachusetts
Newbury House Publishers Inc.
5-42

*Torbe, Mike   1984   "Communication skills and the young school leaver: some notes toward research"
International Journal of the Sociology of Language, 49
Amsterdam
89-110

*Trudgill, Peter   1974   *The Social Differentiation of English in Norwich*
(Abridged and revised version of an unpublished dissertation from 1971)
Cambridge
Cambridge University Press

*Trudgill, Peter   1975a   *Accent, Dialect and the School*
London
Edward Arnold

*Trudgill, Peter   1975b   "Sex, covert prestige, and linguistic change in the urban British English of Norwich"
Thorne, B. & Henley, N. (eds.), *Language and Sex: Difference and Dominance*
(reprinted from *Language in Society*, 1, 1972)
Rowley
Newbury House

*Trudgill, Peter   1979   "Standard and non-standard dialects in the United Kingdom: problems and policies"
International Journal of the Sociology of Language, 21
9-24

*Trudgill, P. & Hannah, J.   1982   *International English. A Guide to Varieties of Standard English*
London
Edward Arnold

*Trudgill, Peter   1983   *On Dialect. Social and Geographical Perspectives*
Oxford
Basil Blackwell

*Trudgill, Peter   1986   *Dialects in Contact*
Oxford
Basil Blackwell

*Tucker, G.R. & Lambert, W.E.   1969   "White and Negro listeners' reactions to various American-English dialects"
Social Forces, vol 47, no 4
University of North Carolina Press
463-468

*Wakelin, Martyn F.   1972   *English Dialects: an Introduction*
London
The Athlone Press

*Wardhaugh, Ronald   1986   *An Introduction to Sociolinguistics*
Oxford
Basil Blackwell

*Warr, P.B., Faust, J. & Harrison, G.J.   1967   "A British ethnocentrism scale"
British Journal of Social and Clinical Psychology, 6
267-277

*Webster, William G. & Kramer, Ernest   1968   "Attitudes and evaluational reactions to accented
English speech"
Journal of Social Psychology, 75
231-240

*Wells, J.C.   1970   "Local accents in England and Wales"
Journal of Linguistics, 6
231-252

*Wells, J.C.   1982   *Accents of English 1-3*
Cambridge
Cambridge University Press

*Widmark, Gun   1980   "Kvinnospråk" ('Women's language')
Jonsson, Inge (ed.), *Språken i vårt språk*
Stockholm
Pan/Norstedts
72-89

*Wigren, G., Nordström, B. & Gahlin, A.   1987   *Lokalradions publik - Radio Jönköping, Radio
Gävleborg, Radio Kristianstad, Radio Dalarna, vecka
6 och 7 1987* (Swedish local radio listener poll)
Stockholm
Sveriges Radio. Publik- och Programforsknings-
avdelningen

*Williams, J.E., Giles, H., Edwards, J.R., Best, D.L. & Daws, J.T.
                                      1977   "Sex-trait stereotypes in England, Ireland and the
United States"
British Journal of Social and Clinical Psychology,
16
303-309

*Windsor Lewis, Jack   1985   "British non-dialect accents"
Zeitschrift für Anglistik und Amerikanistik, 3, 33.
Jahrgang
Leipzig
244-257

Wyld, H.C.   1934   "The best English. A claim for the superiority of
Received Standard English"
Society for Pure English, Tract no. XXXIX
Oxford
Oxford University Press

Appendix 1.

Recording transcripts

These transcripts are arranged in the same order as the presentation of the speakers in table 1, Introduction, i.e. by age, from the oldest to the youngest. The G (Gothenburg) and the B (Brighton) in the speakers' personal codes indicate the location of the recording sessions. The duration of each recording is indicated in brackets after the speaker's personal code.

The transcripts are basically rendered in plain, normalized English. Within that framework, I have however attempted to be as faithful as possible to the spoken forms of the recordings. Brackets are used to indicate non-verbal noises and hesitational cuts in the middle of words or cuts at the end of the recording.

The break in the middle of each recording (to give informants time to think) has been indicated by a break in the transcript.

For further information, see Introduction, particularly the section entitled "The recordings. The voices. What they say".

1. Speaker 7G (90 seconds)

This is a picture of a crossroads. You can see the traffic passing in both directions, but no, it's not passing, it seems to have stopped. There's some sort of trouble in the centre of the crossroads. A man's car has stopped. Yes, he's got a burst tyre. And he's trying to remove the tyre and put on his spare. Two policemen are there. One of them is trying to control the traffic, which is a bit odd, because there are traffic lights, but the car which has stopped is preventing the traffic lights from functioning as they usually do, so two policemen have to come to deal with the traffic jam. A lot of people are looking on. There are men poking their heads out of their cars and shaking their fists

at the culprit. There are women getting off a bus which has been stopped by the car. There are people looking out of windows, looking rather amused, because something's happening at last. There's a little boy carrying a bicycle. He obviously thinks that's the quickest way to get across the road. And there are other people standing at shop doors or just standing on the pavement, watching the whole scene. One of the biggest vehicles which is held up is a lorry which has all kinds of wooden crates on it. And that's almost driving into the side of the stationary car.

2. Speaker 9B (75 seconds)

Well, this picture that I've got in front of me shows a scene of complete chaos, which is probably common to many countries and not necessarily England where it appears to have occurred. The policeman and also the traffic wardens endeavoring to make some order out of the chaos which is concerned seem to be completely lost, and probably have accentuated the problem.

The poor motorist who's suffered the indignity of a puncture is not seen to be receiving help from many of the on-lookers and indeed, they all seem to be so furious at the thought of the inconvenience to which they're subjected at the present time. Quite obviously, the longer he takes to change his wheel, the longer the traffic jam will become, and the greater the chaos will follow. Some of the people appear to be rather amused by the events, and others are completely non-committal as evidence [ ]

3. Speaker 7B (60 seconds)

From this picture I can see that we have total chaos. We have a crossroads operated by traffic signals. A man has a flat tyre and is in the process of making a repair. The police have taken over to direct the traffic.

Other drivers and passengers are becoming very angry at the delay. People are looking out of windows. There are two ladies gossiping on the corner. A cyclist has become tired and is, has decided to carry his bike across the road. A dentist is looking out of his window.

4. Speaker 8G (90 seconds)

This is a picture of absolute chaos. It's a crossroads in the centre of a town and the chaos is caused by the fact that a car has broken down and the poor chap is having to change the wheel in the middle of everything. Behind him a bus has come to a full stop and the passengers in indignation are climbing off. On one side of him, a truck is pressing as near as it possibly can, loaded with crates, and behind the truck a stream of cars tooting away for all they're worth. Of course an accident of this kind attracts spectators and to left and to right out of windows out of doors, we can see people who've turned up to watch.

One or two people though find conversation even more interesting than watching an accident. There are two ladies who've been shopping, vegetables by the look of it, can't for a moment tear themselves away from the interesting things they have to say to one another. They can't afford to give this dramatic situation a single glance. Another young man who seems to be really rather unperturbed by it all is a boy carrying his bicycle. He's obviously got stopped by the traffic jam and has decided to bypass it by lifting it up and moving through as a pedestrian. What's going to come out of this is difficult to say. The police have arrived on the scene. One of them is ridiculously trying to control the traffic and the other one is speaking angrily to the poor fellow who is mending his car. Doesn't seem a very sensible way to help the matter to, to be solved, but no doubt he hopes it is. What else have we got around here? I can see there's a, a bank

5. Speaker 16G (90 seconds)

This is a picture of a street scene. There's a crossing, with traffic lights and a car has broken down in the middle of the crossing, so there's a traffic jam from all four directions. The car that has broken down has got a puncture and the man is trying to mend it. He's actually trying to get the bolts off the, the nuts off the front wheel, back wheel, sorry. There's a policeman standing, glaring at him holding a truncheon in his hand. There's another policeman, who's still trying to direct the traffic, although it's not getting anywhere.

Coming from, well, coming from one direction there's a lorry, an open lorry, with a lot of boxes on it, and behind that, two lines of cars. There are some people standing on the pavement watching this, a man and a woman and a little child. There's a man standing in the doorway of his shop. On the left of the picture, you can see people looking out of windows, there's a dentist and two people looking out from the balcony of the window above him. On the other side of the street, I can see, well, it's a kind of newspaper stand [may-] maybe.

6. Speaker 17G (90 seconds)

This is a picture of a traffic jam. It has been caused by a man who has got a puncture right in the middle of a crossroads and he, he has had to change his tyre there and it seems to be taking a long time for the traffic is piling up all around. And people are getting very angry. There's a policeman talking to him and another one trying to direct the traffic but no one seems to be getting anywhere. Some people are getting off the bus on the right. A boy is carrying his bicycle along I, I should think he is intending to use the the pedestrian crossing.

Two housewives are on the left corner, chatting away as though nothing had happened. There's a man in a newspaper store on the far side of the street. He seems to be looking quite curiously at the scene. No one is buying any newpapers at the moment. There's a family of three on the right hand corner, and they seem to be standing in front of, oh I can't quite see what sort of shop it is. There's a man in an apron standing in the doorway.

7. Speaker 15G (90 seconds)

This is a picture of a crossroads with a traffic jam. In the middle of the crossroads, a man has had a breakdown, because he has had to change his wheel. He's trying to change his wheel, he has got it off, but he hasn't got the new one on, and he's being reprimanded by a policeman, because in fact he's causing a terrible traffic jam. Another policeman is trying to direct the traffic, but is not getting anywhere, because the middle of the crossroads is blocked by the car without the wheel. There is a small boy on the pavement carrying his bicycle, presumably hoping to walk through the traffic carrying his bicycle. There's a small minibus with some very angry-looking ladies on it. They're getting off, presumably to carry on their journey on foot. There are some amused-looking pedestrians on the opposite pavement

obviously enjoying the general problem and confusion. There are some very angry drivers in their cars. One is waving his hand out of the window. Another one looks as if he might be blowing his horn. Behind the one who is blowing his horn, there is another driver who appears to be going to sleep. Perhaps he's been there some time. There are other interested spectators, there's a shopkeeper in a white apron, standing in his doorway. There is another man leaning out of an upstairs window. And a lady in a kiosk watching. And also a man in a bank, peeping through his win[dow]

8. Speaker 11G (90 seconds)

Well, I can see a traffic scene. There's been an accident at a busy road crossing. The, a car or a small bus has bumped into a, no I'm not sure if it is an accident, actually, I think it's a car that's had a breakdown and, yes that's right, it must have had a puncture. It looked as if the car behind or the bus behind have driven into him but he's simply stopped in the middle of the, of the crossing and he's changing the wheel, and there's a policeman looking rather irritatedly at him, because he's holding up all the traffic. There's a line of cars in one direction, with a lorry right in the middle of the crossing

and there's another policeman trying desperately to direct the traffic. There is, cars are, or drivers are hooting and one, two drivers at least are leaning out of their windows, shaking their fists at the man who's causing all the trouble. There's a dentist, evidently, looking out of the window of his surgery, and there's a man and a woman in the flat above also looking out. It's a crossing that's regulated by traffic lights, but I don't think they are of much help at the moment. I can also see the man's got various tools out on the street and also his spare wheel.

9. Speaker 12G (90 seconds)

It's a picture of a crossroads of two rather small streets, and an accident has, no not an accident, a car has got a back wheel puncture in the centre of the crossing and is holding up all the traffic. He is looking very worried and harrassed, because the policeman is getting more and more annoyed, and there are two policemen, one trying to direct the traffic, and the other trying to hurry the man with the puncture along. He's got tools spread out over the road and various people are climbing out of cars and vehicles.

expecting to somehow get past the blockage. Most of the drivers in the cars around are getting very angry and waving their arms and looking infuriated. People are coming out of their shops to look at what's happening and people are getting, are appearing at the windows in the building nearby to look out down into the street. The man who's actually trying to mend the puncture is obviously not being very successful, but he's, he's looking very hot and bothered. There are various vehicles, not just private cars, there is a small bus with elderly people climbing out of it. There is a large lorry with large wooden crates on the back of it.

10. Speaker 15B (105 seconds)

I suppose what this picture is, is a nasty little drawing, from a nasty little book, for English teachers without any bright ideas of their own. They distribute the picture and the kids are supposed to write interesting things from it. I think you'd be unreasonable to expect anybody to write anything very interesting from such a crummy little drawing as this, 'cos this one is. But I guess that's where it's, that's where it comes from. I suppose it's, it's about xenophobia, really, or, or,

maybe not so much hatred of foreigners as hatred of of of well-off people, 'cos the car that's causing all the trouble is fairly clearly supposed to be American. It's got big symbols on the bonnet, and fancy painted signs down the wings, and it's bigger than all the other cars. So I suppose the, the driver who's being idiot enough to change his wheel in the middle of a busy intersection is probably supposed to be American or foreign and all the people he's holding up are kind of right-thinking, sensible, ordinary, modest English people in sensible cars. And maybe if he's not actually American, he's rich enough to buy a fancy American car so that enables all the other people righteously to scream abuse at him and get indignant.

11. Speaker 1G (90 seconds)

Well, the man in the, who's had the car breakdown in the middle of the street's really caused a mess. Looks like a bad puncture and he's got the, the wheel out of the, the boot. He's got all his tools out and hubcap off and a policeman's looking really mad. I think he'll be a long time clearing that away. So he's blocked the junction one way, but the, the man driving the lorry with the packing-cases has caused just as much trouble. He's pulled up right across the road and blocked everybody from going past on the other side too. What a mess. The bus has stopped behind the car with the flat tyre, and all the people are getting off, they must have been waiting for a while,

but they think it'll be quicker to walk. Everybody behind the lorry with the packing-cases is backed up, I can see that their lights are flashing. What a traffic jam. Mind you, the two old ladies outside the greengrocer's are busy chatting away, they don't even seem to have noticed anything. But the dentist over the greengrocer, he's hanging out of a window and having a good look. Hope his patient isn't in the chair. [Eve-] even the grocer across the street's come to the door to have a look, and there are, there's a father and a mother and a small child standing by the traffic lights waiting to cross and they're having a good look too. A small car coming up to the junction where the flat-tyre car i[s]

12. Speaker 3G (90 seconds)

Here we have a very busy street scene. A poor man has a puncture in his back tyre which he's frantically trying to mend. There's a policeman trying to direct traffic, and [ ] The car unfortunately has had its puncture right in the middle of the crossroads, so there are people waiting to turn right, there are a lot of people waiting to go straight on. The bus is completely blocked and the passengers are very angry and they're getting off and they all have cross faces. Everybody, they're tooting their horns. And everybody's waving their arms out of the car,

out of their cars, which I can't imagine helps the poor man who's trying to mend his puncture. In fact it's causing such a stir that people are hanging out of their windows, to see what's going on. There's a lottery seller on the street corner. But there are two ladies standing outside the greengrocer's who don't even seem to have noticed that there's anything going on. They're chatting to each other as if nothing was happening. There's also a small boy on the right hand corner who's decided that the best way to get around it all is to pick up his bi[ke]

13. Speaker 5G (90 seconds)

The picture is about a street scene, and there is a big traffic jam. A poor man has broken down in the centre of the road. He has a puncture and is trying to change his tyre. A policeman is standing next to him who is very angry, because he's causing so much problem. On the left of the picture, there is a man in a kiosk, who is looking very astonished at the scene in front of him. Next to the kiosk

is a bank and one of the bank clerks is looking out very interested to see what's happening. In the, on the left hand side of the picture, bottom left hand corner, there are two ladies quite oblivious of the scene around them. They're standing outside a greengrocer's and gossiping. Above the greengrocer's, there are three very interested people. There's a dentist, who obviously hasn't got very much to do at the moment, looking out. And above, in the flat above him, there are two people also looking out. In the foreground of the picture, there is a milk lorry. Behi[nd]

14. Speaker 12B (80 seconds)

There seems to have been a traffic accident. A man's tyre is flat and the policeman is encouraging him to change it quickly as he's blocking up all the traffic. A boy with a bike is taking advantage of the fact that he has a bike and not a car and walking round. People are getting very angry. People leaning out of windows watching what's going on, and the policeman is trying to sort it all out, two policemen, one handling the man with the car, one directing the traffic. Seems to be an enormous jam with cars. People on the bus are getting so frustrated that they get off the bus to walk.

Two ladies gossiping by the greengrocer's are so busy gossiping that they haven't noticed what's going on. There is one man in a car, with a baby yelling noisily at the back. There are tools lying by the wheel while the man is changing it. He has one tyre that he is to put on to replace the one that's gone flat. Ah, the man, one of the men leaning out of the window is a dentist. The man watching from a bank. Cars seem to be tooting their horns. Generally looks a bit chaotic.

15. Speaker 13G (90 seconds)

A road junction with a certain amount of congestion caused apparently by the car in the middle, suffering from a flat tyre on one of the rear wheels. Poor chap doesn't really seem to understand or care what he's doing, but the police don't seem to be very happy and of course everybody who is not actually involved in the situation is standing looking. There's a bus behind the car where some disgruntled passengers have decided to cut their losses and get off and walk and everyone else appears to be sounding their horns or at least shaking their fists at this

poor chap. Yeah, not really a lot more. The police are making an attempt at directing the traffic and there's one policeman actually speaking to the man, probably trying to give him some sort of encouragement at least. The poor chap's sweating away with all his tools on the ground and the wheel on the floor. The only person who doesn't really seem to be bothered is the chap in the lorry. He's probably on his way to work and doesn't really mind how long it takes

16. Speaker 4G (90 seconds)

Well, here we have a lot of traffic bein' held up. The police are doing what they can, but somebody's decided to repair their tyre in the middle of the high road. All the roads are blocked now. People are getting quite upset. They're jumping out of the buses before they reach their stop. And one little chap has decided that it's quicker to carry his bike than ride it. Even the people are looking out of their windows, so this must have been goin' on for quite a long time now.

I say that, but there's two women still having a good long chat on the corner of the road. They appear to be quite oblivious of what's going on around them. The man standing at the newspaper stand is gettin' a good view of it, and the man standing on the right hand side is come out of his shop to have a look and see what's going on. I think the man whose car has got his tyre doesn't realize the commotion he's causing. And it seems something's going to have to be done. There's a bank on the corner, and with somebody peering over the sign, even they're concerned with the chaos.

17. Speaker 2G (90 seconds)

The picture shows a crossroads with traffic lights. There's a fruit shop on one corner with a dentist above. A bank on the other corner and a, a news vendor's stand next to it. Somebody has had a puncture right in the middle of the crossroads and is mending it. It's caused a very big traffic jam. There's one policeman standing angrily over the man who's trying to mend his puncture. There's another policeman frantically trying to get some order into the traffic. The drivers are hanging out of their windows, shaking their fists, obviously angry at the holdup.

There is a bus just behind the car that's broken down and all the people are getting off it, obviously think it's going to be quicker to walk than to wait on the bus. There's one or two people standing around watching, a man standing at his shop doorway watching, a family. There's two women having a chat on the left hand corner. There's a big lorry full of wooden crates stuck in front of the car that's broken down and a big line of cars behind them all frantically tooting their horns. There is a little boy carrying his bike up the road, he's obviously decided that he can't get through on the road either and it'd be quicker for him to pick up his bike, and walk along.

18. Speaker 6G (90 seconds)

This could be any typical London street on any week day or week end. In the picture we see irate drivers and policemen all shouting at each other and making signs to each other. As usual when people are coming from three or four different directions, an accident like this can always happen. On the side of the streets, you can see the greengrocer's with women just talking with one another, totally unaware of what's happening.

There are also people repairing the breakdown that has arisen. And there are people curious to see what has happened. In the picture we can see two women looking out of the top window, very interested, as this is probably the most exciting thing that has happened during the week; and a dentist underneath with his glasses hanging from the end of his nose, watching what's happened. There are also people in a rush to get to work or to get home and they are extremely irritated by what is happening. Hooters are blaring and people are leaning out of windows, trying to find out when they can continue.

19. Speaker 14B (80 seconds)

Here we have a street scene. Someone has broken down in his car causing terrible chaos. There is a bank on the corner and one imagines if the occurrence has taken place so that someone could rob the bank. Everyone seems to be on the street looking at the goings-on, and the police don't seem to be doing very much about moving them.

Everyone's hooting their horns and getting very angry about the whole affair. People are getting off the bus and going forward to the car driver to see what's going on. A cyclist has given up and he's walking. There are two old ladies on the corner who don't seem to know that the whole thing's going on at all. There's a fruit and vegetable shop. People are looking out of their windows. All the lights seem to be stuck. And the traffic has generally come to a halt.

20. Speaker 9G (90 seconds)

The situation in the picture shows many irate drivers. The reason for the, their anger seems to be that someone has had a flat tyre. He's trying to change the tyre, but his car has come to a halt in the middle of a crossroads. A policeman is standing behind the man with a truncheon in his hand, looking extremely angry. Another policeman is standing in the middle of the crossroads, trying to direct the traffic, but in fact the traffic can't be directed, because all the traffic is stuck and no one is allowing anybody through.

You can see all the drivers in the cars looking extremely frustrated and very angry. No one seems to be able to do anything about the situation. There are bystanders talking about the traffic jam. There are people leaning out of windows to watch with amusement. There are people getting off a bus angrily, because the bus can't go any further. And the poor man changing the, the wheel is perhaps the only person who is sad in the picture and feeling extremely worried. There is a little boy on the pavement looking very grim and carrying his bicycle on his shoulder, which seems rather strange to me, because a bicycle can usually get through a[nyway]

21. Speaker 10G (90 seconds)

[ ] the middle of a town. It seems to have been, well there's a man in the middle with a rather ugly-looking American car, and he's had a flat tyre so he's having to change the wheel. But unfortunately it's at a traffic lights and there seems to be rather a lot of traffic all held up. There's two policemen in the picture, one very angry policeman, shouting or saying something to the man who's changing the wheel. And there's another policeman very, well rather unsuccessfully trying to redirect the traffic. The people around, there seem to be a lot of people in cars, very angry people some of them. Other people seem very puzzled.

There's a boy to the right there, who's obviously decided that with a bike he can pick it up and walk and avoid the, the hold-up. There are quite a lot of people, some people are very interested in what's going on, looking out of the windows and some quite amused of what's happening, particularly the dentist. On the other hand there are some other people who seem totally unaware of what's happening, there seem to be two women to the left outside the greengrocer's who are just happily chatting away, oblivious to what's happening. The people on the bus, there's a bus directly behind the car that's got the flat tyre, and some people have obviously decided that it's time to get off, that they'd be better if they walked.

22. Speaker 14G (90 seconds)

The scene is describing a man who has a flat tyre and he is situated at the centre of a crossroads. He is trying to change the tyre, much to the consternation of both the police and the surrounding traffic, commuters. The policeman to the left is trying to redirect the traffic but failing miserably. The other policeman is trying to tell the motorist that he really must either move his car or find some solution.

Several motorists are shaking their fists at him very angry, very concerned, and there is a traffic jam between three lanes of traffic and a bus directly behind the car which is stationary. A cyclist has given up all attempts of trying to cycle round the incident and has decided to carry his bike instead and several passengers have got off the bus and decided to walk. There is a truck to the right of the broken-down car which has absolutely no hope of getting round the object and is just stationary.

23. Speaker 6B (60 seconds)

The picture centres round a traffic jam at a local crossroads. The car driver has had a puncture and is in the middle of changing his tyre. Policemen are trying to direct traffic. The dentist is looking out of his window wondering what's going on and men are shaking their fists hanging out of the windows of their cars. Two ladies out shopping are standing on the street corner gossiping. And a young boy's so fed up he's carrying his bicycle on his shoulder.

The traffic is at a complete standstill, and people on the local bus are so fed up waiting that they've decided it might be quicker to walk. A little boy is looking up of the back of his father's car, and the local shopkeeper is standing on his doorstep waiting for his next customer. All around cars are honking their horns and waiting for the policeman to direct the traffic and get it going again.

24. Speaker 13B (90 seconds)

The picture seems to be of an accident. To the left of the picture is a policeman frantically trying to organize the traffic from the holdup that has occurred, with another policeman trying to find out whether it has been an accident or mere[ ] well just a [de-], a fault in the car's tyres. It appears that the man is actually trying to change the wheel, although noth[ ] no incident has occurred. And there is a bus behind the car which has stopped and held up the traffic with a lot of angry passengers on. And also a boy carrying a bicycle who seems to be very cross about having to be held up.

Well all the traffic seems to be honking and causing a lot of disturbance. There seems to be people still around watching the [ ] incident, some laughing, some smiling, some very angry about it. Traffic lights still on stop. Many of the shopkeepers are also watching and there are also some, a news agent's bar just on the left hand upper corner. [ ] Outside are some newspaper billboards. There's also a grocery shop and a fruit shop. A lot of the children seem very dismayed about what has happened and everyone seems to be getting very irate. None of the traffic is moving, and it appears to be held up for quite a way.

25. Speaker 8B (40 seconds)

The setting is a very busy crossroads. A motorist has a flat tyre and has stopped in the middle of the road to repair it. This is causing a complete traffic jam. People are looking out of every window and there are a couple of women gossiping on the street corner. All the people in the cars are very tired of waiting and especially the people in a bus behind the broken-down car. They're all getting off the bus. A small child who is on a bike is now fed up and is carrying the bike over his shoulder. Two policemen are trying without much success to control the traffic which is now running right

(This passage was spoken twice on the recording.)

Appendix 2.

Speaker subgroups.

This is a condensed presentation of the speaker subgroups used in the three report sections of the present study (AGE, SEX, REGIONALITY). The underlying figures can be found in table 1, Introduction, p. 59.

Legend:

Id code		Speaker's personal identity code (G and B indicate Gothenburg and Brighton, respectively, i.e. the location of the recording sessions)
Age		Age at the time of the experiment (1982)
Region		Where the speaker spent the major part of the first 20 years of his/her life

1=London
2=South
3=Southwest
4=East
5=Midlands
6=North

Ed. no. yrs	Number of years in education (this figure is based on speakers' subjective reports)
Post-school	Post-school education (academic, non-academic or none)
Occup.	Occupation

1. Professional
2. Intermediate
3. Skilled non-manual
4. Skilled manual
5. Partly skilled
6. Non-skilled
S. Student

% trad. pr.	Percentage of test words pronounced traditionally (see Introduction, "Degree of modernity")

1. Subgroups AGE section.

Subgroup	Id code	Sex	Age	Region	Ed.no.yrs	Post-school	Occup.	% trad
OLD/TRADITIONAL	7G	F	60	1	18	acad	2	93
	15G	F	46	6	22	acad	1	70
	8G	M	53	2	15	acad	2	80
	11G	M	43	2	17	acad	2	77
	1G	F	36	5	15	non-acad	3	70
	5G	F	36	1	16	acad	2	70
	16G	M	52	2	17	acad	2	90
	12G	F	40	5	20	non-acad	2	67
YOUNG/TRADITIONAL	13G	M	34	5	17	acad	2	70
	9G	F	30	1	17	acad	2	70
OLD/MODERN	3G	F	36	5	17	acad	2	60
	15B	M	40	1	18	acad	2	60
	7B	F	54	2	12	non-acad	3	47
	17G	F	47	5	19	acad	2	63
	9B	M	57	2	19	non-acad	1	60
	12B	F	36	5	18	non-acad	2	60
YOUNG/MODERN	14B	M	32	5	14	non-acad	2	57
	2G	F	32	2	14	non-acad	2	47
	10G	M	28	5	16	non-acad	2	53
	13B	F	21	5	16	non-acad	S	50
	14G	F	28	5	16	non-acad	2	40
	4G	F	33	2	15	non-acad	3	53
	6B	F	28	2	11	non-acad	3	43
	6G	M	32	1	15	acad	2	47
	8B	F	17	2	9	- - -	3	50

2. Subgroups SEX section.

Subgroup	Id code	Age	Region	Ed. no. yrs	Post-school	Occup.	% trad. pr.
MALE/TRADITIONAL	8G	53	2	15	acad	2	80
	11G	43	2	17	acad	2	77
	16G	52	2	17	acad	2	90
	13G	34	5	17	acad	2	70
FEMALE/TRADITIONAL	7G	60	1	18	acad	2	93
	15G	46	6	22	acad	1	70
	1G	36	5	15	non-acad	3	70
	5G	36	1	16	acad	2	70
	12G	40	5	20	non-acad	2	67
	9G	30	1	17	acad	2	70
MALE/MODERN	15B	40	1	18	acad	2	60
	9B	57	2	19	non-acad	1	60
	14B	32	5	14	non-acad	2	57
	10G	28	5	16	non-acad	2	53
	6G	32	1	15	acad	2	47
FEMALE/MODERN	3G	36	5	17	acad	2	60
	7B	54	2	12	non-acad	3	47
	17G	47	5	19	acad	2	63
	12B	36	5	18	non-acad	2	60
	2G	32	2	14	non-acad	2	47
	13B	21	5	16	non-acad	S	50
	14G	28	5	16	non-acad	2	40
	4G	33	2	15	non-acad	3	53
	6B	28	2	11	non-acad	3	43
	8B	17	2	9	- - -	3	50

3. Subgroups REGIONALITY section.

Subgroup	Id code	Sex	Age	Region	Ed.no.yrs	Post-school	Occup.	% trad.
SOUTH/TRADITIONAL	8G	M	53	2	15	acad	2	80
	11G	M	43	2	17	acad	2	77
	16G	M	52	2	17	acad	2	90
	7G	F	60	1	18	acad	2	93
	5G	F	36	1	16	acad	2	70
	9G	F	30	1	17	acad	2	70
NORTH/TRADITIONAL	13G	M	34	5	17	acad	2	70
	15G	F	46	6	22	acad	1	70
	1G	F	36	5	15	non-acad	3	70
	12G	F	40	5	20	non-acad	2	67
SOUTH/MODERN	15B	M	40	1	18	acad	2	60
	9B	M	57	2	19	non-acad	1	60
	6G	M	32	1	15	acad	2	47
	7B	F	54	2	12	non-acad	3	47
	2G	F	32	2	14	non-acad	2	47
	4G	F	33	2	15	non-acad	3	53
	6B	F	28	2	11	non-acad	3	43
	8B	F	17	2	9	- - -	3	50
NORTH/MODERN	14B	M	32	5	14	non-acad	2	57
	3G	F	36	5	17	acad	2	60
	12B	F	36	5	18	non-acad	2	60
	10G	M	28	5	16	non-acad	2	53
	17G	F	47	5	19	acad	2	63
	13B	F	21	5	16	non-acad	S	50
	14G	F	28	5	16	non-acad	2	40

Appendix 3.

GÖTEBORGS UNIVERSITET
Engelska institutionen
Mats Mobärg

Acceptability Project

INSTRUCTION TO SPEAKER

1. Fill out the form "Information referring to the speaker".

2. Recording. Try to speak in as natural a voice as possible. Do not put on an accent. If you are 'multi-dialectal' and feel that you must make a choice between different stylistic registers, use the voice that you would consider proper when discussing a serious matter with a stranger, i.e. a fairly neutral, basically non-dialectal, voice. But again: do not put on an accent.

   a) Sentences and text. Read the material through a couple of times so that you can record it without hesitation. Try to read at a natural pace and with a natural intonation. Try not to overdo your pronunciation.

   b) Description. You have 90 seconds at your disposal. Describe the situation in the picture in some detail.

N.B.: BEFORE YOU START READING, SAY: 'THIS IS SPEAKER NO. ....' (you will find your number on the form "Information referring to the informant").

The recordings should be made in the following order:

       1. Sentences
       2. Passage
       3. Picture

with a short break between each.

Appendix 4.

UNIVERSITY OF GÖTEBORG

DEPARTMENT OF ENGLISH
LANGUAGE AND LITERATURE
Lundgrensgatan 7
S-412 56 GÖTEBORG
tel 031/81 04 00

Mats Mobärg: Acceptability Project

Speaker no.: ....

Date: ....

Information referring to the speaker

1. Sex   (‾) Male   (‾) Female

2. Year of birth ....

3. Place of residence at age 0-20 (if more than one, state the one with the longest duration)

....

....

4. Place of residence last ten years (if more than one, state the one with the longest duration)

....

....

5. Place of residence now

....

....

6. Occupation

....

7. Father's (or mother's) occupation

....

8. Husband's/wife's occupation

....

9. Educational background (state no. of years and type of school)

(primary) ....

(secondary) ....

(post-school) ....

....

....

....

Appendix 5.

UNIVERSITY OF GÖTEBORG

REC. NO.: ....

INF. NO.: ....

DATE: ....

PLACE: ....

Can you spare a moment? I am trying to find out how people feel about different English accents, and this is where I need your help.

But first of all, I need some information about you, so I'd be grateful if you would fill out the form on this page. I DO NOT NEED YOUR NAME.

1. Sex :   ( ) Male   ( ) Female   (tick off the right one)

2. Year of birth :.............

3. Place of residence at age 0-20 (town and county; if more than one, state the one with the longest duration):

   ....

4. Place of residence last ten years (town and county; if more than one, state the one with the longest duration):

   ....

5. Place of residence now (town and county):

   ....

6. Occupation: ....

7. Husband's/wife's occupation: ....

8. Father's (or mother's) occupation: ....

9. Your own educational background (state no. of years and type of school):

   (primary): ....

   (secondary): ....

   (post-school): ....

   ....

10. Answer the following questions by ticking off one of the boxes below each question.

    To what extent do you notice a person's accent?
    not at all ( )   a little ( )   quite a lot( )   very much ( )

    To what extent are you influenced by a person's accent?
    not at all ( )   a little ( )   quite a lot( )   very much ( )

    Do you find it easy or difficult to make a rough judgment about where a person comes from by the way he speaks?

very difficult	difficult	fairly difficult	fairly easy	easy	very easy
( )	( )	( )	( )	( )	( )

376

Appendix 6.

UNIVERSITY OF GÖTEBORG

REC.: ....

INF.: ....

DATE: ....

PLACE: ....

Can you spare a moment? I am trying to find out how people feel about different English accents, and this is where I need your help.

But first of all, I need some information about you, so I'd be grateful if you would fill out the form on this page. I DO NOT NEED YOUR NAME.

1. Sex ◯ Male ◯ Female (tick off the right one)

2. Year of birth: ....

3. Where did you live up to the age of 10? (Just give the town and county; if you lived at more places than one, give the one where you lived longest.):

....

4. Where have you lived since then? (Give the town and county; if you have lived at more places than one, give the one where you've lived longest.):

....

5. Where do you live now? (Town and county)

....

6. Your education so far (tick off box):

(a: primary) ◯ Local State School ◯ Private School ◯ Other

(b: secondary) ◯ Local State School ◯ Private School ◯ Other

7. Your father's (or mother's) occupation: ....

8. Answer the following questions by ticking off one of the boxes below each question.

How much do you notice a person's accent?

not at all ◯ a little ◯ quite a lot ◯ very much ◯

How much are you influenced by a person's accent?

not at all ◯ a little ◯ quite a lot ◯ very much ◯

Do you find it easy or difficult to make a rough judgment about where a person comes from by the way he speaks?

very difficult	difficult	fairly difficult	fairly easy	easy	very easy
◯	◯	◯	◯	◯	◯

CH

Appendix 5/6 (back).

<u>INSTRUCTIONS</u>

You are about to hear five different English voices. The speakers all describe the picture you can see below. Each speaker will speak for about <u>80 seconds</u>. After about <u>40 seconds</u>, there will be a one-minute pause (or slightly longer, if necessary). During this pause, you should try to answer the questions on the answer sheet (nos. 1 - 9, front and back). <u>There is one answer sheet for each speaker.</u> After the pause, you will hear <u>another 40 seconds by the same speaker</u>, so that you can make up your mind about doubtful questions.

Then you go on to the next answer sheet and the next voice, and the procedure is repeated; and so on.

Before you start listening, take a quick look at the picture and one of the answer sheets, so that you get acquainted with the material.

THIS IS THE PICTURE THAT THE SPEAKERS DESCRIBE:

(From J.B. Heaton, <u>Composition through Pictures</u> /Longmans/)

Appendix 7.

SPEAKER NO.: ....

Listen carefully

1. How old do you think the speaker is?   Answer: about .... years of age.

2. What part of England do you think the speaker comes from? (Choose between (a), (b) and (c))

   (a) I am fairly certain he/she comes from ....

   (b) I should think he/she probably comes from ....

   (c) I have no idea ($\overline{}$)   (tick off box)

3. What do you think the speaker does for a living? Suggest an occupation that seems reasonable to you.

   Answer: I think he/she is a/an ....

4. What qualities do you think the speaker possesses? (For example, if you think he probably has very high qualities of leadership, you put a tick in the rightmost box; if you think he has high, but not <u>very</u> high qualities, you put a tick in the second box from the right, and so on.)

(a) Leadership	very little ◯	◯	◯	◯	◯	◯	very much
(b) Dependability	very little ◯	◯	◯	◯	◯	◯	very much
(c) Honesty	very little ◯	◯	◯	◯	◯	◯	very much
(d) Sense of humour	very little ◯	◯	◯	◯	◯	◯	very much
(e) Friendliness	very little ◯	◯	◯	◯	◯	◯	very much
(f) Intelligence	very little ◯	◯	◯	◯	◯	◯	very much
(g) Self-confidence	very little ◯	◯	◯	◯	◯	◯	very much
(h) Ambition	very little ◯	◯	◯	◯	◯	◯	very much
(i) Determination	very little ◯	◯	◯	◯	◯	◯	very much
(j) Education	very little ◯	◯	◯	◯	◯	◯	very much

Continued on the back

Appendix 7 (back).

5. How acceptable do you think this speaker's accent would be in different positions? Put a tick in the correct box.

How acceptable would you consider this accent to be in

	not acceptable	◯	◯	◯	◯	◯	◯	highly accept- able
(a) – a teacher of English								
(b) – an actor/actress		◯	◯	◯	◯	◯	◯	
(c) – a grocer's assistant		◯	◯	◯	◯	◯	◯	
(d) – a BBC newsreader		◯	◯	◯	◯	◯	◯	
(e) – a disc jockey		◯	◯	◯	◯	◯	◯	
(f) – a barrister		◯	◯	◯	◯	◯	◯	
(g) – a rock singer		◯	◯	◯	◯	◯	◯	
(h) – a government official		◯	◯	◯	◯	◯	◯	
(i) – a workingman/-woman		◯	◯	◯	◯	◯	◯	
(j) – a fellow worker/student of yours		◯	◯	◯	◯	◯	◯	
(k) – your child (or brother/sister)		◯	◯	◯	◯	◯	◯	

6. How pleasant do you think this accent is?

very unpleasant ◯ ◯ ◯ ◯ ◯ ◯ very pleasant

7. Do you think this accent is heard very often?

(a) – in your part of England   very seldom ◯ ◯ ◯ ◯ ◯ ◯ very often

(b) – in England as a whole   very seldom ◯ ◯ ◯ ◯ ◯ ◯ very often

8. Do you think the speaker's accent would be a disadvantage or an advantage for him/her in a job interview with an employer?

disadvantage ◯ ◯ ◯ ◯ ◯ ◯ advantage

9. Do you think the speaker's accent is like

(a) – your own accent?   very different ◯ ◯ ◯ ◯ ◯ ◯ very like

(b) – the accents of most of your friends?   very different ◯ ◯ ◯ ◯ ◯ ◯ very like